Bare Branches

Praise for *Bare Branches*

"*Bare Branches* is a **tour de force**. It represents **a groundbreaking contribution to the literature on gender and security studies.** Hudson and den Boer call attention to the ticking time bomb of sex ratio imbalances, especially in East and South Asia, and its impact on the likelihood of domestic instability and interstate war. All who address these issues in the future will need to contend seriously with the persuasive arguments made in this book."
—Rose McDermott, Associate Professor of Political Science, University of California, Santa Barbara

"*Bare Branches* reveals a largely overlooked but important variable correlated with war and peace: high ratios of males to females. Through both historical and contemporary analyses, Hudson and den Boer show that in societies where women have low status, peaceful democracies are far less likely to take hold. All those who hope to understand the causes of war—in academe as well as in government—will have to be aware of these findings. **A brilliant contribution to the literature on contemporary world affairs.**"
—Jessica Stern, Lecturer in Public Policy, John F. Kennedy School of Government, Harvard University

"Hudson and den Boer's study is **an exciting, innovative and refreshing work.** The study is **meticulously researched and documented.** It is also **beautifully written and edited.** Most importantly, *Bare Branches* **marks an important contribution at the nexus of the already burgeoning literatures addressing environmental and human security.**"
—Brendan Taylor, *Survival*

"This **well-documented study** shows how female infanticide and prenatal sex selection have caused an alarmingly lopsided gender ratio in China and India. . . . [The authors'] prescriptions for policymakers . . . offer little hope that the balance can be easily restored."
—Susan H. Greenberg, *Newsweek*

"*Bare Branches* is an **impressive and comprehensive** account of sex ratios, especially in China, and may well give us reason to worry more than we have about that country's future and—in a globalized world—our own."
—James Q. Wilson, *Wall Street Journal*

"**Hudson and den Boer make a compelling case.** . . . China's 'daughter dearth' ought to concern us for humanitarian—and quality of life—reasons."
—William R. Mattox, *USA Today*

"Demographers and feminist scholars have written widely in the last decade about the plight of China's missing girls, while criminologists know that violence is disproportionately associated with young, single men. But a controversial new book, *Bare Branches: The Security Implications of Asia's Surplus Male Population* . . . goes one step further, connecting these strands with a government's calculation of how peaceful it can afford to be. If these young men cannot find wives or jobs or become a viable part of their societies, the book argues, they can pose a threat to internal stability and make governments more likely to create military campaigns to absorb and occupy these youths. Given its radical thesis, it is not surprising that *Bare Branches* **has become a flash point for a debate about the link between sex ratios and security.**"
—Felicia R. Lee, *New York Times*

"**A very interesting view [that] urges us to take immediate action** to tackle the problem of disproportion in gender."
—Guo Zi, *China Daily*

"*Bare Branches* **connects the dots of a huge demographic trend that carries international implications.** Policymakers should take note: China, India, and other nations that can't stop this practice might see great social upheavals, such as mass migration of young males or the widespread kidnapping of women."
—*Christian Science Monitor*

Bare Branches

The Security Implications of Asia's Surplus Male Population

Valerie M. Hudson
Andrea M. den Boer

BCSIA Studies in International Security

The MIT Press
Cambridge, Massachusetts
London, England

First MIT Press paperback edition, 2005

© 2004 by the Belfer Center for Science and International Affairs
John F. Kennedy School of Government, Harvard University
Cambridge, Massachusetts 02138
(617) 495–1400

This book was typeset in Palatino by Wellington Graphics and was
printed and bound in the United States of America.

Library of Congress Cataloging-in-Publication Data

Hudson, Valerie M., 1958–
Bare branches: the security implications of Asia's surplus male population/
Valerie M. Hudson, Andrea M. den Boer.
p. cm.—(BCSIA studies in international security)
Includes bibliographical references and index.
ISBN 0-262-08325-6, ISBN 0-262-58264-3 (pb)
1. Sex discrimination against women—Asia. 2. Sex of children, Parental preferences
for—Asia. 3. Sex distribution (Demography)—Asia. 4. Sex of children, Parental
preferences for—Social aspects. 5. Social conflict. I. Boer, Andrea M. den.
II. Title. III. Series.

HQ12375.5.A7H83 2004
304.6'095—dc22   2004040157

10 9 8 7 6 5 4 3

To the missing daughters. Your absence impoverishes our world, and we grieve for the loss.

D&C 123:13–14

The BCSIA Studies in International Security book series is edited at the Belfer Center for Science and International Affairs at Harvard University's John F. Kennedy School of Government and published by The MIT Press. The series publishes books on contemporary issues in international security policy, as well as their conceptual and historical foundations. Topics of particular interest to the series include the spread of weapons of mass destruction, internal conflict, the international effects of democracy and democratization, and U.S. defense policy.

A complete list of BCSIA Studies in International Security appears at the back of this volume.

Contents

Acknowledgments

There are many who deserve our gratitude and acknowledgment in assisting us to bring this book to pass. We wish to acknowledge the financial support and leave provided us by the David M. Kennedy Center for International and Area Studies, the College of Family, Home, and Social Sciences, the Department of Political Science, and the Women's Research Institute of Brigham Young University. We want to thank the able librarians and interlibrary loan specialists of the Harold B. Lee Library, whose talents we exploited to the fullest to obtain esoteric source material.

We would like to recognize the enthusiastic efforts of our research assistants and other students over the years it took to produce this volume. These wonderful young persons include Suzanne Bacon, Emelyn Faulkner, April Fife, Lisa Fry, Stacie Long Glass (without whom the book would literally not exist), Mark Henshaw, Parakh Hoon, Kacey Widdison Jones, Stephanie McWhorter, Kathy Pate, Duan Qing, Jennifer Riddle, Nathan Tolman, and many of Karen Hyer's students from the Foreign Affairs College in Beijing. A special thanks goes to Zhang Qingmin, technically once a student but in reality a beloved peer, not only for assistance with the Chinese translations but also for the work of supplying us with the last two missing provincial data sets from the 1995 Chinese census.

Colleagues at Brigham Young University provided extremely helpful advice and assistance. These friends include Bonnie Ballif-Spanvill, Robert Boden, R. Lanier Britsch, Lynn England, Sterling Hilton, Eric Hyer, Karen Hyer, Paul Hyer, Ruki Jayaraman, Michael Murdock, Susan Quartey, Michael Smart, and David Wright.

Scholars around the world were willing to answer our questions about their research or ask questions about ours. Many of these wonderful individuals also provided greatly needed encouragement over the years it to took write this book. These include Hayward Alker, Judith Banister, James L. Boone III, David Courtwright, Elizabeth Crook, Monica Das Gupta, Jeffrey M. Dickemann, Robert Ford, Daniel Goodkind, Theodore Kemper, William Lavely, Malcolm Litchfield, Peter Mandaville, Allan Mazur, Christian Mesquida, Barbara Miller, Susan Naquin, David Ownby, David Robinson, Denny Roy, James Seymour, James Watson, and Margo Wilson. We also wish to thank Anna Lietti for first identifying our work as of interest to a broader audience, as well as Wu Yenmei for her help in obtaining source material otherwise unavailable to us. In addition, we are grateful to Paul Wiseman of *USA Today* and the anonymous author of the article in the *Economist* for their interest in our work.

It is hard to overstate the contribution that Sean Lynn-Jones, Diane McCree, Rose McDermott, and anonymous reviewers have made to our work. Without their belief in us, where would we be? And without Diane's editing, who would want to read this book?

Last, Andrea wishes to express her gratitude for the support of her husband, Stefan, her son, Nathan, and her parents, Barbara den Boer and Tonny den Boer. Valerie wishes to give special thanks to her family: her husband, Dave, and children Ben, Ariel, Joe, John, Tom, and Jim. They sacrificed many hours and evenings without her so that she could write her chapters of this volume. Any success this book may enjoy belongs to them as an accolade for their support.

Valerie M. Hudson
Provo, Utah

Andrea M. den Boer
Canterbury, United Kingdom

Chapter 1

The Gender Dimension of Environmental and Human Security

Biologists, sociologists, and anthropologists have long assumed that scarcity, whether natural or man-made, is the chief catalyst for both social competition and social conflict. Scarcity may involve tangible items of value, such as cattle or water, or less tangible goods, such as societal status or group identification.

For decades, most international relations research paid little attention to scarcity or the sociobiological roots of competition and conflict, focusing instead on such issues as the ideological differences underpinning the Cold War. The end of the Cold War brought with it a corrective to this perspective: In the absence of great power conflict, scholars have begun to consider more fully the role of scarcity and inequality in producing both domestic and international conflict. This is the research agenda of the relatively new subfield of security studies called environmental security.

A second emerging subfield of security studies, known as human security, calls for a more integrated understanding of how the security of individuals is related to the security of nations.[1] In this approach, security is built from the ground up and from the inside out, individual by individual, family by family, group by group, community by community. National security is derived from the aggregation of these micro levels of security, in addition to standard assessments of external threat. Security thus has two referents—the state and the individual—and what happens

---

1. For an overview of the literature of this subfield, see Andrew Mack, "The Security Report Project Background Paper," Human Security Centre, University of British Columbia, Vancouver, Canada, 2003, http://www.humansecuritybulletin.info/archive/en_v1i2.

at one level profoundly influences what happens at the other. While we intuitively understand how national security can affect individual security, scholars are only now beginning to research how individual security can affect national security. Furthermore, it is intriguing to see the linkages possible between the subfields of environmental security and human security. Issues of scarcity and inequality operate first and foremost, it can be argued, at the subnational levels of interest to human security scholars.

We can begin to see these linkages in the more developed literature of the environmental security subfield. International relations experts are increasingly turning their attention to factors such as nationalism, identity, and migration to explain strife in the post–Cold War world. Writing in 1994, a founder of the environmental security subfield, Thomas Homer-Dixon, declared, "Environmental scarcities are already contributing to violent conflicts in many parts of the developing world. These conflicts are probably the early signs of an upsurge of violence in the coming decades that will be induced or aggravated by scarcity."[2] Some scholars, including Homer-Dixon, predict that this upsurge in violence will lead not only to civil strife but also to international conflict. Another important linkage in environmental security analysis is between scarcity and environmental stress, on the one hand, and large population movements across state borders, on the other, which can produce conflict involving group identity. Since the early 1990s, scholars in the environmental security subfield have documented a growing number of cases of civil and international conflicts arising from these dynamics.[3] Recent efforts by scholars in other fields have buttressed their work.[4] The environmental security subfield

---

2. Thomas F. Homer-Dixon, "Environmental Scarcities and Violent Conflict: Evidence from Cases," *International Security*, Vol. 19, No. 1 (Summer 1994), p. 5.

3. See, for example, Astri Suhrke, "Pressure Points: Environmental Degradation, Migration, and Conflict," Occasional Paper No. 3 (Toronto: Project on Environmental Change and Acute Conflict, University of Toronto and the American Academy of Arts and Sciences, March 1993); Alex de Sherbinin, "World Population Growth and U.S. National Security," *Environmental Change and Security Project Report*, No. 1 (Spring 1995), pp. 24–39; Sanjoy Hazarika, "Bangladesh and Assam: Land Pressures, Migration, and Ethnic Conflict," Occasional Paper No. 3 (Toronto: Project on Environmental Change and Acute Conflict, University of Toronto and the American Academy of Arts and Sciences, March 1993); Thomas F. Homer-Dixon, *Environmental Scarcity and Global Security* (New York: Foreign Policy Association, 1993); and Jeffrey Boutwell and Thomas F. Homer-Dixon, "Environmental Change, Global Security, and U.S. Policy," in Charles F. Hermann, ed., *American Defense Annual* (New York: Lexington, 1994), pp. 201–224.

4. See, for example, Mark Levy, "Global Environmental Degradation: National Security and U.S. Foreign Policy," Working Paper No. 9 (Cambridge, Mass.: Project on the

has even gained some acceptance within the international security community.[5]

Our research is located at the nexus between environmental security and human security. In this book, we argue that both scarcity of resources and unequal access to those resources are the most important sources of conflict at any level of analysis. However, unlike most studies that focus on such common catalysts of environmental security as ozone depletion or deforestation, our study seeks to explain the influence of a factor more associated with the human security agenda that thus far environmental security scholars have overlooked as a source of scarcity and unequal resource access: namely, exaggerated gender inequality. The hallmark of exaggerated gender inequality is the use of violence against females because of their gender. Environmental security (and indeed security studies more generally) is impoverished as an intellectual construct to the extent that it fails to explore the relationship between violence against women and violence within and between societies. This study serves to demonstrate the greater conceptual potential to be found at the intersection of the environmental and human security approaches.

There is probably no society in the world in which females do not ex-

---

Changing Security Environment and American National Interests, John M. Olin Institute for Strategic Studies, Harvard University, November 1994); Joan M. Nelson, "Migrants, Urban Poverty, and Instability in Developing Nations," Occasional Papers in International Affairs No. 22 (Cambridge, Mass.: Center for International Affairs, Harvard University, September 1969); A.S. Oberai, *Population Growth, Employment, and Poverty in Third World Mega-Cities* (New York: St. Martin's, 1993); John Walton and David Seddon, *Free Markets and Food Riots: The Politics of Global Adjustment* (Cambridge, Mass.: Blackwell, 1994); Hans-Georg Bohle, Thomas E. Downing, and Michael J. Watts, "Climate Change and Social Vulnerability: Towards a Sociology and Geography of Food Security," *Global Environmental Change*, Vol. 4, No. 1 (March 1994), pp. 37–48; Mark Duffield, "The Political Economy of Internal War: Asset Transfer, Complex Emergencies, and International Aid," in Joanna Macrae and Anthony Zwi, eds., *War and Hunger: Rethinking International Responses to Complex Emergencies* (London: Zed, 1994), pp. 50–69; Peter H. Gleick, "Water and Conflict: Fresh Water Resources and International Security," *International Security*, Vol. 18, No. 1 (Summer 1993), pp. 79–112; Ted Robert Gurr, "On the Political Consequences of Scarcity and Economic Decline," *International Studies Quarterly*, Vol. 29, No. 1 (March 1985), pp. 51–75; Shaukat Hassan, *Environmental Issues and Security in South Asia*, Adelphi Papers No. 262 (London: Brassey's, 1991); Robert D. Kaplan, "The Coming Anarchy," *Atlantic Monthly*, Vol. 272, No. 2 (February 1994), pp. 44–81; Michael Renner, *National Security: The Economic and Environmental Dimensions*, Worldwatch Paper No. 89 (Washington, D.C.: Worldwatch Institute, 1989); and Arthur H. Westing, ed., *Global Resources and International Conflict: Environmental Factors in Strategic Policy and Action* (Oxford: Oxford University Press, 1986).

5. Steven Greenhouse, "The Greening of U.S. Diplomacy," *New York Times*, October 9, 1995, p. A6.

perience some form of gender inequality—that is, the subordinate status or inferior treatment of females in political, legal, social, or economic matters. Gender inequality exists when females, compared with their male counterparts, are less educated and less well nourished; receive less medical care; cannot make important life decisions; and have fewer political, legal, social, and economic rights and freedoms. Not all societies, however, practice *exaggerated* gender inequality, the subject of this study. For this study, we define exaggerated gender inequality as existing when, because of gender, one infant is allowed to live while another is actively or passively killed. Offspring sex selection, which almost universally favors males, is found in societies where the lives of females hold significantly less value than those of males, or, indeed, when they have no value at all.[6] Offspring sex selection denotes violence against females simply because they are female. There can be no greater evidence of exaggerated gender inequality in a society than prevalent offspring sex selection.

If violence against females within a society bears any relationship to violence within and between societies, then it should be possible to observe this relationship at work in societies where violence against women is exaggerated—that is, in countries where offspring sex selection is prevalent, such as China and India. As the two largest societies in the world, China and India comprise more than 38 percent of the world's population. Because of the socially sanctioned practice of offspring sex selection, both societies have surpluses of young adult males (ages 15–34) larger than any that natural forces could produce. The Chinese have even coined a term for these young males: "bare branches." The imbalance between the numbers of young males and young females in contemporary China and India is arguably larger than in any other historical period.

The masculinization of Asia's sex ratios is one of the overlooked "megatrends" of our time, a phenomenon that may very likely influence the course of national and perhaps even international politics in the twenty-first century. The scale on which sex ratios are being artificially altered in China and India, as well as in Asia more generally, is unprecedented. The time has come for academics and national security policymakers to consider the potential consequences of the vast demographic shift brought on by Asia's spiraling sex ratios. The security logic of high-sex-ratio societies, we argue, differs tremendously from that of nations with normal sex ratios. Indeed gender issues, so long ignored in the

---

6. "Offspring sex selection" should not be confused with "sex selection" as used by evolutionary biologists. Offspring sex selection refers to the selective rearing of children based on sex. Female infanticide and sex-selective abortion are two examples of offspring sex selection.

study of national security, could become a central focus of security scholars as this century continues to unfold.

In this chapter, we explain the methodological and theoretical approach of our research project. We then synthesize the literature on the
origins of offspring sex selection among humans. Following this we explore the persistence of the practice long after the initial catalysts have
subsided, noting in particular the role of religion and the imperatives of
hypergynous social structures.

Methodological Considerations

For our study, we have adopted Homer-Dixon's approach of confirmatory process tracing.[7] According to Homer-Dixon, in highly complex
systems that incorporate both social and physical variables, a confirmatory approach is preferable to a falsificationist approach when a variable
is first identified for study. Only a confirmatory approach allows the researcher to include a variable that may not be necessary or sufficient by
itself, but that is part of a set of sufficient conditions for a given phenomenon. Such a variable may amplify, aggravate, or trigger the phenomenon
through interaction with other variables in the set.

This approach may not satisfy those who would prefer instead a bot-
tom-line statistical analysis that would yield, for example, a statistical
correlation between sex ratio at birth and some indicator of civil or international strife.[8] Because we do not believe that a simplistic linear correlation is at work here, the latter approach would not be useful. Nor do the
amplifying/aggravating/triggering effects of offspring sex selection on
conflict exclude the possibility of significant conflict in societies where
offspring sex selection is not prevalent. Thus, because the relationship between offspring sex selection and societal conflict is complex and includes diverse sets of sufficient conditions, an approach such as process
tracing that can embrace such complexity and nuance is most useful.

Employing process-tracing techniques, we show how a combination
of gender inequality and environmental stress can produce conditions

---

7. Thomas F. Homer-Dixon, "Strategies for Studying Causation in Complex Ecological-Political Systems" (Toronto: Environment, Population, and Security Project, University of Toronto, June 1995).

8. William T. Divale and Marvin Harris do this for a sample of tribal peoples. They
find a very strong relationship between offspring sex selection and bellicosity. Scholars
have continued to debate their methods, data, and theories, however. See Divale and
Harris, "Population, Warfare, and the Male Supremacist Complex," *American Anthropologist*, Vol. 78, No. 3 (September 1976), pp. 521–538.

that encourage offspring sex selection, and how offspring sex selection may contribute to greater violence and disorder within and between societies. We examine the means by which sex ratios are artificially skewed through the practice of female infanticide or sex-selective abortion. To obtain a truer picture of the sex ratio in the young adult populations in China and India, we also consider the effects of differential infant (ages 0–4) and youth (ages 5–14) mortality rates between the sexes, as well as differential suicide rates. The sex ratio of the 15–34 year age group, we argue, is especially interesting to theorists studying societal and intersocietal conflict, given that young men in this age group are responsible for virtually all violent criminal behavior.

Below we review the historical origins of offspring sex selection, noting in particular its prevalence in Asia. We explain offspring sex selection as a response to environmental stress that is eventually sanctioned by religious or other traditional authorities, and that sometimes persists even in the face of declining environmental stress.

The Emergence of Offspring Sex Selection

How and why did offspring sex selection originate in human society, and why has it persisted? The historical literature on offspring sex selection contains a variety of hypotheses and explanations concerning the origins and continuation of this practice. In our literature survey, we found two main environmental stresses—military invasion and chronically fragile subsistence systems—that are consistently linked to the emergence of *prevalent* offspring sex selection. By prevalent, we mean an act practiced by a nontrivial percentage of families at nearly every level of socioeconomic status that continues over time and typically goes unpunished even when such behavior is illegal. These two environmental stresses only initiate the societal move from occasional, idiosyncratic offspring sex selection to prevalent, typical offspring sex selection. Rendering it *persistent* over generations is a dynamic that underpins what we term *malevolently resistant policy*. This dynamic is, in effect, the drive for resource exclusivity through the creation of family/group boundaries that is often accompanied by the manipulation of traditional religious beliefs.

MILITARY INVASION
Military invasion traditionally threatens its victims in two fundamental ways: through physical extermination and through social extermination. The threat of physical extermination of a targeted group is initially felt most acutely through the loss of men—especially young men—who, acting as warriors, risk death to protect the group. Following victory, invad-

ers would often single out surviving warriors and other males of fighting age for execution.

The social extermination of a group, on the other hand, is felt most acutely when the invaders seize women for concubinage, marriage, or slavery. Without women to provide and socialize children, the targeted group is doomed to social extinction within a generation or so.

Preventing the physical loss of men and the social loss of women is therefore vital to group survival. The distinction between physical and social loss is important to understand because, as we show later, preventing the social loss of women is sometimes viewed as best achieved through their physical loss.

Military invasion can also lead to food shortages and disease, with death resulting not only on the battlefield but also in, for example, refugee camps, thus placing huge environmental stress on the targeted group. Although such factors may contribute to a group's decision to engage in prevalent offspring sex selection, these are not the primary cause. Nor do all groups that suffer military invasion choose to practice offspring sex selection. Rather, it is the threat to group identity—often coupled with food shortages and other environmental stresses—that spurs some societies to engage in prevalent offspring sex selection.[9]

At least three dynamics linked to military invasion seem to encourage this practice. The first is the need to stanch the physical loss of men, which in turn puts a greater premium on the birth of male infants. A group suffering such a loss may therefore consider the investment of time and energy required to ensure the survival of a baby (commonly two years, including birth and minimum length of traditional lactational amenorrhea, or suppression of menses) as wasted on a female infant when the real need is to replace lost males. Sex-selective infanticide increases the likelihood that the mother can deliver another child within a year, rather than within two and a half years.

Second, the birth of female infants can increase the vulnerability of the targeted group and thus threaten its identity. The need to protect the honor of girls and prevent their social capture through sexual union with members of the invading army opens the group to further physical loss of men. The more females, the greater the vulnerability. The social loss of these females (and the consequential physical loss of males attempting to protect them) may seem more costly than the physical loss of these women through offspring sex selection during the years of war or occupation.

---

9. See Judith Banister, *China's Changing Population* (Stanford, Calif.: Stanford University Press, 1987).

Third, girls will eventually require suitable marriage partners. To prevent their social loss, the group must find them husbands from within the group or from other acceptable groups. Invaders, on the other hand, seek out women from the targeted group as sexual partners, usually by force, to weaken its morale and sense of identity. Even if the targeted group is able to keep the social capture of its women to a minimum—for example, by secluding them in locations protected by men from the group, the likely loss of some of these men in this endeavor decreases the number of prospective husbands. A further complication is the desire of higher-placed families or clans not to dilute or "pollute" their inheritances by giving their daughters to men from lower-class families or social outcasts, even if they are members of the same group. Thus the obligation to find suitable marriage partners for the women of the targeted group becomes especially onerous during military invasion and occupation. The physical loss of the daughters at birth may therefore seem less serious than their social loss to in-group or out-group undesirables when the group is fighting for its identity.

Not all cultures have responded to military invasion by resorting to female infanticide, however. For example, Jewish lineage is accorded the child of any Jewish woman. Thus even if groups succeeded in the social capture of Jewish women, the offspring of any unions were still considered members of the Jewish community. This alternative response is evident even today. For example, the Imam of Zagreb urged Bosnian Muslim men to marry women raped by Serbian forces during the Bosnian conflict in the 1990s, and to raise any children resulting from such rapes as Bosnian Muslims.[10]

Another response to is to make young females unattractive to invaders. The persistence (though perhaps not the initiation) of foot binding may be related to the desire of Han Chinese to prevent the social capture of their daughters by invading Mongols. Similarly, the Jewish practice of married women shaving their heads bald (and wearing wigs to cover their baldness) is generally understood to have been a response to the continual threat of rape by invaders or during pogroms. When confronted by invaders, the married women would take off their wigs in an effort to repel their attackers. It is also possible that the practice of infibulation, an extreme form of female genital mutilation in which the outer labia are sewn together, arose from similarly threatening historical situations.

In the context of military invasion, then, offspring sex selection repre-

---

10. See Elaine Lutz, "When the Women Cry, Who Will Listen?" *International Relations Journal* (San Francisco State University), Vol. 14, No. 2 (Spring 1993), pp. 29–32.

sents a strategy of resistance (as opposed to adaptation) to the extreme stress produced. It is, in other words, a predatory social practice designed to implement that resistance.

CHRONICALLY FRAGILE SUBSISTENCE SYSTEMS

Societies in chronically fragile subsistence systems may respond to risks from, for example, threatened or real famine by engaging in offspring sex selection. Nature usually takes care of these fragile systems by limiting the fertility of the women in the group. For example, in the early twentieth century, traditional Aboriginal women in Australia were infrequently fertile, ovulating only once every several years. A certain percentage of body fat is required to maintain estrogen levels at the point necessary for female fertility: When body fat is chronically below this percentage, amenorrhea and lack of fertility result.[11] Other types of natural fertility control—such as extended nursing and sexual taboos during lactation—are used in fragile subsistence systems.[12]

In some of these systems, however, the body weight of women may not remain low enough to prevent fertility. Despite lactation-related sexual taboos, women may bear more children than the system can support. In some such cases, offspring sex selection occurs; in others, non-sex-selective infanticide may result. The brief case studies below illustrate this diversity of response.

Arctic peoples such as the Inuit live in one of the world's most inhospitable climes. Historically, survival was a day-to-day struggle. With agriculture all but impossible, hunting and fishing remain the primary means of providing sustenance for the group. Over time, a natural sexual division of labor developed: Men focused on hunting and fishing, while women cared for the children, rendered the meat into usable food, and cured hides for clothing and shelter. Hunting and fishing in Arctic conditions can be treacherous, and men are often killed or disabled in the process. Given the lack of alternative food sources (at least in the past), the strict division of labor along gender lines, and men's physical advantage in procuring food, males became more important to the group. The birth of male babies meant a steady supply of new hunters and fisherman, so that even if some were killed or disabled, others could take their place.

---

11. See Richard B. Lee, "Lactation, Ovulation, Infanticide, and Woman's Work: A Study of Hunter-Gatherer Population Regulation," in Mark Nathan Cohen, Roy S. Malpass, and Harold G. Klein, eds., *Biosocial Mechanisms of Population Regulation* (New Haven, Conn.: Yale University Press, 1980), pp. 321–348.

12. See Herbert Aptekar, *Anjea: Infanticide, Abortion, and Contraception in Savage Society* (New York: William Godwin, 1931).

This ability to feed the entire group required the maintenance of a delicate balance between the number of hunters and the number of nonhunters (i.e., women, children, and the elderly). An excess of nonhunters meant that everyone in the group would experience hunger and perhaps starvation. The Inuit developed a variety of methods to hold down the number of nonhunters: Elderly members might be asked to leave the group, mothers might nurse for years to reduce their fertility levels, and in some cases the group might resort to offspring sex selection. The practice of female infanticide reduced the number of infants who would never become hunters; it also lowered the number of potential mothers. Even today, despite some modern conveniences and sophisticated hunting equipment, the male-to-female ratios in several Inuit groups still exceed normal ratios.[13]

In many societies, the type of food procurement system plays a role in determining the prevalence of female infanticide. Hunting, large animal husbandry, and agriculture involving heavy plowing render sons more valuable than daughters.[14] Male-centered food production systems go hand in hand with patrilocality, wherein a wife not only joins her husband's family upon marriage but also severs daily contact with her natal family. In such cultures, females are usually not allowed to inherit real property, because when they marry, it would fall into the hands of their husbands' families. Even before marriage, girls are viewed not as family members but as houseguests. Investment in their care by their natal families is therefore considered a complete loss: A common proverb in patrilocal cultures is, "Raising a daughter is like watering a plant in another man's garden." Sons, who stay with their families to care and provide for them, are thus considered more valuable.[15]

The combination of male-centered food production systems and patrilocality virtually guarantees not only women's lowly place in society but also the hefty dowries necessary to marry them off. The dowry system furthers erodes any natural affection parents might have for their daughters, for their birth may consign their families to financial ruin.[16]

13. See Eric Alden Smith and S. Abigail Smith, "Inuit Sex-Ratio Variation: Population Control, Ethnographic Error, or Parental Manipulation?" *Current Anthropology*, Vol. 35, No. 5 (December 1994), pp. 595–624.

14. See H. Yuan Tien, *China's Strategic Demographic Initiative* (New York: Praeger, 1991); and Barbara D. Miller, *The Endangered Sex: Neglect of Female Children in Rural North India* (Ithaca, N.Y.: Cornell University Press, 1981).

15. See Fei Hsiao-tung, *Peasant Life in China: A Field Study of Country Life in the Yangtze Valley* (1939; reprint, London: Routledge and Kegan Paul, 1962).

16. See Ho Ping-ti, *Studies on the Population of China, 1368–1953* (Cambridge, Mass.: Harvard University Press, 1956).

According to an old Cantonese saying, "A daughter is a thief." The triple threat of patrilocality, male-oriented food provision systems, and the dowry thus predisposes cultures toward female infanticide as a rational choice. (A logical inference from this hypothesis is that in matrilocal cultures and in cultures where females provide most of the food—for example, rice cultures, sericultures, and small animal cultures—daughters are not a drain on their natal families, but important assets. In these cultures, women are often allowed to inherit real property, and a bride-price system (a type of groom-dowry system) develops in place of a dowry system. In these cultures, such as existed in southern India before independence in 1948, female infanticide was virtually unknown.

As in the case of military invasion, the physical loss of daughters in certain fragile subsistence systems is perceived as less risky than their social loss. The social loss of daughters through patrilocality can bring great costs to the household. Rather than suffer those costs or change to a system where costs are equalized, some groups prefer to accept the physical loss of their daughters through female infanticide. Furthermore, some societies (e.g., the Inuit) perceive this physical loss as the logical outcome of a zero-sum game, where the birth of daughters may imperil the delicate balance between food providers and nonfood providers, both at the time of their birth and well into the future. Resistance to sharing costs and risks equally within a family can thus help to create the predatory social practice of female infanticide.

Occasionally, this resistance to sharing costs and risks has resulted in male infanticide. In China, as the land-to-man ratio fell over succeeding generations, many farming families worried that the survival of several sons to manhood would mean the division of their land into parcels too small to allow for even subsistence agriculture. To avoid this, parents would kill all but one or two of their sons. In so doing, the rest of the family could avoid watching their inheritances dwindle to the point of having to sell off their land.[17]

In some cultures, all infants—whether male or female—are killed when famine strikes.[18] Indeed, in some cases, the infants are also canni-

---

17. See Fei, *Peasant Life in China*.

18.   The following anecdote, from the executive director of World Vision International, indicates that offspring sex selection in time of famine is occurring in cultures not traditionally associated with this practice: "I flew to Kapoeta in southern Sudan. The region was in the midst of famine; 250,000 people had already starved to death. As is common in Africa, when we landed on the dusty runway families came from miles around to see who had arrived. They knew we were from an aid organization, so mothers held up their emaciated children to show us how much they needed our help. It didn't take me long to notice the children's distended stomachs—a sure sign of mal-

balized as a source of food.[19] In other cultures, risks are shared, as entire families choose starvation over killing their infants or other children. As noted above, bringing women into the food provision system may equalize costs to the point where daughters become as valuable as sons, thus obviating the need for female infanticide. In some cases, however, predatory social practices such as female infanticide may achieve cultural acceptance and serve the needs of a malevolently resistant policy, thus ensuring continuation of the practice long after the "rationality" of the choice in the face of environmental or other stress has faded.

The Persistence of Offspring Sex Selection

What causes female infanticide to persist, in some cases outlasting the very conditions that produced it? How do female infanticide and offspring sex selection become such stubborn cultural practices, lasting in some cases hundreds of years past the last military invasion or famine? In the historical literature, two forces appear to encourage the continuation of offspring sex selection. The first is the development of religious sanction for the practice, and the second is the creation of a rigid system of hypergyny (i.e., marriage of a female to a male of higher status) within the society.

THE ROLE OF RELIGION

In some cultures, female infanticide is prevalent even when sacred texts condemn or prohibit the practice. Opposition by religious institutions subsides over time, as religious leaders adopt the practice in their own households during periods of invasion or famine. Tacit religious sanction allows continuation of the practice even after its supposed rationality can no longer be argued. This occurs most often when religious leaders and other prominent individuals derive personal advantage from the practice. The decision of religious leaders to practice female infanticide can thus be viewed as a means to cushion their own households from risk in times of environmental stress.

Nowhere is this dynamic more apparent than in Hinduism. Early

---

nutrition. But it was several minutes before I realized that in this sea of humanity, the mothers were only holding up sons; there were no daughters. In the familial hierarchy, girls were the last to be fed and the first to die. By the time we arrived, they were dead." Quoted in World Vision International, "The Girl Child: Females He Created Them," *World Vision Today*, Spring 1998, p. 2.

19. See, for example, Jasper Becker, *Hungry Ghosts: Mao's Secret Famine* (New York: Free Press, 1996).

Hindu religious texts (the Vedas) appear to hold all human life sacred. Indeed, in pre-Vedic and even Vedic periods, women were more highly valued by society and in religious thought than they are today. Women could be warriors, even generals, and they had a say in government and in their choice of husbands. Marriage involving bride-price was common. Some early Hindu texts appear to proscribe infanticide. For example, Vasishtha warned that only three acts could make a woman impure: becoming an outcast, murdering her husband, or killing her unborn child (Vas. Xxviii.7). According to Gautama, aborting a fetus was just cause for a woman to become an outcast (G.xxi.9).

Following the end of the Vedic period and the subsequent Moghul invasions, new religious texts and interpretations began to emerge. Among the most influential was the Manusamhita, or Code of Manu. Herein was developed the idea that the primary reason for a man to marry was to produce a son who could perform certain rituals for the father's soul after death. Without a son to perform these rituals, the father's soul would be consigned to hell (*put*). In addition, Hinduism began to assume that children were not living souls until approximately two years of age, and that the death of a child before that age was not the death of a complete human being. Causing the death of a child younger than two was thus not considered a religious transgression. Given the strength of son preference in India resulting at least in part from the environmental catalysts discussed above, this evolving religious understanding soothed the moral sensibilities of families that chose female infanticide.

The moral ambivalence displayed toward female infanticide can also be found in Chinese Buddhist culture. As Nicholas Kristof and Sheryl WuDunn write, "A popular moral text that was distributed widely during the sixteenth and seventeenth centuries [in China] orders people not to kill babies. But the injunction against infanticide is simply one on a long list of things that people should not do, such as leaping over food served on the floor; stepping over a person lying on a floor mat; weeping, spitting, or urinating when facing north (the direction of the emperor); spitting at a shooting star; or pointing at a rainbow. If you commit these sins, the Arbiter of Human Destiny would shave three or three hundred days off your life. The text does not indicate that infanticide is any worse than, for example, urinating when facing north."[20]

In another Chinese Buddhist text, infanticide carried a 1,000-point demerit against one's soul, the same level as for writing erotic literature.[21]

---

20. See Nicholas D. Kristof and Sheryl WuDunn, *China Wakes: The Struggle for the Soul of a Rising Power* (New York: Vintage, 1994), p. 227.

21. See Ho, *Studies on the Population of China, 1368–1953*, p. 60.

As in India, specifically female infanticide was most popular to the pre-twentieth-century Chinese mind. For example, one Chinese philosopher, Wang Shih-to (1802–89), advocated mass female infanticide as a way to control population growth.[22] As in Hindu culture, daughters in Buddhist cultures cannot perform the "incense and fire" rites for their ancestors' souls—only a son may perform these important religious duties. In another striking parallel to Indian culture, Chinese culture eventually embraced the view that "infanticide was not considered terrible in part because babies were not considered fully human until they were one year old or had a full set of teeth."[23] One Chinese fable even suggests that the gods smiled on acts of infanticide: "[A young couple] worried that their infant would take food that could better be used by the man's sick mother, so they buried the baby alive. This act of filial piety so touched the gods that they arranged for the couple to find a pile of gold as they dug their baby's grave."[24]

Not all religions have sanctioned offspring sex selection. The practice, once common among the pre-Islamic nomadic tribes of the Arabian Peninsula, was essentially condemned when the prophet Mohammed asked his followers to imagine themselves before God on the day of judgment, then added: "And when the girl-child that was buried alive is asked for what sin she was slain, . . . then every soul will know what it hath produced."[25] The power of that one line of scripture was enough to deny religious sanction to what had become a persistent practice. Without that sanction, practitioners of female infanticide were deemed to be

---

22. See Robert Hans van Gulik, *Sexual Life in Ancient China: A Preliminary Survey of Chinese Sex and Society from ca. 1500 B.C. till 1644 A.D.* (Leiden, Netherlands: E.J. Brill, 1974), p. 249.

23. See Kristof and WuDunn, *China Wakes*, p. 227; and Lillian M. Li, "Life and Death in a Chinese Famine: Infanticide as a Demographic Consequence of the 1935 Yellow River Flood," *Comparative Studies in Society and History*, Vol. 33, No. 3 (July 1991), p. 503.

24. See Kristof and WuDunn, *China Wakes*, p. 227; and Li, "Life and Death in a Chinese Famine," p. 504.

25. Avner Giladi, "Some Observations on Infanticide in Medieval Muslim Society," *International Journal of Middle East Studies*, Vol. 22, No. 2 (May 1990), p. 186. The verse cited is verse 8 of sura 81. In sura 16, verses 57–59, the Koran also passes negative moral judgment on fathers ashamed of the birth of their daughters: "And they assign unto Allah daughters—Be He Glorified!—and unto themselves what they desire [i.e., sons]; When if one of them receiveth tidings of the birth of a female, his face remaineth darkened and he is wroth inwardly, He hideth himself from the folk because of the evil of that whereof he hath had tidings [asking himself]: Shall he keep it in contempt, or bury it beneath the dust? Verily, evil is their judgment." Ibid., p. 187.

beyond the moral order of Muslim society (except in Islamic societies bordering India).

Historically, then, religion has taken a variety of approaches toward offspring sex selection. This suggests that a more fundamental dynamic must be at work in decisions to participate in this practice.

THE IMPERATIVES OF HYPERGYNY

In the absence of military invasion or chronically fragile subsistence systems, it would be difficult for religious sanction alone to perpetuate the practice of female infanticide in certain societies over the course of centuries, if not millennia. A more basic factor must be in play that elucidates the threat inherent in every female birth.

We argue that the answer lies in the family's perceived threat of loss of social boundaries with the birth of every daughter. Social boundaries create divisions among people: divisions of identity, wealth, power (in all its forms), privilege, risk, vulnerability, and security. Boundaries allow the family or group to exclude others from sharing its resources. They also shield it from the suffering that a lack of resources can produce. Only by creating and maintaining social boundaries can families and groups perpetuate inequality in resource accumulation and access. During periods of environmental stress, a family or group with strong social boundaries may not need to make adjustments to guarantee its safety; in fact, they are able to resist making any such adjustments. In contrast, nonfamily or nongroup (i.e., out-group) members are likely to be more vulnerable because they bear the brunt of any sacrifice, suffering, or other adjustment resulting from the environmental stress. Thus the in-group's resistance to making adjustments to environmental stress results in disproportionate adjustment for the out-group. There is, however, an obvious glitch to the logic of social boundaries: The in-group's exclusionary access to resources is always vulnerable because of the human need for exogamy—that is, the need to look beyond one's kin group for suitable marriage partners.

Families, however defined, are the unit around which foundational social boundaries are erected. A family's accumulation of wealth, power, security, and so on can be perpetuated only through inheritance. Without a next generation to maintain the family's social boundaries, and thus the accumulation of resource exclusivity, the effort expended in accumulation is wasted, as are the resources accumulated. This was the dilemma, for example, confronting eunuchs in imperial China: For centuries eunuchs fought for the right to adopt uncastrated sons, who could give them families and to whom the eunuchs could bequeath their riches.

Theoretically, if families could inbreed, resource accumulation would remain intact as long as the family produced both sons and daughters. But because inbreeding produces terrible genetic consequences, a fact recognized in virtually every society throughout history, humans turn to exogamy.

The need to exchange marriage partners outside of the family (generally third cousins and beyond) creates a dilemma. New generations must be produced for social boundaries and resource exclusivity to be maintained, yet the marriages required for such reproduction may compromise those same social boundaries and imperil resource exclusivity. In this light, marriage is both extremely important and extremely perilous.

How can the threat to social boundaries and resource exclusivity be minimized in the context of exogamous marriage? Conceptualizing the choice in this way permits some generalizations about family behavior concerning sons, daughters, marriage, inheritance, and a wide variety of social phenomena that otherwise could not be made. We find that these generalizations hold true in a variety of cultures throughout time, and apply not only to family-based resource exclusivity but also to ethnic-, class-, and caste-based systems of resource exclusivity.

To illustrate how a family or group seeks to minimize the threat to social boundaries and resource exclusivity, we assume the following three conditions: (1) family-based accumulation of resources or resource access of persistent value, (2) the desire to maintain social boundaries that make possible accumulation and resource exclusivity, and (3) the need for exogamous marriage for biological reasons. From these assumptions, we derive seven propositions.

First, in most traditional economies, families do not leave marriage to chance: Rather, they strictly control the choice of mates for their children. In these economies, the family seeks to keep sons within its social boundaries, for at least three reasons: (1) sons are better able to provide physical defense of resource accumulation and resource exclusivity; (2) sons are likely to be the primary creators of additional accumulation in societies centered around hunting, large animal husbandry, harsh land agriculture, or predatory warfare; (3) sons are capable of producing more children than daughters. As H. Yuan Tien, a noted scholar of Chinese demography, writes, "More children, particularly boys, augment productive capacity and future old-age security. Moreover, the need to have a few children (and a son at least) goes beyond these concerns. The rural reality, according to those familiar with the village life, is that one's survival and ability to fend off hostile neighbors or to dominate others has been and still remains a function of one's family size and kinship groups."[26]

---

26. See Tien, *China's Strategic Demographic Initiative*, p. 202.

Second, daughters given in marriage to another family are denied access to the natal family's accumulated wealth so that the social boundaries and resource exclusivity of the natal family can remain intact. Daughters are not allowed to inherit family accumulation to any significant degree, especially not land. Indeed, despite the passage of laws that assert a woman's right to inheritance, many traditional societies continue to favor males in this regard.

Third, to minimize penetration of their social boundaries, families choose their daughters' husbands from families of higher social status (hypergyny).[27] Daughters should not be married off to men from families of lower status. A hypergynous strategy ensures that if social boundaries of the daughter's family are altered, it will be in a positive way. In Indian society, as Ruki Jayaraman, notes, "Higher castes, to maintain their position, made castes rigid. It is this rigid caste system, and the goal to maintain rigid castes, that creates the oppression of women."[28] These sentiments are reflected in proverbs common in hypergynous cultures. For example, in the southeast of China, "the Cantonese and the Hokkiens refer to their daughters as 'goods on which one loses one's capital,' the point being that it costs money and effort to raise and train a girl only for the investment to be handed over to her husband's family when she married."[29] Most benefits to the family of a daughter in a hypergynous marriage may be largely intangible: For example, if the groom's family is favorably disposed toward the bride's family, it could extend to them protection or other forms of assistance. Hypergynous unions thus raise the status of the bride's family. The giving of a daughter in marriage signifies some measure of alliance between the two families, extending a social network that allows the daughter's family to thrive and maintain their accumulation and resource exclusivity.

Fourth, the giving of a daughter in marriage represents a form of tribute from a lower-status party to a higher-status party. A nonreciprocated provision of a bride connotes the subordinate status of the bride's family vis-à-vis the groom's family: thus the Chinese saying, "The family of the

---

27. The most important empirical and theoretical studies of hypergyny are those of Mildred Dickemann, who for many years was an anthropologist at the University of California at Riverside. See, for example, Dickemann, "Paternal Confidence and Dowry Competition: A Biocultural Analysis of Purdah," in Richard D. Alexander and Donald W. Tinkle, eds., *Natural Selection and Social Behavior: Recent Research and New Theory* (New York: Chiron, 1981), pp. 417–438.

28. Ruki Jayaraman, visiting professor of political science at Brigham Young University, 1991–96, communication with authors, April 16, 1996.

29. See Hugh D.R. Baker, *Chinese Family and Kinship* (London: Macmillan, 1979), p. 41.

married daughter holds its head down, while the family of the man whom she has married holds its head up."[30] In the wake of military invasions, for example, daughters were themselves offered as tribute, which is probably at the root of the humiliation felt by families giving their daughters away in marriage. Dowry, or wealth tribute, usually accompanies the bride tribute.

Fifth, in accordance with Mildred Dickemann's theory of hypergyny, in societies that maintain social boundaries, one detects an overall upward movement of women as their families struggle to arrange marriages that will not compromise their own social standing.[31] Many, perhaps most, marriages are isogamous (marriages between spouses of equal social rank); otherwise they will be hypergynous. This results in at least three demographic corollaries: (1) families at the highest level of society cannot marry off their daughters without severely damaging their social boundaries; (2) families in the middle strata can arrange the marriage of a few daughters without suffering critical loss of their status and accumulated wealth; and (3) families on the lowest rungs of the social ladder may not be able to find wives for their sons.

Sixth, when the marriage of daughters would be too costly or socially threatening, families pull them out of the marriage market either by engaging in female infanticide or by promoting female celibacy. In the past, some cultures created elaborate systems of nunneries or secular celibate sisterhoods, where families would often pay a "dowry" to such institutions in return for taking in their daughters. The higher the status or the more exclusive the identity of the family, the more inclusive the disposal of daughters becomes. In Japan, for example, the daughters of several emperors were sent to nunneries. Some Rajput clans in India killed all of their female infants (before the British intervened to stop the practice), as did the tribal Khonds. For the Rajputs, the rationale was societal status; for the Khonds, it was ethnic identity. Middle-class families might make useful alliances by marrying off one or two of their daughters, but beyond that number the burden becomes too great to bear, thus increasing the likelihood of female infanticide.

Seventh, at the lowest levels of society, surfeits of unmarriageable

---

30. See Arthur Henderson Smith, *Village Life in China: A Study in Sociology* (New York: F.H. Revell, 1899), p. 286.

31. See Mildred Dickemann, "The Ecology of Mating Systems in Hypergynous Dowry Societies," *Social Science Information,* Vol. 18, No. 2 (May 1979), pp. 163–195; Mildred Dickemann, "Female Infanticide, Reproductive Strategies, and Social Stratification: A Preliminary Model," in Napoleon A. Chagnon and William Irons, eds., *Evolutionary Biology and Human Social Behavior: An Anthropological Perspective* (North Scituate, Mass.: Duxbury, 1979), pp. 321–367.

males start to develop. The greater the number of daughters taken out of the marriage market and the greater the upward movement of other daughters through hypergynous marriages, the greater the number of unmarriageable males at the lower levels. At these levels, women may be sold into isogamous or hypogynous marriages (i.e., marriages to men of lower status)—bride-price instead of bride dowry may be the norm. At the lowest levels, then, there may be little incentive to dispose of daughters, and the birth sex ratio may be the most normal of any level in society.

COUNTERFACTUAL ANALYSIS

This analysis yields at least two counterfactuals. First, in societies where risk and wealth are shared more equally, or where family accumulation and resource exclusivity cannot persist over time, or where they can change quickly (as in a modern market economy), there should be greater reciprocal exchange of daughters. In such cases, female infanticide is less likely. This is one reason why offspring sex selection in, say, medieval Germanic peasant villages appears to have been almost nonexistent, and why the British promoted *ekdas*—exchange marriage collectives—to stem female infanticide in colonial India. In these cases, reciprocal exchange of daughters was commonplace, and class differences were less extreme.

Second, as previously mentioned, in economies where women are the primary creators of wealth—or at least equal creators of wealth—and where predation is not traditional, some matrilineal inheritance may occur. As a result, daughters become more valuable, and female infants are less likely to be killed. In areas where the economy is based on certain types of rice agriculture or sericulture, for example, women produce the wealth, and female infanticide is rare. As a result, some areas of China, such as the Pearl River Delta, and much of southern India do not exhibit highly skewed sex ratios. The sex ratios in most of Southeast Asia are nearly normal, perhaps again a function of women's greater role in economic productivity.

There is one important caveat regarding these counterfactuals: When social policy mandates that families have no more than one child, even in more modern quasi-egalitarian societies, the overwhelming preference is still for sons, because of their greater potential for protecting and augmenting their families' resources and maintaining their boundaries. Indeed, in societies with one-child policies, the difference between a family unit that endures and one that does not may rest on the birth of that one son. As a result, offspring sex selection may intensify, despite women's seemingly more egalitarian status. This dynamic is playing itself out in, for example, modern China, despite laws that place responsibility for the care of aged parents on both daughters and sons and equalize their inheritance rights.

Conclusion

Historically, prevalent offspring sex selection has been a response to events or conditions that create huge environmental stress, such as military invasion or the presence of a chronically fragile subsistence system. In some cultures, prevalent offspring sex selection persists because it helps to preserve group or family social boundaries and resource exclusivity. In many cases, its persistence has been further guaranteed by religious sanction that evolves over time and by the imperatives that hypergyny forces on households of different social rank. As we discuss in subsequent chapters, however, there is a societal price to be paid for this predatory practice.

Organization of the Book

The remainder of this book is organized into six chapters. In chapter 2, we survey the practice of offspring sex selection throughout human history. We begin with a brief introduction to the practice of infanticide and induced abortion in the animal world, followed by a review of non-sex-selective practices of human infanticide. We then discuss the types of data that indicate the presence of offspring sex selection and the strengths and weaknesses of various data sources. Next we assemble documentation of sex-selective infanticide in ancient Greece and Rome, as well as in historical Europe and other parts of the world. We close with a discussion of contemporary sex-selective practices.

The third and fourth chapters examine offspring sex selection in India and China. For each country, we offer a history of the evolution of the practice, followed by a discussion of its current sex ratios and assessments and comparisons of various data sources. We disaggregate regional, tribal, and urban/rural population data to estimate the number of surplus young adult males, or bare branches, in each society, and then project figures out to the year 2020.

Chapter 5 lays out the theory and history linking the presence of significant numbers of bare branches to increased instability and violence within and between societies. The theoretical literature is diverse, spanning social sciences such as anthropology, biology, criminology, psychology, organization behavior, and sociology. All concur that the existence of sizable numbers of surplus young adult males poses a potential threat to society. Bare branches, who are frequently the least educated and least skilled, also tend to be the most prone to use violence to obtain redress of their low socioeconomic status. Following this discussion, we identify historical cases in which bare branches arguably played a destabilizing role: Case studies include the Nien Rebellion in China, the Reconquista in Portugal, precolonial Oudh in what is now the state of Uttar Pradesh in India, and colonial Taiwan. We then probe additional cases for the presence of bare branches, including the role of eunuchs and monks in pre-twentieth-century China, as well as other cases, such as historical Polynesia.

In chapter 6, we examine China's and India's contemporary bare branches, noting similarity in their characteristics to the bare branches of earlier eras, including transience, low socioeconomic status, congregation, and relative lack of education. In addition, we perform a behavioral analysis of contemporary bare branches, noting their predisposition to substance abuse, violent crime, and collective aggression. Aggregate correlational analysis of sex ratios and violent crime rates demonstrates strong, statistically significant results. We also discuss the logical possibilities for government intervention to counteract the destabilizing nature of high-sex-ratio societies. Many of the logical possibilities turn out to be unsavory or less than effective; others may create greater conflict in the international system. Nevertheless, there are some positive initiatives that may ameliorate the situation over time.

Finally, in chapter 7, we explicate why it is increasingly important for all nations to understand the very different security calculus of high-sex-ratio societies. The extremely low status of women in these societies negatively affects their prospects for both democracy and peace. Given that almost half of humanity resides in this area, the implications for the rest of the world could be profound.

Chapter 2

Offspring Sex Selection in Historical Perspective

From Infanticide to Sex-Selective Abortion and the Problem of "Missing Females"

The abnormally high sex ratios in Asia have generated considerable debate since the late 1980s. Scholars have attributed the high numbers of males and dearth of females to sex-selective practices, particularly female infanticide and abortion. To understand and explain contemporary practices of sex selection, we first review accounts of the killing of infants throughout history with a view to determining the extent and causes of infanticide, and female infanticide in particular. Female sex selection is attributed to a preference for sons, a preference found in many cultures, but most noticeable in parts of Asia. We examine populations in south-central and eastern Asia where son preference is manifested in sex-selective abortions as well as in a gender bias in the care of female infants and children that results in excess female deaths. Finally, we review the debate concerning the "missing females" in Asia to estimate the current number of females "missing" from selected countries.

Non-Sex-Related Selection Practices

To provide perspective for our discussion of human offspring sex-selection practices, an understanding of the ubiquity in nature and culture of non-sex-related infanticide and abortion is useful. For example, such practices are not uncommon in the animal world.[1] Experts have noted the eating of young after birth not only among lower life forms, such as insects, but also among small mammals, such as cats and hamsters. Infanti-

---

1. Most of the following generalizations about non-sex-selective infanticide and abortion in animals come from Glenn Hausfater and Sarah Blaffer Hrdy, eds., *Infanticide: Comparative and Evolutionary Perspectives* (New York: Aldine de Gruyter, 1984).

cide for the purpose of maintaining order in social hierarchies has even been documented among apes and monkeys, and perhaps dolphins. Abortion in animals may, in certain circumstances, be biologically based: Some types of small mammals, such as mice, spontaneously abort fetuses when exposed to the pheromones of an unfamiliar male of the same species. Such abortions, however, may be more than passively induced in other species: For example, usurper stallions often kick pregnant mares of the herd to induce abortion of the deposed stallion's offspring.

Infanticide has also been practiced throughout human history. As anthropologist Laila Williamson notes, "Infanticide has been practiced on every continent and by people on every level of cultural complexity, from hunters and gatherers to high civilizations, including our own [Western] ancestors. Rather than being an exception, then, it has been the rule."[2] The following overview of non-sex-selective infanticide illustrates the scope of this practice and provides a context for our discussion of sex-selective infanticide.

William Sumner, a historian who has studied infanticide in detail, offers a useful explanation for the psychology that underpins this practice: "Children add to the weight of the struggle for existence of their parents. The relation of parent to child is one of sacrifice. The interests of children and parents are antagonistic. The fact that there are, or may be, compensations does not affect the primary relation between the two. It may well be believed that, if procreation had not been put under the dominion of a great passion, it would have been caused to cease by the burdens it entails. Abortion and infanticide are especially interesting because they show how early in the history of civilization the burden of children became so heavy that parents began to shirk it."[3] In this sense, parents may regard their offspring as the unintended but sometimes unavoidable consequence of sexual intercourse. Though in eras of unreliable contraception the birth of children might have been unavoidable, the responsibility of raising them was not.

There have been six main non-sex-related reasons why people have committed infanticide.[4] First, in our survey of the historical literature, vir-

---

2. Laila Williamson, "Infanticide: An Anthropological Analysis," in Marvin Kohl, ed., *Infanticide and the Value of Life* (New York: Prometheus, 1978), p. 61.

3. William Graham Sumner, *Folkways* (New York: Dover, 1959), pp. 309–310.

4. Survey articles on infanticide in various eras and regions include Avner Giladi, "Some Observations on Infanticide in Medieval Muslim Society," *International Journal of Middle East Studies*, Vol. 22, No. 2 (May 1990), pp. 185–200; Mildred Dickemann, "Demographic Consequences of Infanticide in Man," *Annual Review of Ecology and System-*

tually all cultures in every geographic region, including Africa, the Americas, Asia, Europe, and Oceania, have overlooked or even sanctioned the disposal of "imperfect" infants through abandonment (often called "exposure") or infanticide. In some cultures, the mother of a malformed infant might also be killed, ostensibly because the malformation was thought to be a sign of her infidelity. Works of philosophy that call for putting such children to death include Aristotle's *Politics* and Seneca's *De Ira*.

Second, unusual births or the birth of a child with unusual characteristics could also end in infanticide. Among indigenous cultures of the Pacific Islands and the Western Hemisphere, for example, the birth of twins was viewed as an ominous sign that could lead to infanticide of one or both infants.[5] In some cultures, even the mother of twins might also be killed, on grounds that the twin birth symbolized her supposed infidelity. Herbert Aptekar and Edward Westermarck mention other oddities that could lead to infanticide, including position in birth order (e.g., tenth children were always killed among certain African tribes), eruption

---

atics, Vol. 6 (1975), pp. 107–137; William L. Langer, "Infanticide: A Historical Survey," *History of Childhood Quarterly: The Journal of Psychohistory*, Vol. 1, No. 3 (Winter 1974), pp. 353–365; Sumner, *Folkways*; Edward Westermarck, *The Origin and Development of the Moral Ideas* (London: Macmillan, 1924); Williamson, "Infanticide: An Anthropological Analysis"; Kathryn L. Moseley, "The History of Infanticide in Western Society," *Issues in Law and Medicine*, Vol. 1, No. 5 (March 1986), pp. 345–362; Kees de Meer, "Mortality in Children among the Aymara Indians of Southern Peru," *Social Science and Medicine*, Vol. 26, No. 2 (1988), pp. 253–258; "Infanticide," in Maria Leach, ed., *Dictionary of Folklore, Mythology, and Legend*, Vol. 1 (New York: Funk and Wagnalls, 1949), pp. 522–524; Jack Lindsay, *The Ancient World: Manners and Morals* (New York: G.P. Putnam's Sons, 1968); John M. Riddle, *Contraception and Abortion from the Ancient World to the Renaissance* (Cambridge, Mass.: Harvard University Press, 1992); Lloyd deMause, "The Evolution of Childhood," in deMause, ed., *The History of Childhood* (New York: Psychohistory Press, 1974), pp. 1–73; Elise Boulding, *The Underside of History: A View of Women through Time* (Boulder, Colo.: Westview Press 1976); Ruth Oldenziel, "The Historiography of Infanticide in Antiquity: A Literature Stillborn," in Josine Blok and Peter Mason, eds., *Sexual Asymmetry: Studies in Ancient Society* (Amsterdam: J.C. Gieben, 1987), pp. 87–107; Asen Balikci, *The Netslik Eskimo* (New York: Natural History Press, 1970); Sarah B. Pomeroy, "Infanticide in Hellenistic Greece," in Averil Cameron and Amelie Kuhrt, eds., *Images of Women in Antiquity* (Detroit, Mich.: Wayne State University Press, 1993), pp. 207–222; Mary R. Lefkowitz and Maureen B. Fant, *Women's Life in Greece and Rome* (Baltimore, Md.: Johns Hopkins University Press, 1992); and Herbert Aptekar, *Anjea: Infanticide, Abortion, and Contraception in Savage Society* (New York: William Godwin, 1931). Unless otherwise noted, the generalizations about non-sex-selective infanticide in humans that follow in the text appear in these sources.

5. See Gary Granzberg, "Twin Infanticide: A Cross-Cultural Test of a Materialistic Explanation," *Ethos*, Vol. 1, No. 4 (Winter 1973), pp. 405–412; and Ludwik Krzywicki, *Primitive Society and Its Vital Statistics* (London: Macmillan, 1934).

of the upper incisors before the lower teeth (West Africa), or being born on an "evil" day.[6] Occasionally, firstborns were victims of infanticide. In some Southeastern African tribes, if a woman remarried following the death of her husband, her firstborn child would be killed, regardless of his parentage. The belief was that if the child were allowed to live, harm would befall the family.[7] In other cases, the issue was not parentage but rather the special status ascribed to firstborns. Indeed, in his early twentieth-century study of morality, Westermarck, a moral philosopher, remarked on the commonality of traditions concerning the sacrifice of firstborn children among various indigenous peoples of Africa, Australia, China, Europe, India, and North America.[8]

Third, in cultures on every continent, children born outside of social convention could also be at great risk of infanticide. These included children born outside of wedlock, children born as the result of rape or incest, and children born of union with a member of another race. In some cases, the expectant mother might have tried to induce abortion through, for example, the use or herbs or massage; failing that, she might have resorted to infanticide. Some infants were drowned at birth in buckets brought by midwives for this very purpose; others were victims of "overlaying" (in this case, a mother would claim to have accidentally suffocated her child while she was asleep), and still others were simply abandoned. Given the severe consequences that could attend pregnancy out of wedlock in Christian societies, including death by stoning, hanging, drowning, or immolation, the killing of illegitimate infants was widespread where Christianity took root, such as historical Europe. Indeed, a retired sea captain, Thomas Coram, was "so depressed by the daily sight of infant corpses thrown on the dust heaps of London" that he decided to establish one of the city's first foundling hospitals in 1741.[9] Most foundlings, however, succumbed to disease or malnutrition (or a combination of both). Many babies in Europe—about two-thirds of them illegitimate—were given to wet nurses, who were nicknamed "killer nurses" or "angel makers" because of the propensity for their charges to die while in their care.[10]

---

6. See Aptekar, *Anjea;* and Westermarck, *The Origin and Development of the Moral Ideas.*

7. Westermarck, *The Origin and Development of the Moral Ideas,* p. 460.

8. Ibid., pp. 458–459.

9. Langer, "Infanticide: A Historical Survey," pp. 358–359.

10. For more on this, see Lionel Rose, *The Massacre of the Innocents: Infanticide in Britain, 1800–1939* (London: Routledge and Kegan Paul, 1986).

Fourth, infants could be killed if they were thought to be an unacceptable burden on the family. In many cultures, fathers had a legal right to kill any infants born to the family, which could include not only his children (and sometimes grandchildren) but also those of his servants. In ancient Greece and Rome, for example, if a father decided the child was unwanted, it would usually be buried alive. As a result, Greek and Roman families were generally small and had skewed sex ratios. Among the primitive Teutons, if the father picked up the newborn from the ground, it was ordained to live and would be bathed and named. If he did not, it would be exposed. In the seventeenth century, Jesuit missionaries in China were horrified to find that in Beijing alone, "several thousand babies were thrown onto the streets like refuse, to be collected each morning by carriers who dumped them into a huge pit outside the city."[11] On some smaller Pacific islands, tribal leaders, rather than fathers, had the right to decide which infants would live.[12] Though in some cultures abandoned infants could be taken in by other families, in many cases abandonment was a pretext for assuring the infant's death: In nineteenth-century England, thousands of children in the London area were found dead in rivers, canals, and drains; the children had been "abandoned" in water.[13] In other cases, mothers who feared they could not care for their infants would opt instead to kill them. Among some horseback tribes of North America, for example, mothers might have killed infants whose care slowed their ability to keep up with the rest of the tribe.

Fifth, during periods of drought or severe flooding, parents in some cultures might kill infants and young children to prevent them from becoming a drain on scarce resources. The Australian Aborigines, for example, practiced infanticide until brought under British rule, particularly in desert areas and in times of food shortage.[14] This practice was also common in parts of Asia, particularly in China and Japan.

Sixth, perhaps the most common reason given for practicing infanticide has been parents' desire to space their children to avoid having to care for too many infants and toddlers at the same time. In many cul-

---

11. Langer, "Infanticide: A Historical Survey," p. 354, citing a Dr. John B. Beck writing in 1835.

12. William Ellis, *Polynesian Researches, during a Residence of Nearly Eight Years in the Society and Sandwich Islands*, Vol. 1 (London: Henry G. Bohn, 1859).

13. William L. Langer, "Checks on Population Growth, 1750–1850," *Scientific American*, Vol. 226, No. 2 (February 1972), p. 94

14. See Ronald M. Berndt and Catherine H. Berndt, *The World of the First Australians: An Introduction to the Traditional Life of the Australian Aborigines* (London: Angus and Robertson, 1964).

tures, mothers still believe that it is possible to breastfeed only one infant at a time. Thus, babies born to mothers who are still nursing a toddler may be killed. This was true, for example, in historical Aboriginal cultures, whose nomadic lifestyle put a premium on mobility. Indeed, in a survey of cultures, protection of an older nursling was a common reason given for killing a newborn.[15]

Historically, therefore, infant life was generally considered of little value. According to historian William Lecky, disposal of unwanted infants was "practiced on a gigantic scale with absolute impunity [and] noticed by writers with most frigid indifference."[16] Even in Christian societies, where killing of innocents was considered a mortal sin, infant exposure was initially viewed as a lesser offense, becoming a capital crime only in the eighteenth and nineteenth centuries. In his historical study *The Kindness of Strangers: The Abandonment of Children in Western Europe from Late Antiquity to the Renaissance*, John Boswell notes that despite difficulties in data collection, it must be concluded that abandonment and infanticide were common. Boswell suggests that 10–40 percent of urban children in Western Europe were abandoned in the early modern period, a rate presumably similar to that of earlier historical periods.[17] Scholars at various times have referred to prevalent infanticide as "a carnival of infant slaughter," "a massacre of the Innocents," and "the prevailing and stubborn vice of antiquity."[18] Perhaps less well known is that offspring sex-selective practices have also been pervasive throughout human history. It is to that subject this we now turn.

---

15. Susan C.M. Scrimshaw, "Infanticide in Human Populations: Societal and Individual Concerns," in Hausfater and Hrdy, *Infanticide: Comparative and Evolutionary Perspectives*, pp. 439–462. For example, this was cited as a common reason for infanticide among the Yanomamo, a conflict-ridden warrior tribe of ancient origin found in central Brazil. Napoleon A. Chagnon studied them intensively from the 1960s to 1980s. See Chagnon, *Yanomamo: The Fierce People*, 2d ed. (New York: Holt, Rinehart, and Winston, 1977), p. 15.

16. William Edward Hartpole Lecky, *History of European Morals from Augustus to Charlemagne*, Vol. 2 (London: Longmans, Greens, 1869), p. 27.

17. Keith Thomas categorizes Boswell's research in this way in his review of Boswell's book. See Thomas, "Fateful Exposure," *Times Literary Supplement*, August 25–31, 1989, pp. 913–914; and John Boswell, *The Kindness of Strangers: The Abandonment of Children in Western Europe from Late Antiquity to the Renaissance* (Chicago: University of Chicago Press, 1998).

18. See Langer, "Infanticide: A Historical Survey"; Lecky, *History of European Morals from Augustus to Charlemagne*; and Edward Gibbon, *The Decline and Fall of the Roman Empire* (Chicago: Encyclopædia Britannica, 1990).

Offspring Sex Selection

Historically, in almost all cases of offspring sex selection, male infants are selected over females. Offspring sex selection can take place prior to conception through, for example, modern methods of sperm separation. It can occur following conception but prior to birth through sex-selective abortion or other reproductive technologies; or it can happen after birth through active or passive infanticide—that is, denial of proper care in the form of food, clothing, shelter, or health care. Descriptions of methods for determining the sex of fetuses are recorded throughout history, including one Chinese manuscript dating back 4,400 years.[19] The Greek philosophers Anaxagorous and Aristotle taught that the positioning of the male and female bodies during intercourse could control the sex of a baby.[20] To ensure the birth of male progeny, various folk methods claim that the timing of conception (odd days, in the evening with a cold wind blowing, or when the moon is full) as well as the consumption of certain foods (including red meat and salty snacks) could ensure a male fetus. In India, Ayurvedic texts (ancient texts describing methods of complementary medicine) list a number of practices for manipulating the sex of a child in the six weeks following conception, during which time it was believed that the sex of the child was undetermined.[21] Also in India, pregnant women could ingest certain medicines, called *seh palatna*, within the first three months of pregnancy to ensure the birth of a male child.

The reasons underlying the desire for male children vary across cultures and through time. Generally, families in patrilineal cultures prefer to have at least one son, if not a predominance of sons. This preference depends on three sets of factors that determine the value of women: (1) economic factors (including values assigned to women's work, their ability to contribute to family income or labor, and whether they have dowries), (2) social factors (particularly kinship, marriage patterns, and religion), and (3) psychological factors. Cultures differ in the way their preference for sons affects parents' decisions about the size and composi-

---

19. Manuel J. Gordon, "The Control of Sex," *Scientific American,* Vol. 199, No. 5 (November 1958), p. 87.

20. For this and other folklore relating to control of the sex of a baby, see Alison Dundes Renteln, "Sex Selection and Reproductive Freedom," *Women's Studies International Forum,* Vol. 15, No. 3 (May–June 1992), pp. 405–426.

21. Forum against Sex Determination and Sex Pre-selection, "Using Technology, Choosing Sex: The Campaign against Sex Determination and the Question of Choice," *Development Dialogue* (Uppsala, Sweden) Nos. 1–2 (1992), pp. 91–102.

tion of their families. Son preference may result in high fertility rates and large families to ensure the desired number of male offspring; it could result in small families in which the composition and number of children are manipulated through offspring sex selection; or parents may not act at all on their preference for sons. We are primarily interested in populations that use manipulation of various kinds to produce the desired family composition.

How to Determine Skewed Sex Ratios

Ancient texts describing methods of detecting the sex of fetuses suggest a long history for son preference, but how is it possible to determine whether male children were actually selected (i.e., that female children were actively or passively killed because of their sex)? One method is to ascertain the number of males per number of females in a society. Demographers commonly use sex ratios as an indicator of a population's gender balance. Gender balance exists when a population's sex ratio is comparable to standard rates that reflect known "normal" biological patterns. Two key sex ratios are used to suggest gender balance. The first is sex ratio at birth, commonly measured against the standard of 105 to 107 males born per 100 females, although there may be some variation among some populations on the basis of parental age as well as parental diet and nutrition.[22] The second ratio is for the total population, which may vary according to a society's age structure, its overall mortality patterns, and international migration, but is generally expected to be close to 100 males per 100 females.[23]

---

22. Researchers note that the older the father, the lower the sex ratio of offspring, generally speaking. It also appears that the sex ratio of offspring born to vegetarian parents may be lower than average. Populations of African descent also give birth to slightly more females than average; thus their sex ratios at birth are typically between 102.5 and 103.5. See Stephan Klasen, "'Missing Women' Reconsidered," *World Development*, Vol. 22, No. 7 (July 1994), p. 1062. Demographers accept that the 105–107:100 range for birth sex ratios holds for other parts of the world. William H. James, "The Sex Ratio of Oriental Births," *Annals of Human Biology*, Vol. 12, No. 5 (September/October 1985), pp. 485–487. In addition to the sex ratio at birth, it is also possible to refer to sex ratios at conception, which are approximately 160 to 100 in favor of males. Most miscarriages and stillbirths involve male fetuses, however; thus the sex ratio at birth drops to approximately 105 to 107 males born per 100 females. See Klasen, "'Missing Women' Reconsidered," *World Development*, Vol. 22, No. 7 (July 1994), pp. 1061–1071.

23. Generally, women have longer life expectancies than men; thus countries with large elderly populations—such as those in Europe and North America—may have overall sex ratios that favor women. Countries that have lost large numbers of men in war will also exhibit sex ratios that favor women.

Because of greater female longevity, sex ratios of 97–98 males per 100 females are typical in more developed areas. A sex ratio at birth higher than 105–107 males per 100 females indicates possible gender imbalance. Overall sex ratios of 100 or higher would suggest excess female mortality, with the exception of populations with very large childhood populations. Early childhood sex ratios (ages 0–4) higher than 105 might be evidence of selection against females.

Birth and early childhood sex ratios are among the most accurate indicators of gender inequality, whereas overall population sex ratios are often misleading. Some populations exhibit high or low overall sex ratios unrelated to gender inequality. Some countries in the Middle East, for example, may have abnormally high sex ratios if their large numbers of foreign guest workers are included.[24] Similarly, urban sex ratios can lean heavily toward males because of their greater migration to urban centers. Normal overall sex ratios, however, may also mask problems. For example, offspring sex selection may occur in only some segments of a population. Disaggregating data is often the only way to determine whether offspring sex selection is being practiced.

Determining skewed sex ratios is a fairly straightforward task in modern states with reliable record keeping. Sex ratios in the pre–industrial revolution world and sex ratios in contemporary societies with poor record keeping are more difficult to ascertain. Some countries—such as India—may record the sex ratios for the overall population through censuses, but not have a method for recording the sex ratios at birth.

According to some archaeologists and anthropologists, physical evidence from burial grounds since the Pleistocene suggests that the practice of female infanticide was a worldwide phenomenon.[25] Such physical

---

24. For example, 2003 estimates of the sex ratios for Bahrain (135.1), Jordan (108.6), Kuwait (151.3), Oman (135.0), Qatar (173.5), Saudi Arabia (115.9), and United Arab Emirates (185.8) are extremely high given the presence of large numbers of foreign male workers. United Nations Population Division, *World Population Prospects: The 2002 Revision,* http://www.un.org/esa/population/publications/wpp2000/annex-tables.pdf.

25. Henri V. Vallois argues that ancient skeletal remains suggest that female infanticide began early in human history. See Vallois, "The Social Life of Early Man: The Evidence of Skeletons," in Sherwood L. Washburn, ed., *Social Life of Early Man* (New York: Wenner-Gren Foundation for Anthropological Research, 1961), pp. 214–235; and Mark Nathan Cohen and Sharon Bennett, "Skeletal Evidence for Sex Roles and Gender Hierarchies in Prehistory," in Barbara D. Miller, ed., *Sex and Gender Hierarchies* (Cambridge: Cambridge University Press, 1993), pp. 273–296. Some archaeologists and anthropologists debate that such evidence exists. Anthropologist Mildred Dickemann, for example, argues that it is impossible to determine the sex ratios of populations thousands of years ago. According to Dickemann, because male skulls are heavier than female

evidence, however, has only limited value. In the absence of sufficient physical evidence regarding the sex composition of ancient populations, scholars must depend on written records in any historical investigation of offspring sex selection. The practice of sex-selective infanticide in Western cultures, now fairly well documented, appears to be based on reliable sources. Records of sex-selective infanticide in other cultures are not as well documented, although there are some exceptions. Early legal, religious, and other writings from China, India, and ancient Greece and Rome help to reveal much of the history of female infanticide in these imperial civilizations. For other parts of the world, tales, folklore, and accounts from travelers and missionaries suggest an even longer history. As with all such sources, however, care must be exercised in making generalizations. Some sources may be biased, manipulated, or simply erroneous. Nevertheless, the more reliable of these accounts can usually be discerned.

Below is a historical survey of offspring sex selection across regions. Following this is a discussion of contemporary sex-selection practices.

Survey of Offspring Sex Selection

Accounts of the practice of offspring sex selection in Australia and the South Pacific, the Middle East, ancient Greece and Rome, Europe, North and South America, and Asia point to a general undervaluing of the female infant. The most common reason given for the practice of female infanticide—one that plays a part in all of the regions where the practice is prevalent—concerns the role of men in obtaining food for the family or otherwise participating in the economy. Other reasons are specific to the societies studied and include the following: the role of men in conducting war (particularly among tribal societies of the South Pacific, and North and South America), caring for elderly parents (South Pacific and North America), performing religious rites (South Pacific and Asia), as well as continuing the family name (Europe and Asia). Some cultures—such as

---

skulls, male skulls and skull fragments will be more likely to be preserved than those of females. She further suggests that without the pelvic bones to examine, sex identification is extremely difficult. Correspondence with Valerie Hudson, April 10, 1998. Responses to these and other criticisms of paleodemography suggesting that sex identification is possible can be found in Richard S. Meindl and Katherine F. Russell, "Recent Advances in Method and Theory in Paleodemography," *Annual Review of Anthropology*, Vol. 27 (1998), pp. 375–399; and Jane E. Buikstra and Lyle W. Konigsberg, "Paleodemography: Critiques and Controversies," *American Anthropologist*, Vol. 87, No. 2 (June 1985), pp. 316–333.

those of ancient Greece and Rome—undervalued women because of the prevailing belief that women were physically, mentally, and spiritually inferior to men. Also, the economic costs of rearing a daughter were much higher than those for sons because of the expense of the marriage dowry, as was the case in much of Europe. This preference for sons did not always lead to the death of female infants; female survival depended on the desired family composition (both the number of children and their gender) and the costs of rearing children (including the costs of dowries for women in Europe and Asia). Infanticide persisted because of the undervaluing of infant life, although in some regions—such as Europe and the Middle East—the killing of infants ran contrary to religious teachings and thus was banned. Laws pertaining to the practice were introduced in most parts of Europe between the sixteenth and nineteenth centuries, whereas in some cultures—such as the Yanomamo tribes of South America—no such laws exist. The following examples of female infanticide according to region are representative rather than comprehensive.

AUSTRALIA AND THE SOUTH PACIFIC

In the historical literature, the practice of offspring sex selection in Oceania is frequently mentioned. As one woman recounts: "When I was born, and my mother was still in the birth hut, my father came and hung over the fence, and called out, asking what it was, a boy or a girl. My mother replied, 'A girl.' And my father said, 'Break it and throw it away.' But my mother refused, deciding to keep me against his wishes, even though I was a girl. And so I was given my formal name, Letahulozo, Break It and Throw It Away."[26] According to L.L. Langness, the Bena Bena tribe of the New Guinea Highlands has a history of female infanticide.[27] According to Langness, the practice was most common when a mother was still nursing an older infant. The Bena Bena believed that girls were less valuable because they could not become warriors. Also, once married, they would not be available to care for their parents in their old age.[28] Female infanticide also appears to have been widespread in historical Tahiti, where female infants were killed because they did not

---

26. Account of Kilino Aino, Aiposi, Eastern Highlands, Papua New Guinea, 1958. Quoted in Mildred Dickemann, "Concepts and Classification in the Study of Human Infanticide: Sectional Introduction and Some Cautionary Notes," in Hausfater and Hrdy, *Infanticide: Comparative and Evolutionary Perspectives,* p. 427.

27. L.L. Langness, "Sexual Antagonism in the New Guinea Highlands: A Bena Bena Example," *Oceania,* Vol. 38, No. 3 (March 1967), pp. 161–177.

28. Ibid., p. 166.

participate in essential tasks such as fighting wars, performing services to the gods, and providing food for their families.[29]

In his research on Aboriginal Australia, Joseph Birdsell found that the sex ratio among Aboriginal tribes was estimated to be 150 males to 100 females prior to European contact in the late eighteenth century.[30] These tribes practiced infanticide, female infanticide in particular, to control the composition of and spacing within the family. Historically Aboriginal tribes moved a great deal, and the women of the tribes breastfed their children for a long time. Given this, Aboriginal families would seek to have only one child every three years.[31]

James Peggs offers the following account of a missionary's encounter with New Zealand indigenous peoples who practiced female infanticide in the nineteenth century:

> The brethren entered into a free conversation with the natives on the subject, and they spoke of it with pleasure rather than otherwise, and referred them to several of the most respectable females with whom they were acquainted, who had thus destroyed their [female] children. The manner of putting them to death is, by what they call *ro-mea*, or squeezing the nose, as soon as they are born; then the hypocritical mother cuts herself with shells, and makes a great outcry about her dead child. The reasons which they assigned for this practice were two:—The first, and perhaps the principal one, was that they were no good to them in war; for they would only shout and make a noise, but not fight. The other was, that where the offspring is numerous, they make the mother too much work, &c, therefore she kills the girls, but saves the boys.[32]

In addition to not participating in warfare, women required the protection of males who feared they might otherwise be captured or raped.

MIDDLE EAST

References to female infanticide in the Koran suggest its practice among some ancient Middle East populations. For example, sura 16:58–59 de-

---

29. Sumner, *Folkways*, p. 317.

30. See Joseph B. Birdsell, "On Population Structure in Generalized Hunting and Collecting Populations," *Evolution*, Vol. 12, No. 2 (June 1958), pp. 189–205; and Joseph B. Birdsell, "Some Predictions for the Pleistocene Based in Equilibrium Systems among Recent Hunter-Gatherers," in Richard B. Lee and Irven deVore, eds., *Man the Hunter* (Chicago: Aldine de Gruyter, 1968), pp. 229–240.

31. Dickemann, "Demographic Consequences of Infanticide in Man," p. 121.

32. James Peggs, *Cries of Agony: An Historical Account of Suttee Infanticide, Ghat Murders, and Slavery in India* (originally published as *India's Cries to British Humanity*, 1830; reprint, Delhi: Discovery Publishing House, 1984 [page references are to print edition]), p. 27.

scribes the "misfortune" of the birth of a daughter: "When one of them gets a baby girl, his face becomes darkened with overwhelming grief. Ashamed, he hides from the people, because of the bad news given to him. He even ponders: should he keep the baby grudgingly, or bury her in the dust?" Another sura (81:8–9) refers to the burying alive of a female infant: "When the sun is covered, and when the stars darken, and when the mountains are made to pass away, and when the camels are left untended, and when the wild animals are made to go forth, and when the seas are set on fire, and when souls are united, and when the female infant buried alive is asked for what sin she was killed, and when the books are spread, and when the heaven has its covering removed, and when the hell is kindled up, and when the garden is brought nigh, every soul shall (then) know what it has prepared." Although the teachings of the prophet Mohammed dampened enthusiasm for the practice of female infanticide, some Islamic nations (in particular Bangladesh and Pakistan) still have sex ratios well above normal.

GREECE, ROME, AND EUROPE

Throughout much of the history of Western civilization, being female was generally regarded as a disadvantage. Writings of ancient Greek and Roman philosophers describe women as physically and mentally inferior because their body temperature was supposedly lower than that of men—a condition that Aristotle argued affected their powers of reason. Others believed that a woman's soul, like her body, was weaker than a man's. Others (such as Platonists and Stoics) disagreed, arguing instead that a woman's soul was not inferior and that women were just as capable of virtue as men.[33] Daughters were also considered less valuable than sons in part because they needed dowries. (Too many sons, however, could also present a problem when the time came to dividing the family estate.)[34]

Most scholars agree that female infanticide was practiced in ancient Rome; however, the extent to which it was practiced remains the subject of much discussion.[35] Exposure figures prominently in Greek and Roman myths, tragedies, and comedies and seems to have been an accepted

---

33. Gillian Clark, *Women in Late Antiquity: Pagan and Christian Lifestyles* (Oxford: Clarendon, 1994), pp. 120–121.

34. Sue Blundell, *Women in Ancient Greece* (London: British Museum Press, 1995), p. 131.

35. See, for example, Donald Engels, "The Problem of Female Infanticide in the Greco-Roman World," *Classical Philology*, Vol. 75, No. 2 (April 1980), pp. 112–120, who argues that female infanticide was practiced but was not common; and William

practice. Exposure and infanticide are not necessarily the same thing: Most obviously, exposure did not always mean death for the infants. Both Greek and Roman law included provisions for the raising of abandoned infants—whether, for example, they would be cast into slavery or raised in freedom. Some exposed infants might be rescued and adopted by other family members. This was often the case in pharaonic Egypt, but in some places, such as ancient Rome, the adoption of exposed children—even family members—was prohibited.[36]

Legal codes can also be a source of insight into the historical prevalence of offspring sex selection. Laws written in the eighth century B.C. reveal that female infanticide may have been a common practice: Those attributed to Romulus, the founder of Rome (753–716 B.C.), stated that the citizens of Rome should "rear every male child and the first-born of the females."[37] Parents could not kill a female infant at birth unless it was deformed. They could, however, expose the baby after first displaying it to their five nearest neighbors and securing their approval.

Although some Roman census data on papyri have been found indicating that men did outnumber women, experts consider the data to be unreliable. Inscriptions of families given citizenship during the second century B.C., however, reveal sex ratios skewed in favor of males. According to Sarah Pomeroy, this imbalance suggests the prevalence of female infanticide.[38] Inscriptions at Delphi reveal that of six hundred families given citizenship, only 1 percent raised more than one daughter.[39] Milesian records between 228 and 220 B.C. indicate that among seventy-nine families that received citizenship, there were 118 sons and only 28 daughters.[40] In her study of ancient Rome, Aline Rousselle notes that exposure of infants was also widespread, partly due to Augustan laws that limited the number of children per family to just three.[41] Another ex-

---

V. Harris, "The Theoretical Possibility of Extensive Infanticide in the Graeco-Roman World," *Classical Quarterly*, Vol. 32, No. 1 (1982), pp. 114–116, who suggests that female infanticide was more prevalent.

36. Aline Rousselle, "Body Politics in Ancient Rome," in Pauline Schmitt Pantel, ed., *A History of Women in the West*, Vol. 1: *From Ancient Goddesses to Christian Saints* (Cambridge, Mass.: Belknap, 1992), p. 307.

37. Lefkowitz and Fant, *Women's Life in Greece and Rome*, p. 94.

38. Pomeroy, "Infanticide in Hellenistic Greece," pp. 207–222.

39. Jack Lindsay, *The Ancient World: Manners and Morals* (New York: G.P. Putnam's Sons, 1968), p. 168.

40. Ibid.

41. Rousselle, "Body Politics in Ancient Rome," p. 307.

planation for female infanticide was a desire to avoid a surplus of unmarried women.[42] Because the mortality rate for men was generally higher (partly because men often died in war), the probability of a surplus of unwed daughters was high. These daughters were considered an embarrassment to their families. Although both male and female infants were exposed, most scholars agree that more females suffered this fate. The poor in particular typically abandoned their infants, a practice that led to Emperor Constantine's decision in A.D. 315 to provide impoverished parents with food and clothing for their children. Under canon law, infanticide was prohibited throughout Christian Europe by the early fourth century.[43] When the widespread practice of infanticide led to a noticeably declining population in Rome in A.D. 374, infanticide became recognized as a form of murder under Roman law.[44]

Female infanticide was also practiced in ancient Greece. A letter from a Greek citizen named Hilarion to his wife, Alis, in 1 B.C. reads, "If by chance you bear a child, if it is a boy, let it be, if it is a girl, cast it out."[45] The text of a Greek comedy written in the third century B.C. includes the following reference to the exposure of female infants: "Everyone, even a poor man, raises a son, everyone, even a wealthy man, exposes a daughter."[46] Typically the father would place the unwanted infant, usually female, in a crockery pot and leave it on the roadside near the family's home. Given the broad authority that Greek and Roman law accorded to fathers, infanticide was not usually treated as a crime.[47] In cases where women were suspected of practicing infanticide, those who claimed poverty as the cause were often pardoned. The number of individuals actually tried for infanticide was relatively small because of the difficulty of proving that the death was intentional rather than accidental. Children

---

42. See Eve Cantarella, *Pandora's Daughters: The Role and Status of Women in Greek and Roman Antiquity*, trans. Maureen B. Fant with a foreword by Mary R. Lefkowitz (Baltimore, Md.: Johns Hopkins University Press, 1987), p. 44.

43. Claudia Opitz, "Life in the Late Middle Ages," in Christiane Klapisch-Zuber, ed., *A History of Women in the West*, Vol. 2: *Silences of the Middle Ages* (Cambridge, Mass.: Belknap, 1992), pp. 267–317.

44. Ibid., p. 308.

45. From the Papryi Oxyrhynchus 4.744.1–10, quoted in Elaine Fantham, Helene Peet Foley, Natalie Boymel Kampen, Sarah B. Pomeroy, and H.A. Shapiro, *Women in the Classical World: Image and Text* (New York: Oxford University Press, 1994), p. 162.

46. Poseidippus, *Hermaphroditus*, fragment 12, Kassel-Austin, Fantham et al., *Women in the Classical World*, p. 162.

47. John Boswell, *The Kindness of Strangers: The Abandonment of Children in Western Europe from Late Antiquity to the Renaissance* (London: Penguin, 1989), pp. 58–60.

continued to be exposed, eventually necessitating the establishment of the first asylum for abandoned children in Rome in A.D. 787; following this, asylums in other parts of Europe were also established.[48]

As the centuries passed, infanticide came to be seen as a crime that demanded harsher punishment. Because of the growing prevalence of infanticide in France and England, sixteenth-century French law and seventeenth-century English and Scottish law required that all illegitimate pregnancies be declared. Failure to do so was seen as intent to commit infanticide, a crime punishable by burning or hanging.[49] Similar laws were passed in Germany and Switzerland, where, according to Westermarck, a woman found guilty of the crime would be "buried alive with a pale thrust through her body."[50] By the eighteenth or early nineteenth century, infanticide was considered a capital crime throughout all of Europe, with the exception of Russia.[51]

Two key factors that contributed to the practice of infanticide and abandonment were dowries and concern over social status. Dowries for girls were very high throughout Europe: In early fifteenth-century Italy, for example, dowry insurance for daughters was established (parents of daughters were offered the opportunity to invest a sum of money for a fixed number of years, at which time—assuming the daughter was both living and married—the interest would be paid to the daughter's husband for her dowry).[52] Some wealthy families preferred to abandon their daughters rather than risk marrying them to men below their station.[53] Others would send their daughters to nunneries: In so doing, parents of high status but without the accompanying wealth could avoid the expense of dowries and the difficulty of finding suitable marriage partners.[54]

In her research on the ninth-century peasant population of Saint Germain-des-Prés in Paris, France, Emily Coleman suggests that another

---

48. Ibid.

49. Nicole Castan, "Criminals," in Natalie Zemon Davis and Arlette Farge, eds., *A History of Women in the West*, Vol. 3: *Renaissance and Enlightenment Paradoxes* (Cambridge, Mass.: Belknap, 1993), pp. 474–488.

50. Westermarck, *The Origin and Development of the Moral Ideas*, p. 412.

51. Ibid., p. 413.

52. Edith Ennen, *The Medieval Woman*, trans. Edmund Jephcott (Oxford: Basil Blackwell, 1989), p. 230.

53. Ibid.

54. Eileen Power and Michael Moissey Postan, eds., *Medieval Women* (Cambridge: Cambridge University Press, 1975), pp. 89–90.

factor contributing to the killing of female infants was the value assigned to women's labor.[55] In her examination of tax census records, Coleman finds a relationship between the availability of arable land and sex ratios: In general, the larger, more productive farms had more normal sex ratios; on smaller, less productive, and less populous farms, however, sex ratios were skewed in favor of males.[56] Sex ratios for adults ranged from 97.33 for farms with a surface area larger than seventeen bunuaria (a measure of land equivalent to 120 square yards) to 421.05 for farms with less than one bunuarium; sex ratios for children for the same-sized farms ranged from 107.14 to 200.[57] Sex ratios did not decrease in even proportions according to increasing farm size, however, because midrange farms also exhibited high sex ratios of 169 males per 100 females. According to Coleman, the high sex ratios were the result not of underrepresentation of females in the records but of female infanticide. These records, says Coleman, "were relatively sophisticated and carefully constructed tax rolls" and, as such, would not have neglected the taxable females.[58] She concludes that female infanticide reflected a belief that male infants would eventually become more valuable on the farm. The sex ratios may have varied according to the number of adult males living on the land and the type of work performed on a particular piece of land. Areas where forests were cleared to create cultivable fields required more male labor, and thus males in both the adult and child populations would have been favored.[59]

In addition, unlike in other parts of Europe where hypergyny prevailed, Coleman found evidence of hyperandry among the agricultural populations of Saint Germain-des-Près: That is, women's marriage choices did not depend on their social status relative to that of men, as demonstrated by the significant number of marriages in which the women married men of lower social status. Perhaps status in these agricultural communities was not as important as the quality of a man's labor.

We cannot infer from the example of Saint Germain-des-Près that female infanticide was common throughout historical France; as in other

---

55. Emily R. Coleman, "L'infanticide dans le Haut Moyen Age," *Annales: Economies, sociétés, civilisations*, Vol. 29, No. 2 (March–April 1974), pp. 315–335.

56. Ibid., pp. 322–323.

57. Ibid., p. 318.

58. Emily R. Coleman, "Medieval Marriage Characteristics: A Neglected Factor in the History of Medieval Serfdom," in Theodore K. Rabb and Robert I. Rotberg, eds., *The Family in History: Interdisciplinary Essays* (New York: Harper and Row, 1971), p. 5.

59. Ibid., p. 6.

nations, sex ratios varied in different communities. For example, in her study of tax census records of ninth-century Marseilles, Monique Zerner-Chardavoine finds that female children slightly outnumbered male children.[60]

During the late Middle Ages in many parts of Europe, women's changing status is revealed in more normal sex ratios and, in some cases, even female-biased sex ratios. Beginning in the fourteenth century, for example, urban centers began to display a surplus of females among upper and lower classes as the demand for female labor rose. Wealthy families employed female servants, slaves, and wet nurses from lower-class families in their homes.[61] Other young women from similar circumstances found work in cottage industries or agriculture. Around this time, too, women acquired rights to own property, though these rights varied from region to region. Greater economic opportunities and increased rights for women helped to ensure their survival from infancy, although this was not necessarily true throughout all of Europe, as Renaissance historian Richard Trexler's study of Italy reveals.

In his study, Trexler discovered the presence of widespread female infanticide in the dominion of Florence in the fifteenth century.[62] Using data from foundling hospitals and the Florentine Castato (city tax registration lists), Trexler shows that in the year 1427, citywide sex ratios revealed a bias toward male children (114.6 males per 100 females at age 0 and 118.4 males per 100 females at age 1).[63] These figures are similar to dominion sex ratios of 119.7 for ages 0–4 in the same year. David Herlihy, in his analysis of the life expectancies of medieval women, finds even higher sex ratios for children than Trexler quotes when Florence's rural and urban populations are combined. Herlihy reveals that the sex ratio for children aged 0–12 was 123.59.[64] Trexler further reveals a bias of the

60. Monique Zerner-Chardavoine, "Enfants et jeunes au IXe siècle: La démographie du polyptypue de Marseille, 813–814," *Provence historique,* No. 126 (1981), pp. 335–384.

61. For a discussion of female surpluses and opportunities available to women in the workplace, see Mildred Dickemann, "Female Infanticide, Reproductive Strategies, and Social Stratification: A Preliminary Model," in Napoleon A. Chagnon and William Irons, eds., *Evolutionary Biology and Human Behavior: An Anthropological Perspective* (North Scituate, Mass.: Duxbury, 1979), pp. 321–367.

62. Richard C. Trexler, "Infanticide in Florence: New Sources and First Results," *History of Childhood Quarterly: The Journal of Psychohistory,* Vol. 1, No. 1 (Summer 1973), pp. 98–116.

63. Ibid., pp. 100–101.

64. David Herlihy, "Life Expectancies for Women in Medieval Society," in Rosemarie Thee Morewedge, ed., *The Role of Woman in the Middle Ages: Papers of the Sixth Annual*

rich toward male children; parents who were assessed taxes of 400 florins (indicating greater wealth) had a ratio of 124.56 for children aged 0–4.[65] The larger numbers of females in foundling homes in Florence also suggest a bias against female children,[66] and seem confirmed by data from absolution records (i.e., records of parents who, following confession to a priest, received absolution for murdering their infants). Trexler concludes, "In law, in the family, and in the foundling home, European society preferred boys. This meant more deaths for infant girls."[67]

In her study of England in the Middle Ages, Barbara Kellum finds evidence of non-sex-selective infanticide as well as female infanticide.[68] Although detailed data regarding the sex of children killed in England are unavailable, evidence does suggest that female infanticide was practiced at least in some areas. In her review of the *Inquisitions Post Mortem* (public record inquiries undertaken following the death of a feudal tenant to determine his holdings and list his heirs) from 1250 to 1348 and 1430 to 1545, Kellum notes that the ratio of males to females changed from one of relatively equal numbers to 133 males per 100 females. Further evidence from lists of serfs and peasants reveals even higher sex ratios of 170 males per 100 females.[69] Reasons for committing infanticide are not difficult to determine (the stigma associated with raising illegitimate children, the difficulties such children faced in trying to inherit from their fathers' estates, the economic hardship brought on by fines for bearing children out of wedlock, thoughts of unbaptized children as evil, the idea that killing a child was not as heinous as murdering an adult, and general economic and social costs of raising a child). Explanations for female infanticide,

Conference of the Center for Medieval and Early Renaissance Studies, State University of New York at Binghamton, 6–8 May 1972 (Albany: State University of New York Press, 1975), p. 22.

65.   The higher sex ratios among the wealthier families, according to Trexler, suggest that these families were more inclined to keep a male bastard child than an illegitimate female child. See Trexler, "Infanticide in Florence," pp. 101, 112.

66.   See Richard C. Trexler, "The Foundlings of Florence, 1395–1455," *History of Childhood Quarterly: The Journal of Psychohistory*, Vol. 1, No. 2 (Fall 1973), pp. 259–284. From 1404 to 1413, 61.2 percent of the babies left in foundling homes in Florence were female; during the 1430s, considered a period of greater stress in the countryside, the number of female infants increased to 66.3 percent.

67.   Trexler, "Infanticide in Florence," p. 110.

68.   Barbara A. Kellum, "Infanticide in England in the Later Middle Ages," *History of Childhood Quarterly: The Journal of Psychohistory*, Vol. 1, No. 3 (Winter 1974), pp. 367–388.

69.   Ibid., p. 368.

however, are not as obvious. Kellum, for example, does not address the particular motivations of practitioners of female infanticide. One can only infer that it again relates to the status or value of women in the Middle Ages.

The large number of foundling homes and asylums established in historical Europe attests to the many infants abandoned by their parents: By the sixteenth century, nearly every major European city had an institution for abandoned children. Describing such facilities in nineteenth-century France, Langer notes that mortality among these infants was very high. Many were half-dead when they arrived and did not survive; the rest crowded into ill-ventilated quarters and were given whatever food was available. Because of a lack of wet nurses, the majority of infants had to be sent to the provinces for nursing. In the course of being transported, often over long distances and without proper care, most of these foundlings died.[70] Those who survived frequently succumbed to one of the many communicable diseases sweeping the hospitals and hospices. Langer concludes that in the eighteenth and nineteenth centuries, 80–90 percent of foundlings in France died in the first year of life, many within the first few days.[71]

NORTH AMERICA

The practice of infanticide, especially female infanticide, in North America has been the subject of great debate. Instances of female infanticide have been documented among some tribes in the Arctic—including the Netsilik Inuit of Pelly Bay, located northwest of Hudson Bay in the region of Boothia Peninsula. According to Milton Freeman, the historical literature suggests that Inuit fathers typically killed their female offspring because they valued sons more than daughters.[72] The fathers purportedly saw sons as companions and fellow hunters, whereas daughters were seen as being closer to their mothers and therefore a potential threat to paternal dominance.

David Riches suggests that although Freeman may be right in suggesting that male dominance played a role in the decision to kill a female infant, environmental stress may have also been a factor. According to Riches, sex ratios among Inuit tribes fluctuated in the nineteenth and

---

70. Langer, "Checks on Population Growth, 1750–1850," p. 98.

71. Ibid.

72. Milton M.R. Freeman, "A Social and Ecologic Analysis of Systematic Female Infanticide among the Netsilik Eskimo," *American Anthropologist*, Vol. 73, No. 5 (October 1971), pp. 1011–1018.

twentieth centuries according to differing environmental pressures.[73] In addition, Riches argues, female infanticide was closely related to preferential kindred endogamy—that is, a preference for marrying first cousins. The Netsilik would betroth a female infant even before she was named. If not selected for betrothal, she was more likely to be killed. Better that fate, the family believed, than marriage to an unrelated member of the community with whom the family was in competition for scarce resources.[74] Eric and Abigail Smith argue that because Asen Balikci's research of the Netsilik shows that mothers and grandmothers played a part in the decision to kill female infants, the practice cannot be explained solely with reference to male dominance.[75]

Based on census data from 1880 to 1930, female infanticide occurred in the region from Cape Smyth, Alaska (the northwestern Arctic), to Baffin Island.[76] More recently, although scholars have concluded that some Inuit sex ratios were not as severely skewed as might be suggested by the data (in which sex ratios varied from 105 to 224, with a mean of 173 males per 100 females), they nevertheless confirm the practice of female infanticide among the Inuit.[77] Scholars such as Eric and Abigail Smith discount explanations for female infanticide such as a desire to limit population growth. Nor do they view it as an effort to balance the adult sex ratios because of a high number of adult male deaths associated with the dangerous work of hunting for food. The Smiths suggest that female infanticide among the Inuit is best explained by a differential payback hypothesis: Parental investment in male offspring, though greater than that for females, pays higher dividends through males' greater contributions to the family. They suggest that this hypothesis helps to explain female infanticide not just among the Netsilik but also among other Inuit populations.[78]

---

73. David Riches, "The Netsilik Eskimo: A Special Case of Selective Female Infanticide," *Ethnology: An International Journal of Cultural and Social Anthropology*, Vol. 13, No. 4 (October 1974), pp. 351–361.

74. Ibid., p. 358.

75. Eric Alden Smith and S. Abigail Smith, "Inuit Sex-Ratio Variation: Population Control, Ethnographic Error, or Parental Manipulation?" *Current Anthropology*, Vol. 35, No. 5 (December 1994), p. 604.

76. See Asen Balikci, "Female Infanticide on the Arctic Coast," *Man: The Journal of the Royal Anthropological Institute*, Vol. 2, No. 4 (December 1967), p. 615; and Smith and Smith, "Inuit Sex-Ratio Variation," p. 597.

77. Note that in recent literature "Inuit" has replaced "Eskimo," according to indigenous preference. For an in-depth discussion of the census data and problems related to it, see Smith and Smith, "Inuit Sex-Ratio Variation."

78. Ibid.

Skewed childhood sex ratios have also appeared among non-Native American populations. The data here, however, are far from complete. In their study of nineteenth-century childhood sex ratios in the United States, E.A. Hammel and colleagues find that in addition to the role played by immigration, differential child care and mortality patterns also contributed to high sex ratios.[79] They argue that the high sex ratios and excess female childhood mortality (female deaths outnumbered male deaths up to the age of 14) can be explained by "the unequal economic value of boys and girls to a household economy typical of early agricultural modernization."[80] Although both sexes may have been equally valued in urban centers, farm families favored male children for heavy agricultural labor.

SOUTH AMERICA

Several tribes in South America have also practiced offspring sex selection. The most studied case is that of the Yanomamo. The Yanomamo Indians live in southern Venezuela and adjacent portions of northern Brazil in approximately 125 villages. They are considered unique because they still practice tribal warfare. Although the Yanomamo engage in both male and female infanticide, they selectively kill more female than male infants. In his study of the Yanomamo, anthropologist Napoleon Chagnon found high sex ratios among the adult and childhood populations. Demographic data collected from 1964 to 1968 from 7 villages reveals a higher number of males than females: 449 males and 391 females, yielding a sex ratio of 115 males per 100 females.[81] These numbers underrepresent the prevalence of female infanticide, given that more men than women were killed in tribal warfare.[82] According to James Neel and Chagnon, the sex ratios among younger Yanomamo were even higher: The sex ratio for children under the age of 15 was 128.6 males per 100

---

79. E.A. Hammel, Sheila R. Johansson, and Caren A. Ginsberg, "The Value of Children during Industrialization: Sex Ratios in Childhood in Nineteenth-Century America," *Journal of Family History*, Vol. 8, No. 4 (Winter 1983), pp. 346–366.

80. Ibid., pp. 346–347.

81. Chagnon spent a total of nineteen months among the Yanomamo between 1964 and 1968. The sex ratio data for the Yanomamo are given without reference to any particular year. Chagnon, *Yanomamo: The Fierce People*, p. 74.

82. That more men than women die in tribal warfare is supported by cause-of-death data collected by Napoleon A. Chagnon for two different tribes. Among the Shamatari population during the period of study, fifty-two men died in warfare as opposed to five women. During the same period among the Namowei-teri population, forty-four males and nine females died in warfare. See Chagnon, *Studying the Yanomamo* (New York: Holt, Rinehart, and Winston, 1974), p. 160.

females.[83] In Chagnon's view, these figures confirm the Yanomamo practice of sex-selective female infanticide: Parents invested their limited resources in raising sons—who would one day become warriors and hunters—rather than daughters.[84]

An unintended consequence of this practice was an insufficient number of marriageable females, a problem that Yanomamo village leaders exacerbated by practicing polygyny, that is, having more than one mate at a time. This need for mates was a contributing factor to Yanomamo raids on nearby villages.[85]

Other tribes in South America also reportedly practiced female infanticide, including the Sharanahua and Xavante tribes of the Amazon.[86] The sex ratio for the 0–14 population among the Xavante was approximately 124; even higher ratios were found among the Peruvian Cashinahua, where the 0–14 sex ratio was recorded as high as 148.[87] As with the Yanomamo, Mildred Dickemann suggests that "competition for mates is aggravated by polygyny and encourages child betrothal and wife capture."[88]

JAPAN

In his study of the Japanese village of Nakahara in the eighteenth and nineteenth centuries, Robert Eng provides evidence of the practice of female infanticide. According to Eng, through the practice of infanticide—commonly referred to as *mabiki*, or "thinning"—parents manipulated both the size and composition of their families: The "parents' decision to keep or to 'return' (as the euphemism had it) a newborn baby depended in part on the sex of the infant and in part on that of previous children."[89] For example, for families with more male than female chil-

---

83. James V. Neel and Napoleon A. Chagnon, "The Demography of Two Tribes of Primitive, Relatively Unacculturated American Indians," *Proceedings of the National Academy of Sciences*, Vol. 59, No. 3 (March 1968), p. 681.

84. Chagnon, *Yanomamo: The Fierce People*, p. 75.

85. Ibid., p. 125.

86. Warren M. Tern, "Health and Demography of Native Amazonians: Historical Perspective and Current Status," in Anna Roosevelt, ed., *Amazonian Indians from Prehistory to the Present: Anthropological Perspectives* (Tucson: University of Arizona Press, 1994), pp. 123–149.

87. Dickemann, "Demographic Consequences of Infanticide in Man," p. 129.

88. Ibid.

89. Robert Y. Eng, "Fertility and Infanticide," in Thomas C. Smith, ed., *Nakahara: Family Farming and Population in a Japanese Village, 1717–1830* (Stanford, Calif.: Stanford University Press, 1977), p. 66.

dren, the next child was typically female (yielding a sex ratio for the next child of 72 among the sample families); for families with an equal number of male and female children, the next child was male (with a sex ratio of 168).[90] The samples revealed a strong preference for males. Offspring sex selection was most noticeable among smaller families. Families with one to three children exhibited sex ratios of 188; medium-sized families (four to five children) had sex ratios of 130; and large families (six or more children) had sex ratios of 107.[91] During periods when families were large, female infanticide would not have been very prevalent. In the eighteenth and nineteenth centuries, however, small families were the norm.

In his study of population trends in historical and modern Japan, Ryoichi Ishii finds that population pressures led at different times to the widespread practice of infanticide, including female infanticide.[92] According to Ishii, Japan's social history indicates that environmental stress (particularly famine) and economic hardship (poverty among the masses and low fixed hereditary income for many others) led to the use of infanticide to limit family size and composition. Infanticide, he argues, prevailed among all segments of Japan's population.[93]

A late nineteenth-century book titled *Minkan Akushu Jojitsu* (Conditions of Evil Customs among the People) explains the reasons for infanticide during the Tokugawa period:[94] The rearing of more than three children (two male and one female) was considered an unfair drain on both family and community resources, and bearing children at a late age brought shame to the parents. Although the Tokugawa census did not record age groupings (which would enable scholars to examine the sex ratios for infants), such figures are available for the late nineteenth and early twentieth centuries. Sex ratios for children under the age of 5 in Japan from 1884 to 1930 were as follows: 112.5 in 1884, 117.5 in 1893, 128.1 in 1903, 133.4 in 1913, 133.3 in 1920, 138.3 in 1925, and 139.8 in 1930.[95]

Dickemann finds similar results in her studies of Japan's population. She suggests that infanticide in Japan began early in the eighteenth century, following a period of rapid population growth. The practice of fe-

90. Ibid.

91. Ibid., p. 77.

92. Ryoichi Ishii, *Population Pressure and Economic Life in Japan* (London: P.S. King and Son, 1937).

93. Ibid., p. 31.

94. Cited in ibid., pp. 31–32.

95. Ibid., p. 90.

male infanticide permitted parents to raise sons and guarantee perpetuation of the family line. Census data support this finding, beginning with Japan's 1750 census, in which the overall sex ratio was 114 males per 100 females, but declining over the next two centuries until sex ratios normalized in 1950.[96] Offspring sex selection no longer appears as a significant force in Japan.

Contemporary Offspring Sex Selection across Cultures

The preference for sons has remained strong in many parts of the world. In a 1976 cross-cultural survey of parental preferences, Nancy Williamson found that men in the United States, Latin America and the Caribbean, Thailand, and Israel exhibited moderate son preference, as did urban Lebanese and Egyptian women. Rural Lebanese women, urban Indians, Indian Christians, Korean men and women, and Taiwanese men and women exhibited strong son preference. In addition, women in rural Algeria, Egypt, and Tunisia; men in the Indian states of Andhra Pradesh, Gujarat, Jammu and Kashmir, Kerala, and Madhya Pradesh; and women in Gujarat exhibited very strong son preference.[97] The authors of an analysis of the 1983 *World Fertility Survey* examined sex preferences for children in twenty-seven countries. They found a strong preference for sons in six of them (Bangladesh, Jordan, Nepal, Pakistan, South Korea, and Syria), and moderate son preference in eight (Dominican Republic, Fiji, Lesotho, Malaysia, Mexico, Sri Lanka, Sudan, and Thailand).[98]

Son preference can manifest itself in high fertility rates—women will give birth to a large number of children to produce the desired number of sons—as well as in the neglect of female infants and children and, more recently, in sex-selective abortion. Son preference does not always affect reproductive behavior, however, as the *World Fertility Survey* showed: For example, the authors suggest that Arab women, although indicating a

---

96. Dickemann, "Demographic Consequences of Infanticide in Man," p. 129.

97. Nancy E. Williamson, *Sons or Daughters: A Cross-Cultural Survey of Parental Preferences* (London: Sage, 1976).

98. The following regions and countries were represented in the survey: Africa/ Middle East—Jordan, Kenya, Lesotho, Sudan, and Syria; Asia—Bangladesh, Fiji, Indonesia, South Korea, Malaysia, Nepal, Pakistan, Philippines, Sri Lanka, and Thailand; and Americas—Colombia, Costa Rica, Dominican Republic, Guyana, Haiti, Jamaica, Mexico, Panama, Paraguay, Peru, Trinidad, and Venezuela. See John Cleland, Jane Verrall, and Martin Vaessen, *Preferences for the Sex of Children and Their Influence on Reproductive Behaviour,* World Fertility Survey Comparative Studies No. 27 (Voorburg, Netherlands: International Statistical Institute, 1983).

preference for sons, will not alter their reproductive behavior according to the sex composition of the children they already have.[99] Of the countries listed above in which parents revealed a son preference, only in Mexico and the Asian countries (Fiji, Malaysia, Nepal, Pakistan, South Korea, and Sri Lanka) was there a corresponding effect on fertility and contraceptive behavior.[100]

Son preference is not confined to the developing world, as Williamson's research shows. Vijaya Krishnan argues that in developed countries, social changes such as women's participation in the labor force and greater educational opportunities contribute more to decisions about fertility and family size than gender; however, gender may still play a role in a woman's decision to postpone or promote the use of contraception. Krishnan shows that gender plays a role in Canadian women's decisions to use contraceptives—a woman with two sons, for instance, is more likely to use contraception than a woman with two daughters.[101] Data on son preference in the United States are sketchy, with small numbers showing son preference, but equivalent numbers expressing an offsetting daughter preference. Results of an analysis of fertility survey data from 1988 to 1996 for seventeen European countries show a tendency for a mixed composition of sons and daughters or no preference at all, with the exceptions of the Czech Republic, Lithuania, and Portugal, where there was an unexplained slight preference for daughters.[102]

Nowhere has son preference been more noticeable than in Asian populations. In 1994 the United Nations Population Fund and the Government of the Republic of Korea sponsored a symposium at which scholars presented papers on son preference in Asia.[103] Strong son preference was detected in eight countries (Bangladesh, China, India, Nepal, Pakistan, South Korea, Taiwan, and Vietnam), although the participants noted that son preference even within these countries varied according to region or ethnicity. They added that "where son preference existed alongside high or moderately high fertility, even a modest decline in fertility may exacer-

---

99. Ibid., p. 27.

100. See ibid., p. 26, Table 7.

101. Vijaya Krishnan, "Gender of Children and Contraceptive Use," *Journal of Biosocial Science,* Vol. 25, No. 2 (April 1993), pp. 213–221.

102. Karsten Hank and Hans-Peter Kohler, "Gender Preferences for Children in Europe: Empirical Results from 17 FFS Countries," *Demographic Research,* Vol. 2 (January 2000), http://www.demographic-research.org/Volumes/Vol2/1.

103. The symposium, titled "International Symposium on Issues Related to Sex Preference for Children in the Rapidly Changing Demographic Dynamics in Asia," was held in Seoul, South Korea, November 21–24, 1994.

bate the existing discrimination against female babies, children, and now, fetuses."[104] As fertility—and therefore family size—decreased in these parts of Asia, son preference became more noticeable; to have the desired number of sons—usually two—mothers gave birth to four or five children. A drop in overall family size has meant that families have had to adapt their reproductive behavior to have the desired number of sons without producing a large number of daughters. The existing discrimination against females through differential health care, nutrition, and/or sex-selective abortions has resulted in skewed sex ratios for children and overall populations in Asia. Tables 2.1 and 2.2 show the high sex ratios for childhood (ages 0–4) and overall populations for Asia when compared with other regions in the world. We examine the role of son preference in Asia in the remainder of this chapter.

Son Preference in Contemporary Asia

Infanticide still occurs in many parts of Asia, particularly in south-central and eastern Asia. Active female infanticide has been well documented in India and China, but passive infanticide through neglect of female infants and children is more prevalent. As Carol MacCormack indicates in her study of women's health and social power, when women are regarded as having low status, society invests less in them than in males. This preference can be reflected in mortality rates for male and female children.[105]

Males and females experience different patterns of mortality throughout their life cycles.[106] Males are generally more susceptible to death in the first year of life, with a marked difference in mortality rates during this period, and throughout childhood males continue to have higher mortality rates. In addition to increased vulnerability to genetic disorders, male infants are more susceptible to infectious diseases, particularly those of the digestive and respiratory tracts.[107] This increased vulnerabil-

---

104. See Judith Banister, "Son Preference in Asia—Report of a Symposium," at U.S. Census Bureau, http://www.census.gov/ipc/www/ebspr96a.html.

105. Carol P. MacCormack, "Health and the Social Power of Women," *Social Science and Medicine*, Vol. 26, No. 7 (1988), pp. 677–683.

106. The following discussion represents a generalized view of male and female life cycles. A similar, country-specific discussion can be found in Helen R. Ware, "Differential Mortality Decline and Its Consequences for the Status and Roles of Women," in *Consequences of Mortality Trends and Differentials,* Population Studies No. 95 (New York: Department of International Economic and Social Affairs, United Nations, 1986), pp. 113–125.

107. Lauris McKee, "Sex Differentials in Survivorship and the Customary Treatment

Table 2.1. Sex Ratios of the World's Population, Ages 0–4, 2000.

Region	Males	Females	Sex Ratio
Africa	64,431,000	63,156,000	102.0
Asia	192,121,000	179,788,000	106.9
Europe	18,915,000	17,924,000	105.5
Latin America and the Caribbean	28,520,000	27,429,000	104.0
North America	11,371,000	10,818,000	105.1
Oceania	1,404,000	1,327,000	105.8
World	316,763,000	300,442,000	105.4

SOURCE: United Nations, Department of Economic and Social Affairs, Population Division, *World Population Prospects: The 2002 Revision;* and *World Urbanization Prospects: The 2001 Revision,* http://esa.un.org/unpp.

Table 2.2. Sex Ratios of the World's Population, 2000.

Region	Males	Females	Sex Ratio
Africa	395,573,000	400,097,000	98.9
Asia	1,879,417,000	1,800,320,000	104.4
Europe	350,900,000	377,086,000	93.1
Latin America and the Caribbean	257,526,000	262,703,000	98.0
North America	155,239,000	160,676,000	96.6
Oceania	15,585,000	15,459,000	100.8
World	3,054,240,000	3,016,341,000	101.3

SOURCE: United Nations, Department of Economic and Social Affairs, Population Division, *World Population Prospects: The 2002 Revision;* and *World Urbanization Prospects: The 2001 Revision,* http://esa.un.org/unpp.

ity to illness during infancy may be due to the presence of genetic information controlling immunological responses on the X chromosome, of which the male has only one.[108] During childbearing years, women may have higher rates of mortality than men due to the inherent risks of childbirth. As males and females approach old age, males tend to die younger than females; thus women typically have longer life expectancies.

Not all countries exhibit this pattern of mortality, however. In some countries, such as Bangladesh, China, India, and Nepal, infant mortality

of Infants and Children," *Medical Anthropology: Cross Cultural Studies in Health and Illness,* Vol. 8, No. 2 (Spring 1984), pp. 91–108.

108. Ibid., p. 93.

rates (number of deaths per 1,000 live births during the first year of life), as well as child mortality rates (number of deaths per 1,000 ages 1–4), are higher for females. This discrimination against females can even continue for all ages. Helen Ware argues that social factors are responsible for the increased deaths of female children aged 1–4. At this age, according to Ware, "females are most likely to suffer a marked disadvantage" because of their gender; it is "the period when the preference for sons has the greatest impact. Difficult decisions have to be made about the allocation of food or access to expensive medical remedies, and girls are more likely to miss out."[109] The economist Amartya Sen concurs: "It is in the continued inequality in the division of food—and (perhaps even more) that of health care—that gender inequality manifests itself most blatantly and persistently in poor societies with strong antifemale bias."[110]

A 1954 UN Population Division study of infant and early childhood mortality from 1915 to 1949 in 63 countries/regions indicates that nowhere during this period were *infant* mortality rates for females higher than for males.[111] The following exhibited higher rates for *early childhood* mortality (ages 1–4) for females: Ceylon, Ecuador, Formosa (Taiwan), Mexico, Palestine, Puerto Rico, and Venezuela.[112] The United Nations Children's Fund's 1986 *Statistical Review of the Situation of Children in the World* provides data for 45 developing countries, 43 of which exhibited higher mortality rates for girls ages 1–4 than boys in the same age category.[113] The 1998 UN study *Too Young to Die: Genes or Gender?* reported that of the 82 developing countries for which data were collected, girls in south-central Asia—particularly Bangladesh, India, Nepal and, to a slightly lesser extent, Pakistan—were the most severely disadvantaged in terms of health and survival.[114] UN demographers calculated that in the year 2000, 9 countries in the world exhibited infant mortality rates that were higher for females than for males: Bangladesh (68, 66), Brunei

---

109. Ware, "Differential Mortality Decline and Its Consequences for the Status and Role of Women," p. 114.

110. Amartya Sen, *Development as Freedom* (New York: Alfred A. Knopf, 1999), p. 194.

111. United Nations, Department of Social Affairs, Population Division, *Foetal, Infant, and Early Childhood Mortality*, Vol. 1: *The Statistics*, Population Studies No. 13 (New York: United Nations, 1954).

112. Ibid., pp. 64–76, Table 1.

113. UNICEF (United Nations Children's Fund), *Statistical Review of the Situation of Children in the World* (New York: UNICEF, 1986), p. 5.

114. United Nations, Population Division of the Department of Economic and Social Affairs, *Too Young to Die: Genes or Gender?* (New York: United Nations, 1998), p. 13.

Darussalam (9, 8), China (42, 31), India (69, 60), Iran (37, 34), Pakistan (90, 83), Fiji (19, 16), Papua New Guinea (64, 61), and Vanuatu (31, 26).[115] Data collected (and estimated) for 2002 by the U.S. Census Bureau International Data Base suggest that out of 227 countries, 15 exhibited ages 0–4 sex ratios greater than 107 males per 100 females.[116] In particular, China (109.8), Hong Kong (110.7), South Korea (111.1), and Taiwan (108.7) exhibited high sex ratios indicative of differential practices toward male and female children resulting in high death rates for females. Studies have also shown that in Bangladesh and Pakistan, female children experience higher mortality rates.

Son preference is also manifested in the use of sex-selective technology (particularly ultrasound and amniocentesis) to abort female fetuses. The use of sex-selective technology is reflected in the sex ratio at birth, but also through statistics from health clinics regarding the sex of aborted fetuses. This practice is widespread in China, India, South Korea, and Taiwan, whereas there is little evidence of the practice in Bangladesh and Pakistan.

Below we discuss current sex-selection practices in four countries in Asia: Bangladesh, Pakistan, South Korea, and Taiwan. Declining fertility combined with continued son preference in Bangladesh and Pakistan has led to high infant and child mortality rates for females, suggesting discrimination against female offspring that results in infanticide. In Taiwan, however, there is no evidence of differential treatment of male and female offspring, or female infanticide; son preference in this country is manifested in the use of sex-selective technology to abort female fetuses. In South Korea, high mortality rates for female infants and children in the past suggest that female infanticide was widely practiced. Recent statistics, however, indicate that infanticide has been replaced with sex-selective abortion: South Korea's birth sex ratios are high, whereas female infant and child mortality rates are low.

BANGLADESH

According to the 1996–97 Demographic and Health Survey, childhood mortality figures were 27 percent higher for females in Bangladesh, where the preferred family composition, as in other Asian countries, is two sons and one daughter.[117] A study of children in Matlab, Bangladesh,

---

115. United Nations, *The World's Women, 2000: Trends and Statistics,* http://unstats.un.org/unsd/demographic/ww2000/table3a.htm.

116. See Appendix 1 for the sex ratios for all 227 countries.

117. Mortality figures are based on the Bangladesh demographic and health survey, 1996–97, cited in World Health Organization, "Women's Health in South-East Asia,"

showed that girls under the age of 5 were 50 percent more likely to die than boys of the same age.[118] Daughters typically receive less food and health care than sons.[119] Pradip Muhuri and Samuel Preston arrived at similar results in their study. Based on an examination of 14,125 births between 1981 and 1982, they found that mortality rates in Matlab were most affected by the gender composition of the family. Socioeconomic factors, the mother's level of education, and access to health care had no significant influence on child mortality. The study revealed that girls had higher rates of mortality than boys, and that mortality for female infants and young girls was much higher in families with an older female sibling: Girls with an older sister had 5.8 times the risk of dying than girls without an older sister. Male mortality, on the other hand, was not affected by the size or composition of the family unless there were at least two older brothers, but this is not as strongly correlated as the effect of older female siblings on young female siblings.[120]

Despite the higher mortality rates for female infants and children in these studies of Matlab, the current sex ratios in Bangladesh in 2001 do not reflect extreme discrimination against females. The overall sex ratio for Bangladesh is 103.8, a rate that has been decreasing since the recorded level of 109.7 in 1951.[121] The 2001 census, however, reported a sex ratio of 106.1 for the population ages 0–4, showing a significant increase in the sex ratio for children since the 1991 census ratio of 102.9.[122] The 2001 ratio would only reflect higher female infant and child mortality if the sex ratio

http://w3.whosea.org/ women/ch1_2.htm. For son preference and its effect on family composition, see M. Kabir, Ruhul Amin, Ashraf Uddin Ahmen, and Jamir Chowdhury, "Factors Affecting Desired Family Size in Bangladesh," *Journal of Biosocial Science*, Vol. 26, No. 3 (July 1994), pp. 369–375.

118.   M. Shahidullah, "Breast-Feeding and Child Survival in Matlab, Bangladesh," *Journal of Biosocial Science*, Vol. 26, No. 2 (April 1994), pp. 143–154.

119.   Alaka M. Basu, "Is Discrimination in Food Really Necessary for Explaining Sex Differentials in Childhood Mortality? *Population Studies*, Vol. 43, No. 2 (July 1989), pp. 193–210; and Lincoln C. Chen, Emdadul Huq, and Stan D'Souza, "Sex Bias in the Family Allocation of Food and Health-Care in Rural Bangladesh," *Population and Development Review*, Vol. 7, No. 1 (March 1981), pp. 55–70.

120.   Pradip K. Muhuri and Samuel H. Preston, "Effects of Family Composition on Mortality Differentials by Sex among Children in Matlab, Bangladesh," *Population and Development Review*, Vol. 17, No. 3 (September 1991), pp. 415–434.

121.   Bangladesh, Bureau of Statistics, "Population Census 2001 Preliminary Report," http://www.bbsgov.org; and Bangladesh Bureau of Statistics, 1999 Demographic Data, http://www.bbsgov.org/data-sheet/DEMO_DATA.htm.

122.   Bangladesh, Bureau of Statistics, "Population Census, 2001: Preliminary Report"; and Bangladesh Bureau of Statistics, "1991 Population Census," http://www.bbsgov. org/ana_vol1/Projection.htm.

at birth were lower than 106.1. Statistics on birth sex ratios in Bangladesh, however, are often not reliable. One study of 1988–89 births in Matlab stated that the birth sex ratio was 100.2, but another recorded a sex ratio of 113.[123] The problem may be one of underreporting of births, deaths, and number of living children. Further research is required to determine the extent of the effect of son preference on differential child mortality in Bangladesh.

PAKISTAN

Unlike Bangladesh, Pakistan exhibits patterns of son preference similar to those found in the northwestern states of India, where sex ratios are very high (ranging from 109.5 in Rajasthan to 114.5 in Punjab).[124] Although little research has been conducted on the more recent overall sex ratios of the Pakistani population, high juvenile sex ratios suggest that female infanticide is practiced in the country.[125] In 1961 the juvenile (0–9) sex ratio in thirty-seven out of forty-five districts was greater than the normal 105–107, with some ratios as high as 114.6.[126] According to Pakistan's censuses, the juvenile sex ratio was 109.4 in 1961, 109.2 in 1972, 107.7 in 1981, and 106.2 in 1998.[127] The 1998 census recorded an overall sex ratio of 108.5; in the four provinces and two territories, the sex ratio varied from a low of 105 in the North-West Frontier Province to a high of 117 in Islamabad (Capital Territory).[128] In 1999, Sen calculated an overall sex ra-

---

123. Radheshyam Bairagi, Santosh Chandra Sutradhar, and Nurul Alam, "Levels, Trends, and Determinants of Child Mortality in Matlab, Bangladesh, 1966–1994," *Asia-Pacific Population Journal*, Vol. 14, No. 2 (June 1999), pp. 51–68.

124. India, Office of the Registrar General, *Census of India, 2001, Series-1: India, Paper 1 of 2001: Provisional Population Totals* (New Delhi: India, Office of the Registrar General, 2001), http://www.censusindia.net/results.

125. The historical provinces of India that make up Pakistan include regions where female infanticide was widespread in at least the eighteenth and nineteenth centuries.

126. Barbara D. Miller, "Daughter Neglect, Women's Work, and Marriage: Pakistan and Bangladesh Compared," *Medical Anthropology: Cross Cultural Studies in Health and Illness*, Vol. 8, No. 2 (Spring 1984), pp. 114–115.

127. Census data for 1961, 1972, and 1981 come from figures for Pakistan's adjusted census, U.S. Bureau of the Census, International Data Base, 1998. The 1998 sex ratio is from Pakistan's Enumerated Census for 1998, U.S. Bureau of the Census, International Data Base, 2003.

128. Pakistan, Population Census Organization. "Table-1, Area, Population by Sex, Sex Ratio, Population Density, Urban Proportion, Household Size, and Annual Growth Rate, 1998," http://www.statpak.gov.pk/depts/pco/statistics/pop_table1/pop_table1.html.

tio for Pakistan of 111.1 that, if accurate, is worse than the overall population sex ratio of almost any other country.[129] According to Barbara Miller,
Pakistan's high sex ratios are indicative of women's lower status, which
is related to their lesser role in the wheat-dominated agricultural economy, the existence of a hypergynous marriage system, and the high costs
associated with women's dowries (although these costs are not as high as
in India).[130]

The 1990–91 Demographic and Health Survey (DHS) in Pakistan recorded an infant mortality rate of 102.1 for males and 85.5 for females.
As mentioned previously, the UN estimated that in 2002 this rate was actually slightly higher (8 percent) for females than for males. Child mortality rates found in the DHS were 66 percent higher for females than for
males (36.5 for females and 22 for males).[131] This differential mortality
rate is due in part to greater access to health care for males (particularly
immunizations and medicines, and other treatments) as well as to better
nutrition.[132]

SOUTH KOREA

Son preference in South Korea is linked to the country's patriarchal social
structure—sons can carry on the family name, perform rituals of ancestor
worship, and provide economic security for parents.[133] Women's status is
relatively high in South Korea; there is no system of dowries, and yet son
preference continues to influence parental decisions regarding family size
and composition. Demographers Park Chai Bin and Cho Nam-hoon note
that in 1985, South Korea's overall sex ratio at birth suddenly rose.[134] The
rise seems to have begun after 1970, however. Until 1970 the sex ratios at
birth remained between 105 and 107; in 1980 the sex ratio at birth rose to

---

129.   Sen, *Development as Freedom*, p. 104.

130.   Miller, "Daughter Neglect, Women's Work, and Marriage," pp. 121–122.

131.   DHS data recorded in Ian Timœus, Katie Harris, and Francesca Fairbairn, "Can
Use of Health Care Explain Sex Differentials in Child Mortality in the Developing
World?" in United Nations, *Too Young to Die*, p. 156.

132.   Ibid. See also Elisabeth Sommerfelt and Fred Arnold, "Sex Differentials in the
Nutritional Status of Young Children," in United Nations, *Too Young to Die*,
pp. 133–153.

133.   Fred Arnold, "Measuring the Effect of Sex Preference on Fertility: The Case of
Korea," *Demography*, Vol. 22, No. 2 (May 1985), pp. 283–284.

134.   Park Chai Bin and Cho Nam-hoon, "Consequences of Son Preference in a
Low-Fertility Society: Imbalance of the Sex Ratio at Birth in Korea," *Population and Development Review*, Vol. 21, No. 1 (March 1995), pp. 59–84.

108.3, continued to rise slightly in 1985 with a sex ratio of 108.6; and then jumped in the next five years to reach 116.9 in 1990.[135] Bae Wha-oak asserts that the increase in sex ratios is not due to underregistration of females, because South Korea's system of censuses and vital statistics is reliable with an undelayed registration rate.[136] Tougher government enforcement of anti-sex-selection laws may now be influencing sex-selective behavior in South Korea, however: According to the 2000 census, the birth sex ratio is reported to have dropped to 109.6.[137]

The increase in sex ratios corresponds to a decrease in fertility. In 1971 the total fertility rate (i.e., the number of children born per woman) in South Korea was 4.7, a figure that dropped to 2.7 in 1982, and 1.63 in 1990.[138] The effect of son preference on desired family composition is reflected in the 1988 National Fertility and Health Survey: One-half of the women surveyed indicated that a son was essential or better than a daughter; 61 percent of women whose child was male did not want another child, compared with 39 percent of women whose child was female.[139] Since 1974, the sex ratios at birth for higher birth-order children in South Korea have increased to values as high as 228.6 for fourth children in 1992.[140]

The 1991 Fertility and Family Health Survey in South Korea revealed that the sex ratio of first-order births increased dramatically. First-order births in earlier decades typically exhibited normal sex ratios, with only second- and higher-order births exhibiting higher than normal sex ratios, but the 1991 survey revealed a sex ratio for first births of 117.9.[141] According to Park and Cho, "The high sex ratio of first-born children makes us suspect that Korean women now apply sex-choice technology to ensure the outcome of first-order births."[142]

Son preference in South Korea has also manifested itself in differential mortality for female infants and young girls. Even at a time when sex

---

135. See ibid., pp. 61, 66, Tables 1, 6.

136. Bae Wha-oak, "Sex Ratio at Birth in Korea," *Journal of Population, Health, and Social Welfare*, Vol. 11, No. 2 (December 1991), p. 115.

137. South Korea (Republic of Korea), *2001 Report of the National Statistical Office of South Korea* (Seoul: National Statistical Office, July 2001).

138. Bae, "Sex Ratio at Birth in Korea," p. 120.

139. Cited in ibid., p. 121.

140. Park and Cho, "Consequences of Son Preference in a Low-Fertility Society," p. 66, Table 6.

141. Cited in ibid., p. 66, Table 6.

142. Ibid., p. 67.

ratios at birth were normal, sex ratios for children ages 3 and 4 were un-usually high. In 1955, for example, the sex ratio at birth was 105.7, but sex ratios for children ages 3 and 4 were 108.1 and 107.5, respectively.[143] In 1985 the sex ratio at birth was 108.6: thus the expected sex ratio for this age group in five years would be equal to or lower than 108.6 (given higher rates of mortality expected for males in the first year of life), but the sex ratio for this age cohort in 1990 was 111.4.[144] These high sex ratios suggest that female infants and children received less care than male in-fants and were thus subject to higher rates of mortality. The use of sex-selective technology to achieve desired family composition may in fact mean that female infants and children no longer receive differential treat-ment. The 2000 census in South Korea recorded infant and early child-hood mortality rates that were higher for males than females, suggesting that female infanticide is no longer practiced.[145]

TAIWAN

Son preference is considered strong in Taiwan (although perhaps not as strong as in mainland China), for reasons similar to those in South Ko-rea.[146] In 1985, sex screening of fetuses became available in Taiwan.[147] At the same time, Taiwan's sex ratios at birth began to rise, from 106.6 in 1985 to 110.2 in 1990, and then dropped slightly to 109.5 in 2000.[148] An ex-amination of Taiwan's 1990 birth sex ratios according to urban and rural data reveals that the capital city of Taipei had the highest ratio (112), fol-lowed by rural areas (110) and combined cities (109).[149] Scholars have yet to explain Taipei's high sex ratio at birth, but they seem to agree that son

---

143. Ibid., p. 61, Table 1.

144. Ibid.

145. The census recorded death rates per 100,000 as follows: 472.2 females and 491.7 males (age 0); and 41.6 females and 49.8 males (ages 1–4). South Korea (Republic of Korea), "Census Population, 2000" (Seoul: National Statistical Office, 2000), http://www.nso.go.kr.

146. For example, the birth sex ratio for Taiwan in 1990 was 110.2, but it was 114.7 for China in the same year. See Gu Baochang and Krishna Roy, "Sex Ratio at Birth in China, with Reference to Other Areas in Asia: What We Know," *Asia-Pacific Population Journal*, Vol. 10, No. 3 (September 1995), p. 20, Table 1.

147. "Where Have All the Daughters Gone?" *Sinorama Magazine*, n.d., http://www. taiwaninfo.org/info/sinorama/8502/502006e1.html.

148. Gu and Roy, "Sex Ratio at Birth in China," p. 20, Table 1. The sex ratio at birth for 2000 is recorded in Taiwan (Republic of China), *The Republic of China Yearbook— Taiwan, 2002* (Taipei: Ministry of the Interior, 2002), http://www.gio.gov.tw/ taiwan-website/5-gp/yearbook/chpt02–1.htm#1.

149. Gu and Roy, "Sex Ratio at Birth in China," p. 24, Table 3.

preference and sex ratios are generally higher in more traditional and rural areas and lower in large urban centers, where women participate in the labor force and have higher economic value. Where female labor is needed in some agricultural areas, however, sex ratios may be lower. Ronald Freedman, Ming-cheng Chang, and Te-hsiung Sun suggest that son preference in Taiwan has a strong impact on reproductive decisions.[150] Parents' use of contraception increases with the number of sons they have. Similar to South Korea, Taiwan births exhibit high sex ratios at higher orders of parity: The sex ratios for third- and fourth-order births were 118 and 130 in 1991. According to Freedman, Chang, and Sun, the rise in sex ratios is indeed due to increased sex screening and the subsequent abortion of unwanted female fetuses.[151]

The high sex ratio at birth in Taiwan continues to reflect the use of sex-selective technology. There is no evidence to suggest, however, that female infants and children receive less care than males: Mortality rates for the year 2000 for infants and children are slightly higher for males than for females.[152]

Missing Females in Asia

The use of sex-selective technologies and the practice of infanticide—largely through neglect or differential care given to females—have led to a high number of missing females in Asia, a phenomenon that has attracted the interest of scholars for more than a decade. The term "missing females" refers to an estimated number of women (including female infants and girls) who would be alive today in the absence of a gender bias in mortality. In 1990 Amartya Sen calculated that more than 100 million women were missing worldwide.[153] Sen's estimate, one produced by comparing the sex ratios of Asia with the sex ratios of sub-Saharan Africa, was challenged by demographer Ansley Coale the following year. Using mortality and fertility patterns within Asia itself, Coale argued that

150. Ronald Freedman, Ming-cheng Chang, and Te-hsiung Sun, "Taiwan's Transition from High Fertility to Below-Replacement Levels," *Studies in Family Planning*, Vol. 25, No. 6 (1994), pp. 317–331, as cited in ibid., p. 27.

151. Freedman, Chang, and Sun, "Taiwan's Transition from High Fertility to Below-Replacement Levels," as cited in ibid., p. 29.

152. Taiwan's infant mortality rates for males and females were recorded as 7.51 and 6.42, respectively; mortality rates for ages 1–4 were 0.49 for males and 0.45 for females. Ibid., pp. 30–33, Table 16.

153. Amartya Sen, "More Than 100 Million Women Are Missing," *New York Review of Books*, December 20, 1990, pp. 61–66.

the number was closer to 60 million.[154] More recently, economists Stephan Klasen and Claudia Wink have modified Sen's and Coale's methods to arrive at a figure of 93 million missing women worldwide.[155]

As Klasen and Wink indicate, Sen's use of sub-Saharan African sex ratios as a standard by which to measure the expected sex ratios in Asia is problematic because the sex ratios at birth among populations of African descent are slightly lower than in the rest of the world. There are more women in sub-Saharan Africa partly because a higher percentage of females are born each year. Coale's estimates were further calculated by adjusting for excess mortality observed in Asian countries. According to Coale, the sex ratio for populations in Western cultures (in the absence of war or other incidents of gender-specific mortality) should be between 97.9 and 100.3 males per 100 females, which means that because of the female life-expectancy advantage, the number of women should be either more numerous than, or equal to, men.[156] Men outnumber women at birth, but because they generally experience higher mortality than women throughout the life cycle, at some point a crossover occurs and the sex ratio for the overall population begins to favor females. The overall ratio, Coale argued, is determined by the age at which this crossover occurs. A population with a young age structure may have a slightly higher overall sex ratio in the population than a population with an older age structure. He concluded, therefore, that in the absence of excess female mortality caused by discriminatory practices (sex-selective abortion and infanticide in particular), Asian populations, because of their high fertility levels and youthful age structure, should exhibit sex ratios between 101 and 103.[157]

Klasen and Wink contend that some of the assumptions of Coale's approach are questionable. First, they argue that comparing mortality rates in Asia to those in the West underestimates the level of mortality for females in developing countries. Second, they criticize Coale's assumption that the sex ratios at birth in Asian countries would be equal to those in the West: Their research in fact suggests that sex ratios in the West are slightly higher than expected in Asia. Better maternal health and nutri-

154. Ansley J. Coale, "Excess Female Mortality and the Balance of the Sexes in the Population: An Estimate of the Number of 'Missing Females,'" *Population and Development Review,* Vol. 17, No. 3 (September 1991), pp. 517–523.

155. Stephan Klasen and Claudia Wink, "Missing Women: Revisiting the Debate," *Feminist Economics,* Vol. 9, Nos. 2–3 (July–November 2003) Taiwan (Republic of China).

156. Coale, "Excess Female Mortality and the Balance of the Sexes in the Population," p. 518.

157. Ibid.

Table 2.3. Sex Ratios at Birth for Selected Asian Countries.

Country	Expected	Reported	Year and Source of Information
China	105.0	117.00	2000, China CPIRC
		120.00	1999, Chinese Academy of Social Sciences
		116.57	October 1, 1995, SSB (1.04% sample)
		118.65	April 1, 1995, SSB (1.04% sample)
		115.62	October 1, 1994–September 30, 1995, China, SSB (1.04% sample)
		121.01	1993 and 1994, China, State Family Planning Commission of China, *Zhongguo shengyu nianjin, 1996* (China Birth Planning Yearbook, 1996)
		113.8–115.4	1989–90, Zeng et al., 1993
India	103.9	111.0	1996–98, SRS data reported in Premi, 2001
		113.7	1993–1995, Jhunjhunwala, 2001
		132.0	1993, one hospital in Punjab, Booth et al., 1994
		112.2	1981–91, hospital births, India, Office of the Registrar General, 1991
		156.0	1990, town of Rohtak near New Delhi, McDonald, 1991
South Korea	104.7	109.6	2000, South Korea, National Statistical Office, 2001
		115.3	1993, South Korea, National Statistical Office, 2002
		114.0	1992, Park and Cho, 1995
		116.9	1990, Park and Cho, 1995
		117.9	1990, first births only, Park and Cho, 1995
Taiwan	105.2	109.5	2000, Ministry of the Interior
	110.2		1990, Gu and Roy, 1995

tion in Western countries lower the risk of miscarriages and stillbirths, and because more male fetuses are conceived than female fetuses, the sex ratios at birth in developed regions of the world are slightly higher than in less developed regions. The expected sex ratios at birth for Asian countries, according to Klasen and Wink, range between 102.4 and 105.2. Data since the 1980s show that birth sex ratios in China, India, South Korea, and Taiwan are much higher than expected. Few developing countries, particularly those such as India with high fertility rates and large populations, have a reliable system of recording birth statistics. Sampling surveys and other methods, however, have been employed to estimate the overall birth sex ratios in these populations. Table 2.3 provides some of the results of these estimates and compares them with expected figures.

SOURCES: The expected birth sex ratios are calculated in Stephan Klasen and Claudia Wink, "Missing Women: Revisiting the Debate," *Feminist Economics*, Vol. 9, Nos. 2–3 (July–November 2003). Recorded birth sex ratios: China Population Information and Research Council (CPIRC), "China Sees a High Gender Ratio of New-borns," May 14, 2002, http://www.cpirc. org.cn/enews20020514.htm; Chinese Academy of Social Sciences—email communication with the director concerning an article in the *Nando Times* entitled "China Reportedly Has 20 Percent More Males Than Females," January 7, 1999, http://www.nandotimes.com/global/story/body/0,1025,5301–9190–64468–0,00.html; China, State Statistical Bureau (SSB), *China Population Statistics Yearbook, 1996* (Beijing: China Statistics Press, 1996), 1.04 percent samples for October 1994, April 1995, and October 1995; China, State Family Planning Commission of China, *China Birth Planning Yearbook* (Beijing, 1996); Zeng Yi, Tu Ping, Gu Baochang, Xu Yi, Li Bohua, and Li Yongping, "Causes and Implications of the Recent Increase in the Reported Sex Ratio at Birth in China," *Population and Development Review*, Vol. 19, No. 2 (June 1993), pp. 283–302; Mahendra K. Premi, "The Missing Girl Child," *Economic and Political Weekly*, May 26–June 1, 2001, pp. 1875–1880; Bharat Jhunjhunwala, "Sex Ratio Riddles," *Statesman* (India), June 2, 2001; India, Office of the Registrar General, *Compendium of India's Fertility and Mortality Indicators Based on the SRS* (Delhi: Controller of Publications, 1991); Beverley E. Booth, Manorama Verma, and Rajbir Singh Beri, "Fetal Sex Determination in Infants in Punjab, India: Correlations and Implications," *British Medical Journal*, November 12, 1994, pp. 1259–1261; Hamish McDonald, "Unwelcome Sex," *Far Eastern Economic Review*, December 26, 1991–January 2, 1992, pp. 18–19; South Korea (Republic of Korea), *2001 Report of the National Statistical Office of South Korea* (Seoul: National Statistical Office, July 2001); Park Chai Bin and Cho Nam-Hoon, "Consequences of Son Preference in a Low Fertility Society: Imbalance of the Sex Ratio at Birth in Korea," *Population and Development Review*, Vol. 21, No. 1 (March 1995), pp. 59–84; Taiwan (Republic of China), *The Republic of China Yearbook—Taiwan, 2002* (Taipei: Ministry of the Interior, 2002), http://www.gio.gov.tw/taiwan-website/5-gp/yearbook/chpt02–1.htm#1; and Gu Baochang and Krishna Roy, "Sex Ratio at Birth in China, with Reference to Other Areas in Asia: What We Know," *Asia-Pacific Population Journal*, Vol. 10, No. 3 (September 1995), pp. 17–42.

To determine the extent to which sex-selective practices had generated high levels of missing females, Coale, and Klasen and Wink, investigated countries with significant populations and high mortality rates for females. Although Klasen and Wink's assessment included West Asia and sub-Saharan Africa, our study has focused on the high-sex-ratio or high-mortality countries of south-central and eastern Asia, which, according to these scholars, account for 90 percent of the missing females in the world. Although other countries—such as Egypt or Iran—also exhibit sex ratios that indicate the possibility of gender discrimination, further study into these countries is needed to assess the reason for their slightly higher sex ratios. At present, their juvenile sex ratios do not suggest that female infanticide or sex-selective abortion is widely practiced. Klasen and Wink estimate that the overall sex ratios for south-central and eastern Asian populations should range between 96.4 and 100.3. Coupling these expected sex ratios with the most recent census data from selected countries in south-central and eastern Asia, we calculate in Table 2.4 that there are more than 90 million women missing in these regions alone.

Table 2.4. Number of Missing Women for Selected Asian Countries Using Census Data.

Country	Year	Actual Number of Males	Actual Number of Females	Actual Sex Ratio	Expected Sex Ratio	Expected Number of Women	Missing Women
Afghanistan	2000	11,227,000	10,538,000	106.5	96.4	11,646,266	1,108,266
Bangladesh	2001	65,841,419	63,405,814	103.8	99.6	66,105,842	2,700,028
China	2000	653,550,000	612,280,000	106.7	100.1	652,897,103	40,617,103
India	2001	531,277,078	495,738,169	107.2	99.3	535,022,234	39,284,065
Pakistan	1998	68,873,686	63,445,593	108.6	99.2	69,429,119	5,983,526
South Korea	2000	23,068,181	22,917,108	100.7	100.0	23,068,181	151,073
Taiwan	2000	11,386,084	10,914,845	104.3	100.2	11,363,357	448,512
Total							**90,292,573**

SOURCES: Afghanistan—United Nations Population Division, *World Population Prospects: The 2002 Revision*, http://www.un.org/esa/population/publications/wpp2000/annex-tables.pdf; Bangladesh—Bangladesh Bureau of Statistics, *Population Census, 2001: Preliminary Report*, http://www.bbsgov.org; China—National Bureau of Statistics of the People's Republic of China, "Communiqué on Major Figures of the 2000 Population Census," No. 1, April 23, 2002, http://www.stats.gov.cn/english/newrelease/statisticalreports/20020423084.htm; India—Office of the Registrar General, *Census of India, 2001, Series 1: India, Paper 1 of 2001: Provisional Population Totals* (New Delhi: India, 2001), http://www.censusindia.net/results; Pakistan—Population Census Organization, Statistics Division, Government of Pakistan, "1998 Census of Pakistan," http://www.pap.org.pk/population/sec2.htm; South Korea—National Statistical Office, *Republic of Korea Census Population, 2000*, http://www.nso.go.kr; and Taiwan—Statistical Bureau of Taiwan, *Historical Comparison of the Census Results, 2000*, http://www.stat.gov.tw.

China accounts for 45 percent and India for 43 percent of the total number of missing females, and the other five countries account for the remaining 12 percent. Although the actual numbers in some of the remaining countries may be small, in some cases their size relative to the overall national population may be very high. For example, Afghanistan is responsible for just 1 percent of the world's total, yet its number of missing females is 9.5 percent of its overall total female population. This result must be viewed with some caution, however, because unlike the data for the other countries in the table, Afghanistan's population has been estimated by the UN—Afghanistan has not conducted a census since 1979. The figures are consistent, however, with scholars' estimates regarding the level of gender discrimination in the country, particularly in the past decade. China, India, and Pakistan are missing 6.2, 7.3, and 8.6 percent of their respective female populations, while Bangladesh, Nepal, and Taiwan are missing approximately 4 percent of their female populations. South Korea accounts for the lowest number of missing females and also for the lowest percentage relative to its female population—only 0.7 percent.

Given that South Korea's and Taiwan's birth sex ratios are much higher than expected, it is surprising that these countries account for so few of the missing females. The low figures are due mainly to the small populations of these countries—although the births each year are skewed in favor of men, the number of births is relatively small and thus does not have a great impact on the size of the population. For example, in the year 2000, there were 307,200 births in Taiwan, 146,670 of which were female (sex ratio of 109.45).[158] Given that the expected sex ratio for Taiwan is 105.2, we would expect the number of female births to be 149,707, which means that there were 3,037 missing females that year. South Korea's low figure for missing females, however, is in fact misleading. Unlike Taiwan, South Korea's population is heavily skewed in favor of females after the age of 55 and heavily skewed in favor of males in the youth population to the age of 24, which then creates what appears to be a balanced sex ratio for the overall population. With a sex ratio of 110.8 for all ages under 24, there are in fact 475,561 missing females in this age group of the population.[159] Still, this figure represents only 2.1 percent of the females in South Korea.

---

158. Taiwan (Republic of China), *The Republic of China Yearbook—Taiwan*, 2002.

159. South Korea (Republic of Korea), "Census Population, 2000."

Conclusion

Our examination of sex-selective practices shows that female offspring have been undervalued throughout much of history, and in most regions of the world. The most common reason for son preference is economic: Male labor is valued more highly than female labor in areas where son preference is prevalent, and sons contribute to family income even into their parents' old age. High levels of son preference are associated with low female employment opportunities and low levels of female education. In addition, cultural practices such as dowry payments for brides and the roles of men in religious rites increase the desire for sons. A preference for sons is found to some degree in all parts of the world; however, it is most noticeable in parts of Asia, where families use various means to manipulate their composition.

Son preference is demonstrated by the high sex ratios at birth, in early childhood, and in the overall population, as well as by the differences in male and female mortality rates. High birth sex ratios are attributed to the use of sex-selective technology to abort female fetuses. High female infant and childhood mortality rates are indicative of unequal access to health care and nutrition for females, which is a form of infanticide. The countries we examined vary in their methods of sex selection: In Bangladesh and Pakistan, the practice of infanticide has led to the dearth of females, whereas in South Korea and Taiwan, the high sex ratios are primarily due to the practice of sex-selective abortion. The combination of these practices in south-central and eastern Asia—Afghanistan, Bangladesh, China, India, Pakistan, South Korea, and Taiwan—has created populations with much higher numbers of males than females, or to the phenomenon known as the missing females. According to recent estimates, the number of missing females is greater than 90 million.

Given that India and China account for the vast majority of the world's missing females, we have chosen to make them the primary focus of our study. Among the questions we seek to answer are: Have sex ratios in India and China always been this high? What are the causes of these high sex ratios? Are they evenly skewed throughout different age groups within the population—where do we find the fewest number of women per men? Are they evenly skewed throughout the country, or are there regional or other variations? Do current practices suggest that the sex ratio is decreasing, or increasing? Are India's and China's governments and peoples concerned with the rising sex ratios? What are the implications of such high sex ratios for the two most populous countries in the world? We address these questions in chapters 3 and 4, respectively.

Chapter 3

India's "Missing Females"

In 2001 the population of India surpassed 1 billion, making it the second most populous country in the world after China. As the largest contributor to world population growth, adding 18 million people each year, its population will eventually surpass China's.[1] India's population has long attracted study by demographers and other social scientists who have recently turned to analyses of the gender imbalance and especially the question of India's "missing females." In 2001 the sex ratio in India was 107.2; there were 531 million males and 496 million females. Since the 1991 census, the recorded sex ratios at birth have fluctuated between 110.2 and 113.8, although the actual figures may be higher. In this chapter we examine the extent, causes, and implications of this gender imbalance as it pertains to sex selection in India.

The history of sex selection in India is bound up with the history of the country, its religions, the evolution of its social structure, and the changing role of women. The position of women within the family and society has not been uniform throughout history or throughout the country; a woman's status varies according to religion, position within the social hierarchy, region, economy, and even within each family, according to

---

1. Between 1991 and 2001, the Indian population increased by 180.6 million. India, Office of the Registrar General, *Census of India, 2001, Series-1: India, Paper 1 of 2001: Provisional Population Totals* (New Delhi: India, Office of the Registrar General, 2001), http://www.censusindia.net/results. In 1998 the United Nations Population Division published its *World Population Prospects: The 1998 Revision*, in which India surpassed China and all other countries as the top contributor to world population growth. India contributes 20.6 percent to the added world population, and China 14.7 percent. See United Nations, Population Division of the Department of Economic and Social Affairs, "The 1998 Revision of the United Nations Population Projections," *Population and Development Review*, Vol. 24, No. 4 (December 1998), pp. 891–895.

birth order. Understanding the current discriminatory practices against women, including sex-selective abortion, infanticide, and differential mortality, requires an examination of India's unique history, religion, and social structure.

Historical Setting

India comes from the Sanskrit word *sindu*, which was used to describe the Indus River by the Aryan-speaking migrants who traveled from their homeland between the Caspian and Black Seas and eventually settled in the Indian subcontinent.[2] Their arrival in 1500 B.C. disrupted the lives of the existing inhabitants, most of whom were Dravidian speakers. The simple tribal structure of the Aryan people became more complex through processes of conflict and cooperation with the Dravidian-speaking people, as warfare and conquest led to the creation of levels of governance within the tribal system. As Hindu civilization emerged, so did a complex societal structure. Hindu society became organized around the principle of *varna-ashrama-dharma*—class, stages of life (which determine status, goals, duties, and obligations), and righteousness and sacred law—as outlined in Hindu scripture and tradition. Harmony and stability in society were believed to be dependent on the righteousness of all members of the community and the degree to which they fulfilled the obligations coinciding with their age and status.

In addition to the intertribal wars that followed the Aryan invasion, other invaders attempted to encroach on Indian territory from regions beyond present-day Afghanistan and Pakistan. With the exception of the region of Ashoka (even when northern India came under control of Chandragupta Maurya in 326 B.C.), warring within India among Hindu tribes continued until the Mauryan dynasty ended in 184 B.C. and a new period of invasions began.

During the next millennium, several dynasties (composed mainly of Rajput warriors) attempted to gain status and territory but were thwarted by Muslim invaders who, having begun their attacks on India in A.D. 997, gained control over a large portion of the subcontinent in 1175.[3] Rivalry between the resultant Muslim kingdoms and the Hindu empires weakened the regions in the north and northwest, exposing

---

2. Richard F. Nyrop, ed., *India: A Country Study, Foreign Area Studies, the American University* (Washington, D.C.: Superintendent of Documents, U.S. Government Printing Office, 1985).

3. Stanley Wolpert, *A New History of India*, 4th ed. (New York: Oxford University Press, 1993), pp. 106–109.

them to Mughal invasions in 1556. The Mughal empire thrived until 1707, when it disintegrated, finally being removed in 1858. Wars in which other empires, including the Marathas and Sikhs, rose to power marked the years up to the mid-nineteenth century, when the British took over rule of the subcontinent. India would not become independent of British rule until 1947.

India currently consists of twenty-eight states and seven union territories, ranging in population size from 60,000 to 166 million (nineteen states have populations of more than 10 million); there are 15 national languages (including English) and some recognized regional languages as well, chosen from among at least 1,652 spoken languages and dialects. India's 15,200-kilometer border separates it from six surrounding nations: Bangladesh, Bhutan, Burma (Myanmar), China, Nepal, and Pakistan. The Himalayas isolate the Indian subcontinent from the rest of Asia and also form the border between India and the nations to the north. Within India, hills, dense forests, and deserts separate fertile zones from each other, also preventing processes of cultural diffusion and unification. The country is divided into five major regions: north, northwest, east/northeast, west, and south.

As maps 3.1 and 3.2 show, India's state structure changed in the late 1990s. We discuss data both prior to and after this period, so it is useful to know how state boundaries changed.

Religion

Hinduism is the dominant religion in India, followed by 82 percent of the populace. Hinduism is a vast socioreligious system that encourages the acceptance of diverse beliefs and customs; unlike the monotheistic religions of Christianity and Islam, it has no unifying creed, and it recognizes innumerable gods. Hindus accept the notion of an ordained order of the universe and the fulfillment of obligations based on one's age, sex, and status within the social system. The religion relies on the Vedas, composed between 1400 and 1000 B.C., as the most sacred scriptural authority.[4] Most Indians, however, give far more attention to the philosophical *Brahmanas* and *Upanishads*; the historico-mythical *Puranas*; and the epics the *Ramayana* and the *Mahabharata* (which contains the Bhagavad Gita—the most read Hindu scripture).

Islam is the second largest religion in India. Muslims make up 12 per-

---

4. Much speculation surrounds the date of origin of the Vedas. Stanley Wolpert suggests that the Rig Veda was written in approximately 1400 B.C. and that other parts of the Veda were written in 1000 B.C. See ibid., pp. 26–27.

Map 3.1. The States of India, 1996.

cent of the population, and Christianity, Sikhism, Buddhism, Jainism, and other religions make up the remaining 6 percent.[5]

Social Systems

Hinduism provides the religious rationale and sanction for the caste system, the basis of India's social system. The caste system in India is ex-

---

5. India, Office of the Registrar General, *Census of India, 1991, Census Data Online,* Table 23, http://www.censusindia.net/cendat/datatable23.html.

Map 3.2. The State of India, 2003.

tremely complex: Each individual is born into, and remains within throughout life, a *jati* (subcaste), one of many thousands of endogamous kin groups, which is in turn located within one of four *varnas* (castes). Social status, occupation, and opportunities for marriage within India's hierarchical social system are determined by one's jati and varna—both jatis and varnas are hierarchical, with Brahmans atop of the hierarchy and those outside the caste system—the "untouchables"—at the bottom. Rules pertaining to the caste system are discussed (although not to the extent that such rules are currently enforced) in the Code of Manu, or Hindu laws, generally thought to have been written in the fifth century B.C., though others place the date several centuries later.[6] Although Buddhists, Christians, Jains, Muslims, and Sikhs do not participate in the caste system, even members of these religious communities find themselves involved in it because of their proximity to the large Hindu population. Also uncategorizable according to caste are the 8 percent of the population belonging to tribes living primarily along the Himalayas. Tribes vary in size and complexity of social organization; they are often separated by religion, language, economic patterns, and geographical location. Tribes tend to be egalitarian, and leadership can be based on personality rather than heredity. There is no particular marriage pattern at work among the tribes.

To maintain jati purity, all contact with those less pure (of a lower caste)—whether through marriage, eating, or drinking—is controlled. At the village level, kinship underlies the organizations of jatis. There are usually anywhere from two to thirty jatis in each village, and any given jati will necessarily have contacts with thirty-five to forty other jatis to conduct trade or exchange services.[7]

Marriage is the most public statement of jati status. Arranging a proper marriage for a child is one of the greatest duties of parents. Most marriages take place within one's jati, the only exception being the possibility of a woman marrying a man of higher status. Because jati purity is intimately tied to woman's purity, a woman is not permitted to marry beneath her status. Thus the system of marriage in India is hypergynous; women must marry within or above their position in the social hierarchy. Mildred Dickemann explains: "The pyramidal nature of hierarchical societies meant that the higher the status of the subcaste, the fewer options for its daughters: the operation of hypergyny in a pyramidal structure guarantees competition for a resource which is always scarce in relation to demand."[8] In such systems, an Indian woman must bring a dowry with her to the marriage—a form of economic benefit to the groom's fam-

6. William Crooke, *The North-Western Provinces of India: Their History, Ethnology, and Administration* (London: Methuen, 1897), p. 61.

7. David G. Mandelbaum, "Family, *Jati*, Village," in Milton Singer and Bernard S. Cohn, eds., *Structure and Change in Indian Society* (Chicago: Aldine de Gruyter, 1968), p. 41.

8. Mildred Dickemann, "Female Infanticide, Reproductive Strategies, and Social Stratification: A Preliminary Model," in Napoleon A. Chagnon and William Irons, eds., *Evolutionary Biology and Human Social Behavior: An Anthropological Perspective* (North Scituate, Mass.: Duxbury, 1979), pp. 321–367, at p. 326.

ily from the bride's family; the higher the subcaste, the greater the dowry that must be given upon marriage.

Anthropologist Nur Yulman describes the relation among women, marriage, caste, hypergyny, and purity:

Thus the sexuality of men receives a generous *carte blanche*. But it always matters what the women do: (a) They may have sexual relations with superior and "pure" men. No harm comes to them in terms of purity. (b) They may have children from "pure" men; or men from their own caste. . . . But, if they engage in sexual relations with men lower than themselves, then they get "internally" polluted. Moreover, they bear "polluted" children. . . . It is clear that these rules of hypergamy are directly associated with systems in which membership in the group is acquired through both parents, but where the purity of the group is protected through women. . . . Hence, even though caste membership derives through both parents, there is a built-in asymmetry in all these systems.[9]

Thus it is through women that the purity of the caste is maintained, and hence the need to control women's relations, especially marriage.

There are several regional marriage patterns in India. In the north, people must marry endogamously within castes but exogamously within subcastes. Marriage is forbidden among blood relatives, and many jatis refuse to accept brides from the villages to which they send female members of their own villages to marry. Marriages in the south are reciprocal between villages, which reinforces kinship ties with a number of families. Central India follows marriage patterns found in both the north and the south.

Family and kin relationships play an important role in the lives of both women and men in India. One's position within the family is determined primarily by age, sex, and relationship to those in leadership roles. Descent in most of the country is traced through the male line, although there are some exceptions, such as the Nayars of Kerala. Even though the eldest male is the authority, he is not the sole inheritor of property: All males receive a share of property within the family according to Hindu law, though the eldest may receive a larger share. Women generally share in the property only through marriage, despite the existence of property laws that allow for a share of family property.

---

9. Nur Yulman, "On the Purity of Women in the Castes of Ceylon and Malabar," *Journal of the Royal Anthropological Society*, Vol. 93, Pt. 1 (January–June 1963), pp. 42–43, as cited in Mildred Dickemann, "Paternal Confidence and Dowry Competition: A Biocultural Analysis of Purdah," in Richard D. Alexander and Donald W. Tinkle, eds., *Natural Selection and Social Behavior: Recent Research and New Theory* (New York: Chiron, 1981), p. 421.

Women's Status

In India the birth of a son is greeted with much fanfare—drumming, singing, and proud public announcements—whereas the birth of a daughter is quietly observed. Yet this was not always the case. In India's early history, women enjoyed equal status with men: They could become priests, choose their marriage partners, and rule their households; *sati* (the practice of a widow throwing herself upon her husband's funeral pyre) was unknown, and widows were allowed to remarry in the early Vedic period.[10] Folktales from this period (ca. 1500–800 B.C.) extol the beauty, valor, and strength of women. In one such tale, a woman named Satyabhama receives praise for her heroism and bravery: Upon seeing her warrior husband weary from battle and fighting an enemy of superior strength, she took up a weapon and cut off the arms of the enemy, saving her husband's life. Women could accompany men anywhere, and their activities and contributions were considered necessary to the survival of future generations.[11]

Dowry, polygyny, bride-price, and wife capture are mentioned in the Rig Veda, the oldest and most important of the Vedas, in approximately 900 B.C., suggesting that at this time, the status of women began to change, as men began to exert more control over them.[12] This view is reinforced by descriptions of women in the *Ramayana* and the *Mahabharata*, literature of the later Vedic period, in which women appear to have a secondary role.[13] After approximately 600 B.C., women's status gradually deteriorated; they were no longer permitted to be priests, their education was neglected, and their marriageable age was lowered.[14] Hindu literature dating from the sixth century B.C. onward suggests that men must control women. These views are particularly evident in the Code of Manu, which states: "By a young girl, by a young woman or even by an aged one, nothing must be done independently even in her own house. In childhood a female must be subject to her father, in youth to her husband, when her lord is dead to her sons; a woman must never be inde-

---

10. See Richard Lannoy, *The Speaking Tree: A Study of Indian Culture and Society* (Oxford: Oxford University Press, 1971), p. 102; and R. Muthulakshmi, *Female Infanticide: Its Causes and Solutions* (New Delhi: Discovery Publishing House, 1997), p. 2.

11. Har Bilas Sarda, *History of Ancient Hindu Society: An Attempt to Determine the Position of the Hindu Race in the Scale of Nations* (Delhi: Anmol Publications, 1985), p. 101.

12. Dickemann, "Paternal Confidence and Dowry Competition," p. 432.

13. Muthulakshmi, *Female Infanticide*, p. 2.

14. Brij Narain Sharma, *Social Life in Northern India [A.D. 600–1000]* (Delhi: Munshiram Manoharlal, 1966), p. 10.

pendent." Yet despite this control, men are warned that "through [women's] passion for men, through their mutable temper, through their natural heartlessness, they become disloyal towards their husbands, however carefully they are guarded in this [world]."[15] The Code of Manu declares that a girl should be given in marriage in her eighth year, and that she must not remain unmarried beyond age 12. Failure to marry by this age was not only considered a great sin for the parents and elder brothers of the girl, but it also meant that they were assigned to hell.[16] Women of upper classes were also subjected to *purdah*—they were concealed from those other than kin and controlled by male kin—a practice most prevalent in northern India and correlated with polygyny, dowry, and the caste system.

Women's current status in India is reflected in recent figures for literacy and labor force participation. Although women's literacy rates in India increased throughout the twentieth century, there is still a large gap between male and female rates: According to the 1991 census, 53 percent of males were literate compared with 32 percent of females. Generally, literacy is much lower in rural areas as well as in the northern states.[17] The most recent reports on labor force participation indicate that women comprise 29 percent of the country's paid workforce, compared with 55 percent for men, and only 16 percent of the urban labor force compared with 53 percent for men.[18]

Son preference in India is intense, as it is in many other Asian nations. A 1997 study conducted throughout India revealed that son preference is observed in all sections of the population. Son preference typically results from traditional religious beliefs, social customs (dowry, lineage, kinship ties, etc.), and economic benefits, including support for parents in old age. For the population aged 17–41, the average number of sons considered ideal is two for every daughter; however, the ideal number of sons and the intensity of son preference increases in those aged 42–61, which the author of the study explains is due to parental concerns over the costs of dowry and the intensified desire for economic support from sons upon reaching old age. Although preference for sons decreases with increased literacy, the study shows that the intensity of son preference suddenly increases again among men with a university education; per-

---

15. Muthulakshmi, *Female Infanticide*, pp. 3–4.

16. See Sharma, *Social Life in Northern India*, p. 15.

17. Leela Visaria and Pravin Visaria, "India's Population in Transition," *Population Bulletin*, Vol. 50, No. 3 (October 1995), p. 24.

18. Ibid., p. 31.

haps there is a higher representation of upper castes, and thus an intensified desire for sons, among these men.[19]

The 1992–93 National Family Health Survey in India included measurements of son preference. Demographers suggested that the preference for sons was based on three factors: their economic, sociocultural, and religious utility. The researchers explain that "sons are more likely than daughters to provide family labor on the farm or in a family business, earn wages, and support their parents during old age." Sons are also necessary to continue the family line and add status to the family in India's patrilineal and patriarchal system. Finally, according to Hindu tradition, sons are required to "kindle the funeral pyre of their deceased parents and to help in the salvation of their souls."[20] Conversely, daughters appear to be an economic liability because of the dowry and other costs associated with weddings. Also, girls' chastity must be protected and suitable marriage arrangements made; thus a daughter requires more parental effort than a son. Once married, the daughter is typically considered part of her husband's family. Daughters are not wholly undesirable, however, for they also provide emotional support and are needed by parents to "cry at the time of their death."[21]

Female Infanticide—Origins of the Practice

Scholars disagree over the origins of the practice of female infanticide in India. Some suggest that it has been around since time immemorial; others claim that its roots lie in the Muslim invasions of Sind (now southwestern Pakistan); and still others argue that it is associated with the upheaval caused by the disintegration of the Mughal government in the eighteenth century.[22] Although it is difficult to determine a starting date

---

19. Rangamuthia Mutharayappa, Minja Kim Choe, Fred Arnold, and T.K. Roy, "Son Preference and Its Effect on Fertility in India," National Family Health Survey Subject Report No. 3 (March 1997), p. 5. See also K. Mahadevan and R. Jayasree, "Value of Children and Differential Fertility Behaviour in Kerala, Andhra Pradesh, and Uttar Pradesh," in Shri Nath Singh, ed., Population Transition in India (Delhi: B.R. Publishing, 1989), pp. 123–131. The four most popular reasons in their sample for preferring sons were "physical support and staying with parents" (91.9 percent), "economic support during old age" (88.5 percent), "salvation to the parents by doing ritual functions" (87.4 percent), and "provide traditional links (lineage)" (81.3 percent).

20. Mutharayappa et al., "Son Preference and Its Effect on Fertility in India," p. 5.

21. Ibid., p. 6.

22. For the different views, see Muthulakshmi, Female Infanticide, p. 8; Kanti B. Pakrasi, Female Infanticide in India (Calcutta: Editions India, 1970), p. 16; and Lalita

for this practice, it is generally assumed that female infanticide did not occur during the early Vedic period (ca. 1500–800 B.C.), when women generally enjoyed high status within Indian society. Early Hindu texts make no reference to infanticide, although they do imply that the birth of a daughter is not greeted with as much joy as the birth of a son: "Keep aside the girl when she is born and lift up (that is with pride and joy), the son"; and "the wife is indeed a friend, the daughter is distress (or humiliation), the son is light in the highest heaven."[23] Some Hindu texts also indicate the existence of son preference by outlining charms and rituals for ensuring the birth of a male child. We would not expect prevalent female infanticide during this early Vedic period, however, because varna/jati marriage rules were not yet rigidly enforced.

Passages in the Rig Veda suggest that during the later Vedic period (800–500 B.C.), the arrival of female infants may have begun to be viewed as something other than a welcome event. One notable exception to the lack of textual references to Vedic-era infanticide is found in the text of the Yajur Veda from the late Vedic period, which refers to the exposure of female infants after birth.[24] Thus the late Vedic period is the earliest period to which we can reliably trace the origins of the practice.

Female infanticide is tied up with India's caste and hypergynous marriage systems, but these are not the only factors that have led parents to kill their female infants. The value, or burden, of being female has been greatly affected by circumstances in Indian history. As the caste system and notions of purity became firmly entrenched within Indian society, girls themselves (because of the more "polluting" nature of their bodies' functions) came to be seen as sources of pollution themselves; hence they were not allowed to participate in sacred rituals.[25] The purity of one's jati had to be ensured through the careful delineation of boundaries of behavior for men and women. To a society so focused on purity as it pertains to one's social group, "polluting" outsiders would be particularly unwelcome. Given India's history of invasions from the north and northwest, it is perhaps not surprising that female infanticide, when first uncovered by the British in 1789, was most prevalent in the north and

---

Panigrahi, *British Social Policy and Female Infanticide in India* (New Delhi: Munshiram Manoharlal, 1972), respectively.

23. "Dharmasastra" and "The Mahabharata," as cited in Panigrahi, *British Social Policy and Female Infanticide in India*, p. 2.

24. Herbert Hope Risley, *The People of India*, ed. William Crooke (Delhi: Oriental Books Reprint Corporation, 1969), p. 166.

25. Wolpert, *A New History of India*, p. 25.

northwestern provinces. Indian historian Lalita Panigrahi suggests that the seclusion of women became more widespread during the invasions of hordes from Central Asia.[26] The Hindu text *Arthashastra* (322–183 B.C.) speaks of the capture of women in war. The capture of one's wife, mother, sister, or daughter by an invading tribe meant loss of the individual, loss of pride for those whose duty it was to protect her, and loss of the rigidly constructed boundaries drawn around the family, clan, or caste.

The need to seclude and protect women may also have been a function of the anarchy that prevailed in India at the time. Not only were women in danger of being taken captive by, or forced to marry, men of invading groups; they also faced capture by nearby warring tribes. Although Aryan law specifically prohibited the theft of women, Aryan warriors commonly carried away women from other tribes. Hypergyny, which is implicated in the practice of female infanticide, may be linked to the invasions. This form of marriage, which is particularly common in the northwest, has been tied historically to the inflow of conquering tribes to India from this direction. True hypergyny, one author notes, is the gift of a daughter without return; it indicates submission, fidelity toward landlords, or deference, depending on whether the marriage was arranged in time of peace or war.[27]

Indian historian Kanti Pakrasi agrees with the theory that invasions—Muslim invasions in particular—played a large role in the onset of the practice of female infanticide and accepts the explanation constructed by the British on their discovery of the practice among the Rajputs in India's northern provinces.[28] According to this explanation, the Jahreja Rajputs were once the inhabitants of Sind, the site of the first Muslim invasions in the eighth century. Among this group, female infanticide was widespread in the eighteenth and nineteenth centuries. According to historical accounts, the Muslims forced marriage on the daughters of the Rajputs. To marry beneath one's caste was considered shameful enough, but to be forced into a marriage outside of one's social system was disastrous; the Rajput families preferred to kill their daughters rather than face such disgrace. Although the custom of eliminating female children to avoid pollution by invading groups and disgrace may have originated during any of the many invasions, female infanticide was a known practice among the peoples of Arabia; thus it seems plausible to some schol-

---

26. Panigrahi, *British Social Policy and Female Infanticide in India*, p. 4.

27. Alice Clark, "Limitations on Female Life Chances in Rural Central Gujarat," in J. Krishnamurty, ed., *Women in Colonial India: Essays on Survival, Work, and the State* (Delhi: Oxford University Press, 1989), p. 41.

28. Pakrasi, *Female Infanticide in India*, pp. 16–17.

ars that the practice was adopted in India after the invasion and rule by the Muslims. Below we discuss the British discovery of female infanticide in India and their efforts both to understand and to eradicate the practice.

Public Condemnation and Attempts to End Female Infanticide

Female infanticide was first publicly condemned by Emperor Jahangir, who in the early part of the seventeenth century issued a proclamation prohibiting the practice.[29] In 1755 the Rajasthan ruler Raja Jai Singh also attempted to reduce the incidence of female infanticide by setting limits on dowry expenditures, but his efforts were unsuccessful.[30] It was Jonathan Duncan's 1789 disclosure of the practice, and the British response, that had the greatest impact.

Duncan was a civil service officer who, while working with a group of Rajputs in the eastern Benares District along the Ganges River near Oudh (also Oude) in the North-West Province (present-day Uttar Pradesh), discovered that the Rajkumar Rajputs killed their female infants.[31] In his 1789 statement to the Bengal government, Duncan wrote: "It is no unfrequent practice among the Rajkoomars to put their daughters to death. This horrid custom is said to exist also among other tribes, more especially in the Vizier's dominions; it is thought to be founded in the Rajkoomer tribe on the inherent extravagant desire of independency entertained by this race of men, joined, perhaps, to the necessity of procuring a suitable settlement in marriage for these devoted females were they allowed to grow up; and the disgrace which would ensue from any omission in that respect." Duncan touched on several important points in his first description of the practice: The custom did exist among other tribes, as he and others would discover; the practice was related to the high status and "independency" of the Rajputs; and it was connected to the problems associated with marriage customs among the Hindus.[32]

It may seem strange that the British, who had exerted a presence in

---

29. Manmohan Kaur, *Role of Women in the Freedom Movement (1857–1947)* (Delhi: Sterling, 1968), p. 9. Panigrahi also refers to the proclamation of Emperor Jehangir but states that the original reference cannot be traced. See Panigrahi, *British Social Policy and Female Infanticide in India*, p. 5.

30. Kaur, *Role of Women in the Freedom Movement*, pp. 9–10.

31. Crooke, *The North-Western Provinces of India (1857–1947)*, p. 136. See also James Peggs, *Cries of Agony: An Historical Account of Suttee Infanticide, Ghat Murders, and Slavery in India* (originally published as *India's Cries to British Humanity*, 1830; reprint, Delhi: Discovery Publishing House, 1984), p. 133 (page references are to reprint edition).

32. Quoted in Peggs, *Cries of Agony*, p. 133.

India since the 1600s, did not learn about the practice of female infanticide in the country until 1789. Indeed one might think that the dearth of females in some villages would have been immediately noticeable; however, because the Hindus— among whom the practice was most common—were very private, any inquiry into their lives was resented. Furthermore, women of the higher castes—which were more likely to practice female infanticide—were highly controlled and secluded from the public, particularly from men. Even following the discovery of the custom, it was difficult to determine to what extent, and among whom, it was practiced.

The Rajkumars were not the only Rajputs (nor the only caste) to practice female infanticide, nor was the North-West Province the only region in which it was found. The discovery of female infanticide in the Rajput states of Kathiawar and Cutch (now both part of Gujarat) coincided with the British East India Company's attempt to establish a foothold in these northwestern states in the first part of the nineteenth century. Duncan, at this time the governor of Bombay, was told by a Gujarat prince that the Jahreja Rajputs in Cutch practiced wide-scale female infanticide.[33] At the same time, a British officer, Col. Alexander Walker, who had been sent to Kathiawar in 1805 to settle disputes between political groups in the state, observed a lack of females among the Jahreja Rajputs. In fact, he could find only five families who had not killed their daughters.[34]

ORIGINS OF THE PRACTICE

Walker was soon assigned to investigate the extent, causes, and origins of female infanticide in Kathiawar. In an 1808 account, he related several Jahreja legends regarding the early history of the practice. The most commonly cited explanation described how a powerful raja had a daughter of singular beauty and accomplishment for whom his *rajgor*, or family priest, searched for a suitable groom. When no appropriate prince was found, the rajgor urged the raja to kill his daughter rather than suffer the disgrace of her remaining unmarried. Although the raja was at first reluctant to murder his daughter, the rajgor convinced him by offering to assume the consequences for the sin. The daughter was put to death, and the Jahrejas practiced female infanticide from that time on.[35] Regarding this account, Walker commented:

---

33. For a detailed history of the discovery and attempts to abolish the custom in Gujarat, see Pakrasi, *Female Infanticide in India*.

34. Panigrahi, *British Social Policy and Female Infanticide in India*, p. 40.

35. The full text of Walker's account is found in Peggs, *Cries of Agony*, pp. 135–138.

From this narrative curiosity receives little gratification. It resembles the tales of infancy, rather than the grave history of a transaction involving the fate of a numerous portion of the human race. This, however, comprises all the information which the Jahrejas possess of the origin of a custom so contrary to the dictates of nature, and which is justifiable on no plea, as it gratifies no reasonable passion. Notwithstanding this unsatisfactory account of the origin of Infanticide, many absurd institutions like this are dependent less on reason than on particular circumstances, which in the course of many ages, give them importance and influence.[36]

A more probable account, according to Walker, ascribed its origins to the problems experienced by invaders:

It is said that one of the early Mussalman invaders of the Jahrejas' country, who experienced the determination with which they defended their liberties, united policy to arms, and sought to consolidate their interests in the country by demanding the daughters of the Rajahs in marriage. The high-spirited Jahrejas would not brook the disgrace, and pretended they did not preserve their daughters; but fearful of the consequences, and that force would be resorted to in order to obtain what was refused to entreaty they listened to the advice of the Rajgors in this extremity, and, deluded by the fictitious responsibility which they accepted, the practice of Infanticide originated, and has since been confirmed.[37]

When asked why they killed their daughters, other members of the Jahrejas replied that they feared their daughters would become captives or in some way disgrace them.[38] Because their responses seemed to echo the reasons for killing female babies among the "Pagan Arabs," Colonel Walker concluded that "the custom of Infanticide amongst the Jahrejas was a consequence resulting from the Mohamedan conquest of Sind."[39] Because society expected high morality from women, and because women were in danger of capture from outside groups, they became more tightly controlled and could also be considered a liability, particularly among the Rajputs, a warring class who had always held their women in low regard.[40] Panigrahi suggests that the Jahrejas found themselves surrounded by Muslims after the invasion of Sind, which meant that there were no acceptable men to become bridegrooms for their daughters. Traveling great distances to find suitable Rajput husbands

---

36. Cited in ibid., pp. 136–137.

37. Cited in ibid., p. 137.

38. Pakrasi, *Female Infanticide in India*, p. 16.

39. Quoted in ibid., p. 16.

40. Panigrahi, *British Social Policy and Female Infanticide in India*.

would incur large expenses, and because women could not marry within their own group, parents instead chose to put their daughters to death.[41] Despite the existence of Hindu verses proclaiming the sin of murdering infants, the Rajputs felt no sin in committing female infanticide. In fact, they believed it to have been sanctioned by Hindu priests.

THE WIDENING INVESTIGATION

To determine the extent of the practice among the Jahrejas in Gujarat, Walker, deriving figures for the number of families in the area, estimated that the number of female infants killed each year was between 5,000 and 30,000; arriving at a more precise figure was not possible at that time.[42] The first attempt to enumerate the Jahrejas in Kathiawar took place in 1834, although the returns are not considered accurate, because the Jahreja chiefs themselves were asked to fill in the census forms. Nonetheless, the sample census revealed a large majority of males: The number of females of all ages was 696, and the number of males under the age of 20 was 1,422.[43] An 1841 sample revealed 5,760 males and 1,370 females (yielding a sex ratio of 420 males per 100 females), yet even this census is suspected of being an inaccurate portrayal of the population, as it is believed that the census officers were bribed to increase the numbers for women.[44] Similarly, an 1841 sample census of Cutch revealed 2,625 males and 335 females (yielding a sex ratio of 784 males per 100 females).[45]

At first, the British believed that female infanticide was prevalent only among these two clans of Rajputs (Jahrejas and Rajkumars), present in large numbers in the northern and northwestern states. The Rajputs, who were the superior warrior caste in India in the seventh century A.D., can trace their genealogy to the warrior caste of the Vedic tradition as far back as 1000 B.C. Rajput clans together formed part of a complex political system that was present even up to the twentieth century in northwestern India. Because of their superior lineage and status as a warrior and landholding caste, the Rajputs developed a complex social system based on endogamy, where marriage outside the caste meant loss of caste membership.[46] Lineages were carefully maintained so as not to risk losing the

---

41. Ibid., p. 11.

42. Peggs, *Cries of Agony*, pp. 150–151.

43. Panigrahi, *British Social Policy and Female Infanticide in India*, p. 41.

44. Ibid., pp. 41–42.

45. Ibid., p. 42.

46. Robert C. Hallissey, *The Rajput Rebellion against Aurangzeb: A Study of the Mughal*

opportunity to claim legitimacy to the throne of the Rajput kingdoms; thus marriages were endogamous within the caste but exogamous in terms of one's clan and tribe. The Rajputs also had a complex system of property inheritance that created yet another system of hierarchy. The Rajputs thus had difficulty finding suitable marriage partners for their daughters. As Pakrasi points out, the rise in rank consciousness among the Rajputs resulted in clans claiming high descent.[47] No doubt this phenomenon was the result of a policy of resistance to changes in family boundary or status. As L.S. Vishwanath explains, "This warrior/ruler ideology made the Rajputs reject other available means of mobility and lent considerable rigidity to their socio-political hierarchy."[48]

The British would soon discover that not only the Rajkumar and Jahreja clans of the Rajputs (who were of the highest status in their respective regions) killed their female infants, but that other Rajput clans practiced female infanticide as well. By 1818 the British East India Company controlled all of the Rajput states. Knowing that in Cutch and Kathiawar the Rajputs were most responsible for infanticide, the British were eager to determine the extent of the practice in Rajputana (Rajasthan). In 1808 Walker had observed that the Rathor Rajputs of Jaipur and Jodhpur (in central Rajputana) practiced female infanticide, but because the state was not yet under British control, he could not investigate further. Not until Lanncelot Wilkinson's arrival in Rajputana in 1833 would more be learned. Wilkinson, an aide to a British army lieutenant colonel, found that the Minas of Jehazpur, in particular, killed their daughters.[49]

From 1835 to 1854, discovery of female infanticide was made among the Bais, Bhadauri (Bhadawri), Chauhans, Gautams, Kacchwa, Kalhans, Monus, Nanwak, Parihar, Sowan, and Surajbhan clans of Rajputs.[50] As the British inquiry into the practice continued, more Rajput clans were discovered to kill their females: In sixty-two villages visited in 1855, not a single girl under the age of 6 was found. In 1843 there was reportedly not one female child among the Chauhans, who were the proudest Rajputs

Empire in Seventeenth-Century India (Columbia: University of Missouri Press, 1977), pp. 11–12.

47. Pakrasi, *Female Infanticide*, p. 12.

48. L.S. Vishwanath, "Female Infanticide and the Position of Women in India," in A.M. Shah, B.S. Baviskar, and E.A. Ramaswampy, eds., *Social Structure and Change*, Vol. 2: *Women in Indian Society* (New Delhi: Sage, 1996), p. 186.

49. Panigrahi, *British Social Policy and Female Infanticide in India*, pp. 31–32.

50. Ibid., pp. 23–25.

living in Mainpuri (North-West Province).[51] The practice was in fact prevalent among all the upper and middle classes of Rajputs throughout Rajputana, as well as in the Rajput state of Malwa (now part of Madhya Pradesh).[52]

Rajputs were not the only caste with few daughters; the Phatak Ahirs and Gujars in the North-West Province also killed female infants. Panigrahi suggests that these groups imitated Rajput customs to increase their status, although the custom may have originated during a period of hardship, as it did with other clans and castes that practiced female infanticide.[53] The Jetwas, Meanas, and Soomras followed the example of the Jahrejas in Cutch and Kathiawar in killing their female daughters. Vishwanath also notes prevalent female infanticide among the Lewa Kanbis of central Gujarat, also in imitation of the Rajputs.[54] As the British acquired more territory, they learned of the prevalence of the practice in other areas. After taking control of the Trans-Sutlej territories (Punjab), the British discovered the practice among the Bedis (Bedees). These Sikhs, known throughout Punjab as *kuri-mar* (also *kudi-maar*), or the daughter-slaying people, killed all their daughters through neglect.[55] The Bedis were the highest class among the Sikhs, and according to the British, a sense of pride led this group to kill their female infants. The Bedis claimed that the practice originated in the sixteenth century as a result of the insults suffered by the grandson of the founder of the Sikh faith upon the marriage of his daughter to an inferior bridegroom. The girl's father declared that "no Bedee should let a daughter live." Those who did not kill their daughters were excommunicated.[56] The Sodhees, who saw themselves as superior to the Bedis, also killed their daughters as a matter of pride, as did the Manjha and Malwa Sikhs.[57]

In addition to the Sikhs, the Burar Jats, Khatris, Moyal Brahmans, and

---

51. Crooke, *The North-Western Provinces of India*, p. 136.

52. Panigrahi, *British Social Policy and Female Infanticide in India*, pp. 19–32.

53. Ibid., pp. 12–13.

54. Vishwanath, "Female Infanticide and the Position of Women in India," pp. 179–205.

55. Panigrahi, *British Social Policy and Female Infanticide in India*, pp. 25–26.

56. John Cave Browne, *Indian Infanticide: Its Origins, Progress, and Suppression* (London: W.H. Allen, 1857), pp. 115–118. An alternative version of the legend regarding the Bedis suggests that the daughter was treated with less than her due, and on complaining to her father was told that she should die rather than endure such treatment. She accepted this advice and promptly died. The father then declared that no one else should allow a daughter to live and suffer a similar experience.

57. Ibid., p. 119.

Muslims (especially the Goudus and Doghurs) in Punjab killed their daughters to maintain high status.[58] Other minor groups—the Aroras, Kakkars, Kapurs, Khannas, Malhotras, Seths, and Suyals—were included in a detailed 1853 list of castes that practiced female infanticide in Punjab. Rajputs were also present in Punjab, and the high-status Kutoch, Jummoo, and Munha clans all killed their female infants, while the inferior hill clans of the Rajputs saved their daughters.[59]

The people of the Central Provinces (Madhya Pradesh and parts of Orissa) were not immune to the practice. Although apparently absent among the lower classes, higher-class Rajputs (particularly the Bhilchi Rajputs of Khelchipur and the Tomargar, Sakurwari, and Kacchmangar Rajputs of Gwalior), Jats, and Gujars were known to kill their female infants.[60] The widespread existence of female infanticide in Rewa (Madhya Pradesh) among the Rajputs was discovered in 1841.[61] In Oudh (Uttar Pradesh), W.H. Sleeman discovered the extent of the practice during his journey through the kingdom between 1849 and 1850.

EXPLANATIONS OF THE PRACTICE

Sleeman's journal account illustrates the economic problems associated with marriages among the higher castes. In his travels, Sleeman encountered the Rewa raja, who had two daughters and had managed to secure a suitable spouse for his eldest daughter at great cost. For his son, he took five or six women from families a shade lower in caste, but even with the dowry money received, he did not have enough to pay to marry his second daughter to a man of a suitable higher caste.[62] In Oudh, as in the North-West Province, it was primarily Rajputs who killed their female infants. According to Sleeman, almost all clans among the Rajputs practiced female infanticide because of the strict rules of hypergyny and dowry. The Sengers were one of the exceptions.[63] Sleeman gave the following description of his inquiry into the practice:

In my ride this morning I asked the people of the villages, through and near which we passed, whether infanticide prevailed. They told me that it pre-

---

58. Panigrahi, *British Social Policy and Female Infanticide in India*, pp. 28–29.

59. Browne, *Indian Infanticide*, pp. 111–112.

60. Panigrahi, *British Social Policy and Female Infanticide in India*, pp. 36–37.

61. Ibid., p. 37.

62. P.D. Reeves, ed., *Sleeman in Oudh: An Abridgement of W.H. Sleeman's* A Journey through the Kingdom of Oude in 1849–50 (Cambridge: Cambridge University Press, 1971), pp. 132–133.

63. Ibid., p. 169.

vailed amongst almost all the Rajpoot families of any rank in Oude—that very poor families of those classes retained their daughters, because they could get something for them from the families of lower grade into which they married them; but that those who were too well off in the world, to condescend to take money for their daughters from lower grades, and were obliged to incur heavy costs in marrying them into families of the same or higher grade, seldom allowed their infant daughters to live.[64]

To give one's daughter to a clan of a lower status meant loss of caste and thus was not an option for most Rajputs. One further account, told to Sleeman by a Sombunsie (a clan of Rajputs who practiced female infanticide), gives a rare glimpse into the maternal psychological dynamics involved: "Mothers wept and screamed a good deal when their first female infants were torn from them; but after two or three times giving birth to female infants, they become quiet and reconciled to the usage; and said, 'do as you like.'"[65] Rajputs were the dominant caste in Oudh, which is why the practice was so apparent to one traveling throughout the region. The Rajputs claimed that to preserve a daughter would bring calamity on the family and on the caste—it was their duty to kill her. As the above description indicates, strong motivations accompanied the practice, and any objections were easily overcome, including the tender feelings of the mothers.

In the easternmost portion of India, past Bangladesh and near the northwestern border of Burma, is Nagaland. Traveling among the Nagas in the mid-nineteenth century, Col. W. McCulloch came across a village that struck him as remarkably lacking in female children. On inquiry, he was told that there was not a single girl in the village. The girls had been killed to "save themselves from the annoyance of being harried by wife-hunting parties from a stronger clan."[66] In addition to the concern that one's daughter faced capture, there was further worry that having daughters would bring danger to the rest of the family—fathers apparently feared that a man who would capture his daughter might also take away his head as an incidental trophy.[67]

This was also the view among the Khonds, who live in present-day Orissa. The Khonds (also Konds) felt that the number of women in their villages directly affected the risk of being preyed on by their neighbors.[68] The Khonds, descendants of the Dravidians, are neither Muslim nor

64. Quoted in ibid., pp. 201–202.
65. Quoted in ibid., pp. 208–209.
66. Risley, *The People of India*, p. 172.
67. Ibid., p. 174.
68. Ibid., p. 172.

Hindu. They are not unified in their activities or social customs, and are typically divided into three groups based on rites performed: The first group has a history of human sacrifice, both male and female; the second group has a history of female infanticide; and the third group practiced neither.[69] Among those who engaged in female infanticide, only the first daughter was allowed to live; all subsequent girls were killed. The Khonds did not consider this a sin, because they had not yet formally accepted the infants as members of the group—only on the seventh day did a child become a full kin member. They also believed that the souls of girl children killed by the family would not be born again, and hence the number of female children would eventually decrease.[70] In addition, those practicing female infanticide had a strong economic motivation. The Khond system of marriage was unusual in that male infidelity was severely punished, but female infidelity was permissible. Women often took lovers, and there was always a risk that a woman would leave her husband for another. If his wife left him, the husband would keep the large sums he received from the bride's father when they were married. In addition, a similar sum of money had to be given to the second husband. Apparently, two-thirds of the feuds among the Khonds were attributable to unresolved marriage disputes.[71]

Just as the reasons for practicing female infanticide varied from region to region, so did the methods of killing girls. Generally, female infanticide was performed with little ceremony; however, in rural Punjab, when several female children were born in succession, the last one would be killed as part of a ritual. Some *gur* (molasses) would be placed in the baby's mouth and a piece of cotton placed on her chest while the following incantation was repeated two or three times: "Eat gur, spin your thread, we don't want you, but a brother instead." The infant would then be killed by being placed in a water pot and buried in the ground.[72] This was but one way of killing unwanted female infants. Other methods included administering opium; starving the baby to death; placing the umbilical cord in the girl's mouth, causing suffocation; smearing the mother's breast with poison; or placing the infant in a hole dug in the ground filled with milk.[73]

---

69. Barbara M. Boal, *The Konds: Human Sacrifice and Religious Change* (Warminster, U.K.: Aris and Phillips, 1982), p. 47.

70. Risley, *The People of India*, p. 172; and Boal, *The Konds*, p. 67.

71. Boal, *The Konds*, p. 67.

72. Risley, *The People of India*, p. 174.

73. Kaur, *Role of Women in the Freedom Movement*, pp. 8–9.

ATTEMPTS TO END THE PRACTICE

The British attempted to put an end to the practice of female infanticide in India through a system of sanctions, rewards, and education. The results were mixed. The British constantly seemed to find new clans or villages in which daughters were being killed. In regions where preventive measures had long been introduced, numbers of females had increased, but because the females remained unmarried, the practice resumed. In 1868 a special census of clans suspected of commiting infanticide reported that only 22 percent of the population was female.[74] This led to the Female Infanticide Act of 1870, which established rules regarding birth, marriage, and death registration; detection and punishment of the crime; limitation of marriage expenses; and the removal by authorities of any undernourished children from their parents.[75]

Although the British attempted to give accurate counts of rural, village, and town populations, the extent of infanticide in the early years of their rule is not known. In 1872, however, a census was taken in which the sex ratios in Indian provinces were determined, enabling us to hypothesize about the prevalence of the practice. The ratios of children under the age of 12 appear in Table 3.1.

In 1872 the population of India was 190 million, of which 98 million were males and 92 million females, producing an overall sex ratio of 106.4 males per 100 females. By examining the juvenile sex ratios, it is possible to determine where neglect, and in particular infanticide of females, occurred. Juvenile sex ratios are high in all but Mysore and Madras, both southern states. In Bengal (which includes what is now Bangladesh, Bihar, Orissa, and West Bengal), Assam, Oudh, Punjab (Pakistan and northwest India), and the North-West Province, juvenile sex ratios suggest that female infanticide was prevalent. It is in these areas, typically from the northwest, along the border, and including the Central Provinces, that history, social institutions, and customs combined to produce this practice.

The census allowed the British to identify territories in which female infanticide was practiced, but because the census did not include more specific information about caste or clans, only villages could be pronounced guilty. Guilt was determined by comparing the number of females to males in the juvenile population, and penalties were imposed in any village found with less than 40 percent females in the juvenile popu-

74. The size of the population as a whole is not given. See Crooke, *The North-Western Provinces of India*, p. 137.

75. Panigrahi, *British Social Policy and Female Infanticide in India*, pp. 141–142.

Table 3.1. Males per 100 Females for Children under 12 Years of Age in British India, 1872.

Province	Juvenile Sex Ratio
Bengal	120.1
Assam	116.2
Mysore	103.1
Madras	104.1
Central Provinces	108.6
Berar	112.8
Oude	118.6
Bombay	111.8
North-West Provinces	120.1
Punjab	118.6
Coorg	108.3

SOURCE: Barbara D. Miller, *The Endangered Sex: Neglect of Female Children in Rural North India* (Ithaca, N.Y.: Cornell University Press, 1981), p. 59.

lation. For example, when the Infanticide Act was enforced in the North-West Province in 1872, 4,959 villages with a population of 485,938 persons were found guilty because their juvenile female populations were less than 40 percent. Of these villages, 1,013 were declared "blood red," meaning that the juvenile female population constituted less than 25 percent of the total juvenile population.[76] Once the guilty villages were determined, the castes, clans, and families found practicing female infanticide were also identified and carefully watched. The constant vigilance and punishment of the crime led to a decrease in its prevalence among the families under surveillance. In 1874 in the North-West Province, 389,697 members of the population were under surveillance, and the sex ratio of the juvenile population was 231 males per 100 females. Six years later, the number of people under surveillance had dropped to 285,860, and the sex ratio among the surveilled population had decreased to 159 males per 100 females. By 1882 the juvenile sex ratio had plummeted to 114.[77] By 1890 the number of girls and boys under the age of 5 was equal, and the practice of female infanticide appeared to have ended, with the exception of a few isolated villages.[78]

76. Ibid., pp. 162–163.

77. Ibid., p. 188.

78. Ibid., pp. 189–190.

The British also encouraged the formation of *ekdas*, meaning circles of families (as large as could be created) that all agreed to intermarry. Ekdas prohibited hypergyny because all of their units were considered equals. Wedding expenses were also tightly regulated, and "exchange marriages" were not uncommon. Unfortunately, defection from ekdas by families who sought higher status undermined the system.[79] Nevertheless, the British practice of placing a cap on permissible dowry helped at every level lower than the highest castes or subcastes. The key variable was whether the cap was enforceable.

One unforeseen consequence of British intervention to normalize sex ratios was an increasing number of never-married females. As Vishwanath puts it, "The Jadejas were forced to preserve their female daughters, but did not know where to marry them."[80] Forced celibacy was thus the fate of many daughters saved from infanticide.

The story of infanticide in India does not end here, however. India's 1901 census, which listed the overall sex ratio for the country at 102.9 males per 100 females, seemed evidence that the British had put an end to the practice. As Figure 3.1 shows, however, the sex ratio has risen in 2001 to a level of 107.2 males per 100 females for the overall population.

In addition to the rise in sex ratio in the overall population, there were indications that female infanticide had never been fully eradicated. Even in 1901, when the population seemed to exhibit a fairly normal sex ratio for a country with high fertility and low life expectancy, many Indian states had sex ratios that were far from normal. In the following states and territories, sex ratios were higher than expected in 1901: Assam (108.8), Delhi (116.0), Haryana (115.3), Himachal Pradesh (113.1), Jammu and Kashmir (113.3), Punjab (120.2), Rajasthan (110.5), Sikkim (109.2), Tripura (114.4), and Uttar Pradesh (106.7).[81] Even if one takes into account the long history of female infanticide and the probability of high sex ratios among the older adult population, these ratios suggest that female infanticide may not have ceased.

Vishwanath demonstrates that even after 1901, sex ratios were still skewed in castes with a history of female infanticide: "The 1911 census also showed that among castes having a tradition of female infanticide (such as Rajputs and Jats), the proportion of girls to boys under 5 years

---

79. Vishwanath, "Female Infanticide and the Position of Women in India," p. 195.

80. Ibid., p. 189.

81. India, Office of the Registrar General, *Census of India, 1991, Series-1: India, Paper 2 of 1992: Final Population Totals: Brief Analysis of Primary Census Abstract* (New Delhi: India, Office of the Registrar General, 1992), pp. 102–105.

Figure 3.1. India's Sex Ratios (number of males per 100 females), 1901–2001.

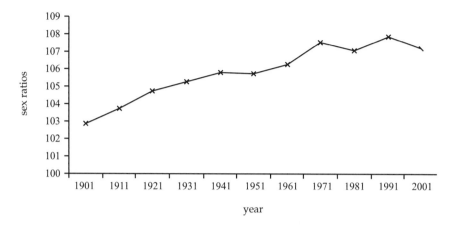

SOURCES: India, Office of the Registrar General, *Census of India, 1991, Series-1: India, Paper 2 of 1992: Final Population Totals: Brief Analysis of Primary Census Abstract* (New Delhi: India, 1992); and India, Office of the Registrar General, *Census of India, 2001, Series 1: India, Paper 1 of 2001: Provisional Population Totals* (New Delhi: India, 2001), http://www.censusindia.net/results.

of age was 832 in Punjab [120.2 male-to-female ratio], while among castes which have no such tradition it was 1005 to 1052 [99.5–95.1 male-to-female ratio]. The census reports of 1921 and 1931 showed a continuing disproportion of females to males among castes known to practice female infanticide during the nineteenth century. . . . This shows that castes which practiced female infanticide during the nineteenth century continued that tradition through the neglect or killing of females well into the twentieth century."[82]

This discussion of the history of female infanticide among many of the castes and groups in India's north and northwestern regions points to a tradition of sex selection at birth, neglect of female infants, and seclusion of women. These forms of discrimination were rooted in a history of invasions, a complex social system based on a hierarchy of power and status, notions of purity and impurity, marriage patterns (with emphasis on the role of hypergyny), and economics (particularly pertaining to the value of women and the dowry). British attempts to end the killing of female infants did affect numerous families, clans, and villages, but because they were unable to attack the roots of the problem, female infanti-

---

82. Vishwanath, "Female Infanticide and the Position of Women in India," p. 200.

cide has continued to varying degrees throughout much of northern India.

The Current Situation

In this section we examine the current sex ratios in India, focusing on the phenomenon of rising sex ratios at birth, differential treatment of male and female infants, and other manifestations of gender inequality that contribute to an artificially skewed sex ratio. Following this discussion, we identify factors that contribute to what is commonly referred to as India's "missing females," or "surplus males," and make projections for the male and female populations in the year 2020.

We base much of our analysis of India's current population on figures from the 1991 and 2001 censuses.[83] But how accurate are India's censuses? According to statistician and demographer Pravin Visaria, the India censuses have a very low undercount, translating to 0.7 percent in 1961, 1.7 percent in 1971, and 1.8 percent in 1981. He claims that the low percentage of urban population in India (25.7 percent in 1991) accounts for the low undercount.[84] Demographer Tim Dyson disputes this claim, contending that the census has been undercounted by as much as 4 percent.[85] The 1981 post-enumeration check (PEC) revealed an undercount of males by 1.710 percent and of females by 1.885 percent.[86] The higher undercount of females would change the total of females from 329,954,637 to 336,174,282 and the male total from 353,374,460 to 359,417,163. The resulting sex ratio would change from 107.07 males per 100 females to 106.95 males per 100 females, only a slight decrease in the overall sex ratio. Results from the PEC of the 1991 census suggest that there was an omission of 17.3 per 1,000 males and 17.9 per 1,000 females in the population, which would once again produce little change in the overall sex ratio: The total number of males would be 446,829,145 (instead of 439,230,458), and the total number of females would be 414,358,823 (instead of 407,072,230), producing an overall sex ratio of

83. Although the 2001 census preliminary results were published at the time of writing, only general population figures are available, thus preventing an analysis of the detailed census data.

84. Pravin M. Visaria, "Indian Population Problem: Emerging Perspective after the 1991 Census," *Demography India*, Vol. 20, No. 2 (July–December 1991), pp. 273–295.

85. Tim Dyson, "On the Demography of the 1991 Census," *Economic and Political Weekly*, December 17–24, 1994, pp. 3235–3239.

86. P.N. Mari Bhat, Samuel H. Preston, and Tim Dyson, *Vital Rates in India, 1961–1981* (Washington, D.C.: National Academy Press, 1984), p. 18.

107.84 (instead of the recorded ratio of 107.90). It is still too early to determine the accuracy of the 2001 census.

RISING SEX RATIOS IN INDIA

As Figure 3.1 indicates, India's sex ratios have been rising over the past 100 years. According to the preliminary results of the 2001 census, there are 531,277,078 males and 495,738,169 females in India, yielding an overall sex ratio of 107.2. This is a slight decrease in the overall sex ratio from that recorded in 1991, when, according to the census, there were 439,230,458 males and 407,072,230 females, for an overall sex ratio of 107.9 (or 107.8 according to the PEC). The 1991 and 2001 figures are slightly higher than the sex ratio reported in 1981, which was 107.1. Although the high sex ratio observed in some parts of the world reflects an influx of male workers, according to the Registrar General's Office, there is "no evidence to suggest differential male immigration into India to upset the sex ratio of population."[87] Furthermore, although undercounting of females in India's census probably does exist, it cannot account for the steady increase in the Indian sex ratio. As Amitabh Kundu and Mahesk Sahu note, "Increase in the bias against female census enumeration can explain the [rise] in sex ratio in a decade, but not a [rising] trend over a period of 90 years. It would be difficult to sustain a thesis of progressive undercounting of females from one census to the other."[88] The high sex ratio in India for the overall population is our first indication of discriminatory practices against women that lead to higher numbers of males than females. An examination of census figures, fertility surveys, and smaller studies helps us determine where and among whom the sex ratios are highest and assists in identifying the various practices—including abortion, infanticide, and differential mortality—that have contributed to these high sex ratios.

Table 3.2 provides state and territory figures for sex ratios in India according to the 2001 census. The figures are arranged according to descending sex ratios, thus making it easy to observe states and territories where the sex ratios are particularly high. Table 3.3 disaggregates state sex ratios according to urban and rural areas for 1991, allowing us to see further variations.

---

87.   India, Office of the Registrar General, *Census of India, 1991, Paper 2*, p. 10.

88.   Amitabh Kundu and Mahesk K. Sahu, "Variation in Sex Ratio: Development Implications," *Economic and Political Weekly*, October 12, 1991, p. 2341. In the original, Kundu and Sahu speak of *declining* sex ratios because their unit of analysis is number of females per 100 males, whereas our unit of analysis is number of males per 100 females.

Table 3.2. Sex Ratios in India by State and Union Territory, 2001.

India/State/Union Territory*	Sex Ratio
Daman and Diu*	141.01
Chandigarh*	129.42
Dadra and Nagar Haveli*	123.31
Delhi*	121.87
Andaman and Nicobar Islands*	118.19
Haryana	116.12
Punjab	114.46
Sikkim	114.25
Uttar Pradesh	111.30
Jammu and Kashmir	111.14
Arunachal Pradesh	110.98
Nagaland	110.00
Madhya Pradesh	108.74
Bihar	108.63
Gujarat	108.62
Rajasthan	108.45
Maharashtra	108.44
Assam	107.29
India	**107.17**
West Bengal	107.11
Mizoram	106.61
Jharkhand	106.23
Lakshadweep*	105.57
Tripura	105.22
Goa	104.14
Karnataka	103.78
Uttaranchal	103.68
Himachal Pradesh	103.12
Orissa	102.86
Meghalaya	102.60
Andhra Pradesh	102.26
Manipur	102.20
Tamil Nadu	101.38
Chhattisgarh	101.05
Pondicherry*	99.91
Kerala	94.49

SOURCE: India, Office of the Registrar General, *Census of India, 2001, Series-1: India, Paper 1 of 2001: Provisional Population Totals* (New Delhi: India, Office of the Registrar General, 2001), http://www.censusindia.net/results.

Table 3.3. Sex Ratios in India According to Total, Rural, and Urban Populations, 1991.

Region/State	Total	Rural	Urban
Arunachal Pradesh	116.4	113.6	137.4
Haryana	115.6	115.8	115.2
Sikkim	113.9	112.1	133.3
Uttar Pradesh	113.8	113.2	116.2
Punjab	113.4	112.7	115.2
Nagaland	112.9	109.1	133.5
Rajasthan	109.9	108.8	113.7
Bihar	109.8	108.5	118.5
West Bengal	109.1	106.4	116.6
Mizoram	108.6	109.6	107.3
Jammu and Kashmir	108.3	107.2	112.0
Assam	108.3	107.1	119.4
India	107.9	106.6	111.9
Madhya Pradesh	107.4	106.0	112.0
Maharashtra	107.1	102.8	114.3
Gujarat	107.1	105.4	110.2
Tripura	105.8	106.2	104.4
Meghalaya	104.7	103.5	109.9
Manipur	104.4	105.2	102.6
Karnataka	104.2	102.7	107.6
Goa	103.4	100.7	107.6
Orissa	103.0	101.2	115.4
Andhra Pradesh	102.9	102.3	104.3
Tamil Nadu	102.7	101.9	104.1
Himachal Pradesh	102.5	101.0	120.3
Kerala	96.5	96.4	96.7

SOURCES: Sex ratios were calculated from population totals according to total, rural, and urban populations recorded in the 1991 census. Similar figures for the 2001 census are not yet available. India, Office of the Registrar General, *Census of India, 1991, Series-1, Part 2-B(i)*, Vol. 1: *Primary Census Abstract, General Population* (New Delhi: India, Office of the Registrar General, 1994).

Tables 3.2 and 3.3 indicate that India's sex ratios are not uniform throughout the country; sex ratios vary according to geographical location as well as by urban and rural populations. Given that approximately 75 percent of India's population is rural, rural sex ratios have a greater impact on the sex ratios of the nation. Overall, sex ratios in the urban areas are much higher (111.9) than in rural areas (106.6), but the overall sex ratio is raised only slightly by the high urban ratios. The larger proportion of males in urban areas is typically attributed to migration, although we will see that other factors, including sex-selective abortion, play a part in this high ratio as well.

As Table 3.2 shows, the sex ratio is particularly high (above 106) in twenty-two states and territories. In addition, the sex ratio is very low only in Kerala, and only slightly above normal in a few states, including Andhra Pradesh, Goa, Orissa, and Tamil Nadu, which are southern states (with the exception of Orissa). Interestingly, the twenty-one states and territories with high sex ratios comprise the regions where infanticide was known to be prevalent during the nineteenth century—the north and northwest regions. In 1872, 4,959 villages with a population totaling 485,938 were under surveillance because of low sex ratios. Today the population of this area is much greater, comprising approximately 70 percent of India's total (594 million people in 1991, 707 million in 2001).

MISSING FEMALES

Although there may no longer be entire villages without females, as in India's past, the number of females missing from the population has increased greatly as the population soared. If one assumes, as most scholars do, that the numbers of males and females in the overall population should be relatively equal, then the number of females missing from India's population has increased to 35,538,909 in 2001 from 32,158,228 in 1991. The number of missing females may be much higher, however, as Stephan Klasen and Claudia Wink argue. As discussed in chapter 2, the fertility levels, age-structure, and mortality patterns of Asian countries vary, as do the expected sex ratios at birth and for the overall population. Klasen and Wink calculate that the expected birth sex ratio in India is 103.9, and the expected overall sex ratio is 99.3.[89] Using these figures, there were 39,284,065 women missing from the population in 2001. Although this figure may be a more accurate representation of the number of missing women, we use the more conservative estimate above for ease of comparison with the calculations of other scholars.

The contributions made by individual states to the total of missing females in the population are found in Table 3.4. Of the twenty-one states and territories with high sex ratios, five (Chandigarh, Sikkim, Mizoram, Daman and Diu, and Dadra and Nagar Haveli) have populations of less than 1 million and thus contribute only a small portion (less than 1 percent) to the missing females in India. The other sixteen high-ratio states and territories, however, contribute to a great degree; Uttar Pradesh alone contributes 25 percent (despite the fact that its population is but 16 per-

---

89. Stephan Klasen and Claudia Wink, "'Missing Women': Revisiting the Debate," *Feminist Economics*, Vol. 9, Nos. 2–3 (July–November 2003), Table 3.

Table 3.4. State Contributions to "Missing Females" in India, 2001.

India/State/Union Territory*	Total Population	Total Males	Total Females	Missing Females	Contribution to Missing Females (%)	Share of Total Population (%)
India	**1,027,015,247**	**531,277,078**	**495,738,169**	**35,538,909**	**100.00**	**100.00**
Jammu and Kashmir	10,069,917	5,300,574	4,769,343	531,231	1.49	0.98
Himachal Pradesh	6,077,248	3,085,256	2,991,992	93,264	0.26	0.59
Punjab	24,289,296	12,963,362	11,325,934	1,637,428	4.61	2.37
Chandigarh*	900,914	508,224	392,690	115,534	0.33	0.09
Uttaranchal	8,479,562	4,316,401	4,163,161	153,240	0.43	0.83
Haryana	21,082,989	11,327,658	9,755,331	1,572,327	4.42	2.05
Delhi*	13,782,976	7,570,890	6,212,086	1,358,804	3.82	1.34
Rajasthan	56,473,122	29,381,657	27,091,465	2,290,192	6.44	5.50
Uttar Pradesh	166,052,859	87,466,301	78,586,558	8,879,743	24.99	16.17
Bihar	82,878,796	43,153,964	39,724,832	3,429,132	9.65	8.07
Sikkim	540,493	288,217	252,276	35,941	0.10	0.05
Arunachal Pradesh	1,091,117	573,951	517,166	56,785	0.16	0.11
Nagaland	1,988,636	1,041,686	946,950	94,736	0.27	0.19
Manipur	2,388,634	1,207,338	1,181,296	26,042	0.07	0.23
Mizoram	891,058	459,783	431,275	28,508	0.08	0.09
Tripura	3,191,168	1,636,138	1,555,030	81,108	0.23	0.31
Meghalaya	2,306,069	1,167,840	1,138,229	29,611	0.08	0.22
Assam	26,638,407	13,787,799	12,850,608	937,191	2.64	2.59
West Bengal	80,221,171	41,487,694	38,733,477	2,754,217	7.75	7.81
Jharkhand	26,909,428	13,861,277	13,048,151	813,126	2.29	2.62
Orissa	36,706,920	18,612,340	18,094,580	517,760	1.46	3.57

Table 3.4. (*continued*)

India/State/Union Territory*	Total Population	Total Males	Total Females	Missing Females	Contribution to Missing Females (%)	Share of Total Population (%)
Chhattisgarh	20,795,956	10,452,426	10,343,530	108,896	0.31	2.02
Madhya Pradesh	60,385,118	31,456,873	28,928,245	2,528,628	7.12	5.88
Gujarat	50,596,992	26,344,053	24,252,939	2,091,114	5.88	4.93
Daman and Diu*	158,059	92,478	65,581	26,897	0.08	0.02
Dadra and Nagar Haveli*	220,451	121,731	98,720	23,011	0.06	0.02
Maharashtra	96,752,247	50,334,270	46,417,977	3,916,293	11.02	9.42
Andhra Pradesh	75,727,541	38,286,811	37,440,730	846,081	2.38	7.37
Karnataka	52,733,958	26,856,343	25,877,615	978,728	2.75	5.13
Goa	1,343,998	685,617	658,381	27,236	0.08	0.13
Lakshadweep*	60,595	31,118	29,477	1,641	0.00	0.01
Kerala	31,838,619	15,468,664	16,369,955	(901,291)	(2.54)	3.10
Tamil Nadu	62,110,839	31,268,654	30,842,185	426,469	1.20	6.05
Pondicherry*	973,829	486,705	487,124	(419)	(0.00)	0.09
Andaman and Nicobar Islands*	356,265	192,985	163,280	29,705	0.08	0.03

SOURCE: Population totals required for calculating total populations are from India, Office of the Registrar General, *Census of India, 2001, Series 1: India, Paper 1 of 2001: Provisional Population Totals* (New Delhi: India, Office of the Registrar General, 2001), http://www.censusindia. net/results.

cent of the country's total). The state of Kerala, on the other hand, has more women than men. In 2001 women outnumbered men by more than 900,000 in this state. Kerala has a high net migration of young men, most who leave to work in the Middle East.[90] Kerala is also unique in that it has the highest number of female-headed households, high literacy rates for women, and a high number of women among the elderly due to long life expectancy.[91]

Grouping the major states geographically, we are able to observe further patterns (see Table 3.5). By grouping the most populous states into regions, Table 3.5 helps to further show patterns in variations in sex ratios. The north comprises 40 percent of India's total population, yet it is responsible for 17 million missing females in 1991 and 2001—approximately half of the total. The west and east/northeast rank second and third in 2001, followed by the northwest and the south. When their contributions to the missing females are compared with their overall population size, the following pattern emerges: The north and northwest contribute more to the missing females than one would expect, given their population size; and the south contributes to a much lesser extent. In general, the north and northwest regions, which together comprise approximately 45 percent of the country's total population, have the highest sex ratios (109.8 and 115.2) and contribute to approximately 57 percent of the missing females.

Examination of figures for missing females and population size alongside fertility data points to further patterns. The north and northwest have the highest fertility rates for the country; thus they will continue to contribute to the high sex ratios. The highest fertility rate, 5.2, is found in Uttar Pradesh, which has one of the highest sex ratios and largest populations, with 166 million people. Its neighbor to the east, Bihar, has the third-greatest population size, with 83 million people, and the second highest fertility rate, 4.6. These two states will continue to be responsible for a large segment of the missing females of India. The south, however, has more normal sex ratios and much lower fertility rates.

By further disaggregating the census data, we can observe other patterns according to "scheduled" tribes and castes, and the general population (see Table 3.6). Scheduled castes are the members of the lowest socioeconomic classes in India—the former "untouchables" who are now protected and given advantages by the Indian government. Scheduled tribes are non-Hindus and generally live in resource-poor parts of India.

---

90. S. Irudaya Rajan, "Heading towards a Billion," *Economic and Political Weekly*, December 17, 1994, p. 3205.

91. Ibid.

Table 3.5. Sex Ratios, Total Fertility Rates, and Contribution to "Missing Females" in India by Region and State, 1991 and 2001.

Region/State	Sex Ratio 1991	Sex Ratio 2001	Total Fertility Rate 1991	Missing Females 1991	Missing Females 2001	Contribution to Missing Females 1991 (%)	Contribution to Missing Females 2001 (%)
INDIA	107.9	107.2	3.7	32,158,000	35,539,000	100.00	100.0
North	111.0	109.8	—	17,425,000	17,128,000	54.19	48.2
Bihar	109.8	108.6	4.6	4,030,000	3,429,000	12.53	9.7
Madhya Pradesh	107.4	108.7	4.6	2,353,000	2,529,000	7.32	7.1
Rajasthan	109.9	108.4	4.5	2,080,000	2,290,000	6.47	6.4
Uttar Pradesh	113.8	111.3	5.2	8,962,000	8,880,000	27.87	25.0
East/Northeast	107.3	106.0	—	4,314,000	4,209,000	13.42	11.8
Assam	108.3	107.3	3.4	902,000	937,000	2.80	2.6
Orissa	103.0	102.9	3.3	469,000	518,000	1.46	1.5
West Bengal	109.1	107.1	3.2	2,943,000	2,754,000	9.15	7.8
South	102.2	101.2	—	2,086,000	1,350,000	6.49	3.8
Andhra Pradesh	102.9	102.3	3.0	941,000	846,000	2.93	2.4
Karnataka	104.2	103.8	3.1	927,000	979,000	2.88	2.8
Kerala	96.5	94.5	1.8	521,000	901,000	−1.62	2.5
Tamil Nadu	102.7	101.4	2.2	739,000	426,000	2.30	1.2
West	107.1	108.5	—	4,115,000	6,007,000	12.80	16.9
Gujarat	107.1	108.6	3.2	1,401,000	2,091,000	4.36	5.9
Maharashtra	107.1	108.4	3.0	2,714,000	3,916,000	8.44	11.0
Northwest	112.1	115.2	—	2,465,000	3,210,000	7.67	9.0
Haryana	115.6	116.1	3.9	1,191,000	1,572,000	3.70	4.4
Punjab	113.4	114.5	3.1	1,274,000	1,637,000	3.96	4.6

SOURCES: Sex ratios and population totals required for calculations are from the 1991 census. India, Office of the Registrar General, *Census of India, 1991, Series-1: Part 2-B(i)*, Vol. 1: *Primary Census Abstract General Population* (New Delhi: India, Office of the Registrar General, 1994); total fertility rates (average number of children a woman will have during her lifetime) found in Leela Visaria and Pravin Visaria, "India's Population in Transition," *Population Bulletin*, Vol. 50, No. 3 (October 1995), p. 22. Missing females for these five regions do not add up to the total for India, because only the most populous states are listed here. Figures for 2001 were calculated from India, Office of the Registrar General, *Census of India, 2001, Series 1: India, Paper 1 of 2001: Provisional Population Totals* (New Delhi: India, Office of the Registrar General, 2001), http://www.censusindia.net/results.

Table 3.6. Males per 100 Females in India According to Caste and Tribe, 1991.

Region/State	Total Sex Ratio	Scheduled Caste Sex Ratio	Scheduled Tribe Sex Ratio	Nonscheduled Caste–Scheduled Tribe Sex Ratio
INDIA	**107.9**	**108.5**	**102.9**	**108.3**
North	**111.0**	**111.9**	**103.1**	**111.8**
Bihar	109.8	109.4	103.0	110.5
Madhya Pradesh	107.4	109.3	101.5	109.2
Rajasthan	109.9	111.2	107.5	110.0
Uttar Pradesh	113.8	114.0	109.4	113.8
East/Northeast	**107.3**	**106.4**	**96.1**	**109.4**
Assam	108.3	108.8	103.4	109.2
Orissa	103.0	102.6	99.8	104.3
West Bengal	109.1	107.4	103.7	110.0
South	**102.2**	**102.5**	**104.0**	**102.5**
Andhra Pradesh	102.9	103.2	104.2	102.7
Karnataka	104.2	104.0	104.1	104.3
Kerala	96.5	97.2	100.4	96.3
Tamil Nadu	102.7	102.2	104.2	102.8
West	**107.1**	**106.5**	**110.6**	**107.7**
Goa	103.4	103.4	112.5	103.4
Gujarat	107.1	108.1	103.4	107.6
Maharashtra	107.1	105.9	103.3	107.8
Northwest	**112.1**	**113.6**	**101.9**	**112.7**
Haryana	115.6	116.3	—	115.5
Himachal Pradesh	102.5	103.4	101.9	102.2
Punjab	113.4	114.5	—	113.0

SOURCES: Sex ratios for each state according to scheduled caste, scheduled tribe, or non-scheduled caste–scheduled tribe are found in India, Office of the Registrar General, *Census of India, 1991: Series-1, Part 2-B(i)*, Vol. 1: *Primary Census Abstract, General Population* (New Delhi: Office of the Registrar General, 1994). Regional ratios were calculated using population totals found in S.B. Agnihotri, "Missing Females: A Disaggregated Analysis," *Economic and Political Weekly*, August 19, 1995, p. 2075.

Analyzing the contributions of these groups to the overall sex ratio of India's population sheds further light on the problem of where, and by whom, offspring sex selection is practiced.

In the population as a whole, 16 percent belong to a scheduled caste, and 8 percent to a scheduled tribe. Because of the small percentage of people belonging to scheduled tribes, this group has little effect on the sex ratio for India as a whole, although it can have state or regional effects. In Nagaland, 88 percent of the population belongs to a scheduled tribe; similarly, 86 percent of Meghalaya's population belongs to a scheduled tribe. In these states, the sex ratio of the scheduled tribe can have a great impact on the overall sex ratio. In Himachal Pradesh and Punjab, where more than 25 percent of the population belongs to scheduled castes, these groups can also have an effect on the overall sex ratio.

Several patterns emerge when sex ratios are examined according to caste and tribe. In the north, east/northeast, and northwest, the scheduled tribes have the lowest sex ratios of the three groups and thus act to lower the overall sex ratio. In the north and northwest, scheduled castes have high sex ratios, but these ratios are only slightly higher than those for nonscheduled castes/tribes. Tribes and castes have mixed effects on the southern and western populations. Historically, only a few tribes were known to practice female infanticide; those that did, such as the Khonds, had reasons peculiar to their own group. Because there were no general causes for the practice among them, we would expect to find the sex ratio among the tribes lower than that among the Hindu castes. The high sex ratios among the scheduled castes are unusual in that we might have expected these low-ranking castes to refrain from the practice of infanticide, which is highly linked with hypergyny and dowry. An examination of the scheduled caste sex ratios, however, reveals that their sex ratios are high only in areas where female discrimination is most acute and has become customary—in the north and northwest. Throughout these regions in India's history, even lower-ranking castes were found to kill their daughters due to long-standing tradition and their desire to imitate the higher castes.

Although sex ratios are a good indicator of gender imbalance in the population, without knowing the exact sizes of the different populations, it is difficult to determine where gender inequality is most prevalent. Examining population totals according to the number of males and females helps to ascertain which states, and groups within states, contribute most to the missing population of females.

Table 3.7 highlights several characteristics about India's population and the contribution of different groups to the missing females. The table shows that the scheduled castes contribute to a larger portion of missing females than is expected from their population size: They account for 17.52 percent of the missing females, although they constitute only 16.33 percent of the total population. Conversely, the data show that scheduled tribes contribute less than would be expected from the size of their populations: They account for 3.01 percent of the missing females, though their populations contribute 8.01 percent to the overall population size. The scheduled castes and tribes account for 24.34 percent of India's population and contribute to 20.5 percent of the missing female population. This means, then, that the general population, which comprises 75.66 percent of the population, contributes 79.5 percent of the missing females.

Table 3.7. Missing Females in India by Total, Scheduled Caste, and Scheduled Tribe, 1991.

Region/State	Total Missing Females	Scheduled Caste Missing Females	Scheduled Caste Percentage of Total Population	Scheduled Caste Percentage of Missing Females	Scheduled Tribe Missing Females	Scheduled Tribe Percentage of Total Population	Scheduled Tribe Percentage of Missing Females
INDIA	**32,158,000**	**5,635,000**	**16.33**	**17.52**	**968,000**	**8.01**	**3.01**
North	**17,425,000**	**3,325,000**	**17.60**	**19.08**	**427,000**	**8.28**	**2.45**
Bihar	4,030,000	567,000	14.54	14.07	98,000	7.66	2.43
Madhya Pradesh	2,353,000	429,000	14.55	18.23	117,000	23.27	4.97
Rajasthan	2,080,000	407,000	17.29	19.57	199,000	12.44	9.57
Uttar Pradesh	8,962,000	1,922,000	21.04	21.45	13,000	0.21	0.15
East/Northeast	**4,314,000**	**707,000**	**18.72**	**16.39**	**268,000**	**10.92**	**6.21**
Assam	902,000	70,000	7.41	7.76	49,000	12.83	5.43
Orissa	469,000	64,000	16.20	13.65	6,000	22.21	1.28
West Bengal	2,943,000	573,000	23.62	19.47	311,000	5.04	10.57
South	**2,086,000**	**386,000**	**16.07**	**18.50**	**137,000**	**3.57**	**6.57**
Andhra Pradesh	941,000	167,000	15.93	17.75	86,000	6.31	9.14
Karnataka	927,000	143,000	16.38	15.43	38,000	4.26	4.10
Kerala	521,000	41,000	9.92	-7.87	1,000	1.10	0.19
Tamil Nadu	739,000	117,000	19.18	15.83	12,000	1.02	1.62

Table 3.7. (continued)

Region/State	Total Missing Females	Scheduled Caste Missing Females	Scheduled Caste Percentage of Total Population	Scheduled Caste Percentage of Missing Females	Scheduled Tribe Missing Females	Scheduled Tribe Percentage of Total Population	Scheduled Tribe Percentage of Missing Females
West	**4,135,000**	**372,000**	**9.75**	**9.00**	**219,000**	**11.10**	**5.30**
Goa	20,000	0	2.10	0.00	0	0.00	0.00
Gujarat	1,401,000	119,000	7.41	8.49	102,000	14.92	7.28
Maharashtra	2,714,000	253,000	11.09	9.32	117,000	9.27	4.31
Northwest	**2,529,000**	**656,000**	**24.58**	**25.94**	**2,000**	**0.52**	**0.08**
Haryana	1,191,000	245,000	19.75	20.57	0	0.00	0.00
Himachal Pradesh	64,000	22,000	25.33	34.38	2,000	4.22	3.13
Punjab	1,274,000	389,000	28.32	30.53	0	0.00	0.00

SOURCES: Population totals required for calculating total populations are from India, Office of the Registrar General, *Census of India, 1991, Series-1, Part 2-B(i)*, Vol. 1: *Primary Census Abstract, General Population*, (New Delhi: India, Office of the Registrar General, 1994). Totals for scheduled tribes and castes were obtained from S.B. Agnihotri, "Missing Females: A Disaggregated Analysis," *Economic and Political Weekly*, August 19, 1995, pp. 2074–2084.

Over the past thirty years, the sex ratios among the scheduled castes have risen at a higher rate than for scheduled tribes or the general population. In 1961 the overall sex ratio in India was 106.3; in 1991, it had risen to 107.9. During the same period, the sex ratios for scheduled tribes rose from 101.3 to 102.9; those for the general population rose from 107.1 to 108.3; and for scheduled castes, the sex ratio rose from 104.5 to 108.5.[92] The sharp rise in sex ratio among the scheduled caste population requires further research.

JUVENILE SEX RATIOS

One additional disaggregation of the data further shows patterns emerging within India's population: Comparing the juvenile (age 0–6) sex ratios to those of the overall population points to regions in which a normal sex ratio masks the presence of high juvenile sex ratios. Conversely, there may be regions in which the overall sex ratio is high, but the juvenile sex ratio is not, which can be an indication of male in-migration or other factors. Table 3.8 compares juvenile sex ratios with total sex ratios for 1991 and 2001; to observe states where the juvenile sex ratio is highest, the states appear in descending value for the 0–6 sex ratio in 2001.

Using juvenile ratios, we can surmise where sex ratios reflect gender inequality and where the figures might be high because of immigration of males or other factors. For example, the territory of Daman and Diu has a very high overall sex ratio (141), but this is not exhibited in the juvenile population, where the sex ratio is moderately high (108). On the other hand, we are also able to see areas where, although the overall sex ratio is low, the high juvenile ratio suggests the presence of gender inequality in the form of sex-selective practices. Uttaranchal and Himachal Pradesh are examples of such an area: The overall sex ratios for the two states are 103.7 and 103.1, respectively, but their juvenile ratios are 110.4 and 111.5. Overall, there are sixteen states and territories in which the juvenile sex ratio is greater than 106—an increase of 100 percent since 1991, when only eight states exhibited such juvenile sex ratios. Eight of these states—Punjab, Haryana, Chandigarh, Delhi, Gujarat, Himachal Pradesh, Uttaranchal, and Rajasthan—have sex ratios greater than 110. Although the slight decrease in India's overall sex ratio in 2001 may suggest to some that there has been a decrease in sex-selective practices, the continued increase in the juvenile ratio from 103.95 in 1981 to 107.85 in 2001 is cause for concern.

Even these sex ratios hide the fact that districts and villages within

92. S.B. Agnihotri, "Missing Females: A Disaggregated Analysis," *Economic and Political Weekly*, August 19, 1995, p. 2075.

Table 3.8. Juvenile Sex Ratios in India, 1991 and 2001.

India/State/Union Territory*	Total Population 2001	0–6 2001	Total Population 1991	0–6 1991
India	**107.17**	**107.85**	**107.87**	**105.82**
Punjab	114.46	126.11	113.38	114.29
Haryana	116.12	121.96	115.61	113.77
Chandigarh*	129.42	118.35	126.58	111.23
Delhi*	121.87	115.60	120.92	109.29
Gujarat	108.62	113.89	107.07	107.76
Himachal Pradesh	103.12	111.49	102.46	105.15
Uttaranchal	103.68	110.39	106.84	105.49
Rajasthan	108.45	110.02	109.89	109.17
Uttar Pradesh	111.30	109.17	114.16	107.87
Maharashtra	108.44	109.04	107.07	105.71
Daman and Diu*	141.01	108.07	103.20	104.38
Madhya Pradesh	108.74	107.64	109.65	106.27
Goa	104.14	107.20	103.41	103.73
Jammu and Kashmir	111.14	106.72	—	—
Bihar	108.63	106.57	110.25	104.93
Tamil Nadu	101.38	106.46	102.67	105.49
Karnataka	103.78	105.32	104.17	104.17
Orissa	102.86	105.21	102.99	103.41
Pondicherry*	99.91	104.40	102.15	103.84
Manipur	102.20	104.05	104.38	102.67
Arunachal Pradesh	110.98	104.04	116.41	101.83
Kerala	94.49	103.89	96.53	104.38
West Bengal	107.11	103.84	109.05	103.41
Andhra Pradesh	102.26	103.77	102.88	102.56
Assam	107.29	103.74	108.34	102.56
Andaman and Nicobar Islands*	118.19	103.61	122.25	102.77
Jharkhand	106.23	103.56	108.46	102.15
Mizoram	106.61	103.01	108.58	103.20
Dadra and Nagar Haveli*	123.31	102.79	105.04	98.72
Lakshadweep*	105.57	102.65	106.04	106.27
Tripura	105.22	102.60	105.82	103.41
Nagaland	110.00	102.55	112.87	100.70
Meghalaya	102.60	102.52	104.71	101.42
Chhattisgarh	101.05	102.52	101.52	101.63
Sikkim	114.25	101.41	113.90	103.63

SOURCE: India, Office of the Registrar General, *Census of India, 2001, Series 1: India, Paper 1 of 2001: Provisional Population Totals* (New Delhi: India, Office of the Registrar General, 2001), http://www.censusindia.net/results.

states in India have varying sex ratios. Madhya Pradesh, for example, has a juvenile sex ratio of 107.64 (106.27 in 1991). A study in the mid-1990s of the Bhind and Morena Districts, comprising 2,170 villages within Madhya Pradesh, indicated that juvenile sex ratios in many of the districts were extremely high despite the lower overall state sex ratio: 53 had sex ratios above 156; 131 between 139 and 156; and 271 between 125 and 138. The sex ratio at birth in this area was 119 males per 100 females for all births, and 129 for live births.[93] Further study into the districts and villages with such high sex ratios is needed to determine the extent of sex-selective practices within India's states.

The means through which the female sex is selected against have changed over time. Although sex-selective infanticide may still contribute to skewed sex ratios, sex-selective abortion and neglect of female infants are the prevailing methods of selecting against female children in India. We now turn to an examination of how the sex ratio has risen to its current level.

RISING SEX RATIOS AT BIRTH

As discussed in chapter 2, 105–107 males per 100 females is generally taken as the worldwide standard for the sex ratio at birth. A 1964 countrywide analysis of hospital births confirms that this figure applies to India.[94] Although the India census does not include statistics on sex ratios at birth, three other sources do: the Civil Registration System (CRS), which relies on reports from parents following a birth; the Medical Registration System (MRS), which records births in hospitals and other health-care facilities; and the Sample Registration System (SRS), which conducts its own surveys throughout the country. Recorded sex ratios at birth vary greatly among these three reporting systems.

From 1978 to 1980, the Civil Registration System recorded sex ratios at birth of 89.4, 95.9, and 85.1 males per 100 females for India, a number that does not correspond to the levels of 107.0, 111.2, and 106.7 that the

---

93. Mahendra K. Premi and Saraswati Raju, "Born to Die: Female Infanticide in Madhya Pradesh," *Search Bulletin*, Vol. 13, No. 3 (July–September 1998), pp. 94–105.

94. Study cited in R.K. Sachar, J. Verma, V. Prakash, A. Chopra, R. Adlaka, and R. Sofat, "Sex-Selective Fertility Control—An Outrage," *Journal of Family Welfare*, Vol. 36, No. 2 (June 1991), pp. 30–35. The Registrar's office also indicates that India conforms to the standard of 105 male births per 100 female births. It should be noted at this point that sex ratios in India are typically given as number of females per 1,000 males. Although census and other official data are provided in this format, it is difficult to make comparisons between India and other nations given the unique method of reporting this statistic. For ease of comparison, all Indian sex ratios have been changed to reflect number of males per 100 females.

MRS noted in some states. What accounts for the difference between these two sets of data? The CRS is estimated to cover 70 percent of the population, but this coverage is particularly poor in the rural areas of Bihar, Rajasthan, and Uttar Pradesh, and only moderate in Andhra Pradesh, Karnataka, and West Bengal—all of which have traditionally high sex ratios. Comparisons with the SRS indicate that underregistration occurs for 40–50 percent of births at the national level.[95] If the problem is underregistration, then it appears that males are registered less often than females, because the recorded sex ratios are much lower than expected. Some suggest that parents are less likely to register male babies, to protect them from evil spirits.[96] Mildred Dickemann argues that a more plausible reason for underregistering males is to hide the extent of female infanticide.[97] Whatever the reason, the figures collected by voluntary registration do not appear representative of the sex ratio at birth for the population.

The SRS, a dual-record system that began in the mid-1960s, has become the most important source of demographic information in India.[98] As Table 3.9 shows, Sample Registration data for 1981–88 recorded ratios from 108.1 to 112.2.[99] SRS data are verified to prevent any systematic bias in birth records. In addition to the Sample Registration data, the Office of the Registrar General recently collected data on live births in urban hospitals around the country. From 1981 to 1991, the office recorded 6 million live births, with a mean sex ratio of 112.2 males per 100 females.[100] This high sex ratio was reported for all zones in which data were collected. This figure is much higher than figures collected through the SRS in which the average sex ratio from 1981 to 1988 was 109.7. According to the Registrar General's Office, the sex ratio at birth of 112.2 collected in urban hospitals more accurately reflects the birth sex ratio for India, suggesting that the SRS has been affected by a reporting bias absent in the figures collected from hospital births.[101] The 2001 census includes a graph depict-

95. For a more thorough discussion of the problems of the civil registration system, see Bhat, Preston, and Dyson, *Vital Rates in India*, pp. 28–29.

96. For a discussion of reasons for underregistration of males in other parts of Asia as well, see Swapan Seth, "Two-Way Movement of Sex Ratio," *Economic and Political Weekly*, October 5, 1996, pp. 2730–2733.

97. Mildred Dickemann, correspondence with Valerie Hudson, April 10, 1998.

98. For a discussion of how the SRS operates, see Bhat, Preston, and Dyson, *Vital Rates in India*, pp. 29–34.

99. India, Office of the Registrar General, *Census of India 1991, Paper 2*, p. 12.

100. India, Office of the Registrar General, *Census of India 1991, Paper 2*.

101. Ibid., p. 11.

Table 3.9. Sex Ratios at Birth in India According to Total, Rural, and Urban Populations, 1981–88.

Years	Total	Rural	Urban
1981–83	108.9	108.9	108.8
1982–84	109.8	110.0	109.1
1983–85	110.4	110.0	112.2
1984–86	109.6	109.1	111.5
1985–87	109.6	109.4	110.9
1986–88	109.6	110.1	108.1

SOURCE: India, Office of the Registrar General, *Census of India, 1991, Series-1: India, Paper 2 of 1992: Final Population Totals: Brief Analysis of Primary Census Abstract* (New Delhi: Office of the Registrar General, 1992).

ing the same three-year averages in births from SRS data. Table 3.10 lists the sex ratios recorded by this sampling system.

It is unfortunate that the India census does not include information about births, because the SRS figures do not provide data according to state or region. We can only assume that sex ratios at birth would be high in states with corresponding high overall sex ratios, or in states that also exhibit high infant mortality, for which state-level data exist. Our discussion on sex-selective abortion, therefore, focuses solely on the nationwide level.

SEX-SELECTIVE ABORTION

In 1971 the government of India passed the Medical Termination of Pregnancy Act, allowing physicians to terminate a pregnancy "where there is a risk to the life or mental health of the mother, a risk that the child will be born handicapped, or where the pregnancy is the result of rape or the failure of a contraceptive device."[102] The belief that the fetus has no life prior to the third month may contribute to the high number of abortions; thus there is little moral stigma associated with terminating a pregnancy in the first trimester. This attitude is reflected in the expressions used when a fetus is miscarried: Prior to the end of the third month, the term *charhna* (meaning "the days extend"—i.e., a late menstrual cycle) is used to refer to the event; after the third month, however, the phrase *bucha girna* (meaning "a baby falling") is used to refer to a miscarriage.[103]

102. Odesa Gorman-Stapleton, "Prohibiting Amniocentesis in India: A Solution to the Problem of Female Infanticide or a Problem to the Solution of Prenatal Diagnosis?" *ILSA Journal of International Law*, Vol. 14, No. 23 (1990), p. 30.

103. Roger Jeffery, Patricia Jeffery, and Andrew Lyon, "Research Note: Female Infan-

Table 3.10. Sex Ratios at Birth in India, 1987–98 (3-year averages).

Years	Sex Ratio
1987–89	109.9
1988–90	109.8
1989–91	110.2
1990–92	111.1
1991–93	111.9
1992–94	113.0
1993–95	113.8
1994–96	113.3
1995–97	112.2
1996–98	111.0

SOURCE: India, Office of the Registrar General, *Census of India, 2001, Series 1: India, Paper 1 of 2001: Provisional Population Totals* (New Delhi: India, Office of the Registrar General, 2001), http://www.censusindia.net/results, Figure 13a.

Of greater interest to us, however, is the number of fetuses aborted because of their gender. Is there evidence, as Roger and Patricia Jeffery suggest, that in India the "cultural obstacles" to prenatal sex testing and female fetus abortion "would be small"?[104] The evidence appears to be plentiful. In 1975 the All India Institute of Medical Sciences, a government-run medical research center and hospital, conducted tests to diagnose fetal abnormalities through amniocentesis. Of the fifty women who volunteered for the tests, forty-eight decided to abort their fetuses after learning that they were female.[105] The government of India issued a partial ban on sex determination in 1976 following a protest by women's groups and other activists concerned by the high percentage of women who wished to abort female fetuses once their sex was known.[106] Prenatal sex-determination testing was subsequently banned from all government institutions; however, a privatized industry soon emerged to meet the continuing demand for this service. Between 1982 and 1987, the number

ticide and Amniocentesis," *Social Science and Medicine,* Vol. 19, No. 11 (1984), pp. 1207–1212.

104. Roger Jeffery and Patricia Jeffery, "Female Infanticide and Amniocentesis," *Economic and Political Weekly,* April 16, 1983, pp. 655–656.

105. Manju Parikh, "Sex-Selective Abortions in India: Parental Choice or Sexist Discrimination?" *Feminist Issues,* Vol. 10, No. 2 (Fall 1990), pp. 19–32.

106. Forum against Sex Determination and Sex Pre-selection, "Using Technology, Choosing Sex: The Campaign against Sex Determination and the Question of Choice," *Development Dialogue* (Uppsala, Sweden), Nos. 1–2 (1992), p. 93.

of clinics for sex-determination testing multiplied rapidly—in Bombay alone, it increased from 10 to 248.[107] A 1985 study of Bombay gynecologists reported that 84 percent were performing amniocentesis for the purpose of sex determination and that some had been doing so for ten to twelve years, while the majority had been performing the test for five years.[108] Sex-determination clinics are found throughout India, using one of three types of tests to determine the sex of the fetus: amniocentesis, chorion villi biopsy, or ultrasound. Bombay and Delhi are the major centers for such tests, but even clinics in small cities and towns have the facilities for amniocentesis, and mobile diagnostic teams now take ultrasound technology to smaller towns and villages.[109] Even remotely located peasants can have access to the technology if they are able to travel to a village.

The costs of sex-determination technology have dropped considerably since the 1980s. For example, amniocentesis, which in the 1980s cost 1,500 to 2,000 rupees ($88 to $117), now costs from 200 to 500 rupees ($12 to $30).[110] Sensational ads stating "Better Rs. 500 now than Rs. 5 lakhs [500,000 rupees] later" warn parents of the expense of raising a daughter and one day paying a large dowry instead of a small sum to abort her.[111] Against claims that only the urban rich take advantage of prenatal testing, one author notes: "Districts which lack such basic amenities as potable water and electricity have prenatal sex-determination clinics. Rural health centres with no facilities for testing of sputum for T.B. or to maintain the cold-chain for oral polio vaccine send samples of amniotic fluid in ice packs to district towns for sex-determination tests. A study showed that even marginal farmers and landless labourers were willing to take loans at 25 percent compound interest to avail themselves of these tests."[112]

---

107. Dolly Arora, "The Victimising Discourse: Sex Determination Technologies and Policy," *Economic and Political Weekly*, February 17, 1996, p. 420.

108. Forum against Sex Determination and Sex Pre-selection, "Using Technology, Choosing Sex," p. 95.

109. See Hamish McDonald, "Unwelcome Sex," *Far Eastern Economic Review*, December 26, 1991–January 2, 1992, pp. 18–19; and Vibhuti Patel, "Sex Determination and Sex Preselection Tests in India: Modern Techniques for Femicide," *Bulletin of Concerned Asian Scholars*, Vol. 21, No. 1 (January–March 1989), pp. 2–11.

110. Parikh, "Sex-Selective Abortions in India," pp. 21–22.

111. Srikanta Ghosh, *Indian Women through the Ages* (New Delhi: Ashish Publishing House, 1989), p. 121.

112. Nivedita Menon, "Abortion and the Law: Questions for Feminism," *Canadian Journal of Women and Law*, Vol. 6, No. 1 (1993), p. 108.

The consequences of easily available ultrasound technology can be seen in the case of Rohtak, a town 50 kilometers from New Delhi. As reported by the *Far Eastern Economic Review*, "Rohtak's sex ratio rose from 113.7 to 115.5 over the past decade. A recent report for the UN Population Fund by New Delhi's Mode Research reports the sex ratio at birth was 156 males to 100 females—a massive imbalance, even before mortality factors are included. Nor is Rohtak's record all that extraordinary: four other Haryana towns have worse sex ratios at birth." The article goes on to report that staff at the Rohtak Medical College have developed the slogan, "The mother's womb should not be the daughter's tomb."[113]

A new campaign against sex-determination tests began in 1982, coinciding with a public outcry against the accidental abortion of a male fetus in a hospital in Amritsar. Results of research on sex-selective abortions surprised the public: For example, a 1984 study found that out of 8,000 cases, 7,999 aborted fetuses were female; another Bombay study indicated that of 1,000 cases, 97 percent were female.[114]

In 1988, Maharashtra became the first state to pass a law banning abortions following sex-determination tests; however, those desiring the tests are still able to go to neighboring states or to physicians who will perform the tests illegally. In 1996 the Indian government issued a law banning the abortion of healthy female fetuses, but only three states— Haryana, Punjab, and Rajasthan—have passed the law. It is not known how common fetal testing is in India, and the illegality of testing makes studies very difficult. Parents are typically unwilling to let researchers know that they have had the tests performed. One study, however, conducted from May 1990 to December 1991 at a hospital in Punjab, attempted to determine the extent of fetal testing by interviewing women who came to the hospital.[115] The study was instigated by the increasing

---

113.   These sex ratios correspond to an increase from 113.8 to 115.5 for the town of Rohtak. See McDonald, "Unwelcome Sex," p. 18.

114.   For these and other examples of statistics regarding female fetuses aborted during the 1980s, see Patel, "Sex Determination and Sex Preselection Tests in India"; Parikh, "Sex-Selective Abortions in India," pp. 22–24; Ghosh, *Indian Women through the Ages*, p. 121; Radhika Balakrishnan, "The Social Context of Sex Selection and the Politics of Abortion in India," in Gita Sen and Rachel C. Snow, eds., *Power and Decision: The Social Control of Reproduction* (Cambridge, Mass.: Harvard University Press, 1994); and K.P. Srikumar, "Amniocentesis and the Future of the Girl Child," in Leelamma Devasia and V.V. Devasia, eds., *Girl Child in India* (New Delhi: Ashish Publishing House, 1989), pp. 51–65.

115.   Beverley E. Booth, Manorama Verma, and Rajbir Singh Beri, "Fetal Sex Determination in Infants in Punjab, India: Correlations and Implications," *British Medical Journal*, November 12, 1994, pp. 1259–1261.

sex ratio observed by hospital staff: The sex ratio rose from 107 boys/100 girls in 1982 to 132 boys/100 girls in 1993. The physicians encountered reticence, yet 13.6 percent of the mothers of boys and 2.1 percent of the mothers of girls admitted to having undergone prenatal sex tests.[116] Despite the small number of women willing to admit to the practice, the physicians concluded that fetal sex determination is common. They suggested that use of fetal testing increased with household monthly income, and that all those who underwent testing had had some formal schooling—the largest percentage of women having six to ten years of education (24 percent), followed by those who had had at least ten years of formal schooling (20 percent). Women with no children represented only 2 percent of those who had undergone prenatal sex determination; the presence of one daughter but no son increased testing to 18 percent; and the presence of more than one daughter and no sons accounted for 63 percent of testing. The presence of even one son greatly decreased the likelihood of sex-determination testing. Of the mothers who underwent testing, none had more than one son.[117]

Not all researchers agree that sex-selective abortion is the primary cause of India's declining sex ratio. In *Economic and Political Weekly*, India's leading journal for social science research, demographers and other social scientists have argued over the contributions of sex-selective abortions to the country's high sex ratios.[118] Irudaya Rajan claims that abortions are common only in the large cities of Bombay, Calcutta, Delhi, and Madras, arguing that to increase the sex ratio by even one point, from 106 to 107, 60,000 female fetuses would have to be aborted.[119] Given the statistics cited earlier, this does not appear to be impossible. Rajan proposes that double counting of males is at the root of the problem. Post-

---

116.   The mothers who gave birth to girls after having had a prenatal sex determination test were told that they either had a male twin or were incorrectly diagnosed as having a male fetus.

117.   Booth, Verma, and Beri, "Fetal Sex Determination in Infants in Punjab, India," pp. 1259–1260.

118.   See, for example, S. Irudaya Rajan, "Decline in Sex Ratio: An Alternative Explanation?" *Economic and Political Weekly*, December 21, 1991, pp. 2963–2964; Saraswati Raju and Mahendra K. Premi, "Decline in Sex Ratio: An Alternative Explanation Re-examined," *Economic and Political Weekly*, April 25, 1992, pp. 911–912; S. Irudaya Rajan, U.S. Mishra, and K. Navaneetham, "Decline in Sex Ratio: Alternative Explanation Revisited," *Economic and Political Weekly*, November 14, 1992, pp. 2505–2508; and Padma Prakash, "Decline in Sex Ratio," *Economic and Political Weekly*, December 19–26, 1992, p. 2670.

119.   Rajan, "Heading towards a Billion," pp. 3201–3205.

enumeration checks in the past, however, have not indicated double counting; in fact, males and females are both undercounted. Furthermore, according to another article in *Economic and Political Weekly*, "The Registrar General of India has admitted to abortion of 3.6 lakh (360,000) female foetuses in India in 1993–94."[120] This figure is probably too conservative, but in the absence of concrete data on the numbers of female and male births throughout India, it is difficult to determine accurately the number of females missing in the infant population. Data collected by the Sample Registration System and Office of the Registrar General for the years 1990 to 1995 reveal a sex ratio at birth ranging between 111.1 and 113.8. The average birth sex ratio for this period is 112.6, which, when coupled with an average number of births of 28 million for the same period, corresponds to 13.2 million female births instead of an expected 14.1 million if the sex ratio were at a normal level. This high birth sex ratio means that 953,000 females are missing from the birth population every year. In other words, at least 953,000 fetuses may be aborted annually in India on the basis of gender.[121] Given that the total number of abortions in India is estimated at 11 million per year, 60 percent of which are induced, this figure does not seem improbable. The number of sex-selective abortions may in fact be much higher.[122]

INFANT MORTALITY

As the previous discussion shows, many females in India do not survive the fetal stage. Son preference is still strong in northern India, and direct or indirect infanticide still occurs. The names sometimes given to female children reflect their parents' disappointment: Akki ("fed up"), Kauri ("bitter"), or Beant ("endless") point toward their undesirability,[123] as do the high rates of female infant deaths. Normally, during the first year of life, male infants throughout the world tend to die at a higher rate than females, particularly during the neonatal period; India is one of the few countries (along with China) where female infant deaths occur more often than male infant deaths.

---

120. Arora, "The Victimising Discourse," p. 420.

121. If one uses Klasen and Wink's expected birth sex ratio for India (103.9), then 1.1 million females are missing from the birth population annually. Klasen and Wink, "'Missing Women': Revisiting the Debate."

122. For abortion statistics, see Visaria and Visaria, "India's Population in Transition," p. 38; and M.E. Khan, Sandya Barge, and George Philip, "Abortion in India: An Overview," *Social Change*, Vol. 26, Nos. 3–4 (September–December 1996), pp. 208–225.

123. Sachar et al., "Sex-Selective Fertility Control—An Outrage," p. 30.

The infant mortality rate, given as the number of deaths per 1,000 in an infant (age 0–1) population, was 79.5 for males and 80.4 for females in India in 1990, and 63.89 for males and 62.44 for females in 2000.[124] Although the infant mortality rates for 1990 and 2000 show a marked improvement from 1980 (113.9 for males, 119.0 for females), these mortality rates are still extremely high.[125] Given that male mortality rates in the first year of life are expected to be 30 percent higher than female rates, we calculate that there are 175,000 excess female deaths in the first year of life.[126] With few exceptions, female infant and early childhood mortality rates have persisted at levels higher than those for males since the early 1980s. It is not just during the initial year of life that female death rates are unusually high; these rates persist throughout childhood. The imbalance between the deaths of boys and girls is one of the major causes of India's skewed sex ratios.

A 1996 study conducted by the World Health Organization, the World Bank, and Harvard University reveals differential patterns in deaths among males and females in India.[127] According to data collected on children ages 0–4 for the year 1990, 1,650,000 female deaths and 1,600,000 male deaths occurred. Fifty thousand more girls in India died than boys from the following causes: infectious and parasitic diseases (including tuberculosis, sexually transmitted diseases, diarrheal diseases, childhood-cluster diseases such as tetanus and measles, and malaria); respiratory infections, perinatal conditions, nutritional deficiencies (protein-energy malnutrition, iodine deficiency, vitamin A deficiency, and iron-deficiency anemia); cardiovascular diseases; respiratory diseases; and self-inflicted injuries. In fact, female deaths outnumber male deaths until ages 30–34. Thus, for the first thirty years of life, Indian females are at a disadvantage compared to males; this situation, however, is most marked in the first five years of life. More deaths occur during these first

---

124. U.S. Bureau of the Census, International Data Base, 1998, http://www.census.gov/ipc/www/idbnew.html.

125. For example, infant mortality rates in Canada are 6.08 for males and 5.06 for females, and corresponding rates in the United States are 7.43 and 5.40. Ibid.

126. Demographers Sten Johansson and Ola Nygren calculate that the male-to-female ratio for infant mortality rates should be 130:100. See Johannson and Nygren, "The Missing Girls of China: A New Demographic Account," *Population and Development Review,* Vol. 17, No. 1 (March 1991), p. 48.

127. Christopher J.L. Murray and Alan D. Lopez, eds., *Summary of the Report: The Global Burden of Disease: A Comprehensive Assessment of Mortality and Disability from Diseases, Injuries, and Risk Factors in 1990 and Projected to 2020* (Geneva: World Health Organization, 1996).

years than in the next fifty-five, and the problem may be greater than these numbers suggest, because many infant deaths may go unrecorded.

Of the causes of death for infants in India, infectious and parasitic diseases account for the greatest proportion (42 percent of deaths before the age of 5). Differential death rates from disease are often attributed to differential health care afforded male and female children, which has historical precedents. Following the introduction of the 1870 prohibition against female infanticide, the number of girls in most villages increased, but girls did not always receive the same care as boys. A government report in 1873 provides the following anecdote about parents' attitudes toward their male and female children in Mathura: "A rumor was afloat in some villages that the effect of smallpox vaccination was dangerous to the health of the child. As a result, it was found that most of the girls of the villages were brought forward for vaccination. When experience showed that the female children were better off on account of this the parents withdrew their daughters and presented the sons instead to be vaccinated."[128]

Indian parents are more willing to invest in costly health care for male infants. In her oft-cited book *The Endangered Sex*, Barbara Miller summarizes eleven studies of hospital records and finds that, in India, males are treated much more frequently than females (ranging from 1.2 times as often in Tamil Nadu to 2.6 times in Punjab) and are usually given more attention and time during visits.[129] The lack of medical attention given to girls was also observed by researchers involved in the National Family Health Survey in India in 1992–93; not only are parents less likely to attend to a daughter's illness, but they also vaccinate their daughters less often.[130] The incidence of acute and chronic malnutrition is much higher for girls, evidenced by the higher female death rates from malnutrition. Female babies are likely to be breast-fed less and for a shorter period of time than male babies.[131] The National Family Health Survey report suggests that mothers do not stop breast-feeding females out of intentional neglect, but because they want to hasten the onset of menses to allow them to become pregnant and again try to produce sons.[132] Boys

128. Cited in Panigrahi, *British Social Policy and Female Infanticide in India*, p. 166.

129. For a detailed discussion of differential health care and infant mortality in northern India, see Barbara D. Miller, *The Endangered Sex: Neglect of Female Children in Rural North India* (Ithaca, N.Y.: Cornell University Press, 1981).

130. Mutharayappa et al., "Son Preference and Its Effect on Fertility in India," p. 12.

131. Sachar et al., "Sex-Selective Fertility Control—An Outrage," pp. 30–35.

132. Mutharayappa et al., "Son Preference and Its Effect on Fertility in India," p. 12.

and girls may have equal access to cereal and vegetables, but studies indicate a bias in feeding boys dairy products. Foods may also be allotted according to whether they are considered heat-generating or cooling; it is taboo for girls to eat foods considered heat-generating (meat, fish, and eggs) because of the association made between heat and sexuality.[133] In Rajasthan and Uttar Pradesh, women and girls eat only after the men and boys have eaten, generally eating much smaller portions than the males.

Child mortality, like the overall sex ratios in India, is not uniform throughout the country but follows regional patterns. According to the 1992–93 National Family Health Survey, Assam, Bihar, Madhya Pradesh, Orissa, and Uttar Pradesh have the highest estimated under-5 mortality rates. Infant mortality rates (the number of infant deaths per 1,000) in India in 1993 ranged from 13 in Kerala to 56–59 in Punjab, Tamil Nadu, and Maharashtra, and to 98 to 114 in Uttar Pradesh, Madhya Pradesh, and Orissa.[134] State-level data are not available according to sex, however; thus we can only estimate regions where infant mortality rates are higher for females. In general, child mortality is higher for both sexes in the north than in the south, and it follows observed sex ratio patterns discussed earlier.[135] Several studies have successfully correlated a number of factors with infant mortality, including family composition—sex, age, and number of siblings, as well as parental preference; fertility; education; poverty; female labor force participation; urbanization; and tribal status. It is important to note that high infant-mortality rates often imply passive infanticide, or killing children through neglect. A 1987–89 study in the southern state of Tamil Nadu revealed that the practice of female infanticide still occurs, even in regions where infanticidal rates were traditionally low.[136] In areas in the north where sex ratios are very high and mortality rates are also high, we can infer that sex-selective abortion, infanticide, and neglect contribute to the lack of females. In the Madurai District, a 1986 study of the Usilampatti government hospital reported

---

133.   Malavika Karlekar, "The Girl Child in India: Does She Have Any Rights?" *Canadian Woman Studies*, Vol. 15, Nos. 2–3 (Spring/Summer 1995), pp. 55–57.

134.   Visaria and Visaria, "India's Population in Transition," pp. 18–19.

135.   See Tim Dyson and Mick Moore, "On Kinship Structure, Female Autonomy, and Demographic Behavior in India," *Population and Development Review*, Vol. 9, No. 1 (March 1983), pp. 35–60. Barbara Miller notes the same regional variations between northern and southern India; see Miller, *The Endangered Sex*.

136.   Sabu George, Rajaratnam Abel, and Barbara D. Miller, "Female Infanticide in Rural South India," *Economic and Political Weekly*, May 30, 1992, p. 1153.

that castes with a tradition of female infanticide probably still practice it: "Nearly 600 female births in the Kallar caste in the Usilampatti government hospital occur every year. Of these, about 570 female babies 'vanish with their mother.' According to hospital sources, nearly 80 percent of these 'vanishing babies' are killed."[137]

One of the most important keys to understanding India's skewed sex ratios is family composition: The choices parents make are greatly affected by the number of children they wish to have, as well as their birth order and gender. Female children are not equally discriminated against; that is, parents do not look upon a daughter who is the first child in the same way they would regard the second or third daughter. In fact, many consider the ideal family to be composed of one daughter and at least one or two sons. In a study of Ludhiana District, Punjab, Monica Das Gupta discovered that parents discriminate selectively against their female children.[138] Das Gupta found that infant mortality rates for females increased according to the number of siblings (particularly females) in the family. Thus, if one or two girls were already present, a second or third daughter born would likely receive insufficient care and thus have a greater chance of dying than a first daughter. These same results were found by others investigating infant mortality based on the 1981 census for all of India.[139] Applying an economic model to family planning, a group of researchers concluded that mortality rates are determined by parents' desired family size and sex composition and their budget constraints. Parents are shown to make allocative decisions that directly affect the mortality of their children.[140] According to researchers, "If 'Fate' is unkind enough to give couples a family sex-balance radically different from what is wanted, a sizeable minority will move toward their desired pattern through the neglect of their 'surplus' girls."[141]

137. Vishwanath, "Female Infanticide and the Position of Women in India," p. 201.

138. Monica Das Gupta, "Selective Discrimination against Female Children in Rural Punjab, India," *Population and Development Review*, Vol. 13, No. 1 (March 1987), pp. 77–101.

139. Katherine L. Bourne and George M. Walker, "The Differential Effect of Mother's Education on Mortality of Boys and Girls in India," *Population Studies*, Vol. 45, No. 2 (July 1991), pp. 203–219.

140. George B. Simmons, Celeste Smucker, Stan Bernstein, and Eric Jensen, "Post-Neonatal Mortality in Rural North India: Implications of an Economic Model," *Demography*, Vol. 19, No. 3 (August 1982), pp. 371–390.

141. Jeffery, Jeffery, and Lyon, "Research Note: Female Infanticide and Amniocentesis," p. 1210.

Fertility has an interesting effect on infant mortality and differential treatment of male and female children. In cultures with a strong son preference, the desire for male offspring can result in a skewed sex ratio among the children or a larger family size to ensure a certain number of males. In India, offspring sex-selective practices, including abortion, infanticide, and differential mortality, are greatest in areas where fertility is highest—in the north. Using district-level data from the 1981 census, a group of researchers noted a correlation between high fertility and increased mortality for females, showing that chances of survival for female infants is lower in areas of high fertility.[142] Because the areas of highest fertility are in the north and northwestern states, which also have the highest sex ratios and largest populations, one would expect a strong correlation between female infant mortality and high fertility. Shelley Clark's empirical analysis concludes that "on average, girls [in India] belong to larger families because families with girls tend to become large in an effort to have boys . . . produc[ing] a large group of girls who are unwanted: those who belong to large families that become large in an effort to have sons. It seems plausible that these unwanted girls would experience an unusually high risk of dying young."[143]

But what happens as fertility rates decline, as they have in recent years in most parts of India? A study by Monica Das Gupta and P.N. Mari Bhat reveals that as fertility declines, gender bias intensifies, because the total number of children desired decreases at a faster rate than the decline in son preference.[144] Das Gupta and Bhat explain: "When fertility declines, the total number of children couples desire falls more rapidly than the total number of desired sons. The differences in speed of these two trajectories narrows the space left for daughters, and results in greater pressure to remove girls."[145] In the 1980s, fertility in India fell by 20 per-

142. Mamta Murthi, Anne-Catherine Guio, and Jean Dreze, "Mortality, Fertility, and Gender Bias in India: A District-Level Analysis," *Population and Development Review*, Vol. 21, No. 4 (December 1995), pp. 745–782.

143. Shelley Clark, "Son Preference and Sex Composition of Children: Evidence from India," *Demography*, Vol. 37, No. 1 (February 2000), p. 106. Clark also notes that the sibling cohort sex ratio is strongly associated with religion, Hindu and Muslim families having the highest such ratios in India.

144. Monica Das Gupta and P.N. Mari Bhat, "Fertility Decline and Increased Manifestation of Sex Bias in India," *Population Studies*, Vol. 51, No. 3 (November 1997), pp. 307–315. See also Monica Das Gupta and P.N. Mari Bhat, "Intensified Gender Bias in India: A Consequence of Fertility Decline," Working Paper No. 95.03 (Cambridge, Mass.: Harvard Center for Population and Development Studies, May 1995).

145. Das Gupta and Bhat, "Fertility Decline and Increased Manifestation of Sex Bias in India," p. 307.

cent, but the desired number of sons fell by only 7 percent. In the absence of pressures regarding total family size, if a family desires at least two sons, then they may have four or five children to ensure the desired number of male offspring; the sex ratio in such a family will not necessarily be skewed. If, however, a family desires only three children but still wants two sons, it will use whatever means available to ensure the composition they are seeking. Thus in periods of fertility decline, areas with strong son preference may practice increased discrimination against females in the form of sex-selective abortion, infanticide, or increased neglect of females.

Between 1981 and 1991, Das Gupta and Bhat found that "for a given fertility decline the sex ratio of children increased more in the Northern states," particularly in Madhya Pradesh, Punjab, and Rajasthan.[146] Clark's analysis of the 1992–93 National Health Survey produced similar results: Clark found a sex ratio of 140 in *completed* families. Generally, the smaller the family size, the worse the sex ratio. For families of eight or more children, the sex ratio was 98. For families with only two children, the sex ratio was 154.[147] This is strong evidence that fertility decline in India is linked to significant increases in the sex ratio of children.

Female literacy, female education, and female labor-force participation all have positive effects on female infant mortality (they also affect male infant mortality, but not as markedly) because they reduce antifemale bias.[148] The states in India with the lowest literacy rates for women in 1991 also corresponded to the states contributing the most to the overall number of missing females: Bihar, Madhya Pradesh, Rajasthan, and Uttar Pradesh all have female literacy rates less than 30 percent.[149] The correlation between literacy and sex ratio is not clear, however, because Maharashtra, Punjab, and West Bengal are also among the states with high sex ratios and large numbers of missing females, but their literacy rates are well above the national rate of 39 percent with rates of 52, 50, and 47 percent, respectively. In fact, education can have the opposite effect: Adhering to standard family planning once an "ideal" family is reached requires skillful manipulation. Das Gupta shows that it is not backward or uneducated women who employ such

146. Ibid., p. 313.

147. Clark, "Son Preference and Sex Composition of Children," p. 103, Table 6.

148. Murthi, Guio, and Dreze, "Mortality, Fertility, and Gender Bias in India," pp. 764–765.

149. United Nations Development Programme, *India: The Road to Human Development*, India Development Forum, Paris, France, June 23–25, 1997, document of the United Nations Development Programme, New Delhi, http://www.undp.org.in/REPORT/IDF97/default.htm.

strategies; rather those with education may be better able, or more motivated, to manipulate fertility and their child's mortality. Urbanization
also amplifies female disadvantage, according to Das Gupta, increasing
female infant mortality rates. The higher sex ratios exhibited in urban
areas are not solely due to the migration of males from rural areas.[150]

Poverty also has an effect on female bias. As was the case in India's
past, daughters are less likely to be discriminated against within poor
families and are more likely to be considered a burden among wealthy or
high-status families. In their analysis of district-level data from the 1981
census, Mamta Murthi, Anne-Catherine Guio, and Jean Dreze discover
an inverse relationship between poverty and female infant mortality; as
poverty increases, female infant mortality decreases.[151] This view is also
held by N. Krishnaji, who found greater discrimination against female infants and adults among the landowning classes than among the poor.
Like Das Gupta, Krishnaji suggests that the richer classes may have
greater motivation to be discriminatory because of the high cost of
finding a suitable marriage partner for a daughter.[152] Additionally,
women among the poorer castes may be valued for the contributions of
their labor. This does not mean, however, that female infanticide is absent
among the poorer classes. As our previous discussion of the castes and
scheduled castes shows, sex ratios are high among scheduled castes, suggesting the practice of female infanticide; they are not, however, as high
as the sex ratios among the nonscheduled caste population.

A higher proportion of scheduled tribes reduces discrimination
against female infants, which corresponds to the positive effect observed
earlier of tribes on overall sex ratios within states and regions in India.
The fact that tribal groups do not follow Hindu marriage patterns means
that a daughter is not lost to the family after marriage; thus daughters
may be considered more valuable among tribal populations. Other factors, such as property rights accorded to females among tribes, also tend
to decrease bias against females.

Finally, a note about regional variations: The same regional variations
observed for sex ratios apply to differential infant mortality rates. The
north and northwest states, where the highest sex ratios were observed,
also correspond to areas of high infant mortality. The southern regions,
on the other hand, are areas of lower sex ratios and lower infant mortality

150. Das Gupta, "Selective Discrimination against Female Children in Rural Punjab,
India."

151. Murthi, Guio, and Dreze, "Mortality, Fertility, and Gender Bias in India," p. 765.

152. N. Krishnaji, "Poverty and Sex Ratio: Some Data and Speculations," *Economic
and Political Weekly*, June 6, 1987, pp. 892–897.

rates. Marriage and property customs, religion, caste, and agricultural methods are factors that influence the variation between the two regions. In the northern regions, agriculture is more typically large-scale, not labor-intensive as in the south, where female labor is valued. Marriages in the north tend to be exogamous; brides leave their families and often move to other villages. This contributes to the view that "raising a daughter is like watering another man's garden." In the south, the bride typically does not move far away and is able to visit her family; she can continue to care for her parents in their old age, which mitigates son preference.[153] In addition, historical legacy contributes greatly to current practices of discrimination against females in India. Historically, female infanticide was most prevalent in the northern provinces within clans and castes of high status. Despite government attempts to end the practice, more female infants continue to die in these regions.

It is not only female infants who die at higher rates than males, however. As stated previously, female deaths outnumber male deaths until age 30. Among the causes of mortality, death by fire figures prominently. According to the 1996 study by the World Bank, World Health Organization, and Harvard University on global mortality, Indian women "face an appallingly high risk of dying in fires": In 1990 alone, 87,000 women (compared with 37,000 men) died in fires. Fifty-three thousand of those deaths were of women between the ages of 15 and 44.[154] Although some of these deaths may be due to the hazards of cooking in the kitchen or near an open fire, a more plausible reason suggested by the age at which these deaths occur relates to the problems of marriage and dowry. Bride burnings, or dowry deaths, gained publicity in India in the 1970s, when feminists became involved in several cases made known to the public —cases in which husbands or in-laws had attempted to burn women to death because of the insufficient dowry they brought to the marriage. As Elisabeth Bumiller notes, "Usually the burning occurs in the first year of an arranged marriage, after it has become clear that the bride's parents will not meet the demands of the in-laws for more wedding gifts. Once the woman is disposed of, a new bride, who presumably will fulfill the dowry demands, is found."[155] These deaths are yet another example of practices of extreme gender discrimination, and they contribute to the overall phenomenon of low life expectancy for women in India. Through-

153. Celia W. Dugger, "Modern Asia's Anomaly: The Girls Who Don't Get Born," *New York Times*, May 6, 2001, sec. 4, p. 4.

154. Murray and Lopez, *Summary of the Report: The Global Burden of Disease*.

155. Elisabeth Bumiller, *May You Be the Mother of a Hundred Sons: A Journey among the Women of India* (New York: Fawcett Columbine, 1990), p. 49.

out the rest of the world, women have a higher life expectancy than men, the only exception being southern Asia. For example, 1990–95 figures for the United States give a life expectancy of 79 years for women and 73 for men. Even in very poor countries, such as Mauritania, the female life expectancy of 50 is higher than the male life expectancy of 46.[156] In Bangladesh, India, Nepal, and Pakistan, however, the life expectancy for women is equal to or less than that of men.

In most countries, women tend to live longer than men, but as Table 3.11 shows, in India there is no difference between the life expectancy for women and men: It is 55.9 years for both. In Bihar, Haryana, Orissa, and Uttar Pradesh, the life expectancy for women is less than that for men. Once again, greater discrimination occurs against women in the north, where it affects female mortality.

Missing Females, Surplus Males—Past, Present, and Future

India's 2001 census indicated that males outnumber females by 35 million. In addition to determining where and among which groups this male surplus (or deficit of females) is found, we are interested in identifying the age groups most affected. We also want to know what the future holds for India's male and female populations, given that the sex ratio seems to be constantly rising. In particular, we are most interested in the age group 15–35. Table 3.12 shows the sex ratios and population sizes according to gender from 1961 to 1991.

Between 1961 and 1981, the population aged 15–35 in India rose dramatically, with a corresponding large increase in the excess number of males. The rate of population increase had slowed, however, by the time of the 1991 census.[157] Given that in the past fifteen years the sex ratios at birth have increased greatly, we would expect to see greater differences between future male and female populations in the 15–35 age group as

---

156. United Nations, *The World's Women, 1995: Trends and Statistics* (New York: United Nations, 1995), pp. 84–88, Table 6.

157. The cause of the decrease in surplus males in 1991 is not clear; it will be useful to compare 1991 figures with the 2001 census when such figures become available. Interestingly, however, the 7 million surplus males are all found within the same northern states with the highest birth sex ratios. The missing females in this age group can be attributed to the following ten states: Assam (120,421), Bihar (555,094), Gujarat (404,894), Haryana (413,358), Madhya Pradesh (681,066), Maharashtra (926,454), Punjab (376,620), Rajasthan (601,047), Uttar Pradesh (2,425,329), and West Bengal (857,825). These ten states have a total of 7,362,108 surplus males aged 15–35, a number that is in fact slightly higher than the all-India figure of 7,267,923. See India, Office of the Registrar General, *Census of India, 1991, Series-1: India, Part 4 A-C Series: Socio-Cultural Tables*, Vol. 2 (New Delhi: India, Office of the Registrar General, 1998), pp. 380–395, Table C-6.

Table 3.11. Life Expectancy in India by State, 1991.

State	Males	Females
India	**55.9**	**55.9**
Andhra Pradesh	57.3	60.3
Arunachal Pradesh	—	—
Assam	52.4	52.5
Bihar	54.9	52.3
Goa	—	—
Gujarat	55.9	57.9
Haryana	61.5	59.5
Himachal Pradesh	58.5	62.9
Jammu and Kashmir	60.2	60.7
Karnataka	59.8	62.4
Kerala	65.9	72.2
Madhya Pradesh	50.6	51.8
Maharashtra	60.1	62.8
Manipur	—	—
Meghalaya	—	—
Mizoram	—	—
Nagaland	—	—
Orissa	53.6	53.1
Punjab	63.0	64.7
Rajasthan	53.5	54.3
Sikkim	—	—
Tamil Nadu	57.4	58.5
Tripura	—	—
Uttar Pradesh	52.3	49.6
West Bengal	57.9	59.1

SOURCE: India, Office of the Registrar General, *Census of India, 1991* (New Delhi: Office of the Registrar General, 1991).

well as in other age groups. We would also expect that future populations will exhibit higher sex ratios and have a larger surplus population of males than present or past populations. The sex ratios and relative sizes of the young male and female populations in India support this: According to the 1991 census, there were 161,727,446 males and 150,637,216 females under the age of 15, or 11,090,230 excess males in this small portion of the population alone.[158] Examining all surplus males aged 0–19 in 1991, the calculated surplus of young males ages 15–35 in the year 2006 is conservatively 16.5 million. Future populations will exhibit higher sex ratios and have a larger surplus population of males than present or past

158. Ibid.

Table 3.12. Surplus Male Population in India, 1961–91 and 2006 Estimates.

Year	Total Male Population Ages 15–35	Surplus Male Population Ages 15–35	Surplus Males Total Population
1961	75,845,000	6,566,000	18,180,000
1971	96,676,000	9,201,000	24,264,000
1981	125,534,886	10,500,152	25,470,776
1991	144,209,649	7,267,923	32,158,228
2006 (est.)	203,950,520	16,509,449	—

SOURCES: 1961–81—U.S. Bureau of the Census, International Data Base, 1998, http://www.census.gov/ipc/www/idbnew.html; and 1991—India, Office of the Registrar General, *Census of India, 1991, Series-1: India, Part 4 A-C Series: Socio-Cultural Tables*, Vol. 2 (New Delhi: Office of the Registrar General, 1998). Estimates for 2006 were calculated using the data for the male/female population aged 0–19 in the 1991 Indian census.

populations because of the increase in sex ratios at birth and the rising sex ratios for juvenile populations. It is obvious that India is currently experiencing a problem of too many men and too few women, particularly if men desire to marry women of their own age group. If the sex ratios continue to be as high as they now are (a conservative assumption), and the differential mortality between male and female infants continues as it has, what will this population look like in the year 2020?

Tables 3.13A and 3.13B provide two scenarios for India's population in 2020, based on two different sex ratios at birth. The first scenario is based on a conservative sex ratio at birth of 109.65, whereas the second scenario utilizes what we believe is a more probable sex ratio of 112.23. Our estimates are conservative because they assume a constant, rather than a rising, sex ratio at birth. The two scenarios produce different figures for the surplus male population for the age group 15–35 in 2020: The figures range from 28 million in Table 3.13A to 32 million in Table 3.13B. These figures are not implausible when compared with the change in this same age group between 1961 and 1981: During this period, the 15–35 surplus male population increased by 3.9 million, a 60 percent jump. A similar increase in each subsequent twenty-year period would take us to the year 2021 with a surplus population of 26.9 million men. Table 3.14 compares our projections with those of the World Bank and the United Nations.

Population totals based on our estimates are within the range of estimates made by both the World Bank and the United Nations. Given differences in assumptions regarding current and future sex ratios, there is great variation, however, among each of the estimates in the surplus male population for the 15–35 age group in the year 2020. The World Bank's estimates are based on an extremely conservative estimate for India's sex ratios; to achieve a sex ratio of 104.5 males per 100 females, the sex ratio at birth would have to be much lower than this figure, because differential mortality rates act to reduce the number of women in the population at a greater rate than men. Even the UN's sex ratio of 107.4 is highly improbable, given the current indications of high sex ratios at birth and high rates of female mortality. Research suggests that the problem will only worsen. Even our estimates for a surplus male population of between 28 and 32 million may be well below the actual size of the 15–35 age group in twenty years.

Conclusion

Throughout this discussion of infanticide, abortion, differential mortality, and other practices that have contributed to India's missing females, it has often been necessary to generalize. In the nineteenth century, when the British set out to learn the extent and causes of infanticide, they conducted their research at the level of families and individuals, recording the names of the heads of families that had practiced female infanticide. This type of research is no longer possible for a number of reasons, not the least of which is the immense size of India's population. Yet one cannot speak in generalities about the problem of the "girl child" in India, for not all females in the country are equally discriminated against, as this discussion has shown. There are great variations in women's status and treatment between north and south, between rural and urban areas, between castes and tribes, within castes and clans, according to socioeconomic status and education, and even within families according to a female's birth order and the desired family composition.

Still, generalizing about high sex ratios at the state level can show where female mortality (whether fetus, infant, or child) is greatest. For example, the four neighboring northern states of Bihar, Madhya Pradesh, Rajasthan, and Uttar Pradesh together contribute to one-half of the missing females of India. Focusing on these four states alone would go far toward stopping continued discrimination against females. Researchers can no longer create lists of clans that continue to kill their daughters, but it can be assumed that because both the caste structure has remained rigidly in place and hypergyny continues to be practiced, the same upper castes and clans find it necessary to practice female abortion or infanticide, or discriminate in other ways against their female children.

One of the questions not addressed here is why these practices have become increasingly prevalent in India. In some areas, there have been significant increases over the last twenty years in levels of infant mortal-

Table 3.13A. Population Projection, Ages 15–35, India, 2020: Sex Ratio of 109.65 Males per 100 Females.

Years	Sex Ratio at Birth[a]	Total Births[b]	Male Births	Female Births	LTSR Males to 2020[c]	LTSR Females to 2020[d]	Male Population 2020	Female Population 2020
1985–90	109.65	129,965,000	67,972,000	61,993,000	0.80973	0.77931	55,039,000	48,312,000
1990–95	109.65	139,695,000	73,060,000	66,635,000	0.81889	0.79519	59,829,000	50,994,000
1995–2000	109.65	139,975,000	73,207,000	66,768,000	0.82485	0.81057	60,648,000	54,120,000
2000–05	109.65	137,515,000	71,920,000	65,595,000	0.83694	0.82258	60,193,000	53,957,000
Total							**235,709,000**	**207,383,000**

Missing females   28,326,000

Table 3.13B. Population Projection, Ages 15–35, India, 2020: Sex Ratio of 112.23 Males per 100 Females.

Years	Sex Ratio at Birth[e]	Total Births	Male Births	Female Births	LTSR Males to 2020	LTSR Females to 2020	Male Population 2020	Female Population 2020
1985–90	112.23	129,965,000	68,751,000	61,214,000	0.80973	0.77931	55,670,000	47,704,000
1990–95	112.23	139,695,000	73,899,000	65,796,000	0.81889	0.79519	60,515,000	52,321,000
1995–2000	112.23	139,975,000	74,047,000	65,928,000	0.82485	0.81057	61,344,000	53,439,000
2000–05	112.23	137,515,000	72,745,000	64,770,000	0.83694	0.82258	60,884,000	53,278,000
Total							**238,413,000**	**206,742,000**

Missing females   31,671,000

[a]Sex ratio at birth of 109.65 males per 100 females is equal to the figure of 912 females per 1,000 males as determined by the Sample Registration System for 1984 to 1988. Although the sex ratio at birth has been rising, we use this conservative estimate of a constant ratio over time. Source: India, Office of the Registrar General, Census of India, 1991, Series-1: India, Paper 2 of 1992: Final Population Totals: Brief Analysis of Primary Census Abstract (New Delhi: India, Office of the Registrar, 1992).

[b]United Nations, Department of International and Economic Social Affairs, World Population Prospects, 1990, Population Studies No. 120 (New York: United Nations, 1991).

[c]Lifetime survival ratios (LTSRs) were obtained, with adjustments, from the U.S. Bureau of the Census, International Data Base, 1998, http://www.census.gov/ipc/www/idbnew.html, Life Table Values: India/1980/Total/Male. The nqx values for infant mortality (ages 0–1) were adjusted according to the change in infant mortality in India. The infant mortality rate in 1980 was 113.9, which dropped to 79.50 for males in 1990, according to the U.S. Bureau of the Census. The life table was then adjusted in accordance with this reduction in mortality for the first year of life. No further adjustments are possible at this time because the India census has not yet been made available according to age intervals other than that of 0–6 and 7+. Data collected by the Sample Registration system in India, however, indicate no change in the ratio of male/female age-specific death rates for the ages of 0–4 between 1979 and 1991 (Monica Das Gupta and P.N. Mari Bhat, "Intensified Gender Bias in India: A Consequence of Fertility Decline," Working Paper No. 95.03 [Cambridge, Mass.: Harvard Center for Population and Development Studies, May 1995]). The lifetime survival ratios were obtained as $LTSR_x = 5L_x / 5L_x$ where x = age intervals of 15–20, 20–25, 25–30, and 30–35.

[d]LTSR calculated as above in [c]. According to the U.S. Bureau of the Census, the infant mortality rate dropped from 119.0 to 80.40, thus the corresponding probability rate of nqx for ages 0–1 was adjusted accordingly. Original values from U.S. Bureau of the Census, International Data Base, 1998, Life Table Values: India/1980/Total/Female.

[e]Table 3.13B is calculated with a sex ratio of 112.23, which compares with that of 891 females per 1,000 males, the sex ratio calculated by the office of the Registrar General, India, through data collected from 1981 to 1991, based on 6 million births in various parts of the country. India, Office of the Registrar General, Census of India, 1991: Final Population Totals: Brief Analysis of Primary Census Abstract.

Table 3.14. Comparison of Population Projections, Ages 15–35, India, Year 2020.

Type of Estimate	Total Population	Male Population	Female Population	Sex Ratio Population (females per 1,000 males)	Male Surplus
United Nations medium variant estimates[a]	450,069,000	233,096,000	216,973,000	107.4	16,123,000
United Nations high variant estimates	467,984,000	242,360,000	225,624,000	107.4	16,736,000
United Nations low variant estimates	432,136,000	22,3823,000	208,313,000	107.4	15,510,000
World Bank estimates[b]	442,408,000	226,040,000	216,368,000	104.5	9,672,000
Estimates based on sex ratio at birth[a]	443,092,000	235,709,000	207,383,000	113.7	28,326,000
Estimates based on sex ratio at birth[b]	445,155,000	238,413,000	206,742,000	115.3	31,671,000

[a]United Nations, Department for Economic and Social Information and Policy Analysis, Population Division, *The Sex and Age Distribution of the World Populations: The 1994 Revision* (New York: United Nations, 1994).

[b]World Bank, *World Population Projections, 1994–95 Edition: Estimates and Projections with Related Demographic Statistics* (Washington, D.C.: World Bank, 1994).

ity and in the overall sex ratios. The rise in the sex ratio for ages 0–6 from 1991 to 2001, in particular, requires further study. The cause may be a decline in fertility accompanied by only a moderate decline in son preference, environmental stresses, or socioeconomic changes brought on by development policies implemented in a particular area that have adversely affected the value of women's labor or their overall status.[159]

Much research still needs to be done on rising sex ratios at birth and in the overall population, at both national and regional levels. As of 2001, at least 35 million females were missing from India's population, with the number rising every year. Conversely, there is a surplus of 35 million men in India, half of whom are found in the four populous states in the north. We calculate that there will be approximately 16.5 million surplus males ages 15–35 by the year 2006, and if trends continue as they have, a conservative estimate is that there will be approximately 28–32 million surplus young males in India by the year 2020.

---

159. For a discussion of the effect of development programs on the community of Karimpur in Uttar Pradesh, see Susan S. Wadley, "Family Composition Strategies in Rural North India," *Social Science and Medicine*, Vol. 37, No. 11 (December 1993), pp. 1367–1376.

Chapter 4

China's "Missing Females"

With approximately 1.3 billion citizens—one-fifth of the world's population—the People's Republic of China is the most populous nation on earth. China's population policies have long attracted world interest, from the launching of its "one-child policy" in the late 1970s to attempts to address the country's high sex ratios at birth. Rising sex ratios, in particular, have captured the interest of the media worldwide: Popular newspapers and journals refer to the "missing girls," or girls who are being "weeded out," "rationed," and "rejected" by the "return of the baby killers" in China.[1] Television programs on the BBC and American news stations have broadcast from "the dying rooms"—orphanages in China where unwanted children, primarily females, are left to die. In addition to emphasizing the dearth of females, headlines also refer to the "glut" or "army" of bachelors, estimating that between 80 and 111 million Chinese men will not be able to find wives.[2] How valid are such claims?

According to the preliminary results of China's 2000 census, there are 106.74 males for every 100 females. This is a slight increase over the total

---

1.   See, for example, Nicholas D. Kristof, "Chinese Turn to Ultrasound, Scorning Baby Girls for Boys," *New York Times*, July 21, 1993, p. A1; Jonathan Mirsky, "Return of the Baby Killers," *New Statesman*, March 21, 1986, p. 19; Park Chai Bin, "Asia's Female Populations Fall amid Sex-Selection Abortions: Technology Used to Reject Daughters," *Washington Times*, June 30, 1995, p. A19; and Bob Herbert, "China's Missing Girls," *New York Times*, October 30, 1997, p. A31.

2.   See Ren Meng, "Confronting Three Populations of 80 Million," *Inside China Mainland*, Vol. 19, No. 1 (January 1997), pp. 78–81; Graham Hutchings, "Female Infanticide 'Will Lead to Army of Bachelors,'" *London Daily Telegraph*, April 11, 1997, http://www.telegraph.co.uk/htmlContent.jhtml?html=/archive/1997/04/11/wchi11.html;   and "China Has 20 Percent Male Surplus," Agence France-Presse, January 7, 1999.

sex ratio of 105.98 recorded in the 1990 census. The sex ratio for the overall population tells only part of the story, however; the sex ratio for children under the age of 5 is reported in official publications to be 118.38.[3] Unlike India, the problem of missing females in China was not constant throughout the twentieth century; present in the early part of the century, the problem lessened following the 1949 communist revolution and then intensified with the onset of the one-child policy. Thus it has not yet affected all age groups. In addition to determining the validity of journalists' claims regarding China's large bachelor populations, we are interested in explaining the recent dramatic rise in the sex ratio at birth. To do this, we examine the factors affecting women's social status, the prevalence of son preference, the history of sex selection, and current gender politics in China.

China and Its People

China's citizens are a relatively homogeneous people: The population is 92 percent affiliated with the Han culture, and 94 percent speak a Sinitic language or dialect. The world's fourth largest country, China is divided into twenty-two provinces, five autonomous regions, four independent municipalities (Beijing, Chongqing, Shanghai, and Tianjin), and two special administration regions (Hong Kong and Macau). Map 4.1 shows the provinces of China. Throughout China's history, geographical barriers that have helped to preserve the country's unique culture have generally demarcated its borders.

Women in China

The historical record of women's positions within Chinese society is more mixed than that of Indian women. As with India, one can identify periods of greater and lesser mobility and power, with differences among the various strata of society as well as regional and rural/urban differences. Unlike India, however, there are more exceptions to general trends. The Empress Dowager Cixi, or "dragon lady," who ruled male-dominated Manchu China from 1861 to 1908, is but one example. The history of women in China also differs from that of women in India because of the effects of the communist revolution, which greatly altered the role of women in society.

As Laurel Bossen notes, the "traditional" portrait of Chinese women

---

3. China, State Statistical Bureau, *China Population Statistical Yearbook, 1996* (Beijing: China Statistics Press, 1996).

Map 4.1. The Provinces of China.

is "a generalized and timeless abstraction that ignores processes of historical change and regional variation in the ways gender was experienced."[4]
Bossen correctly points out that Chinese women are typically portrayed
as a unified group sharing the same experiences of infanticide, foot binding, devaluation, subordination to males, and other effects of living in a
patriarchal society with patrilineal descent. Yet subtle, and at times significant, shifts in women's status are evident throughout China's history
and among different groups, classes, and regions. For example, during
periods in which women seemed to be heavily controlled by men, such as
the Song dynasty (A.D. 960–1279)—when female infanticide, foot binding,
and widow suicide were common—women gained the right to inherit
property and control their dowries, even taking them into second mar-

4. Laurel Bossen, "Women and Development," in Robert E. Gamer, ed., *Understanding Contemporary China* (Boulder, Colo.: Lynne Rienner, 1999), p. 294.

riages. In the brief chronological summary that follows, we review China's gender experience.

Archaeological evidence from Neolithic times and extending to the Shang dynasty (1766–1122 B.C.) suggests that patriarchy was not as dominant as it would be in later periods.[5] For example, most people were buried in the graveyard of their mother's family. Other indications suggest the presence of a matriarchal order, or matrilineal society: Records of ancient folklore contain stories of heroes identified by their mother's names as opposed to their father's; mothers were honored through a special sacrificial ceremony during the Shang dynasty; and inheritance was determined by the mother's surname.[6] During the Shang, women, along with men, were warriors, and could lead military campaigns against invaders.

During the Zhou dynasty (1122–221 B.C.), traces of matriarchy remained: Women's surnames were still considered the family name, and men were given only personal names according to their place of birth or occupation.[7] Women were generally not secluded. With the exception of women of royalty and nobility, who ate separately from men and observed public life from behind screens, women could choose their husbands, divorce, and remarry.[8] During the latter period of this dynasty, ancestor worship was better codified and disseminated throughout society, and Confucius (551–479 B.C.) reapplied a moral system of thought to the Chinese after the chaotic times of the Warring States period (475–221 B.C.). The ideas of Confucius, China's preeminent moral philosopher, permanently altered the societal structure and affected the status of women within society.

Confucian thought is associated with the teachings of nine texts known as "The Four Books" and "Five Classics," which include texts attributed to Confucius, such as *The Analects of Confucius,* and those attributed to other authors, such as the *Book of Changes.* Confucius urged the Chinese people to consult the "Five Classics" as a source of moral guidance. One of the primary teachings of these texts is that a fundamental difference between male and female must be maintained to preserve the

---

5. Esther S. Lee Yao, *Chinese Women: Past and Present* (Mesquite, Tex.: Ide House, 1983), p. 13.

6. In fact, the Chinese roots for the word "surname" are "woman" and "birth." Ibid., pp. 14–16.

7. Lin Yutang, *My Country and My People* (New York: Reynal and Hitchcock, 1935), p. 137.

8. Robert Hans van Gulik, *Sexual Life in Ancient China: A Preliminary Survey of Chinese Sex and Society from ca. 1500 B.C. till 1644 A.D.* (Leiden, Netherlands: E.J. Brill, 1974).

cosmic order.[9] Confucius's teachings reinforced the belief that women were inferior to men: He taught that women's supposed temperamental nature and limited intellectual capacity make them unequal to men. Confucian virtues stressed the need for women to be quiet, obedient, neat, chaste, and industrious within their homes, which contributed to the seclusion of women.[10] Women were considered to have been given an equal position with men, because they were both allocated spheres of influence, yet they came to be viewed as subordinate to men.

During the Zhou dynasty, women were increasingly seen as a commodity. The wedding ceremony evolved during the late Zhou dynasty, and three types of marriages resulted: captured, purchased, and arranged. Captured and purchased brides had the least freedom. Having no rights, these women were essentially slaves, whose main functions were to serve their husbands and carry on the male line.[11] Also believed to have originated in the Zhou dynasty was the clan system, which further contributed to the subordination of women—the higher a woman's status within a clan, the more restricted she became and the more norms she had to follow.[12]

The veiling of women became a common practice during the Qin and Han dynasties (221 B.C.–206 B.C. and 202 B.C.–A.D. 220), and the feminine virtues of obedience and loyalty (to one's father, husband, and son) were codified. During the Han, the cult of chastity became more institutionalized. Women were allowed to marry only once, and premarital or extramarital sexual relations were punishable by death. The state erected memorials to women who remained chaste despite great challenges, such as widowhood in youth. Arranged marriages gained prominence and were accompanied by the payment of dowries, as well as betrothal gifts, from the groom's family. Female infanticide may also have become more widely practiced, given the high costs to the family of marrying off a daughter.[13] Many books, such as *Records of Virtuous Women* and *Admonition to Women* were published describing women's duties and further restricting women's activities. Despite the greater constraint on women's

---

9. Richard W. Guisso, "Thunder over the Lake: The Five Classics and the Perception of Women in Early China," in Guisso and Stanley Johannesen, eds., *Women in China: Current Directions in Historical Scholarship* (Youngstown, N.Y.: Philo, 1981), p. 48. These sayings derive largely from the interpretations of neo-Confucianists in the Song dynasty period.

10. Lin, *My Country and My People*, p. 139.

11. Yao, *Chinese Women*, p. 17.

12. Ibid., p. 29.

13. Ibid., p. 48.

activities during the Han, this period also saw Empress Lu's de facto reign after her husband's death.

In the subsequent period of the Three Kingdoms (220–280), Jin (265–420) and Southern and Northern dynasties (420–588), the social caste system developed, restricting marriages according to caste level and discouraging remarriage for women. In 480, as the tradition of chaste widowhood became entrenched, a religious retreat was constructed at Tang-chou for childless widows.[14] The high cost of weddings during this time prohibited marriage for many, resulting in a growing number of bachelors and increased infanticide.[15] The Tang dynasty (618–907) provided a less restrictive environment for women. There were a number of strong women in the Tang, including the only woman to rule in her own name (Wu Zetian, who ruled from 655 to 705, also kept a harem of men). The Tang was also a more cosmopolitan time in Chinese history, where Buddhism made great inroads into society and lessened the power of the Confucianists.

Emperor Li of the Five dynasties (907–960) is believed to have introduced foot binding by designing a special shoe for his favorite concubine.[16] This practice became more common during the subsequent Song dynasty, which more than any other period in China's history is synonymous with the subordination of women. Seclusion was imposed on upper-class women, the shape of women's bodies was concealed by their clothing, and female infanticide was prevalent. Practiced among the upper classes, foot binding was a symbol of status and beauty—a small foot symbolized a beautiful woman. Women of lower classes would not bind their feet because the restricted movements it imposed would prevent them from laboring for the family. Regional differences to these practices existed, however; in the southeast region of China, for example, foot binding was virtually unknown.[17]

Dowry came to play a more important role in the wedding ceremony during the Song dynasty (960–1279). During the Tang dynasty, betrothal gifts were used to prepare the dowry, resulting in a fairly equal exchange of money between families. During the Song, the expected size of dowries grew, resulting in financial hardship on families with daughters.[18] In

---

14. Ibid., p. 46; and Lin, *My Country and My People*, p. 140.

15. Yao, *Chinese Women*, p. 52.

16. Ibid., p. 93.

17. Yao, *Chinese Women*, p. 94.

18. Patricia Buckley Ebrey, *The Inner Quarters: Marriage and the Lives of Chinese Women in the Sung Period* (Berkeley: University of California Press, 1993), p. 101.

response, leaders posted signs, established laws, and exacted punishments to ensure that marriage was not used as a means to acquire wealth.[19] Neo-Confucianists of the late Song developed sayings such as *nan zun nu bei*, meaning "treat men as superior, women as inferior," and *san rong side*, "three types of obedience and four virtues (for women)," the three types of obedience being to father before marriage, to husband while married, and to son when a widow.

From the fourteenth to the nineteenth centuries—during the Yuan, Ming, and Qing dynasties—middle- and upper-class women became increasingly secluded. Even physicians were not allowed to see their bodies, and there were heavy penalties for touching women or entering their quarters. Medical texts explained techniques for conceiving males.[20] Dowry competition, female infanticide, and polygyny were all prevalent.[21] Lack of control over their lives was reflected in women's loss of control over their dowries.

In the late nineteenth and early twentieth centuries, the role of women changed in much of Chinese society. Missionaries and Western-educated Chinese questioned assumptions about women's roles, and some traditional practices harmful to women came to an end. Female political activists, such as Qiu Jin, brought attention to female infanticide, wife beating, widow chastity, polygamy and concubinage, and other social problems. The seclusion and veiling of women became less common, and foot binding ceased in most areas. These changes primarily affected urban women or those from wealthy families. New laws giving women the right to choose their husbands and inherit property were created.[22] Rural women also experienced change, becoming more active politically through participation in rebel organizations during the Taiping Rebellion (1851–64), the Boxer Rebellion (1900), and the Red Spears Movement (1911–49).[23] The Taiping Rebellion, which swept through China from south to north, challenged conceptions of male-female inequality. The rebels included women in high-ranking positions in their army. Increased

---

19. Ibid., pp. 101–103.

20. See Charlotte Furth, *A Flourishing Yin: Gender in China's Medical History, 960–1665* (Berkeley: University of California Press, 1999), pp. 210–216.

21. Mildred Dickemann, "Paternal Confidence and Dowry Competition: A Biocultural Analysis of Purdah," in Richard D. Alexander and Donald W. Tinkle, eds., *Natural Selection and Social Behavior: Recent Research and New Theory* (New York: Chiron, 1981), p. 434.

22. Patricia Buckley Ebrey, *The Cambridge Illustrated History of China* (Cambridge: Cambridge University Press, 1996), pp. 279–281.

23. Bossen, "Women and Development," p. 297.

contact with the West during the nineteenth and early twentieth centuries was another source of pressure to provide women with access to education, and to abolish foot binding and infanticide. Despite these efforts, changes affecting the entire population were brought about only with the communist revolution in 1949.

History of Infanticide and Offspring Sex Selection

The history of infanticide and offspring sex selection in China, as in India, must be pieced together from fragmented and sometimes contradictory sources. Pinpointing the origins of the practice is difficult, because Chinese scholars seldom referred to it, and population records are unreliable for most of China's early history. One author suggests that offspring sex selection in China dates to approximately 2000 B.C., when girls were the primary victims of infanticide in times of environmental stress.[24] The earliest written reference to infanticide is found in *The Book of Songs*, dating between 800 and 600 B.C., and describes attempts to kill a male child. Yet another of the *Songs* opines:

When a son is born
Let him sleep on the bed,
Clothe him with fine clothes.
And give him jade to play with.
How lordly his cry is!
May he grow up to wear crimson
And be the lord of the clan and the tribe.

When a daughter is born,
Let her sleep on the ground,
Wrap her in common wrappings,
And give her broken tiles for playthings.
May she have no faults, no merits of her own.
May she well attend to food and wine,
And bring no discredit to her parents.[25]

In the *Tso Chuan* (Commentaries on Spring and Autumn Annals), written in the fifth century B.C., a case is recorded of an abandoned baby girl found under a dike.[26]

---

24. Elisabeth J. Croll, *Feminism and Socialism in China* (London: Routledge and Kegan Paul, 1978).

25. Ibid., p. 32.

26. Yao, *Chinese Women*, p. 91.

Both male and female infants were killed to control family size and composition, yet a prevailing preference for males, at least in some areas, suggests that more females may have been killed. Han Fei (d. 233 B.C.), a well-known legalist thinker of the latter part of the Zhou dynasty, referred to female infanticide: "When [parents] bear a son they congratulate each other, but when they bear a daughter they kill her. Both come from the parents' love, but they congratulate each other when it is a boy and kill it if it is a girl because they are considering their later convenience and calculating their long-term interests."[27]

Yet another reference suggests that when food and necessities were scarce, parents killed both male and female offspring. A passage in the *Hou Han shu* (History of the Later Han [A.D. 25–220]) states that "when Sung Tu became governor of Ch'ang-sha, the people were much in need of clothes and food and did, therefore, not bring up their infants. Sung Tu severely reprimanded the village elders (*san-lao*) and prohibited infanticide."[28] Parents used infanticide and abandonment to control family size, and it may have been a common practice among the poor despite the belief that killing a child meant the forfeiture of blessings from heaven.

Infanticide did not become a crime until the twelfth century. Moral and legal texts reveal that officials recognized that infanticide, and female infanticide in particular, were problems throughout the Qin, Han, Song, Yuan, and later dynasties.[29] Whereas evidence of female infanticide in the Qin, Han, and subsequent dynasties is scarce, references to the practice during the Song dynasty are frequent, largely due to changes in attitudes toward women. The killing of infants, both male and female, is recorded as a common practice during the Song dynasty; it was known as *hao-tzu*—weeding out children. If a family had too many sons, they risked having to make too many divisions of property, but too many daughters meant having to pay large sums of money for dowries; thus smaller families were desired. In addition, once children became of age

---

27. Quoted in Bernice J. Lee, "Female Infanticide in China," in Guisso and Johannesen, *Women in China*, p. 164.

28. Quoted in Werner Eichhorn, "Some Notes on Population Control during the Sung Dynasty," in *Etudes d'histoire et de littérature chinoises offertes au Professeur Jaroslav Prusek*, Bibliothèque de l'institut des hautes études chinoises, Vol. 24 (Paris: Presses Universitaires de France, 1976), p. 90.

29. For a discussion of the criminal texts, see Sharon K. Hom, "Female Infanticide in China: The Human Rights Specter and Thoughts towards (An)other Vision," *Columbia Human Rights Law Review*, Vol. 23, No. 2 (Summer 1992), pp. 249–314. For a discussion of normative texts, see Ann Walter, "Infanticide and Dowry in Ming and Early Qing China," in Anne Behnke Kinney, ed., *Chinese Views of Childhood* (Honolulu: University of Hawaii Press, 1995), pp. 193–217.

(usually 16), parents had to pay a head tax on their behalf, which was cited as yet another reason for disposing of infants.[30]

A law prohibiting infanticide was brought forward in 1110 by imperial decree. Revisions to the decree just two years later indicate that small landowners and independent peasants practiced infanticide throughout the southern part of the empire in what was then Eastern and Western Chiang-nan and Northern and Southern Ching-hu.[31]

Although direct infanticide occurred primarily through drowning, a large number of girls also died from neglect during childhood. Beginning in the twelfth century, the government began to establish foundling homes. Abandoned females had little chance of adoption, however, whereas abandoned males would be adopted by families without sons to perpetuate the family name.

That females were killed more often than males is also suggested by an order given in the thirteenth century prohibiting the killing of female babies in Ganzhou (city in Jiangxi), where it is recorded that all female infants were eliminated because the people "despised girls."[32] In addition to a daughter's inability to carry on the family name and provide the necessary worship for her parents, the expense of her dowry, and the head tax, a daughter also needed protection. After the Song scholar Cheng Yi's assertion that "to starve to death is a very minor matter, but to lose one's chastity is a major matter," an increasing emphasis was placed on women's chastity.[33] As one author asks, "Could it be that some parents, confronted with the prospect of raising a daughter who might bring shame to the family by losing her chastity, preferred to kill her rather than take the risk?"[34]

As the clan system once again became important during the Song dynasty, patriarchal figures sought to end discriminatory practices against female members. Parents were expected to regard children and women as members of the group; to do otherwise would reflect unfavorably on the clan.[35] Records that survive from the Song and later dynasties state that thirty clans had punished family members for committing what were considered "serious default of parental responsibility," including:

---

30. Eichhorn, "Some Notes on Population Control during the Sung Dynasty," p. 90.

31. Ibid., p. 89.

32. Lee, "Female Infanticide in China," p. 166.

33. Ibid., p. 175.

34. Ibid.

35. Liu Hui-chen Wang, *The Traditional Chinese Clan Rules* (Locust Valley, N.Y.: J.J. Augustin, 1959), pp. 58–59.

"infanticide of daughter by drowning"; "mistreating patrilocal fiancée of the son"; "marrying daughter off as concubine"; and "selling daughter into prostitution."[36]

A law in the Yuan dynasty (a Mongolian dynasty) punished anyone who killed a baby girl with confiscation of half their property;[37] no such law existed with reference to males, suggesting that the problem of female infanticide was more acute. T'ien Ju-k'ang contends that female infanticide was "rampant" during the Ming and Qing dynasties in China's most densely populated areas, despite the fact that

Infanticide has in fact been constantly condemned throughout Chinese history. Numerous exhortative books and tracts have been published as moral correctives and various penalties, although in general ineffectively carried out, have been imposed by successive dynasties. During the Sung [Song] Dynasty, the crime of infanticide was considered analogous to, and punished as, premeditated filicide. In the legal codes of the Yuan Dynasty, the punishment was to confiscate half of the family's property. In the Ming, the statutes of the successive rulers from 1500 to 1585 invariably made this an offence punishable by servitude on a military station one thousand *li* away from home. Many individuals also spared no personal effort, whenever possible, to reform this degenerate custom. Nonetheless, all these endeavors were entirely inadequate in proportion to the magnitude of this abominable practice.[38]

---

36. Ibid., p. 59.

37. The law stated, "Anyone who kills a baby girl is liable to have half his family property confiscated for the army." See Lee, "Female Infanticide in China," p. 166.

38. T'ien Ju-k'ang, *Male Anxiety and Female Chastity: A Comparative Study of Chinese Ethical Values in Ming-Ch'ing Times* (New York: E.J. Brill, 1988), pp. 28–30. T'ien recounts the efforts of several individuals to decrease the incidence of this practice. We mention only two here, both of which appear in ibid., p. 29. "The well-known Chia Piao of the middle of the second century A.D. devoted his strongest endeavors to the forbidding and elimination of infanticide when he was magistrate of Hsin-hi (the present Hsi County in Honan). As heavy a penalty was imposed on perpetrators of infant murder as on those convicted of any other homicide. One day, two criminal cases occurred in the district: a robber murdered someone in the southern part of the county, and a woman killed her baby in the northern part. While Chia Piao was preparing to examine the cases, his subordinates suggested that priority should be given to the case of robbery. The magistrate was indignant at this suggestion, saying it was normal for robbers to kill someone, but the crime of infanticide was in defiance of nature itself. Therefore, he went to the northern part first for the examination. The effect of Chia's open moral indignation was to induce the robber to give himself up. Within several years' time, thousands of babies were saved in Chia's district. People regarded him as a local patriarch and established the custom of calling all newborn children 'Chia's son,' or 'Chia's daughter.'" "From 1659 to 1661, Magistrate Chang Chuo-shih through strong exhortative measures saved some ten thousand baby girls in Hsiao-kan, Hupei."

Outside the town of Fuzhou in Kiangsi (Jiangxi), a stone over a small pool read, "Girls may not be drowned here."[39] A sixteenth-century observer noted, "There was also a custom in Kiangsi of killing baby girls, and as a result, there were not enough females for the males to marry at their proper age. . . . The governor asked for an imperial decree prescribing severe punishment for those practicing infanticide. Imperial permission was granted."[40]

An Italian priest who lived in China from 1583 to 1610 wrote that parents would justify killing their daughters by citing a belief in the transmigration of souls, which they claimed would enable the child to be born into a family with greater wealth.[41] Scholar-officials throughout the Qing gave accounts of the continued practice of female infanticide, leading, once again, to an imperial decree against the practice in 1697. In the eighteenth century, Jesuit missionaries were horrified to find that in Peking (Beijing) alone, several thousand babies (almost all female) were thrown into the streets like refuse, to be collected each morning by carriers who dumped them into a huge pit outside the city.[42] During this period, any family that raised two daughters was rewarded with a wooden tablet that extolled virtue.

T'ien notes that the prevalence of female infanticide in China led to other consequences in the seventeenth and eighteenth centuries: "The disproportionate ratio of the sexes resulting from female infanticide undoubtedly led to a shortage of marriageable women at a later date. Some estimates of the situation in Fukien are quite alarming. During the period 1649–59 in Chien-ning prefecture, nearly half of the male population were said to be bachelors. Later, in 1743, in the county of Te-hua, of ten male adults, six or seven remained unmarried. There is a saying in China: "'When something is scarce, it is precious.' This, however, did not apply to the situation of women in China. The 'preciousness' of females led to their being treated as assets for exploitation, no matter what their status, as maidens, wives, or widows."[43]

In the nineteenth century, anecdotal accounts of female infanticide were amply recorded by missionaries and scholars in China, as well as by

---

39. Julie Jimmerson, "Female Infanticide in China: An Examination of Cultural and Legal Norms," *Pacific Basin Law Journal*, Vol. 8, No. 1 (Spring 1990), pp. 47–79, at p. 50.

40. Quoted in T'ien, *Male Anxiety and Female Chastity*, p. 24.

41. Lee, "Female Infanticide in China," p. 167.

42. William L. Langer, "Infanticide: A Historical Survey," *History of Childhood Quarterly: The Journal of Psychohistory*, Vol. 1, No. 3 (Winter 1974), pp. 353–365.

43. T'ien, *Male Anxiety and Female Chastity*, p. 31.

the Chinese themselves. In 1838 the lieutenant-governor of Guangdong, learning that the killing of female infants was common in his province, sent instructions to all departments to put a stop to the practice.[44] One missionary, the Rev. David Abeel, attempted to determine the extent of female infanticide in the district of Tongan in Fujian Province in 1843. He found that as few as 10 percent, or as many as 70 to 80 percent of baby girls were killed, depending on the area, with little variation according to economic status.[45]

Several scholars have had some success calculating sex ratios during the Ming and Qing dynasties, despite the undercounting of females in most official records. One Chinese historian and demographer, Ho Ping-ti, has provided figures for several periods from 1368 to 1953 that show highly skewed sex ratios favoring males. While the sex ratios fluctuate to highs of 125.9 males per 100 females for Hunan in 1381 (with a children's ratio of 161.4 and an adult ratio of 109.2), the overall sex ratios for the period average 110 males per 100 females, indicating widespread female infanticide.[46] The registration of the Chinese population under the Ming emperor T'ai-tsu (1368–98) provided the first representative count; the system of registration used by the emperor was not equaled until the census of 1776. Registration during this intervening period was based on tax-paying units and was not representative of the entire population. In particular, the returns indicate a severe undercounting of females as well as an undercounting of males.

There is no countrywide sex ratio data for the Ming period; registrations from 1381 to 1391 gave accounts of the number of households, number of mouths, and size of landholdings, but did not always reveal the gender of the population. A few surviving provincial or county histories do provide such data, which suggest the presence of sex-selective practices that led to more males than females. Registration laws changed in 1391, however, to include the gender of the population to ensure that males would be enlisted in labor services once they reached 16 years of age. Because the registration's emphasis was on males, females were severely underregistered. To avoid labor service, males were also underregistered. Thus the enumerations after 1391 do not accurately reflect the actual population.

A famine in 1775 in Hupei (Hubei) alerted the emperor to the degree

---

44. Lee, "Female Infanticide in China," p. 168.

45. Ibid., p. 169.

46. Ho Ping-ti, *Studies on the Population of China, 1368–1953* (Cambridge, Mass.: Harvard University Press, 1959).

of underregistration in the province, and potentially in the country: The number of people in need of relief exceeded the registered population by 100,000.[47] A new system of registration was devised, with severe punishment for falsification of numbers. Registration would no longer be linked to the *ting*—the identification of males between the ages of 16 and 60 who were required to pay a labor tax through service. Yet underregistration continued in rural areas, particularly in the south. Records from 1776 to 1850 still point to some underregistration, particularly of females, but the low number of females may also reflect the widespread practice of female infanticide during the Ming and Qing dynasties. In other areas, the high sex ratios were due to an influx of male migrants who worked the fields, resulting in areas with two to three times the expected number of males to females.[48] The dearth of women, coupled with the practice of taking concubines, led to a large number of males unable to find wives. Eighteenth-century officials such as Chen Hongmou and Zhu Chun noted that in Jiangsu, local bullies abducted young widows as brides. This period was characterized as "an endemic 'marriage crunch' felt most keenly by lower class males" (see Table 4.1).[49]

Population data after 1851 are difficult to interpret. Following the outbreak of the Taiping Rebellion in 1851, the registration system became synonymous with enlisting men for militia service.[50] In Shanghai, for example, registration was not required of the wealthy, or great clans; it covered only poor adult males who could not escape military service. Women and children were left out of the registrations; thus late nineteenth-century enumerations again show ratios of more than 400 males per 100 females in some areas.[51] Through his analysis of household data from nineteenth-century Qing China, Gilbert Rozman concludes that the figures provide a reasonably accurate account of the age and sex distribution of the population in Chihli and Shantung, which may suggest regional patterns in the north of China at that time. In Shantung (Shandong) Province in 1837, the sex ratio for adults in one county was 134 males per 100 females; in the same county that year, the sex ratio for children was 147. Overall sex ratios in Chihli Province were 117 for adults and 124 for children; in Shantung Province, sex ratios averaged 112 for

---

47. Ibid., p. 47.

48. Ibid., p. 57.

49. Walter, "Infanticide and Dowry in Ming and Early Qing China," pp. 193–217.

50. Ho, *Studies on the Population of China, 1368–1953*, pp. 67–68.

51. For example, the sex ratio for children in Ch'ang-hsing in Chekiang was 431.9 males per 100 females. See ibid., p. 68.

Table 4.1. Male and Female Population Sizes and Sex Ratios in China, Selected Provinces, 1773–1833.

Province	Year	Total Population	Sex Ratio	Males	Females	Place
Chihli	1778	20,746,519	118.8	11,264,563	9,481,956	
Chihli	1773	1,432,031	120.6	782,878	649,153	Yung-p'ing P
Chihli	1777	196,576	108.3	102,204	94,372	Yung-ch'ing C
Shantung	1837	4,086,511	111.5	2,154,354	1,932,157	Chi-nan P
Shantung	1826	400,237	115.7	214,684	185,553	Chi-ning C
Shensi	1803	93,990	126.7	52,530	41,460	Lo-ch'uan C
Shensi	1784	234,456	125.0	130,253	104,203	Chou-chih C
Shensi	1783	158,310	154.2	96,032	62,278	Ch'eng-ch'eng C
Shensi	1829	115,392	156.4	70,387	45,005	Ning-shan-t'ing C
Kiangsu	1820	5,908,436	134.4	3,387,772	2,520,664	Su-chou P
Kiangsu	1793	525,617	135.1	302,045	223,572	Ch'ang-shu
Kiangsu	1816	2,472,974	128.1	1,388,812	1,084,162	Sung-chiang P
Kiangsu	1816	261,898	131.1	148,571	113,327	Feng-hsien C
Chekiang	1785	513,878	118.3	278,478	235,400	I-wu C
Anhwei	1826	617,111	120.7	337,496	279,615	She-hsien C
Kwangsi	1835	877,337	109.5	458,560	418,777	Hsun-chou P
Yunnan	1845	95,451	110.9	50,192	45,259	Ta-yao C
Szechwan	1843	2,071,695	112.8	1,098,154	973,541	Ch'ung-ch'ing P
Szechwan	1814	184,679	107.2	95,548	89,131	San-t'ai C
Szechwan	1795	135,788	101.1	68,265	67,523	Ch'iung-chou
Szechwan	1810	134,488	111.5	70,900	63,588	Pi-hsien C
Szechwan	1815	386,397	125.7	215,198	171,199	Ch'eng-tu C
Szechwan	1833	113,963	116.5	61,324	52,639	Shih-ch'uan C
Total		**41,763,734**	**120.6**	**22,829,204**	**18,934,530**	

SOURCE: Ho Ping-ti, *Studies on the Population of China, 1368–1953* (Cambridge, Mass.: Harvard University Press, 1959), pp. 58–59.
"P" refers to prefecture, and "C" refers to county.

adults and 119 for children.[52] Later, in 1877, sex ratios were even higher. In his study of 435 settlements in Hebei, Rozman found that twenty-one settlements had adult sex ratios of 160 or greater, and ninety-five settlements had either no girls at all or sex ratios greater than 160. The overall sex ratio in Chihli in 1877 was 119 for adults and 120 for children.[53] Figures for 1906, however, provide only a partial picture of China's population and point to a severe undercounting of both males and females. The only girls under the age of 15 included in the count were those few

52. Gilbert Rozman, *Population and Marketing Settlements in Ch'ing China* (New York: Cambridge University Press, 1982), p. 75.

53. Ibid., pp. 49–51.

who were already married.[54] Attempts to enumerate the entire population were not made until the twentieth century.

Because few studies of China's imperial population provide accounts of infant mortality, we can only presume that given the high child sex ratios, females were not only the victims of direct infanticide but also experienced indirect infanticide through neglect. In their study of the population of the province of Liaoning from 1774 to 1873, James Lee, Cameron Campbell, and Guofu Tan were able to derive accounts of infant mortality (including differential mortality of females) and fertility, revealing that both mortality and fertility were responsive to changes in economic circumstances.[55] As Lee and his coauthors suggest, "The Chinese apparently regarded infanticide as a form of postnatal abortion through which they could choose the number, spacing, and sex of their children in response to short-term economic conditions as well as their long-term family-planning goals."[56] An analysis of population data for these years indicates marked differences in mortality rates and life expectancies for males and females. Life tables computed from data collected over a seventy-year period indicate that females had a shorter life expectancy than males for the first thirty-five years of life, after which life expectancies were similar for both genders. For example, for children ages 1–5, life expectancy for females was 28.0 years, but life expectancy for males was 35.2.[57] In times categorized as economically hard, Lee, Campbell, and Tan found that life expectancy dropped dramatically for females and less dramatically for males: Females ages 1–5 had a life expectancy of 18.4 years, while males had a life expectancy of 28.9 years.[58]

The pattern of mortality in Liaoning Province, the authors suggest, indicates a system of resource allocation in which females are given a much smaller share. Information regarding mortality in the first year of life is not available because children under Chinese age 2 were not registered. (In Chinese reckoning, when a child is born, he or she is 1 year of age.) In fact, the average age upon registration in the province was 6.[59] Children who died before they reached this age, particularly female children, were not registered. Thus Lee, Campbell, and Tan note that mor-

---

54. Ibid., p. 144.

55. Lee, Campbell, and Tan, "Infanticide and Family Planning in Late Imperial China," p. 146.

56. Ibid., p. 147.

57. Ibid., p. 152.

58. Ibid., pp. 153–154.

59. Ibid., p. 150.

tality rates in the first year of life were probably much higher than the registered population indicates. The imbalance in mortality is exhibited in the sex ratios of children during this period.[60] In single-child families, the sex ratio was 576 males per 100 females. For two-child families, the sex ratio was 211 for the first child and 450 for the second child. For families with three children, the sex ratio was 156 for the first child, 294 for the second child, and 324 for the third child. Similar sex ratios were observed for families with four children, but sex ratios were lower for families with five or more children (from a sex ratio of 88 for the first child to 162 for the fifth child).[61] Although some of the missing females may be explained by underregistration, as Lee and his coauthors note, "The closer a girl's birth order was to the completed family size, the less likely she was to survive to registration. The pattern is too systematic to be explained by registration."[62] Thus wide-scale female infanticide and neglect of females seem to be the cause of the observed high sex ratios in the province.

Whether a girl survived infancy in Liaoning depended on the desired family size and composition, family wealth, and general economic conditions. Prices of essential food items varied according to weather and harvest yields in the area. Increases in prices of grains appear to have affected the availability of food in Liaoning, and in turn influenced population behavior. Fertility decisions were made at the time of birth rather than at conception. If prices were high, then fewer children were allowed to live, particularly fewer female children, unless the family was wealthy and not as affected by food prices.[63]

In another study, James Lee, Wang Feng, and Cameron Campbell examine Qing nobility and find that even daughters in comfortable circumstances were not immune to active or passive infanticide. They determine that as many as one-tenth of all daughters of the imperial lineage fell victim to these practices, and that in the late eighteenth century in particular, as many as one-fifth were killed.[64]

Map 4.2 displays what we know about the regional incidence of female infanticide in the Song and Qing dynasties. A province is shaded

---

60. The calculations for sex ratios by birth order are for families that registered their children between 1792 and 1840. Registrations after 1840 were not included because of underregistration of females after that time. See ibid., p. 154.

61. Ibid.

62. Ibid., p. 156.

63. Ibid., p. 167.

64. James Lee, Wang Feng, and Cameron Campbell, "Infant and Child Mortality among Qing Nobility: Implications for Two Types of Positive Checks," *Population Studies*, Vol. 48 (1994), pp. 395–411.

Map 4.2. Female Infanticide in the Song and Qing Dynasties.

only if there is reliable historical evidence of the practice. Thus it is still possible that female infanticide may have taken place in the unshaded provinces.

Twentieth-Century Changes

Equality, including gender equality, was one of the primary aims of the communist revolution of 1949. As the government put it, "The People's Republic of China shall abolish the feudal system that fettered women. Women shall enjoy equal rights with men in all spheres of life, political, economic, cultural and social, including family life. Men and women shall enjoy the freedom to choose their own spouse."[65]

---

65. Information Office of the State Council, *Protection of Chinese Women's Rights and Interests* (Beijing: New Star, 1993), pp. 1–2.

The Chinese communist revolutionaries recognized the marriage issue for its political importance in the context of high sex ratios. In the Kiangsi Soviet period of the early 1930s, Mao Zedong proclaimed that the communist revolution would liberate concubines, who would then be free to marry, as Judith Stacey puts it, "the 30 percent of poor peasant and artisan men, the 90 percent of the lumpen proletariat, and the 99 percent of the hired farm hands in Kiangsi whom Mao estimated to be bachelors."[66] With the new Marriage Law, drafted in 1949, the Chinese government attempted to abolish concubinage, dowries, female infanticide, selling of children (particularly daughters), prostitution, and the general subordination of women through patriarchal structures.

The communist revolution declared equality for men and women; its effect on the treatment of women, however, was mixed. For example, equal access to education as a principle of law resulted in equal rates of enrollment in primary education for boys and girls. The Marriage Law of 1949 also gave women the right to hold and inherit property, but in reality, there was little recognition of the law.[67] Another mixed example involves the freedom to choose one's spouse. Instead of the former system in which marriage was an arranged contract between families, it was now seen as a voluntary contract between two individuals, but with some unforeseen consequences in the early years. Women who had been married prior to 1950 by arranged marriage could divorce their husbands, although attempting to do so led to violence against women from husbands unwilling to accept the law. On the other hand, some women found themselves in the position of unwanted spouse by husbands seeking a divorce. Women who were reluctant to end their marriages were turned over to village militia by their husbands and subjected to violence for opposing the new law and the Chinese revolution.[68] In the first year of the Marriage Law, more than 10,000 women were killed in South China; 11,500 women were killed in East China from 1950 to 1952; and China-wide figures reached 70,000–80,000 deaths per year from marriage-related issues.[69]

---

66. Judith Stacey, *Patriarchy and Socialist Revolution in China* (Berkeley: University of California Press, 1983), p. 161.

67. Bossen, "Women and Development," pp. 302–303; and Rubie S. Watson, "Afterword: Marriage and Gender Inequality," in Watson and Patricia Buckley Ebrey, *Marriage and Inequality in Chinese Society* (Berkeley: University of California Press, 1991), p. 362.

68. Bossen, "Women and Development," p. 303.

69. Kazuko Ono, *Chinese Women in a Century of Revolution, 1850–1950* (Stanford, Calif.: Stanford University Press, 1989), p. 181, quoted in ibid.

Other mixed results could be found in the area of labor. Rural women were provided opportunities to participate in collective-labor organizations, where they worked alongside men, earning points from the collective (although women's points were typically fewer [or worth less] than points earned by men for the same work). However, this labor was in addition to their domestic labor of hauling water, tending fires, doing laundry, and participating in cottage industries.[70] Urban women, on the other hand, were given access to the industrial labor force, where they were likely to be assigned to small industries with fewer benefits than those offered to men in larger industries.[71] China is extremely proud of the participation of its women in the labor force. In 1999, women constituted 46.5 percent of the workforce, and women's income was 80.4 percent of men's income.[72]

The reforms made on behalf of women have had mixed effects on the degree to which women are able to control their own lives. Women may work in the fields, but have little control over the land that they farm—land is still allocated to households headed by married males and cannot be purchased or sold to others.[73] Yet women have gained the ability to control their own money and choose their occupations. With regard to choices concerning their own bodies, however, women lost control over family planning in the late 1970s.

Despite some government attempts to improve women's lives and increase their value within the family and community, the continuing practice of female infanticide and high mortality levels for female infants indicate that women continue to be undervalued. Data on infant mortality rates since 1957 show that females have higher mortality rates in the first year of life.[74] Figures from the 1982 One-per-Thousand fertility survey, as well as the 1988 Two-per-Thousand survey, demonstrate a pattern of sex ratios at birth that show normal rates only over a brief period in the 1960s (see Figure 4.1). As the graph shows, the sex ratio reported for births remained consistently above the normal level of 105. Given that sex-selective abortion was not practiced at this time (the technology was

---

70.   Ibid., p. 304.

71.   Ibid., p. 305.

72.   We obtained these statistics from a Chinese government white paper released December 18, 2000. See "China's Population and Development in the 21st Century," Information Office of the State Council of the People's Republic of China, Beijing, December 18, 2000, http://www.china.org.cn/e-white/21st/.

73. Bossen, "Women and Development," pp. 307–308.

74.   Yasuko Hayase and Seiko Kawamata, *Population Policy and Vital Statistics in China* (Tokyo: Institute of Developing Economies, 1991), p. 66.

Figure 4.1. Sex Ratio at Birth in China According to Fertility Surveys, 1936–40 to 1985–88.

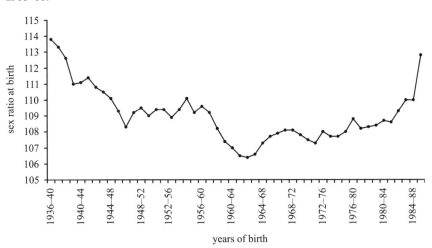

years of birth

SOURCE: 1982 One-per-Thousand Fertility Survey; 1988 Two-per-Thousand Fertility Survey; and 1990 Census Data, reported in Ansley J. Coale, "Excess Ratio of Males to Females by Birth Cohort in the Census of China 1953 to 1990 and in the Births Reported in the Fertility Surveys, 1982 and 1988," OPR Working Paper No. 93-6 (Princeton, N.J.: Office for Population Research, Princeton University, July 1993), Table 4.

not yet available), what can account for the high sex ratios at birth? The fertility surveys for 1982 and 1988 asked a large sample of married women (311,000 aged 15–67 in 1982 and 459,000 aged 15–57 in 1988) about their own birth and the births of each of their children. Ansley Coale suggests that when asked about the births of their children, the respondents did not include births of infants who had died in the first year of life; thus the sex ratios are more indicative of surviving infants' ratios than of sex ratios at birth.[75] The high sex ratios must therefore mean that a high proportion of female infants were dying within the first year of life. Terence Hull, who argues that the sex ratios at birth were closer to the expected norm, suggests that female infants "died soon after birth as a result of deliberate action by parents or through neglect to the point of fatal illness."[76] Female infanticide accounts for the high sex ratios from

75. Ansley J. Coale, "Excess Ratio of Males to Females by Birth Cohort in the Census of China 1953 to 1990 and in the Births Reported in the Fertility Surveys, 1982 and 1988," OPR Working Paper No. 93–6 (Princeton, N.J.: Office for Population Research, Princeton University, July 1993).

76. Terence H. Hull, "Recent Trends in Sex Ratios at Birth in China," *Population and Development Review*, Vol. 16, No. 1 (March 1990), p. 72.

1936 to the 1980s; thus despite beliefs that the communist revolution altered attitudes toward gender and put an end to female infanticide, the practice persisted.

The One-Child Policy and Son Preference

China's first national census, taken in 1953, recorded a population of 583 million, but by 1975, the population was estimated to be more than 900 million. The following factors caused the government to reexamine Mao's assertion that more children would lead to a stronger nation: the large increase in population between the 1950s and early 1970s; the famine of the early 1960s; a lack of housing, food, and jobs; and the declining health of the population.[77] In the early 1970s, the government adopted a policy known as *wan, xi, shao* ("later, farther apart, and fewer") and encouraged couples to limit the number of children to two (in urban areas) or three (in rural areas).[78] This policy was then adapted in 1979, when China introduced the strategic demographic initiative known as the "one-child policy," which aimed to reduce population growth. The one-child policy was part of a family planning law to be presented to the Fifth National People's Congress in 1980, but it was not formally enacted until the twenty-fifth session of the Standing Committee of the National People's Congress in December 2001. Although the one-child policy did not become a law until September 2002, from 1979 on government at all levels throughout China acted as though the policy were law and attempted to enforce its rules and penalties. Family planning has become a fundamental part of Chinese life and is even written into the constitution, which states that it is the duty of a husband and wife to practice family planning, and that their rights may not infringe on the interests of the state, the society, or the collective.[79]

The 2002 Population and Family Planning Law states that couples can have only one child. A second child, if requested, may be arranged

---

77. Mao reasoned that "every mouth comes with two hands." Cited in Lisa B. Gregory, "Examining the Economic Component of China's One-Child Family Policy under International Law," *Journal of Chinese Law,* Vol. 6, No. 1 (Spring 1992), p. 48. Another popular slogan following the 1949 revolution was, "The more babies the more glorious are their mothers." Cited in Li Xiaorong, "License to Coerce: Violence against Women, State Responsibility, and Legal Failures in China's Family-Planning Program," *Yale Journal of Law and Feminism,* Vol. 8, No. 1 (Summer 1996), p. 148.

78. Li, "License to Coerce," p. 148.

79. Lisa B. Gregory, "Examining the Economic Component of China's One-Child Family Policy under International Law: Your Money or Your Life," *Journal of Chinese Law,* Vol. 6, No. 1 (Spring 1992), pp. 50–51.

but is "subject to law and regulation."[80] The circumstances under which couples may actually be permitted to have a second child are unclear. Under the previous one-child policy, regulations regarding fertility varied in rural and urban areas. In urban areas, the one-child policy was applied with strictness, whereas in rural areas the policy was to encourage one birth, control second births, and prevent third births. Even this policy varied depending on the gender of the births. A woman with two daughters was often permitted the chance to have a third child in the hope that it would be a boy. Other exceptions to the rule of the one-child policy were made for parents whose first child had a nonhereditary disability, for parents who were both the only child of their parents, for spouses who had both returned from overseas, for minorities, and for residents of regions where there was a shortage of labor.[81] The legal marriage age in China is 20 for women and 22 for men; in rural areas, however, men were not permitted to marry until age 25, and women could marry only when they reached 23. Also in rural areas, first children could follow immediately after marriage, but subsequent children had to be spaced four years apart.[82] Most universities prohibited undergraduates from marrying and placed limits even on the marriage of graduate students. Failure to follow these rules resulted in heavy fines, ranging from a one-time payment to payments over several years.[83] Couples who had unauthorized children could also be denied government aid, such as poverty assistance, access to farming materials, technology training programs, and even health care

---

80. Article 18 of the 2002 Population and Family Planning Law declares: "The state shall maintain its current fertility policy encouraging late marriage and child bearing and advocating one child per couple; arrangements for a second child, if requested, being subject to law and regulation. Specific measures shall be enacted by the People's Congress or its standing committee in each province, autonomous region, and municipality. Ethnic minorities shall also practice family planning. Population and Family Planning Law of the People's Republic of China, http://www.unescap.org/pop/database/law_china/ch_record052.htm.

81. Li, "License to Coerce," p. 154.

82. Sulamith Heins Potter, "Birth Planning in Rural China: A Cultural Account," in Nancy Scheper-Hughes, ed., *Child Survival: Anthropological Perspectives on the Treatment and Maltreatment of Children* (Dordrecht, Netherlands: D. Reidel, 1987), pp. 41–42.

83. Nicholas D. Kristof and Sheryl WuDunn provide the following example of a man who failed to space his children four years apart. In 1983, following the birth of a second child three years after his first child was born, a grade school teacher was fined $2,456 by the government. This fine was seventeen times the teacher's annual salary at the time. For the next ten years, 80 percent of the teacher's salary was deducted to pay the fine. For similar stories, see Kristof and WuDunn, *China Wakes: The Struggle for the Soul of a Rising Power* (New York: Vintage, 1994), pp. 237–239.

and education for the children.[84] It is too early to determine whether the penalties under the new family planning law will be the same as those in the past.

Since the one-child initiative was introduced, China's birth rate has decreased and the use of birth control, including sterilizations, intrauterine devices, and abortions, has greatly increased.[85] The number of killed or abandoned infants, particularly female infants, however, has also risen, so much so that the 2001 Marriage Law and the 2002 Population and Family Planning Law both contain prohibitions against infanticide.[86] Li Xiaorong argues that local government policies and campaigns have exacerbated the problem of female infanticide and abandonment of infant girls by forcibly detaining women for abortions and sterilizations, demolishing houses, and generally terrorizing women.[87] It is not simply parents who are making decisions regarding family planning; in some cases, local family planning officials have the last word. Article 22 of the Population and Family Planning Law in fact points to the mistreatment of even the mothers who give birth to females: "Discrimination against and mistreatment of women who give birth to female children or who suffer from infertility are prohibited. Discrimination against, mistreatment, and abandonment of female infants are prohibited."

The one-child policy has reinforced the tradition of son preference. To understand the people's response to China's family planning policies, we must understand the role of children—in particular, sons—within the Chinese family, and examine the politics surrounding the difficult reproductive decisions of parents.

---

84. Li, "License to Coerce," pp. 158–159.

85. For a discussion of the increase in abortion rates, sterilizations, and birth control, see H. Yuan Tien, Zhang Tianlu, Ping Yu, Li Jingneng, and Liang Zhongtang, "China's Demographic Dilemmas," *Population Bulletin,* Vol. 47, No. 1 (June 1992), p. 12. The central government's resolutions regarding the one-child policy outline the following: Couples must apply for a birth permit before trying to conceive; following the birth of the permitted number of children, at least one spouse has to use contraception and women are required to use an intrauterine device; and any unauthorized pregnancies, especially after the birth of the permitted number of children, must be terminated, or, if the birth occurs, one spouse must be sterilized. See Li, "License to Coerce," pp. 152–153.

86. Article 21 of the 2002 Marriage Law states that "infant drowning, deserting and any other acts causing serious harm to infants and infanticide shall be prohibited." Marriage Law of the People's Republic of China, http://www.fmprc.gov.cn/eng/28840.html. Population and Family Planning Law of the People's Republic of China, http://www.unescap.org/pop/database/law_china/ch_record052.htm.

87. Li, "License to Coerce," pp. 145–191.

In Chinese culture, children are viewed as the means of family continuity, the basis of prosperity, and the source of care for the aged. Caring for the financial needs of parents is one of the primary roles of sons. Daughters do not play a role in carrying on the family name, nor is their labor thought to be equally valuable, although in some cases women produce and earn more than men.

The need to produce sons is particularly evident in rural areas, where males are considered more valuable as laborers. The system of farming adopted in the 1970s changed the focus from the collective to the family. Families with sons seem to have an economic advantage because males are given tasks of heavy agricultural work and also handle disputes over land boundaries or allocation of resources. Females, on the other hand, are given less strenuous farming jobs not considered as valuable to the family's welfare.[88] As H. Yuan Tien notes, "This preference for male children, contrary to the explanation offered most often by scholars and others in China, is not simply an expression of feudalistic mentality. It is very much dictated by highly labor-intensive agricultural and related pursuits. Even during the days of collective farming under the People's Commune, more males enabled a family to earn more work points and, hence, to better its standard of living."[89]

There are additional economic advantages to having sons in rural areas: At least 90 percent of rural populations are pensionless and must rely on sons to meet the economic needs of aged parents.[90] A daughter typically marries and then moves into the home of her husband's family, where she becomes responsible for the care of her in-laws. Anthropologist Sulamith Heins Potter describes living conditions for those without children who rely on government support as "pitiable," adding that these old men and women live in decrepit buildings with little food and must depend on the goodwill of neighbors to provide water and fuel.[91]

---

88. See ibid., p. 173. In their research in rural China, Susan Greenhalgh and Li Jiali also found that because "village culture continued to see women and girls as lesser beings, girls were restricted from engaging in some crucial agricultural activities, making sons prized members of the family labor force." See Greenhalgh and Li, "Engendering Reproductive Practice in Peasant China: The Political Roots of the Rising Sex Ratios at Birth," Working Paper No. 57 (Beijing: Population Council Research Division, 1993), p. 15.

89. H. Yuan Tien, *China's Strategic Demographic Initiative* (New York: Praeger, 1991), p. 202.

90. Potter, "Birth Planning in Rural China," p. 35.

91. Ibid.

The Rising Sex Ratio at Birth

As a result of the one-child policy and the politics surrounding it, sex ratios at birth in China have increased greatly. As discussed previously, the sex ratios at birth between 1936 and 1989 reported in the 1982 and 1988 fertility surveys stayed above the expected norm of 105–107. According to Chinese demographers, the sex ratio at birth between 1970 and 1980 remained close to normal levels; since that time, however, sex ratios have risen well above the norm and are still increasing. Yet the precise sex ratio at birth is difficult to ascertain. Unlike India, where data on number and sex of births are not collected by census surveyors, they are collected in China. Unlike India, however, where each member of the population is counted, censuses in China are actually samplings of the population. The Fourth National Population Census of July 1, 1990, was merely a 10 percent sample, as was the 2000 census. Figures for 1995 are based on a 1.04 percent sample survey, and 1994 figures are taken from a 0.63 percent sample survey. Because these small sample surveys may not accurately represent the population of China, calculations based on them are imprecise.

Figure 4.2, based on calculations by Chinese demographers Gu Baochang and Li Yongping, depicts the rising sex ratio at birth for the total population of China. Since 1980 and the implementation of the one-child policy, sex ratios at birth have continued to rise. In some areas, the sex ratio is rising to much higher levels than the figure suggests, and in other areas, the sex ratio at birth is closer to the norm.

Table 4.2 shows a breakdown of the sex ratio at birth in the years 1982, 1989, and 1995, according to province, autonomous region, and municipality. As the table shows, the birth sex ratios in China have increased from 108.5 to 115.6, with sex ratios exhibited as high as 130.3 in one province in 1995. Unlike India, where there was a marked difference between north and south, the only difference we find in China is in the outlying autonomous regions of Guizhou, Tibet, and Xinjiang, which, for reasons we discuss later, consistently exhibit birth sex ratios within or below the norm.

Using the sex ratios at birth and the totals for male and female births, it is possible to calculate and then compare the number of missing females from China's birth population (see Table 4.3). For example, in 1985 the overall sex ratio at birth was 111.4, and there were 11.6 million male births and 10.42 million female births. Using an expected birth sex ratio of 105, 11.05 million females should have been born, suggesting that there are 628,000 females missing from the population that year. Between 1985

Figure 4.2. Sex Ratio at Birth in China 1980–95.

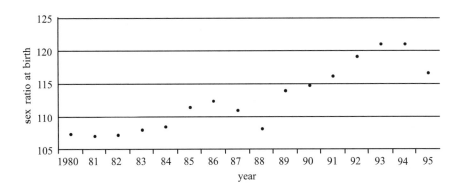

SOURCES: 1980–91: Gu Baochang and Krishna Roy, "Sex Ratio at Birth in China, with Reference to Other Areas in East Asia: What We Know," *Asia-Pacific Population Journal*, Vol. 10, No. 3 (September 1995), p. 20, Table 1; 1992–95: China, State Family Planning Commission, *China Birth Planning Yearbook*, Beijing, 1996, p. 483, reported in William Lavely, "Unintended Consequences of China's Birth Planning Policy," University of Washington, July 14, 1997.

and 1995, the number of missing females ranges from 342,000 to 1.47 million, which represents 3 to 15 percent of female births. In total, 10.68 million females are missing from China's birth population during this period.

The number of births in China has remained relatively constant since 1981, with 20–25 million births each year, but because the sex ratio has increased steadily in this same period, the number of missing females has also increased. In Tables 4.4 and 4.5, the missing female population is examined for 1989 and 1995 births, showing the increase in the number of missing females from 700,000 to 800,000. Based on the data available since 1995, an average of more than 1 million females are "missing" each year from the birth population alone.

A strong regional pattern of high sex ratios and missing females emerges from the north coastal province of Liaoning to the southern coastal province of Guangxi, and to the south-central province of Sichuan. All the provinces covered in this area exhibit high sex ratios at birth and also contribute the greater percentages to the total missing female population in China. In addition to geographic variations in sex ratios at birth, other factors, including education and ethnicity, play a role in sex ratio variations among localities. In their analysis of 1990 figures, Gu Baochang and Xu Yi suggest that the regions that exhibit normal sex

Table 4.2. Sex Ratios at Birth in China by Region, 1982–95.

Region	1982	1989	1995
China	**108.5**	**111.3**	**115.6**
Beijing	107.0	107.1	112.4
Tianjin	107.7	110.4	110.5
Hebei	108.2	110.9	115.2
Shanxi	109.4	110.1	112.0
Inner Mongolia	106.8	108.5	110.0
Liaoning	107.1	110.5	111.4
Jilin	107.8	107.8	109.6
Heilongjiang	106.9	107.3	110.0
Shanghai	105.4	104.1	104.8
Jiangsu	107.9	113.8	123.4
Zhejiang	108.8	116.7	115.2
Anhui	112.5	111.3	116.4
Fujian	108.6	109.9	122.3
Jiangxi	107.9	110.4	115.4
Shandong	109.9	115.0	118.8
Henan	110.3	116.2	126.7
Hubei	107.0	109.5	130.3
Hunan	107.6	110.1	116.4
Guangdong	110.5	111.3	123.1
Guangxi	110.7	117.4	119.1
Hainan	—	116.1	124.5
Sichuan	108.0	112.1	110.1
Guizhou	106.8	103.4	99.1
Yunnan	106.2	107.3	108.5
Tibet	101.3	103.6	100.7
Shaanxi	109.2	110.3	123.1
Gansu	106.3	108.4	108.6
Qinghai	106.2	104.6	107.1
Ningxia	106.2	109.7	107.4
Xinjiang	106.1	104.1	102.0

SOURCES: 1982—China, Population Census Office under the State Council and the Department of Population Statistics of the State Statistical Bureau, *The 1982 Population Census of China (Major Figures)* (Hong Kong: Economic Information Agency, 1982); 1989—China, State Statistical Bureau, *10 Percent Sampling Tabulation on the 1990 Population Census of the People's Republic of China* (Beijing: China Statistics Press, 1991); 1995 sex ratio at birth for China is from China, State Statistical Bureau, *China Population Statistical Yearbook, 1996* (Beijing: China Statistics Press, 1996); and regional figures are from the 1995 1 Percent Population Sample Survey in China, State Statistical Bureau, *China Population Statistical Yearbook, 1997* (Beijing: China Statistics Press, 1997), Table 2-32.

Table 4.3. Missing Females in China's Birth Population, 1985–95.

Year	Sex Ratio at Birth	Number of Births	Males	Females	Expected Females	Missing Females	Missing Females (%)
1985	111.4	22,020,000	11,600,000	10,420,000	11,047,619	627,619	6.0
1986	112.3	23,840,000	12,610,000	11,230,000	12,009,524	779,524	6.9
1987	111.0	25,220,000	13,270,000	11,950,000	12,638,095	688,095	5.8
1988	108.1	24,570,000	12,760,000	11,810,000	12,152,381	342,381	2.9
1989	113.9	24,070,000	12,820,000	11,250,000	12,209,524	959,524	8.5
1990	114.7	23,910,000	12,770,000	11,140,000	12,161,905	1,021,905	9.2
1991	116.1	22,580,000	12,130,000	10,450,000	11,552,381	1,102,381	10.5
1992	119.0	21,190,000	11,510,000	9,680,000	10,961,905	1,281,905	13.2
1993	121.0	21,260,000	11,640,000	9,620,000	11,085,714	1,465,714	15.2
1994	121.0	21,040,000	11,520,000	9,520,000	10,971,429	1,451,429	15.2
1995	115.6	20,630,000	11,060,000	9,570,000	10,533,333	963,333	10.1
1985–95	114.7	250,330,000	133,690,000	116,640,000	127,323,810	10,683,810	9.2

SOURCES: 1985–90 sex ratios at birth are from Gu Baochang and Krishna Roy, "Sex Ratio at Birth in China, with Reference to Other Areas in Asia: What We Know," *Asia-Pacific Population Journal*, Vol. 10, No. 3 (September 1995), p. 20; 1991–94 sex ratios at birth are from William Lavely, "Unintended Consequences of China's Birth Planning Policy," University of Washington, July 14, 1997; and 1985–95 birth totals and 1995 sex ratios at birth are from China, State Statistical Bureau, *China Population Statistical Yearbook, 1996* (Beijing: China Statistics Press, 1996), p. 372.

Table 4.4. Missing Females among China's Birth Population by Province, 1989 (a 10 percent sample of the population).

Region	Males	Females	Sex Ratio	Expected Females	Missing Females	Contribution to Missing Females (%)	Missing Females (%)
China	**1,299,880**	**1,168,165**	**111.28**	**1,238,032**	**69,867**	**100**	**6.0**
Beijing	8,003	7,469	107.15	7,622	153	0.2	2.0
Tianjin	7,682	6,959	110.39	7,316	357	0.5	5.1
Hebei	69,616	62,756	110.93	66,300	3,544	5.1	5.6
Shanxi	34,039	30,904	110.14	32,417	1,513	2.2	4.9
Inner Mongolia	21,878	20,156	108.54	20,836	680	1.0	3.4
Liaoning	33,261	30,104	110.49	31,678	1,574	2.3	5.2
Jilin	25,355	23,524	107.78	24,147	623	0.9	2.6
Heilongjiang	33,055	30,797	107.33	31,480	683	1.0	2.2
Shanghai	8,224	7,897	104.14	7,832	−65	−0.1	−0.8
Jiangsu	74,182	65,185	113.80	70,648	5,463	7.8	8.4
Zhejiang	33,623	28,805	116.73	32,023	3,218	4.6	11.2
Anhui	73,090	65,642	111.35	69,612	3,970	5.7	6.0
Fujian	38,353	34,905	109.88	36,527	1,622	2.3	4.6
Jiangxi	48,024	43,516	110.36	45,737	2,221	3.2	5.1
Shandong	90,205	78,444	114.99	85,907	7,463	10.7	9.5
Henan	121,502	104,553	116.21	115,715	11,162	16.0	10.7
Hubei	70,131	64,019	109.55	66,793	2,774	4.0	4.3
Hunan	76,482	69,490	110.06	72,839	3,349	4.8	4.8
Guangdong	76,047	68,352	111.26	72,427	4,075	5.8	6.0
Guangxi	52,194	44,447	117.43	49,709	5,262	7.5	11.8

Table 4.4. (continued)

Region	Males	Females	Sex Ratio	Expected Females	Missing Females	Contribution to Missing Females (%)	Missing Females (%)
Guangxi	52,194	44,447	117.43	49,709	5,262	7.5	11.8
Hainan	8,608	7,417	116.06	8,198	781	1.1	10.5
Sichuan	102,953	91,817	112.13	98,052	6,235	8.9	6.8
Guizhou	40,482	39,139	103.43	38,554	−585	−0.8	−1.5
Yunnan	45,194	42,126	107.28	43,041	915	1.3	2.2
Tibet	3,478	3,356	103.64	3,313	−43	−0.1	−1.3
Shaanxi	42,429	38,484	110.25	40,408	1,924	2.8	5.0
Gansu	29,461	27,183	108.38	28,058	875	1.3	3.2
Qinghai	5,337	5,102	104.61	5,083	−19	0.0	−0.4
Ningxia	6,174	5,628	109.70	5,880	252	0.4	4.5
Xinjiang	20,818	19,989	104.15	19,827	−162	−0.2	−0.8

SOURCE: Figures are based on the 10 percent Fourth National Population Census on July 1, 1990—China, State Statistical Bureau, *China Population Statistical Yearbook, 1991* (Beijing: China Statistics Press, 1991).

Table 4.5. Missing Females among China's Birth Population by Province, 1995 (a 1.04 percent sample of the population).

Region	Males	Females	Sex Ratio	Expected Females	Missing Females	Contribution to Missing Females (%)	Missing Females (%)
China	**95,144**	**82,293**	**115.62**	**90,616**	**8,323**	**100.0**	**10.1**
Beijing	562	459	122.44	535	76	0.9	16.6
Tianjin	496	449	110.47	472	23	0.3	5.2
Hebei	4,249	3,687	115.24	4,047	360	4.3	9.8
Shanxi	2,760	2,464	112.01	2,629	165	2.0	6.7
Inner Mongolia	1,917	1,743	109.98	1,826	83	1.0	4.7
Liaoning	2,720	2,441	111.43	2,590	149	1.8	6.1
Jilin	1,794	1,637	109.59	1,709	72	0.9	4.4
Heilongjiang	2,627	2,389	109.96	2,502	113	1.4	4.7
Shanghai	455	434	104.84	433	−1	0.0	−0.2
Jiangsu	4,832	3,915	123.42	4,602	687	8.3	17.5
Zhejiang	3,003	2,607	115.19	2,860	253	3.0	9.7
Anhui	5,116	4,396	116.38	4,872	476	5.7	10.8
Fujian	2,485	2,032	122.29	2,367	335	4.0	16.5
Jiangxi	4,200	3,641	115.35	4,000	359	4.3	9.9
Shandong	4,342	3,655	118.80	4,135	480	5.8	13.1
Henan	6,230	4,918	126.68	5,933	1,015	12.2	20.6
Hubei	5,091	3,907	130.30	4,848	941	11.3	24.1
Hunan	4,123	3,542	116.40	3,927	385	4.6	10.9
Guangdong	7,033	5,714	123.08	6,698	984	11.8	17.2
Guangxi	3,998	3,356	119.13	3,808	452	5.4	13.5

Table 4.5. (continued)

Region	Males	Females	Sex Ratio	Expected Females	Missing Females	Contribution to Missing Females (%)	Missing Females (%)
Guangxi	3,998	3,356	119.13	3,808	452	5.4	13.5
Hainan	768	617	124.47	731	114	1.4	18.5
Sichuan	9,881	8,979	110.05	9,411	432	5.2	4.8
Guizhou	3,901	3,938	99.06	3,715	−223	−2.7	−5.7
Yunnan	4,192	3,864	108.49	3,992	128	1.5	3.3
Tibet	293	291	100.69	279	−12	−0.1	−4.1
Shaanxi	2,943	2,391	123.09	2,803	412	4.9	17.2
Gansu	2,565	2,362	108.59	2,443	81	1.0	3.4
Qinghai	525	490	107.14	500	10	0.1	2.0
Ningxia	521	485	107.42	496	11	0.1	2.3
Xinjiang	1,521	1,491	102.01	1,449	−42	−0.5	−2.8

SOURCE: Figures are based on the 1 Percent Population Sample Survey of 1995. China, State Statistical Bureau, *China Population Statistical Yearbook, 1997* (Beijing: China Statistics Press, 1997), p. 183, Table 2-32. Births are from October 1, 1994 to September 30, 1995.

ratios are at opposite poles: Either economically and socially advanced for a long time with more modern attitudes about gender or economically and socially backward.[92]

The China Population Information and Research Center, through its examination of the 1990 census, found that there was also a difference in the sex ratio at birth according to nationality. Differences in culture and religious practices may affect attitudes toward gender and practices of offspring sex selection. The Han nationality, which comprises more than 90 percent of the Chinese population, recorded a high average birth sex ratio of 111.71. Minority nationalities, on the other hand, exhibited a sex ratio at birth of 107.5, no doubt due to the more lenient family planning quotas for minorities. (For example, Inner Mongolians may have three children, Uighurs five, and Tibetans an unlimited number.) Within these nationalities, the sex ratio at birth also varies, with some groups exhibiting stronger son preference through higher sex ratios; among the eighteen nationalities with more than 1 million people, Dong, Hani, Man, and Xhuang have birth sex ratios above 110.[93]

As the above tables show, sex ratios at birth in China vary by province or area, but they also differ according to urban, town, or county residence. As Figure 4.3 demonstrates, urban populations exhibit the lowest sex ratio at birth, while the towns exhibit a sex ratio that is slightly higher than that of rural areas. Chinese demographers Gu and Xu note that townships comprise populations transitioning from rural to urban areas, so the high ratios present in towns are cause for concern.[94]

Sex ratios also vary according to birth order and family composition: Sex ratios increase for second, third, and later children. For example, in 1989, the sex ratio at birth for the firstborn child was 105.2, but this value jumps to 121.0 for the second child. From the overall sex ratios for the country, it becomes apparent that the majority of the population is not stopping at just one child. In addition, as in India, gender bias does not come into play strongly with the first child, despite the one-child policy. With the first child, most parents are willing to avoid sex selection; however, sex selection must be occurring with subsequent pregnancies to produce highly skewed overall sex ratios. Table 4.6 displays birth sex ratios according to birth order from 1981 to 1993.

Some families are willing to have only one child, although they are the minority. During its first few years of implementation, the One-

92.   Gu Baochang and Xu Yi, "A Comprehensive Discussion of the Birth Gender Ratio in China," *Chinese Journal of Population Science*, Vol. 6, No. 4 (1994), p. 423.

93.   Ibid.

94.   Ibid., p. 422.

Figure 4.3. Birth Sex Ratios for City, Town, Country, and Total Births, China, 1994–95.

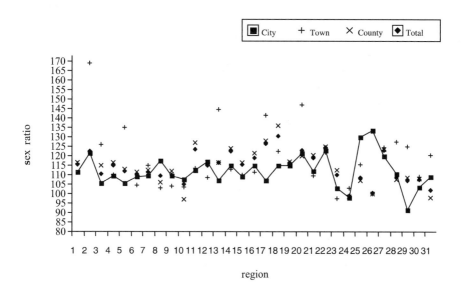

region

SOURCE: Figures are from the 1995 1 Percent Population Sample Survey in China, State Statistical Bureau, *China Population Statistical Yearbook, 1997* (Beijing: State Statistics Press, 1997), Tables 2-32, 2-33, 2-34, 2-35.

per-Thousand fertility survey indicates that the number of women who had accepted a one-child certificate (attesting to determination to have only one child, whereupon the family received various advantages in education and work) was extremely low: 3.8 percent of the rural women sampled, and 14.4 percent of urban women sampled, had accepted the certificate.[95] Of the mothers accepting one-child certificates, 60 percent had a male child and only 40 percent had a female child. In rural areas, 64 percent of the women accepting certificates had sons, compared with 55 percent of urban women. As Trent Wade Moore writes, "Though there are strong penalties associated with not signing the one-child certificate, e.g., less food rations and fewer educational and occupational opportunities for the children, etc., . . . many rural Chinese have chosen to accept penalties and forego the rewards associated with signing the one-child

95. Li Jieping and Shao Wei, "Single Children and Their Mothers," in China Population Information Center, *Analysis on China's National One-per-Thousand Population Fertility Sampling Survey* (Beijing: China Population Information Center, 1984), p. 147.

Table 4.6. Reported Sex Ratio at Birth in China by Birth Order, 1981–93 (males per 100 females).

Year	1st	2d	3d	4th	5th+	Total Births
1981	105.1	106.7	111.3	106.5	114.1	107.1
1982	106.6	105.2	109.4	112.9	109.9	107.2
1983	107.8	107.2	109.5	104.7	112.1	107.9
1984	102.5	113.3	113.0	115.3	127.3	108.5
1985	106.6	115.9	114.1	126.9	117.3	111.4
1986	105.4	116.9	123.1	125.3	123.5	112.3
1987	106.8	112.8	118.9	118.6	124.6	110.0
1988	101.5	114.5	117.1	123.1	108.7	108.1
1989	105.2	121.0	124.3	131.7	129.8	113.9
1990	—	—	—	—	—	114.7
1991	110.8	122.6	124.3	—	—	116.1
1992	106.7	125.7	126.7	—	—	114.2
1993	105.6	130.2	126.1	—	—	114.1

SOURCE: Gu Baochang and Krishna Roy, "Sex Ratio at Birth in China, with Reference to Other Areas in Asia: What We Know," *Asia-Pacific Journal*, Vol. 10, No. 3 (September 1995), p. 24, Table 3.

certificate by having more than one child."[96] In 1991 only 18 percent of married women of child-bearing age had signed the certificate, and as Moore points out, it is not surprising that two-thirds of these women have given birth to sons as their one child.[97] Despite family planning programs and pressures since that time, few parents are willing to have only one child: Although the fertility rate in China is dropping, the total fertility rate in 1990 was 2.25, and estimates for 1997 fell between 2.0 and 2.1.[98]

96.   Trent Wade Moore, "Fertility in China, 1982–1990: Gender Equality as a Complement to Wealth Flows Theory," *Population Research and Policy Review*, Vol. 17, No. 2 (April 1998), pp. 197–222, at p. 198.

97.   Ibid., p. 198.

98.   For the 1990 total fertility rate, see Gu Baochang and Krishna Roy, "Sex Ratio at Birth in China, with Reference to Other Areas in Asia: What We Know," *Asia-Pacific Population Journal*, Vol. 10, No. 3 (September 1995), p. 22. Although the Chinese government claims that the 1997 total fertility rate was 1.8, Chinese demographers disagree. At the International Union for the Scientific Study of Population (IUSSP) meeting held on October 12, 1997, in Beijing, Xu Yi, of the Beijing Institute of Information Control consistently referred to 2.1 as the total fertility rate in China. Xu's use of 2.1 as the total fertility rate was defended by Feng Jiuxhang, director of the Department of Demography in Nanjing, which trains family planning cadres, and by others present.

In their examination of the 1989 census, Chinese scholars Li Yong-ping and Gao Ling found that the gender of second- or higher-birth-order babies is positively correlated with the number of existing female and male children. Among the rural population, Li and Gao found the sex ratio of second children in families in which the first child was a female to be 138; the sex ratios for third, fourth, and fifth children when no sons were yet present were 188, 182, and 204, respectively. For families whose first child was a son, the sex ratios for subsequent children were 101, 108, and 128 for fourth or later children. For families with two or more sons, the sex ratio for additional births tended to be low.[99] As observed in India, as fertility decreases, son preference intensifies, leading to higher sex ratios at lower birth orders.

In addition to geographic and ethnic factors that influence sex ratios at birth, level of education also plays a role. An examination of the 1989 census by Chinese scholars uncovered a correlation between level of education of mothers and the observed sex ratios at birth. For women with less than a primary school education, the sex ratio at birth was 112.5; for those with primary school education, the ratio was 114.2; for women with junior high school education, the ratio was 116.2; and it was only 110.7 for those with a college or secondary vocational education.[100] Unlike the India case, education may thus provide the means to change attitudes about gender and practices harmful to women.

Explaining the Rising Sex Ratios

Most researchers do not agree on the extent of sex selection in China. Despite recent claims of large numbers of females missing from the population, some demographers suggest that undercounting of females in general and a failure to count adopted females in particular explains the statistical discrepancy. Other social scientists, meanwhile, trace what they view as an accurate report of skewed ratios to sex-selective abortion and female infanticide.

Beijing University Professor Zeng Yi (who is also on the advisory committee to the State Family Planning Commission) claims that the figure is only slightly lower, at 2.0. For a summarized report of the IUSSP meeting, see "China's One Child Policy, Two Child Reality," a report from the U.S. embassy, Beijing, October 1997, http://www.usembassy-china.org.cn/english/sandt/fert21.htm.

99. Cited in Gu and Xu, "A Comprehensive Discussion of the Birth Gender Ratio in China," p. 424.

100. Ibid., p. 422.

UNDERCOUNTING OF FEMALES

Zeng Yi, Tu Ping, Gu Baochang, Xu Yi, Li Bohua, and Li Yongping, of Beijing University's Population Institute and the China Population Information and Research Center, claim that undercounting of females is responsible for China's skewed sex ratios—that parents are more willing to report the birth of a son, regardless of his birth order and any penalties that may be inflicted on them, to produce a legal heir. According to this argument, parents will not consider it worthwhile to report a female birth and risk penalty. The parents will then "hide" the female infant from the authorities by putting her up for adoption, reporting her later as an immigrant, or simply not reporting her at all.[101] In his study of the fertility survey responses for the provinces of Hebei and Shaanxi, Wen Xingyan argued that because most births occurred outside of a hospital, unassisted by doctors, nurses, or midwives, it would be easy to hide births of females.[102]

Gu and Xu offer a variation on the theme of underreporting: Not only will parents withhold the truth from officials, but officials will also mislead local political leaders.[103] There is ample opportunity for parents to hide births from family planning cadres, and for the cadres to hide them from other family planning officials. But do they? The findings of Zeng and his colleagues are representative of the official Chinese position on the problem of China's missing females: Their calculations of 1989 census data led them to conclude that errors in birth statistics (i.e., underreporting of females) account for 50–75 percent of the abnormal sex ratio at birth.[104]

---

101.   Zeng Yi, Tu Ping, Gu Baochang, Xu Yi, Li Bohua, and Li Yongping, "Causes and Implications of the Recent Increase in the Reported Sex Ratio at Birth in China," *Population and Development Review,* Vol. 19, No. 2 (June 1993), p. 290.

102.   Wen Xingyan, "Effect of Son Preference and Population Policy on Sex Ratios at Birth in Two Provinces of China," *Journal of Biosocial Science,* Vol. 25, No. 4 (October 1993), p. 518.

103.   Gu and Xu, "A Comprehensive Discussion of the Birth Gender Ratio in China," p. 424.

104.   The findings of the team from Beijing University and the China Population Information and Research Center were first presented at the Fourth Population Census Beijing International Conference, October 19–23, 1992, and later published as Zeng Yi, Gu Baochang, Tu Ping, Xu Yi, Li Bohua, and Li Yongping, "Analyses on the Origins and Consequences of the Increase in China's Gender Ratio at Birth," *Population and Economy,* Vol. 1 (1993). Another article presenting their findings was published in *Population and Development Review* under the title "Causes and Implications of the Recent Increase in the Reported Sex Ratio at Birth in China," Vol. 19, No. 2 (June 1993),

As Gu and Xu note, however, statistical factors cannot explain the missing females in all regions and areas of the country. Data from Zhejiang and Shandong Provinces show that underreporting of infants occurs equally for both male and female births, and that it occurs with greater frequency in reports by local leaders than in reports by parents. Although local leaders suggest that underreporting of male births actually exceeds that of female births, Gu and Xu dispute this claim. Parents are more likely to underreport the birth of a female "for fear of having an 'oviduct ligation' committed on women who have only girls."[105] Against claims that underreporting does not occur, Zeng and his coauthors use a reverse survival method to estimate that underreporting of births does occur for 2.26 percent of male births and 5.94 percent of female births.[106] Western demographers Ansley Coale and Judith Banister disagree, however, stating that figures from the 1990 census point to an equal undercounting of males and females in the 1982 census.[107] Undercounting in the 1990 and 1995 censuses, however, has not yet been examined in a comprehensive manner. There may have been some undercounting of female births between 1985 and 1989, but statistics appear to be accurate for births after 1990.

It should also be noted that parents' underreporting of females born is accompanied by local officials' overreporting of females born. William Lavely, comparing micro data from the 1990 Chinese census with published tabulations, found credible evidence of significant overreporting of infant females in one locale.[108] If this case is indicative of a national trend, then the underreporting of female infants by families may in some cases be exceeded by official overreporting of female infants. For all of these reasons, we argue that underreporting cannot account in large part for the skewness, and the increase in skewness, of China's sex ratios.

---

pp. 283–301. It was also published in the *Economist* as "The Lost Girls," September 18, 1993, pp. 38–41. As Gu and Xu note, the Chinese researchers sought to correct the biases in international opinion regarding the causes of the increasing birth sex ratio. See Gu and Xu, "A Comprehensive Discussion of the Birth Gender Ratio in China," p. 429. This article represents the first Chinese attempt to address the problem of birth sex ratios to a Western audience.

105.   Gu and Xu, "A Comprehensive Discussion of the Birth Gender Ratio in China," p. 424.

106.   Zeng et al., "Causes and Implications of the Recent Increase in the Reported Sex Ratio at Birth in China," p. 285.

107.   Ansley J. Coale and Judith Banister, "Five Decades of Missing Females in China," *Demography*, Vol. 31, No. 3 (August 1994), p. 476.

108.   William Lavely, communication with Valerie Hudson, September 26, 2000.

ADOPTION

Sten Johansson and Ola Nygren estimate that half of the missing females in China in the 1980s were adopted children and thus were not reported as live births by their mothers.[109] This conclusion parallels that of Sten Johansson, Zhao Xuan, and Ola Nygren, who calculate that the number of children adopted in 1987 was approximately 500,000, with 80 percent of those adoptees being female.[110] This would account for more than half of the missing girl births that year. In their study of infants abandoned between 1995 and 1996, Kay Johnson, Huang Banghan, and Wang Liyao find that gender, birth order, and gender composition of siblings were the key determinants in abandonment. Of the 237 abandoned infants in their study, 90 percent were female, 87 percent had no brothers, and 95 percent were second, third, or fourth daughters.[111] Thus the typical profile of an abandoned child is a healthy newborn girl who has one or more older sisters and no brothers. She is abandoned because her birthparents already have daughters and want a son. These birth parents routinely say they did not want to abandon the child but that given their desire for a son, birth planning policies left them 'no choice.'"[112]

This matter is difficult to clarify, however. The fertility surveys did ask questions about adopted children but did not ask the date of adoption; thus demographers have not been able to conclude whether some of these adoptions correspond to underreported births. As one demographer notes, more female than male babies were adopted in the provinces of Hebei and Shaanxi (sex ratios of adopted children were 38.9 and 73.6, respectively); the number of adopted children, however, was small (75 for Hebei and 158 for Shaanxi), suggesting that even adopted children are underreported or that adopted children cannot account for the numbers of missing girls in these, or perhaps other, provinces.[113] Coale and Banister agree that child adoption cannot explain the missing females in census data because "they are members of the adopting house-

---

109. Sten Johansson and Ola Nygren, "The Missing Girls of China: A New Demographic Account," *Population and Development Review,* Vol. 17, No. 1 (March 1991), pp. 35–51.

110. Sten Johansson, Zhao Xuan, and Ola Nygren, "On Intriguing Sex Ratios among Live Births in China in the 1980s," *Journal of Official Statistics,* Vol. 7, No. 1 (1991), http://www.jos.nu/Articles/abstract.asp?article=7125.

111. Kay Johnson, Huang Banghan, and Wang Liyao, "Infant Abandonment and Adoption in China," *Population and Development Review,* Vol. 24, No. 3 (September 1998), pp. 469–481, at p. 475.

112. Ibid., p. 477.

113. Wen, "Effect of Son Preference and Population Policy on Sex Ratios," p. 51.

hold and presumably would be listed in the household to qualify for benefits."[114]

SEX-SELECTIVE ABORTION AND INFANTICIDE

Underreporting and adoption are no doubt occurring in China, but the steady increase in sex ratios since 1980 seems to imply that something more is going on. As Coale and Banister note, "Foreign demographers had not widely accepted conjectures that the sex ratio at birth increased in the 1980s because of increased recourse to sex-selective abortion. It was believed that the technical means for identifying the sex of the fetus were not available, except perhaps in major cities. In 1992, however, the Chinese government and Chinese scholars revealed previously unreported evidence that adequate technology may be widely available, and that the sex ratio at birth has risen."[115] China began importing ultrasound machines in the late 1970s and imported them on a massive scale in the 1980s, when it also started to manufacture its own machines, according to Chinese demographers.[116] Moreover, by the end of 1991, 2,227 county-level family planning facilities had been established; in addition, there were 29,000 planning clinics in townships and towns, with an average of 12 ultrasound machines per county in some areas. Gu and Xu estimated that in 1994 there were more than 100,000 ultrasound machines throughout China. If only a small number of facilities use these to determine the gender of a fetus—despite the fact that the use of ultrasound to determine fetal sex, and sex-selective abortion itself, are both illegal in China—the effect could be huge.[117]

Judging from data collected for seven Chinese provinces, cities, townships, and counties in 1989, ultrasound machines are already having a huge impact on the population. Sex ratios for Shandong, Henan, Guangdong, Jiangsu, Fujian, Jiangxi, and Shanxi climbed to a range from 109.40 to 115.60.[118] In 1993 Nicholas Kristof reported that the sex ratio at

---

114. Coale and Banister, "Five Decades of Missing Females in China," p. 475.

115. Ibid.

116. Gu and Xu, "A Comprehensive Discussion of the Birth Gender Ratio in China," p. 425.

117. Ibid.

118. Ibid., p. 427. In the first few years of the one-child policy, abortion rates also soared. In 1978, 5,391,000 abortions were performed, but that number increased to 12,412,000 by 1982. The number of abortions throughout the 1980s remained fairly constant, averaging 11,010,000 abortions per year. By 1989, 632 abortions were being performed for every 1,000 live births in China, ranging from a low of 181 for the province of Liaoning to a high of 2,022 for Shanghai.

birth in China rose to 118.5 in 1992, a statistic he claims is based on an official survey of 385,000 births that the government kept secret.[119] While in Xiamen, China, Kristof recorded villagers' accounts of sex-selective abortion: "'Last year we had only one girl born in the village—everybody else had boys,' villager Y.H. Chen said in a tone of awe, as the others nodded agreement." He explained that "for a bribe of $35 to $50, a doctor will tell whether a woman is pregnant with a boy or a girl. Then, if it's a girl, 'you get an abortion.'" In fact, Kristof discovered that the gift of a carton of cigarettes would encourage a physician to say whether a fetus is male or female.[120]

Xu Song points to hospital surveys to estimate the effects of ultrasound technology on the sex ratio. Asserting that a hospital survey precludes underreporting, abandonment, or infanticide, Xu notes that the Huaxi Medical Hospital found a birth sex ratio across twenty-nine provinces and 945 hospitals of 108.0 in 1986–87, rising to 109.7 in 1991.[121] Of course, it could be argued that women who knew through ultrasound they were carrying daughters declined to give birth in hospitals so that underreporting, abandonment, or infanticide could take place away from the scrutiny of officials. But that would not easily explain the *rise* in the birth sex ratio over the five-year period that Xu studied.

Although the number of ultrasound machines and abortions performed each year in China suggests that sex selection through testing and abortion is occurring, hard data are difficult to obtain. According to Gu and Xu, "The areas with high birth ratios are also areas with the greatest popularity of ultra-sound equipment."[122] Banister estimates that between the mid-1980s and 1990, 1.5 million female fetuses were selectively aborted in China.[123] This figure is low when compared with the numbers of missing females among the birth population in any give year in the 1980s.

In addition to sex-selective abortion, infanticide—active or passive—contributes to China's high sex ratios. The China Population and Information Research Center acknowledges that drowning is still a problem, despite being strictly forbidden by law. Abandonment also contributes to

119.   Kristof, "Chinese Turn to Ultrasound," p. A4.

120.   Ibid.

121.   Xu, "A Quest on the Causes of Gender Imbalance in China."

122.   Gu and Xu, "Comprehensive Discussion of the Birth Gender Ratio in China," p. 426.

123.   Quoted in Rick Weiss, "Anti-Girl Bias Rises in Asia, Studies Show: Abortion Augmenting Infanticide, Neglect," *Washington Post,* May 11, 1996, p. A1.

the high sex ratios for male infants, because the victims are primarily female. Many abandoned female infants are placed in orphanages, but because of the poor care received in these "dying rooms," few survive.

Although female infanticide received little attention in the first three decades following the 1949 communist revolution, it gained recognition again in 1982 when newspapers throughout China published articles informing the public of the practice.[124] In 1983 China's Central Committee's Propaganda Department called for "the protection of infant girls, and also of women who had given birth to daughters, from social ostracism and physical cruelty at the hands of husbands, parents-in-law, or other kinfolk."[125] The practice of infanticide is not always confined to the female gender: Reports of doctors killing third children or any infant born without permission from the mother's work unit are common.[126] Women with unauthorized pregnancies often have little choice but to undergo an abortion, even when the pregnancy is well advanced. When the fetuses survive a late abortion, physicians or health-care workers will smother and kill the babies to avoid punishment of "refusing to carry out family-planning policy."[127] The risk of punishment for not killing the child can be much greater than the risk of punishment for killing it. Laws regarding female infanticide generally vary from province to province and are often left to the discretion of the working unit of those accused of the crime. As Li Xiaorong notes, the government has generally failed to carry out punishment for female infanticide.[128]

Government Concern about Skewed Sex Ratios

The government's population policies have focused on reducing China's overall population without undue concern for gender composition. In the past decade, however, the government has conducted five nationwide surveys related to childbirth, which have paid attention to the increasing

---

124. Article titles included the following (translated into English): "Young Worker Wan Chuwen Sentenced to 13 Years in Prison for Murdering His Own Infant Daughter"; "Strictly Prohibit the Killing of Girl Babies"; "Cases of Abandoning of Girl Babies Occur Frequently in Yancheng, Jiangsu"; and "Phenomenon of Discarding Baby Girls Becomes Serious in Fujian." Cited in John S. Aird, *Slaughter of the Innocents: Coercive Birth Control in China* (Washington, D.C.: AEI Press, 1990).

125. H. Yuan Tien, "Provincial Fertility Trends and Patterns," in Elisabeth Croll, Delia Davin, and Penny Kane, eds., *China's One-Child Family Policy* (New York: St. Martin's Press, 1985), p. 131.

126. See Aird, *Slaughter of the Innocents*, pp. 91–92.

127. Li, "License to Coerce," p. 163.

128. Ibid., pp. 167–168.

sex ratio at birth. The government has passed legislation to ban the practice of prenatal sex identification, stating that "identification of the sex of a fetus through technological means is strictly forbidden unless it is necessary on medical grounds," and threatening to take away the medical license of anyone who violates the law.[129] In 1991 Peng Peiyun, director of the State Family Planning Committee, suggested that the upcoming five-year plan include research on birth gender ratio. In March 1993 the Party Central Committee met for a family planning working seminar, at which Peng spoke of the problematic rising birth ratio. The meeting received news coverage in the *China Population Daily* and the *People's Daily*. This was the first coverage state-level newspapers in which top leaders in China acknowledged a problem with birth sex ratios.[130]

Chinese and Western interpretations of China's population figures differ. Chinese scholars tend to believe that faulty statistics are the cause of the county's high sex ratios at birth, whereas Western scholars cite sex-selective abortion and infanticide as the primary causes.[131] Current sex ratios in China, female infanticide, and sex-selective abortion are highly political issues. Tien suggests that these issues "have been cited by critics outside the country in their clamor for ending support for crucial international efforts in the population field generally and assistance to China in particular."[132] Nevertheless, the Chinese government's official statements continue only to hint at recognition of the problem of skewed sex ratios. The White Paper on Population and Development released by the Information Office of the State Council of the People's Republic of China on December 18, 2000, made reference to the need to change attitudes toward female children and denounced the mistreatment of girls, including the practice of infanticide. No mention was made of sex-selective abortions, however. Despite the lack of official open discussion, some provinces have taken legal measures to prevent widespread sex-selective abortions of females.

The politicization of China's population figures may be having negative effects on the quality of the government's data. In a recent study on China's fertility, Herbert Smith and his coauthors discuss the problem of assessing government population and family planning statistics: "The idea of statistical systems as disinterested observational devices—both in

---

129. Ibid., pp. 169–170.

130. Gu and Xu, "A Comprehensive Discussion of the Birth Gender Ratio in China," p. 429.

131. Ibid., p. 419.

132. Tien, *China's Strategic Demographic Initiative*, p. 190.

China and elsewhere—is a common one. However, in official statistical systems, political judgment often determines the choice of what to measure, how to measure it, and how to interpret statistical results."[133] Figures must be transmitted to officials up the administrative ladder, processed, represented, and disclosed. At any stage during collection, processing, or transmission, errors and misrepresentation of the data can occur, particularly if pressures for the figures to conform to some predetermined pattern are strong.

In addition to pressure within China to achieve population goals, there are pressures from the international community. The United States, in particular, has taken a great interest in China's efforts to control its population. False reports have been circulated regarding Chinese population figures. The press, both within China and without, has been quick to publish information that exaggerates the current population problems. They often do this (perhaps unintentionally) by taking sex ratios at birth and misrepresenting them as sex ratios for the total population.

Chinese demographers seem anxious to gain as accurate an assessment of China's population as possible and discredit any misrepresentation of population or family planning statistics by their government. At the 1997 International Union for the Scientific Study of Population meeting in Beijing, Chinese demographers were quick to assert that government statements regarding the fertility rate were too low. In addition, they avoided using the 1.04 percent sample census survey of 1995 in their population calculations, claiming that the survey contained too many inaccuracies. Instead the demographers relied on the more accurate 1990 census. The Chinese experts commented that the size of China's population, its fertility rate, and other relevant statistics are not possible to determine with precision at this point.[134]

Infant Mortality

As discussed in the chapter on India, infant mortality is normally higher for males than for females; in the first year of life, 130 male infants typically die for every 100 female infants due to the increased probability of congenital illness for the male infant.[135] In China, as in India, however, more female infants die. Complete data on infant mortality rates are not

133. Herbert L. Smith, Tu Ping, M. Giovanna Merli, and Mark Hereward, "Implementation of a Demographic and Contraceptive Surveillance System in Four Counties in North China," *Population Research and Policy Review*, Vol. 16, No. 4 (August 1997), p. 292.

134. "China's One-Child Policy, Two-Child Reality."

readily available, and neither Western nor Chinese demographers appear to agree on the current rate. According to Gu and Xu, a recent study showed that in 1989, a higher proportion of female infants died—the infant mortality rate between 1981 and 1990 decreased from 38.84 to 35.5 for males, but the rate for females increased from 36.87 to 40.4 deaths per 1,000.[136] As with figures for the sex ratio at birth, infant mortality rates vary depending on the source. For example, the U.S. Bureau of the Census International Data Base lists the infant mortality rate for China in 1990 as 39.69 for males and 65.88 for females. U.S. demographer Judith Banister, however, suggests that the infant mortality rate is much lower; at the International Seminar on China's 1990 Population Census in Beijing, held in 1992, Banister presented a paper in which she suggests that the infant mortality rate for males is 28.2 and the infant mortality rate for females is 32.7.[137] Banister's data, like that of Gu and Xu, indicate that the infant mortality rate for males is decreasing at a much higher rate than for females, such that the female infant mortality rate is now higher than the male rate. Revised infant mortality figures from the 1990 census suggest that the infant mortality rate is 32.2 for males and 36.8 for females.[138] Figure 4.4, derived from data collected by Banister in addition to data from the most two recent censuses, depicts the decrease of infant mortality for the male population, as well as the recent increase in the rate for the female population.

Regardless of the source, current infant mortality rates for females are higher than they are for males. Depending on which source is used, however, the sex ratio of infant deaths in the first year of life in China varies from 88 to 61 (male deaths per 100 female deaths) and not the expected ratio of 130. As Table 4.7 indicates, an excess number of female infants died in China between 1989 and 1990; and we suggest that similar,

---

135. Swedish researchers Sten Johansson and Ola Nygren obtained this figure by computing the sex ratio among infant deaths for a large number of developed countries as well as for developing countries, revealing a consistent pattern of 130 male deaths for every 100 female deaths. See Johansson and Nygren, "The Missing Girls of China," p. 48.

136. Gu and Xu, "A Comprehensive Discussion of the Birth Gender Ratio in China," pp. 426–427.

137. Judith Banister, "Implications and Quality of China's 1990 Census Data," paper presented at the International Seminar on China's 1990 Population Census, Beijing, China, October 1992. Cited in Daniel Goodkind, "On Substituting Sex Preference Strategies in East Asia: Does Prenatal Sex Selection Reduce Postnatal Discrimination?" *Population and Development Review*, Vol. 22, No. 1 (March 1996), p. 117.

138. Reported in William Lavely, "Unintended Consequences of China's Birth Planning Policy," University of Washington, July 14, 1997.

Figure 4.4. China's Male and Female Infant Mortality Rate (per 1,000), 1966–95.

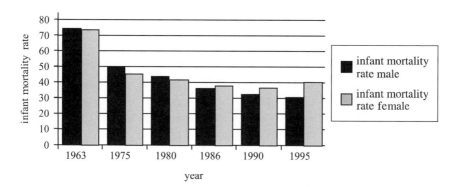

SOURCES: 1963—Yasuko Hayase, and Seiko Kawamata, *Population Policy and Vital Statistics in China* (Tokyo: Institute of Developing Economies, 1991), Table 8; 1975, 1980, and 1986—China, State Statistical Bureau, *China Population Statistical Yearbook, 1989* (Beijing: China Statistics Press, 1989); 1990—adjusted rate for 1990 census, reported in William Lavely, "Unintended Consequences of China's Birth Planning Policy," University of Washington, July 14, 1997; and 1995—China, State Statistical Bureau, *China Population Statistical Yearbook, 1996* (Beijing: China Statistics Press, 1996), Table 3-9.

if not increasing, numbers of females have died each year since and will continue to do so.

As with sex ratios at birth, infant mortality varies with birth order. Although both sexes have less chance of surviving neonatal infancy if they are higher in birth order, the odds for males surviving are much greater. In his study of three provinces in China, Steve Ren found that the survival rate of fourth- and higher-order females was 41 percent of that of first-order births. In contrast, for boys of fourth- and higher-order births, the odds of surviving neonatal infancy were 63 percent of that of first-order births.[139] Competition for resources necessary for survival would more adversely affect those of higher birth orders, because parents would be more willing to spend resources on those children in whom they had already invested. Survival also depends on the education of the mother. Although a mother's education has little effect on the survival of male infants, Ren's study showed that it can have an effect on the survival of female infants, suggesting that "mother's education, an indicator of

139.   Xinhua Steve Ren, "Sex Differences in Infant and Child Mortality in Three Provinces in China," *Social Science and Medicine*, Vol. 40, No. 9 (May 1995), pp. 1263–1264.

Table 4.7. Excess Female Deaths in China in the First Year of Life, 1989–90.

Data Source	Male Infant Mortality Rate[a]	Female Infant Mortality Rate	Number of Female Births	Expected Infant Mortality Rate[b]	Estimated Deaths[c]	Expected Deaths[d]	Excess Deaths
Banister	28.2	32.7	11,655,803	22.0	381,145	256,428	124,717
SSB	32.2	36.8	11,655,803	24.8	428,934	289,064	139,870
Gu and Xu	35.5	40.4	11,655,803	28.0	470,894	326,362	144,532
U.S. International Data Base	39.7	65.9	11,655,803	31.0	768,117	361,330	406,787

SOURCES: Number of female births from *1990 China Population Census Data*, reported in Gu Baochang and Xu Yi, "A Comprehensive Discussion of the Birth Gender Ratio in China," *Chinese Journal of Population Science*, Vol. 6, No. 4 (1994), pp. 417–431; Judith Banister, reported in Daniel Goodkind, "On Substituting Sex Preference Strategies in East Asia: Does Prenatal Sex Selection Reduce Postnatal Discrimination?" *Population and Development Review*, Vol. 22, No. 1 (March 1991), pp. 111–125; Gu and Xu, "A Comprehensive Discussion of the Birth Gender Ratio in China"; and U.S. Bureau of the Census, International Data Base, 1998.

[a]Infant mortality rate is the number of deaths per 1,000 births.

[b]Expected infant mortality rate is calculated by assuming a ratio of male infant mortality rate/female infant mortality rate of 130.

[c]Estimated deaths are estimated using number of births and recorded infant mortality rate for females.

[d]Expected deaths are calculated using the expected infant mortality rate.

women's status, is essential for females to survive neonatal infancy."[140] It may be that, unlike in India, an educated mother in China has a greater sense of women's worth and therefore places value on her female offspring.

Statistics suggest that from ages 1 to 4, male children normally die at a rate that is 1.11 to 1.24 times higher than that for females. Throughout the first two years of life, however, females in China continue to die at a higher rate than males. Chinese data from 1995 reveal that in the second year of life, the probability of dying for females is 3.123, and for males it is 3.081. In the third year of life, these probability rates drop to 1.918 for females and 2.228 for males; in the fourth year of life, they drop further to 1.410 for females and 1.426 for males; and in the fifth year, the rates drop to normal levels of 0.894 for females and 1.041 for males.[141] Thus, only in the third and fifth years of life are these rates within the normal range, evidence that in the first, second, and fourth years, female children experience higher levels of differential mortality and continuing discrimination. By comparing these figures with the sex ratios at birth for 1989, we can observe that the sex ratio remains high throughout the first four years of life, whereas in normal populations, the sex ratio would decrease significantly over the first year of life, plateauing below the normal 105–107 birth sex ratio. Table 4.8 illustrates the increase in the sex ratio in the first year of life for most years, as well as the abnormally high-sex-ratio plateau during the first four years of life between 1953 and 1996.

Missing Females and China's Bachelors

How many women are missing from the entire population of China? According to the 2000 census, there were 653 million men and 612 million women in China, indicating that 41 million females are missing, or that there are 41 million surplus men. In 1990, this number was 35 million. Almost half of this surplus is found in the population ages 15–34; Table 4.9 shows that this number is increasing.[142]

In particular, the large number of unmarried males in China has attracted interest in the press. As one journalist notes, there were 48 million unmarried men in China in 1992 (for men of all ages above

---

140. Ibid., pp. 1265–1266.

141. Data from China, State Statistical Bureau, *China Population Statistical Yearbook, 1996* (Beijing: China Statistics Press, 1996), p. 77, Table 3–9.

142. The age breakdown for the 2000 census is not yet available; thus we cannot provide surplus figures for any particular age group.

Table 4.8. Sex Ratios in China, Ages 0–4, 1953–96.

Year	Age 0	Age 1	Age 2	Age 3	Age 4	Ages 1–4
1953	104.88	105.58	106.59	108.62	109.38	107.32
1957	105.41	—	—	—	—	106.45
1963	105.59	—	—	—	—	105.44
1964	103.83	105.31	106.38	106.96	108.68	106.47
1975	106.63	—	—	—	—	104.86
1982	107.63	107.82	107.35	106.71	106.19	107.00
1987	112.24	114.74	110.39	95.88	101.13	110.05
1989	112.54	110.26	108.03	110.59	108.75	109.38
1990	111.68	111.68	110.13	109.28	108.36	109.88
1994	116.30	119.43	119.58	115.18	113.07	116.30
1995	116.57	121.08	121.26	119.17	115.01	118.82
1996	116.16	120.89	121.32	120.83	120.94	120.99

SOURCES: 1953, 1964, and 1982—China, Population Census Office under the State Council and the Department of Population Statistics of the State Statistical Bureau, *The 1982 Population Census of China (Major Figures)* (Hong Kong: Economic Information Agency, 1982); 1957, 1963, 1975, and 1987—Yasuko Hayase and Seiko Kawamata, *Population Policy and Vital Statistics in China* (Tokyo: Institute of Developing Economies, 1991); 1989—China, China Statistical Bureau, *China Statistical Yearbook, 1990* (Beijing: China Statistics Press, 1990); 1990—China, State Statistical Bureau, *China Population Statistical Yearbook, 1991* (Beijing: China Statistics Press, 1991); 1994—China, State Statistical Bureau, *China Statistical Yearbook, 1995* (Beijing: China Statistics Press, 1995); 1995—China, State Statistical Bureau, *China Population Statistical Yearbook, 1996* (Beijing: China Statistics Press, 1996); and 1996—China, State Statistical Bureau, *China Population Statistical Yearbook, 1997* (Beijing: China Statistics Press, 1991).

---

25), and he suggests that this number will increase easily to 80 million in the near future if current sex ratios at birth continue.[143] Similarly, an-

---

143. Ren, "Confronting Three Populations of 80 Million." Ren obtained this figure of 80 million by using 1991 statistics suggesting that of the 23 million births that year, 13.3 million were male and 9.7 million were female (for an overall sex ratio of 137 males per 100 females), indicating a surplus of 3.6 million males. Projecting this into the future, the author predicts that within ten years (or by the end of the twentieth century), there would be a surplus of 36 million males. Added to the current figure of 48 million bachelors, the author concludes that in the near future, China will have 80 million bachelors. There are several problems with this approach to estimating the population. First, 1991 statistics reveal that the sex ratio at birth in 1991 was 115 and not 137; thus a possible 1.6 million more males than females were born that year, not 3.6 million. Thus the author's use of a sex ratio at birth for 1991 of 137 is inaccurate, but it is even more inaccurate to assume that the sex ratio at birth for the rest of the decade would be so unusually high. In addition, as we have seen, figures for the number of bachelors are very different from the actual number of surplus males. Although there may be 48 million bachelors in China, many of them will marry at some point. We feel that calculating the number of surplus males in China gives a more realistic, if conservative, picture of the single male population in China.

other source suggests that China may already have 90 million bachelors.[144]

How might the increasing sex ratios at birth affect this population in twenty years? The current number of surplus males is small when compared to the already large surplus in the infant population, because those within the 15–34 age range were, for the most part, born prior to the implementation of family planning policies of the 1980s and 1990s. To project to populations in the year 2020, we have utilized statistics for number of births and the sex of those births between 1985 and 1995. For births after 1995, we use conservative predictions for the decreasing number of births to 2004 and for sex ratios at birth. We have used lifetime survival ratios from China's life tables to estimate the number of individuals from among those births who will still be alive in the year 2020. Our results appear in Tables 4.10 and 4.11, with Table 4.11 utilizing what we believe are more accurate infant mortality rates. Calculations from these tables suggest that China will have a surplus of between 29 and 33 million males in the age group 15–34—more than twice the number of the current surplus population of this same age group.

Table 4.12 provides a comparison of our estimates with those of the United Nations and World Bank. Our estimates for the overall population ages 15–34 are comparable to their projections. The sizes of our estimated male populations are also similar to those of the UN and only slightly higher than the World Bank's. The similarities end there, however. Key differences can be noted in the sex ratios and the size of the female populations. Although all of the projections have sex ratios in favor of the male population, the UN and World Bank estimates have sex ratios of approximately 107 males per 100 females. To produce sex ratios so low, the sex ratio at birth would have to drop to corresponding levels, and differential mortality between male and female infants and children would have to end. But such a change is not likely, particularly since the majority of the male and female population of the age group 15–34 in the year 2020 will have been born years ago into birth populations with high sex ratios and very high rates of differential mortality).

What does the Chinese government predict for its future population? In its December 2000 White Paper on China's population, the government laid out its plans: By 2010, "Informed choice of contraceptive mea-

---

144. Hutchings, "Female Infanticide 'Will Lead to Army of Bachelors.'" Hutchings cites a Chinese journal that quotes statistics of a sex ratio at birth for China of 131 males per 100 females, a total number of births each year of 25 million, and a current bachelor population of 46 million for the overall population. The birth sex ratio used in this example is also much higher than official statistics suggest. In addition, the number of births since 1990 has been much less that 25 million, and is decreasing.

Table 4.9. Surplus Male Population in China, 1964–2000.

Year	Total Male Population Ages 15–34	Surplus Male Population Ages 15–34	Total Male Population All Ages	Surplus Males Total Population
1964	110,357,642	10,677,546	356,517,011	18,452,263
1982	191,184,794	13,193,750	519,406,895	30,661,653
1990	226,020,631	14,857,587	585,476,497	35,877,844
2000	—	—	653,550,000	41,270,000

SOURCES: 1964 and 1982—China, Population Census Office under the State Council and the Department of Population Statistics of the State Statistical Bureau, *The 1982 Population Census of China (Major Figures)* (Hong Kong: Economic Information Agency, 1982); 1990—China, State Statistical Bureau, *China Population Statistical Yearbook, 1991* (Beijing: China Statistics Press, 1991); and 2000—calculations based on preliminary figures for the 2000 census.

Table 4.10. Projections for China's Male and Female Population Ages 15–34, Year 2020, Adjusted Lifetime Survival Ratio (LTSR).

Years	Sex Ratio at Birth[a]	Total Births[b]	Male Births	Female Births	LTSR Males to 2020[c]	LTSR Females to 2020[d]	Male Population (15–34) in 2020	Female Population (15–34) 2020
1985–89	111.3	119,720,000	63,061,983	56,658,017	0.9140	0.88605	57,638,652	50,201,836
1990–94	118.2	109,980,000	59,578,594	50,401,406	0.9212	0.89380	54,883,800	45,048,777
1995–99	115.4	101,900,000	54,597,887	47,302,113	0.92825	0.90088	50,680,488	42,613,528
2000–04	115.0	98,895,000	52,897,326	45,997,674	0.93356	0.90574	49,382,827	41,661,934
Total							**212,585,768**	**179,526,075**
Missing females								**33,059,694**

[a]For sex ratio at birth, 1985–95, see Table 4.2 in this chapter; 1996 sex ratio at birth from China, State Statistical Bureau, *China Population Statistical Yearbook, 1997* (Beijing: China Statistics Press, 1997); and 1997–2004 sex ratio at birth estimated from current sex ratio at birth.

[b]Total births 1985–96 from China, State Statistical Bureau, *China Population Statistical Yearbook, 1997*, Table 4-10; 1997–99 births estimated from current birth totals; 2000–04 birth estimates from United Nations, Department of International and Economic Social Affairs, *World Population Prospects, 1990*, Population Studies No. 120 (New York: United Nations, 1991).

[c]LTSR was determined by an adjusted form of the U.S. Bureau of the Census, International Data Base, 1998, http://www.census.gov/ipc/www/idbnew.html, Life Table Values: China/1981/Total/Male. The $_nq_x$ values for infant mortality (age 0–1) were adjusted according to 1990 data for infant mortality rates of 39.69 male deaths per 1,000, as per the U.S. Bureau of the Census, International Data Base, 1998. LTSR was obtained as $LTSR_x = 5L_x/5L_x$ where x = age intervals of 15–20, 20–25, 25–30, and 30–35.

[d]U.S. Bureau of the Census, International Data Base, 1998, Life Table Values: China/1981/Total/Female. LTSR calculated as above in note 3, with an adjusted $_1q_0$ value based on 1990 U.S. Bureau of the Census, International Data Base estimates of infant mortality of 65.88 female deaths per 1,000.

Table 4.11. Projections for China's Male and Female Population Ages 15–34, Year 2020, Adjusted Lifetime Survival Ratio (LTSR).

Years	Sex Ratio at Birth	Total Births	Male Births	Female Births	LTSR Males to 2020[a]	LTSR Females to 2020[b]	Male Population (15–34) 2020	Female Population (15–34) 2020
1985–89	111.3	119,720,000	63,061,983	56,658,017	0.92345	0.91853	57,638,588	50,042,088
1990–94	118.2	109,980,000	59,578,594	50,401,406	0.93220	0.92766	55,539,165	46,755,369
1995–99	115.4	101,900,000	54,597,887	47,302,113	0.93737	0.92789	51,178,421	43,891,158
2000–04	115.0	98,895,000	52,897,326	45,997,674	0.94454	0.93525	49,963,640	43,019,325
Total							**214,915,814**	**185,707,940**

Missing females 29,207,874

SOURCES: Sources are the same as in Table 4.10, with the exception of the $1q_0$ and $4q_1$ values for the life table.

[a] As with Table 4.10, the U.S. Bureau of the Census, International Data Base, 1998, http://www.census.gov/ipc/www/idbnew.html, Life Table Values: China/1981/Total/Male was used as the basic life table, but with an adjusted $1q_0$ value of 28.2 and a $4q_1$ of 9.3 for 1990, according to Judith Banister's 1990 data in Daniel Goodkind, "On Substituting Sex Preference Strategies in East Asia: Does Prenatal Sex Selection Reduce Postnatal Discrimination?" *Population and Development Review*, Vol. 22, No. 1 (March 1991), p. 117, Table 1. This life table was then used to calculate LTSR for the years 1985–94. For 1995–2004, a different life table was created using an adjusted $1q_0$ value of 30.45 according to the 1995 1.04 percent sampling survey figures in China, State Statistical Bureau (SSB), *China Population Statistical Yearbook, 1996* (Beijing: China Statistics Press, 1996), p. 77, Table 3-9.

[b] Female life table values were obtained from the U.S. Bureau of the Census, International Data Base, 1998, Life Table Values: China/1981/Total/Female, but with an adjusted $1q_0$ value of 32.7 and a $4q_1$ of 9.8, also according to Banister's data in Goodkind, "On Substituting Sex Preference," p. 117, Table 1. The life table was then used to determine LTSR for the years 1985–94. For 1995–2004 figures, another life table was constructed using $1q_0$ value adjusted to 40.84, according to the 1995 sample survey in China, SSB, *China Population Statistical Yearbook, 1996*, p. 77, Table 3-9.

Table 4.12. Comparison of Population Projections in China, Ages 15–34, Year 2020.

Type of Estimate	Total Population	Male Population	Female Population	Sex Ratio Population	Male Surplus
United Nations medium variant estimates	417,548,000	216,130,000	201,418,000	107.3	14,712,000
United Nations high variant estimates	456,044,000	235,971,000	220,073,000	107.2	15,898,000
United Nations low variant estimates	381,699,000	197,653,000	184,046,000	107.4	13,607,000
World Bank estimates	410,030,000	211,709,000	198,321,000	106.8	13,388,000
Estimates in Table 4.10	392,634,000	214,916,000	179,526,000	118.4	33,060,000
Estimates in Table 4.11	400,624,000	214,916,000	185,708,000	115.7	29,208,000

SOURCES: United Nations, Department for Economic and Social Information and Policy Analysis, Population Division, *The Sex and Age Distribution of the World Populations: The 1994 Revision* (New York: United Nations, 1994); and World Bank. *World Population Projections, 1994–95 Edition: Estimates and Projections with Related Demographic Statistics* (Washington, D.C.: World Bank, 1994).

sures is to be practiced widely and the sex ratio at birth is expected to gradually become normal." No information is provided regarding why the sex ratio at birth is expected to decline. The report merely states that "the whole society should be mobilized to help girl children, disabled girls, children in single parent families and in poverty, and street children. Any action of maltreating, drowning and discarding girls is forbidden, and such crimes as mistreatment and trafficking of children ought to be severely punished."

The U.S. Census Bureau concurs with official Chinese expectations of a lowered sex ratio at birth; according to its predictions, the ratio will decline to 106 by 2020. The primary researcher for Asia's population at the bureau, Daniel Goodkind, claims that "evidence from [South] Korea and Taiwan do suggest that SRBs [sex ratios at birth] have declined from their peaks," and he expects that China's sex ratios at birth will soon follow suit.[145] There is no evidence to suggest that China's sex ratios have peaked, however, and all recent reports on the sex ratios at birth in Taiwan and South Korea suggest that their sex ratios have plateaued, but remain high. Although it may be possible for the sex ratios at birth to reach a peak in the near future and then decline, it is highly unlikely that sex ratios in China will then return to normal levels, especially as attitudes toward son preference show no sign of altering.

Conclusion

In this chapter, we have attempted to show that gender inequality resulting in various forms of offspring sex selection was evidenced throughout much of China's history, as in India, and continues to exist. Economic, political, and social reforms in the latter half of the twentieth century combined to produce a culture in which traditional son preference, coupled with declining fertility and politicized family planning policies, resulted in increasing resort to female infanticide and sex-selective abortion. It is likely that these practices will persist. Our calculations suggest that by 2020, there will be 29–33 million surplus males aged 15–34 in China. In chapters 5, 6, and 7, we discuss some of the consequences of the increasing masculinization of China's and India's populations and provide suggestions for policymakers confronting this harmful and potentially dangerous phenomenon.

---

145. Daniel Goodkind, correspondence with Andrea den Boer, April 26, 2001.

Chapter 5

Bare Branches of High-Sex-Ratio Societies

Theory and Cases

Artificially high sex ratios pose potentially grave problems for society.[1] They also create vexing policy dilemmas for governments. James Boone explains, "Reproductive strategies have an important effect on the development of state political organization, and . . . there is a fundamental contradiction between individual (or familial) reproductive interests and the social reproduction of the state political structure."[2] It is to this contradiction that we now turn.

The sex ratios in the world's two most populous countries, China and India, are increasing as sex-selective practices continue to produce unprecedented numbers of surplus males. A confluence of factors—including female infanticide, sex-selective abortion, higher female mortality in youth, and a rise in female suicide rates—have helped to create this outcome. These variables are contributing to a larger syndrome of exaggerated gender inequality in both countries.

In this chapter, we outline a theory of surplus young adult male behavior that synthesizes theoretical insights and empirical findings from a variety of disciplines. In keeping with the Chinese vernacular of the nineteenth century, we refer to surplus young adult males as "bare branches," or *guang gun-er*. Bare branches are males who will never have families be-

---

1. This volume addresses the problems of high-sex-ratio societies, a case can be made, however, that there are negative societal consequences to very low-sex-ratio societies as well.

2. James L. Boone, "Parental Investment and Elite Family Structure in Preindustrial States: A Case Study of Late Medieval–Early Modern Portuguese Genealogies," *American Anthropologist*, Vol. 88, No. 4 (December 1986), p. 859.

cause they cannot find spouses.[3] As one contemporary Chinese citizen put it: "This is a metaphor, which indicates that the unmarried men have nothing attached, just like bare branches. Bare branches give people an impression of bleakness and loneliness. It is quite similar to the lives of the unmarried men. They have no warm families, which can give them support and comfort; they have no children, who can take care of them when they become old."[4]

Characteristics of Bare Branches

In high-sex-ratio societies, surplus males share several characteristics. First, they belong predominantly to the lowest socioeconomic class. Unlike men of higher standing, surplus males have little or no bargaining power in the marriage market and thus frequently end up alone. The evidence for this assertion is ample: Beginning with nonhuman primate studies and moving up the evolutionary chain to humans, when females are scarce, the only reproductive failures are low-status males.[5] As noted in chapter 1, the upward movement of women who marry—hypergyny—results because men with greater status and wealth are better able to attract mates. Indeed the phrase "bachelor herd," originating in the study of mammals, refers to low-status males who lack access to females and who congregate at the outer edges of society waiting for their chance to overthrow the group's alpha male.[6] As Martin Daly and

---

3. Elizabeth Perry, *Rebels and Revolutionaries in North China, 1845–1945* (Stanford, Calif.: Stanford University Press, 1980). *Guang* means shiny/bare/naked/bald/crazy; *gun-er* means branch/club/stick/truncheon/rascal/villain/ruffian. To this day, *guang gun-er* is slang for a bachelor, and *lao guang gun-er* is slang for an old bachelor. We are indebted to David Wright of Brigham Young University for this linguistic explication.

4. Quoted in Ren Feng, "Bare Branches among Rural Migrant Laborers in China: Causes, Social Implications, and Policy Proposal," Foreign Affairs College, Beijing, March 1999, p. 6.

5. See, for example, John H. Crook, "Sexual Selection, Dimorphism, and Social Organization in the Primates," in Bernard Campbell, ed., *Sexual Selection and the Descent of Man* (Chicago: Aldine de Gruyter, 1972), pp. 231–281; Irven deVore, "Male Dominance and Mating Behavior in Baboons," in Frank Ambrose Beach, ed., *Sex and Behavior* (New York: Wiley and Sons, 1965), pp. 266–289; Mildred Dickemann, "The Ecology of Mating Systems in Hypergynous Dowry Societies," *Social Science Information*, Vol. 18, No. 2 (May 1979), pp. 163–195; Mildred Dickemann, "Female Infanticide, Reproductive Strategies, and Social Stratification: A Preliminary Model," in Napoleon A. Chagnon and William Irons, eds., *Evolutionary Biology and Human Social Behavior: An Anthropological Perspective* (North Scituate, Mass.: Duxbury, 1979), pp. 321–367.

6. See, for example, S.M. Mohnot, "Peripheralization of Weaned Male Juveniles in Presbytis entellus," in David John Chivers and J. Herbert, eds., *Recent Advances in*

Margo Wilson put it, "Top males keep other males down—underdeveloped, out of circulation, out of the breeding population. In song birds, for example, there are always 'floater' males ready to take the place of any territory holder that should disappear. In many monkey species there are solitary males and all-male groups ever eager to break into the mixed-sex groups in which breeding occurs."[7]

Second, in economies with market features, bare branches are more likely to be underemployed or unemployed. They are also more likely to be chosen for low-status jobs that are dangerous, menial, labor intensive, or seasonal.[8] A 1990 Chinese survey indicates that of the 94 percent of Chinese unmarried adults who were male, 73.8 percent had failed to graduate from high school.[9]

In nonmarket economies, bare branches generally do not have land or other resources that would increase their chances of marrying. For this reason, second, third, and higher birth-order sons in primogeniture societies are likely to become bare branches. Even in nonprimogeniture societies, such as China's, eldest sons are more likely to have access to the resources needed to attract wives. Like those at the bottom of the socioeconomic ladder, higher birth-order sons of the upper classes frequently engage in risky ventures to acquire the resources and status they lack. The most common route is through military service, a path also taken by low-status bare branches. According to Boone, "Many males at the lower end of the scale lead lives of enforced celibacy in what for them is a seller's market and are furthermore engaged in production, construction, and military occupations that tend to raise their mortality rates through occupational hazards and unhealthful conditions. Their poor socioeconomics position and reproductive prospects make them perennial as-

---

Primatology, Vol. 1: *Behavior* (London: Academic Press, 1978), pp. 87–91; J.K. Russell, "Exclusion of Adult Male Coatis from Social Groups: Protection from Predation," *Journal of Mammalogy*, Vol. 62, No. 1 (February 1981), pp. 206–208; and Thad Q. Bartlett, Robert W. Sussman, and James M. Cheverud, "Infant Killing in Primates: A Review of Observed Cases with Specific Reference to the Sexual Selection Hypothesis," *American Anthropologist*, Vol. 95, No. 4 (December 1993), pp. 958–990.

7. Martin Daly and Margo Wilson, *Sex, Evolution, and Behavior: Adaptations for Reproduction* (North Scituate, Mass.: Duxbury, 1978), p. 201.

8. See David T. Courtwright, *Violent Land: Single Men and Social Disorder from the Frontier to the Inner City* (Cambridge, Mass.: Harvard University Press, 1996).

9. That is, they either were illiterate (17.24 percent), had received only an elementary education (23.13 percent), or had graduated only from junior high school (33.36 percent). Figures refer to 1987 and are from Zhang Ping, "Issues and Characteristics of the Unmarried Population," *Chinese Journal of Population Science*, Vol. 2, No. 1 (1990), pp. 87–97.

pirants in large-scale expansionist and insurgent military campaigns through which they might hope to achieve higher positions."[10]

Third, bare branches are typically transients with few ties to the communities in which they look for work. Because they move repeatedly to find jobs, they possess a high degree of anonymity.[11] This anonymity and lack of community attachment combine to loosen the psychological constraints of bare branches against engaging in criminal behavior. Also, they have a lower probability of being identified or apprehended in the event they do commit a crime. Two criminologists explain this dynamic in modern China:

[China's] stable social order before economic reform was built upon the interaction of three factors: a strict restriction on population movements; efficient informal control mechanisms, including the resident committee, where one lives (the *danwei*), where one works, and the school where one studies; and an ideological and moral consensus in conjunction with the three mechanisms. However, the massive movement of [the] transient population has directly disrupted this arrangement. Criminal opportunities have greatly increased due to the disturbance of the neighborhoods by the introduction of temporary workers. Eighty million people, who are on the move, have left their villages, work units, and communities, where they are deeply attached, and become free persons who are subject to no supervision in a new environment. Ideological and moral norms have seriously declined in that they were built upon collective brainwashing and reinforced education, which are difficult to continue among mobile population[s]. All these changes have drastically undercut the control mechanisms that functioned effectively in the past. As the external control weakened, increase in crime became inevitable.[12]

Fourth, bare branches live and socialize with other bare branches, creating distinctive bachelor subcultures.[13] Predictably, the rest of the

---

10. Boone, "Parental Investment and Elite Family Structure in Preindustrial States," p. 862.

11. See Courtwright, *Violent Land;* Joan M. Nelson, "Migrants, Urban Poverty, and Instability in Developing Nations," Occasional Papers in International Affairs No. 22 (Cambridge, Mass.: Center for International Affairs, Harvard University, September 1969); Howard M. Bahr, ed., *Disaffiliated Man: Essays and Bibliography on Skid Row, Vagrancy, and Outsiders* (Toronto: University of Toronto Press, 1970); and Gregory R. Woirol, *In the Floating Army* (Chicago: University of Illinois Press, 1992). The mobility of low-status male laborers was also a common theme in medieval Europe.

12. Yingyi Situ and Liu Weizheng, "Transient Population, Crime, and Solution: The Chinese Experience," *International Journal of Offender Therapy and Comparative Criminology*, Vol. 40, No. 4 (December 1996), p. 297.

13. See Lionel Tiger, *Men in Groups* (London: Marion Boyars, 1984); Courtwright, *Violent Land;* John C. Burnham, *Bad Habits: Drinking, Smoking, Taking Drugs, Gambling, Sex-*

community treats them as social outcasts. Historically, James Rooney argues, "the continuous development of a distinctive single man's culture was associated with increasing differentiation, isolation, and opposition from the stable, family-oriented community. The unattached men could not be included in the status groups of the resident community because of the differences of values stemming from the former's lack of structured responsibility, particularly as expressed in the lack of restraint in recreation, pursuit of immediate pleasure, and lack of concern for the future."[14]

These four features are classic hallmarks of surplus male behavior in high-sex-ratio societies. Interestingly, these features may also be found among the lowest-status males in other kinds of communities, including: frontier outposts,[15] male labor colonies,[16] and itinerant male "societies"

---

ual Misbehavior, and Swearing in American History (New York: New York University Press, 1993); George Gilder, Naked Nomads: Unmarried Men in America (New York: Quadrangle, 1974); Bell I. Wiley, The Life of Billy Yank: The Common Soldier of the Union (Baton Rouge: Louisiana State University Press, 1978); J.S. Holliday, The World Rushed In: The California Gold Rush Experience (New York: Simon and Schuster, 1981); Joe B. Frantz and Julian Ernest Choate Jr., The American Cowboy (Norman: University of Oklahoma Press, 1960); Murray Melbin, "Night as Frontier," American Sociological Review, Vol. 43, No. 1 (February 1978), pp. 3–22; Murray Melbin, Night as Frontier: Colonizing the World after Dark (New York: Free Press, 1987); and Sanyika Shakur, Monster: The Autobiography of an L.A. Gang Member (New York: Atlantic Monthly Press, 1993).

14. See James F. Rooney, "Societal Forces and the Unattached Male," in Bahr, Disaffiliated Man, p. 18.

15. Courtwright, Violent Land, is arguably the definitive work on this matter. See also David Dary, Cowboy Culture: A Saga of Five Centuries (Lawrence: University Press of Kansas, 1989); Frantz and Choate, The American Cowboy; David H. Breen, The Canadian Prairie West and the Ranching Frontier: 1874–1924 (Toronto: University of Toronto Press, 1983); Robert Wooster, Soldiers, Sutlers, and Settlers: Garrison Life on the Texas Frontier (College Station: Texas A&M University Press, 1987); and Ray A. Billington, America's Frontier Culture (College Station: Texas A&M University Press, 1977). The Argentine gaucho era is also a case in point.

16. Australia started out as one such colony; other examples include the California Gold Rush labor camps, the labor camps involved in the construction of the transcontinental railroad in the United States, and the Chinatown male labor camps of early California. See, for example, Ged Martin, ed., The Founding of Australia: The Argument About Australia's Origins (Sydney: Hale and Iremonger, 1978); Holliday, The World Rushed In; Charles Ross Parke, Dreams to Dust: A Diary of the California Gold Rush, 1849–1850, ed. James E. Davis (Lincoln: University of Nebraska Press, 1989); James McCague, Moguls and Iron Men: The Story of the First Transcontinental Railroad (New York: Harper and Row, 1964); Gunter Barth, Bitter Strength: A History of the Chinese in the United States, 1850–1870 (Cambridge, Mass.: Harvard University Press, 1964); Lucie Cheng and Edna Bonacich, eds., Labor Immigration under Capitalism: Asian Workers in the United States before World War II (Berkeley: University of California Press, 1984); and

in which females never amount to more than 3–5 percent of the population.[17]

In sum, most bare branches in high-sex-ratio societies historically did not choose their bachelorhood. Some, though, did make this choice, among them, men in celibate religious orders and many of China's eunuchs. The status of these men was higher—much higher in some cases—than that of the involuntary bachelor.

Behavioral Tendencies of Bare Branches

Typically, bare branches are more likely than other males to turn to vice and violence.[18] Unable to achieve satisfaction in socially approved ways, they spend their meager wages on gambling, alcohol, drugs, and prostitutes in short (but intense) sprees.[19] The disorder created during these sprees predictably has a negative impact on society, but it is the violence that surplus males engage in during these episodes that arguably has the greatest negative effect. Consider the following seven facts.

First, males are more violent than females. One of the few social science verities, confirmed through experiments and anthropological observation over the last 100 years, is that males are more aggressive

---

Sian Rees, *The Floating Brothel: The Extraordinary True Story of an Eighteenth-Century Ship and Its Cargo of Female Convicts* (New York: Theia/Hyperion, 2002).

17.   Itinerant males, usually former soldiers, were common in both medieval and Renaissance Europe. Indeed many of the central characters in Anderson's and Grimms's fairy tales are bare branches. See, for example, "The Tinder Box," "The Twelve Dancing Princesses," and "The Robber Bridegroom." For the situation in the Middle Ages, see James L. Boone, "Noble Family Structure and Expansionist Warfare in the Late Middle Ages," in Rada Dyson-Hudson and Michael A. Little, ed., *Rethinking Human Adaptation: Biological and Cultural Models* (Boulder, Colo.: Westview, 1983), pp. 79–96. Itinerant males were also commonplace in the United States until World War I. See, for example, Eric H. Monkkonen, *Walking to Work: Tramps in America, 1790–1935* (Lincoln: University of Nebraska Press, 1984); Roger Bruns, *Knights of the Road: A Hobo History* (New York: Methuen, 1980); and Woirol, *In the Floating Army*. This category of itinerant male groups includes mobile armies. See, for example, Olive Knight, *Life and Manners in the Frontier Army* (Norman: University of Oklahoma Press, 1978).

18.   Theodore D. Kemper has constructed an elegant theory of this dynamic. He discusses how low-status, unmarried young males have few opportunities to achieve dominance or eminence, and thus engage in behavior that will bring them the "T surge" that they cannot achieve any other way. See Kemper, *Social Structure and Testosterone: Explorations of the Socio-Bio-Social Chain* (New Brunswick, N.J.: Rutgers University Press, 1990). Such behavior includes physical aggression, drug and alcohol abuse, risk taking, and sexual misconduct.

19.   See Courtwright, *Violent Land*, especially chap. 5.

than females. This is also one of the few sex differences that has a firm biological basis. In addition, male sex hormone levels can be manipulated to increase or decrease the intensity of male aggression.[20] Sex differences in aggression appear early in life, arguably before socialization.

Although in some instances females may be as aggressive as males (e.g., when their offspring are threatened), males generally inflict more serious injuries. Indeed males are responsible for the vast majority of violent deaths.[21] As Richard Wrangham and Dale Peterson note, "Male criminals specialize in violent crime. In the U.S., for example, a man is about nine times as likely as a woman to commit murder, seventy-eight times as likely to commit forcible rape, ten times as likely to commit armed robbery, and almost six and a half times as likely to commit aggravated assault. Altogether, American men are almost eight times as likely as women to commit violent crime."[22]

Second, males engage more often than females in other types of antisocial behavior. For example, in the American case,

Men are nearly thirteen and a half times as likely to commit fraud, thirteen times as likely to be arrested for carrying or possessing a weapon, more than ten times as likely to burgle, nine times as likely to steal a car, eight and a half times as likely to find themselves collared for drunkenness, and well over

---

20. Eleanor Emmons Maccoby and Carol Nagy Jacklin, *The Psychology of Sex Differences* (Stanford, Calif.: Stanford University Press, 1974), pp. 227–247.

21. The literature here is immense. Illustrative works include D. Benton, "Do Animal Studies Tell Us Anything about the Relationships between Testosterone and Human Aggression?" in Graham C.L. Davey, ed., *Animal Models of Human Behavior* (Chichester, U.K.: Wiley, 1983), pp. 281–298; Marie-France Bouissou, "Androgens, Aggressive Behaviour, and Social Relationships in Higher Mammals," *Hormone Research*, Vol. 18, Nos. 1–3 (1983), pp. 43–61; John M.W. Bradford and D. McLean, "Sexual Offenders, Violence, and Testosterone: A Clinical Study," *Canadian Journal of Psychiatry*, Vol. 29, No. 4 (June 1984), pp. 335–343; Kerrin Christiansen and Rainier Knussmann, "Androgen Levels and Components of Aggressive Behavior in Men," *Hormones and Behavior*, Vol. 21, No. 2 (June 1987), pp. 170–180; James M. Dabbs Jr. and Robin Morris, "Testosterone, Social Class, and Antisocial Behavior in a Sample of 4,462 Men," *Psychological Science*, Vol. 1, No. 3 (May 1990), pp. 209–211; Bruce B. Svare, ed., *Hormones and Aggressive Behavior* (New York: Plenum, 1983); Janet Shibley Hyde, "Gender Differences in Aggression," in Janet Shibley Hyde and Marcia C. Linn, eds., *The Psychology of Gender: Advances through Meta-Analysis* (Baltimore, Md.: Johns Hopkins University Press, 1986); Kenneth E. Moyer, "Sex Differences in Aggression," in Richard C. Friedman, Ralph M. Richart, and Raymond L. Vande Wiele, eds., *Sex Differences in Behavior* (New York: Wiley, 1974), pp. 335–372; and Dolf Zillmann, *Connections between Sex and Aggression* (Hillsdale, N.J.: Lawrence Erlbaum, 1984).

22. Richard Wrangham and Dale Peterson, *Demonic Males: Apes and the Origins of Human Violence* (New York: Houghton Mifflin, 1996), p. 113.

eight times as likely to be pinched for vagrancy. They are eight times as likely to vandalize, nearly seven and a half times as likely to fence stolen property, seven times as likely to commit arson, six and a half times as likely to be arrested for gambling offenses, six and a half times as likely to be stopped for drunk driving, and some five and a half times as likely to be hauled in for sex offenses (excluding prostitution and forcible rape). And they are five times as likely to be taken in for drug abuse offenses, four and a half times as likely for offenses against children and the family, over twice as likely for larceny, almost twice as likely for forgery or counterfeiting, and one and a half times as likely for embezzlement.[23]

In addition, younger males exhibit more antisocial behavior than older males. The ages of greatest commission of violence are 15 to 35, with violent criminal behavior (indeed all criminal behavior) peaking in late adolescence and early childhood, then declining to a low plateau around age 40.[24] Younger males are also responsible for the vast majority of crimes that result in violent death.[25] In China, perhaps more than 80 percent of incarcerated males in the 1990s were younger than 30.[26] Young men in all societies monopolize violence and violent crime.[27] The higher potential of young males to commit violent acts exists at both the individual and collective levels. In their analyses of interstate and intrastate episodes of collective aggression since the 1960s, Christian Mesquida and Neil Wiener write, "[There is] a consistent correlation between the ratio of males 15 to 29 years of age per 100 males 30 years of age and older, and the level of

---

23. Ibid., pp. 113–114.

24. Travis Hirschi and Michael Gottfredson, "Age and the Explanation of Crime," *American Journal of Sociology* (November 1983), pp. 552–584.

25. See, for example, Dan Olweus, Ake Mattsson, Daisy Schalling, and Hans Loew, "Circulating Testosterone Levels and Aggression in Adolescent Males: A Causal Analysis," *Psychosomatic Medicine*, Vol. 50, No. 3 (May–June 1988), pp. 261–272; Margo Wilson and Martin Daly, "Competitiveness, Risk Taking, and Violence: The Young Male Syndrome," *Ethology and Sociobiology*, Vol. 6, No. 1 (1985), pp. 59–73; Derral Cheatwood and Kathleen J. Block, "Youth and Homicide: An Investigation of the Age Factor in Criminal Homicide," *Justice Quarterly*, Vol. 7, No. 2 (June 1990), pp. 265–292; and Christian G. Mesquida and Neil I. Wiener, "Human Collective Aggression: A Behavioral Ecology Perspective," *Ethology and Sociobiology*, Vol. 17, No. 4 (July 1996), pp. 247–262. Males aged 15–35 are responsible for the vast majority of homicides. Within that age group, males between 20 and 29 commit most of the homicides. See Wilson and Daly, "Competitiveness, Risk Taking, and Violence."

26. James D. Seymour and Richard Anderson, *New Ghosts, Old Ghosts: Prisons and Labor Reform Camps in China* (London: M.E. Sharpe, 1998), p. 115. These figures can only be approximated from representative cases for which data are available.

27. Satoshi Kanazawa and March C. Still, "Why Men Commit Crimes (and Why They Desist)," *Sociological Theory*, Vol. 18, No. 3 (2000), pp. 434–447.

coalitional aggression as measured by the number of reported conflict-related deaths."[28]

Third, unmarried males commit more violence than married males.[29] As David Courtwright notes, "It is when young men cannot or do not marry that socially disruptive behavior is intensified."[30] According to Robert Wright,

Womanless men . . . compete with special ferocity. An unmarried man between twenty-four and thirty-five years of age is about three times as likely to murder another male as is a married man the same age. Some of this difference no doubt reflects the kinds of men that do and don't get married to begin with, but . . . a good part of the difference may lie in "the pacifying effect" of marriage. Murder isn't the only thing an "unpacified" man is more likely to do. He is also more likely to incur various risks—committing robbery, for example—to gain the resources that may attract women. He is more likely to rape. Abuse of drugs and alcohol . . . compound the problem by further diminishing his chances of ever earning enough money to attract women by legitimate means.[31]

Allan Mazur and Joel Michalek have determined that T (serum testosterone) levels in men who marry drop relative to men who are single: "Changing T levels may explain the low criminality found among married men. . . . Married men, living stably with their wives, are less prone

---

28. Mesquida and Wiener, "Human Collective Aggression," p. 247.

29. See ibid.; John H. Laub, Daniel S. Nagin, and Robert J. Sampson, "Trajectories of Change in Criminal Offending: Good Marriages and the Desistance Process," *American Sociological Review,* Vol. 63, No. 2 (April 1998), pp. 225–238; Robert J. Sampson and John H. Laub, Crime *in the Making: Pathways and Turning Points through Life* (Cambridge, Mass.: Harvard University Press); Daly and Wilson, *Sex, Evolution, and Behavior;* Courtwright, *Violent Land;* Kemper, *Social Structure and Testosterone;* Robert Wright, *The Moral Animal* (New York: Pantheon, 1994); Laura Betzig, "Despotism and Differential Reproduction: A Cross-Cultural Correlation of Conflict Asymmetry, Hierarchy, and Degree of Polygny," *Ethology and Sociobiology,* Vol. 3, No. 4 (1982), pp. 209–221; Martin Daly and Margo Wilson, *Homicide* (Hawthorne, N.Y.: Aldine de Gruyter, 1988); Martin Daly and Margo Wilson, "Killing the Competition: Female/Female and Male/Male Homicide," *Human Nature,* Vol. 1, No. 1 (1990), pp. 81–107; Napoleon A. Chagnon, "Is Reproductive Success Equal in Egalitarian Societies?" in Chagnon and Irons, *Evolutionary Biology and Human Social Behavior,* pp. 374–401; David Buss, *The Evolution of Desire: Strategies of Human Mating* (New York: Basic Books, 1994); Frank A. Pedersen, "Secular Trends in Human Sex Ratios: Their Influence on Individual and Family Behavior," *Human Nature,* Vol. 2, No. 3 (1991), pp. 271–291; and Randy Thornhill and Nancy Thornhill, "Human Rape: An Evolutionary Analysis," *Ethology and Sociobiology,* Vol. 4, No. 3 (1983), pp. 137–173.

30. Courtwright, *Violent Land,* p. 202.

31. Wright, *The Moral Animal,* p. 100.

to crime than unmarried men. Married men are less likely than single men of the same age to kill an unrelated male."[32] According to Mazur and Alan Booth, T has been found to be significantly related to antisocial behavior, including criminal activity and alcohol and substance abuse. When T falls, so does the propensity to engage in this kind of behavior.[33]

Psychologist Satoshi Kanazawa argues that men's psychology is attuned to marriage as a cue to cease criminal behavior: "Criminologists have known that one of the strongest predictors of desistance from criminal careers is a good marriage. Criminals who get married, and especially those who maintain strong marital bonds to their wives, subsequently stop committing crime, whereas criminals at the same age who remain unmarried tend to continue their criminal careers."[34]

Mazur and Michalek suggest some of the dynamics that underlie this tendency:

Single men spend more time in male company than do married men, and they are more likely than married men to encounter confrontations and challenges. Lacking the social support of a wife, they are more likely to face situations where they must protect their social prestige in competitive encounters with other males. These are precisely the kinds of situations in which T elevates. The marriage ceremony is the culmination of a more gradual period of courtship and engagement, in which a man accepts the support and consortship of his partner, removing himself from competition with other men for sexual partners. As a result, according to the reciprocal model, his T declines.[35]

Thus, according to the analyses of Mazur and his colleagues, the larger the number of men who are unable to marry, the higher their circulating T, and the greater amount of violent and antisocial behavior they will exhibit. Kanazawa concurs: "The sudden drop in testosterone after their marriage and the birth of their children might provide the biochemical reason why men's psychological mechanism to commit crime . . .

---

32. Allan Mazur and Joel Michalek, "Marriage, Divorce, and Male Testosterone," *Social Forces*, Vol. 77, No. 1 (September 1998), p. 315.

33. See Allan Mazur and Alan Booth, "Testosterone and Dominance in Men," *Behavioral and Brain Sciences*, Vol. 21, No. 3 (June 1998), pp. 353–397. The debates over the effects of testosterone on behavior have been numerous. Some suggest that it is testosterone's transformation into estradiol that provides the effect. Others dispute that any effect exists at all. See, for example, David France, "Testosterone, the Rogue Hormone, Is Getting a Makeover," *New York Times*, February 17, 1999, p. G3.

34. Satoshi Kanazawa, "Why Productivity Fades with Age: The Crime-Genius Connection," *Journal of Research in Personality*, Vol. 37 (2003), pp. 257–272, at p. 269.

35. Mazur and Michalek, "Marriage, Divorce, and Male Testosterone," p. 327.

'turns off' when they get married and become fathers and simultaneously why the same mechanism does not 'turn off' when the men do not get married."[36] As George Gilder puts it, "Individual life assumes a higher value within the monogamous marriage than it does in the male group."[37] This is not a new phenomenon: The scriptural *Ben Sira* in Jewish tradition, for example, declares, "Without a hedge, the vineyard is laid waste, and without a wife, a man is a hopeless wanderer. Who trusts an armed band of vagabonds?"[38]

Fourth, low-status males commit more violence than high-status males. Again, this empirical finding has found wide confirmation in human societies.[39] As Theodore Kemper notes, "A careful examination of the social science literature supports the view that the lower class is physically more aggressive and more violent in its social relations than the middle class, whether one looks at child rearing, adolescent and young adult peer groups, street encounters, domestic relations, conflict resolution, or crime."[40] In a study by Wilson and Daly, unemployed males, when compared with employed males, were more than four times as likely to commit homicide.[41] Courtwright finds the correlation between unemployment and violent death to be 0.73, and the correlation with homicide to be 0.65; both are statistically significant.[42] In addition, Mazur and Booth cite a study in which unemployed males had the highest T levels among males categorized according to occupation.[43]

Fifth, males commit more violence under the influence of alcohol and certain drugs than males not under such influences. Young unmarried

---

36.   Kanazawa, "Why Productivity Fades with Age," p. 270.

37.   Gilder, *Naked Nomads*, p. 152.

38.   We are indebted to Theodore Kemper for bringing this to our attention. *Ben Sira* is the book of Ecclesiastes. The language of the King James version does not, however, accurately reflect the Hebrew nuances of this passage in chapter 36.

39.   The literature on this subject is immense, so we provide only a sampling here: Wilson and Daly, "Competitiveness, Risk Taking, and Violence"; Mesquida and Wiener, "Human Collective Aggression"; Kemper, *Social Structure and Testosterone*; Courtwright, *Violent Land*; Betzig, "Despotism and Differential Reproduction"; Laura Betzig, *Despotism and Differential Reproduction: A Darwinian View of History* (New York: Aldine de Gruyter, 1986); Daly and Wilson, *Sex, Evolution, and Behavior*; and William H. Durham, "Resource Competition and Human Aggression," *Quarterly Review of Biology*, Vol. 51, No. 3 (September 1976), pp. 385–415.

40.   Kemper, *Social Structure and Testosterone*, p. 73.

41.   Wilson and Daly, "Competitiveness, Risk Taking, and Violence."

42.   Courtwright, *Violent Land*.

43.   Mazur and Booth, "Testosterone and Dominance in Men," p. 361.

males use all such substances more than married males, older males, or females.[44] Alcohol especially, but also drugs such as crack cocaine, methamphetamine, and PCP, are often associated with higher levels of violence.[45] According to one report, 80 percent of U.S. prisoners in 1996 were abusing alcohol or drugs at the time of their arrest.[46]

On the other hand, some drugs (e.g., opium) tend to diminish their users' violent tendencies; still, users may resort to violence to get money to buy more drugs. Writing about Chinese immigrants in nineteenth-century California, Courtwright observes, "Opium, the Chinese intoxicant of choice, was a powerful tranquilizer. Those who were under its influence seldom exhibited the irritable aggressiveness of men drinking liquor in saloons, nor did they beat women and children. But opium smoking did lead to theft by impoverished addicts, especially after prohibitory federal legislation drove up the price of the drug. The opium traffic was also an indirect cause of criminal violence in the form of rivalry among the tongs, secret Chinese organizations that fought for control of the vice industry."[47]

Sixth, transient males commit proportionately more violence than nontransient males; they also tend to be victims of violent crime more of-

---

44. Wilson and Daly, "Competitiveness, Risk Taking, and Violence."

45. See Judith Roizen, "Issues in the Epidemiology of Alcohol and Violence"; Kai Pernanen, "Alcohol-Related Violence: Conceptual Models"; Klaus A. Miczek, Elise M. Weerts, and Joseph F. DeBold, "Alcohol, Aggression, and Violence: Biobehavioral Determinants"; and Alan R. Lang, "Alcohol-Related Violence: Psychological Perspectives," all in Susan E. Martin, ed., *Alcohol and Interpersonal Violence: Fostering Multidisciplinary Perspectives*, NIAAA Research Monograph No. 24 (Rockville, Md.: National Institutes of Health, 1993), pp. 30–36, 37–69, 83–119, and 121–147. See also James J. Collins, "Alcohol Use and Expressive Interpersonal Violence"; David Levinson, "Social Setting, Cultural Factors, and Alcohol-Related Aggression"; Richard E. Boyatzis, "Who Should Drink What, When, and Where If Looking for a Fight," all in Edward Gottheil et al., ed., *Alcohol, Drug Abuse, and Aggression* (Springfield: Charles C. Thomas, 1983), pp. 5–25, 1–58, and 314–329; as well as A. James Giannini, Robert H. Loiselle, and Brian H. Graham, "Cocaine-Associated Violence and Relationship to Route of Administration," *Journal of Substance Abuse Treatment*, Vol. 10, No. 1 (January–February 1993), pp. 67–69; Norman S. Miller, Mark S. Gold, and John C. Mahler, "Violent Behaviors Associated with Cocaine Use: Possible Pharmacological Mechanisms," *International Journal of the Addictions*, Vol. 26, No. 10 (1991), pp. 1077–1088; and P.M. Marzuk, K. Tardiff, D. Smyth, M. Stajic, and A.C. Leon, "Cocaine Use, Risk Taking, and Fatal Russian Roulette," *JAMA*, May 20, 1992, pp. 2635–2637.

46. Christopher Wren, "Drugs or Alcohol Linked to 80% of Inmates," *New York Times*, January 9, 1998, p. A14.

47. Courtwright, *Violent Land*, pp. 165–166. See also David T. Courtwright, *Dark Paradise: Opiate Addiction in America before 1940* (Cambridge, Mass.: Harvard University Press, 1982).

ten than nontransients. In 1997 Ren Meng reported, "In the Jinqiao area of Shanghai's Pudong region [in China], with the rise of the migrant population, migrants now account for over 90% of crimes, compared to 30% in 1990." In addition, migrants are overwhelmingly likely to be poor, which is consistent with the characteristics of bachelor subcultures.[48]

Mazur and Booth again offer a psychological rationale for the synergy between transience, on the one hand, and openness to violent behavior, on the other:

There may be a general hypersensitivity to insult in any subculture that is (or once was) organized around young men who are unconstrained by traditional community agents of social control, as often occurs in frontier communities, gangs, among vagabonds or bohemians, and after breakdowns in the social fabric following wars or natural disasters. When young men place special emphasis on protecting their reputations, and they are not restrained from doing so, dominance contests become ubiquitous, the hallmark of male-to-male interaction. . . . Hormone levels [T levels] should be elevated in young men who are constantly vigilant against assaults on their reputations.[49]

Seventh, males who are predisposed to risk taking (i.e., men who are young, unmarried, low status, or substance abusing) exhibit even more exaggerated risky and violent behavior when in groups.[50] Experiments have shown that this "risky shift," or the willingness to take greater risks collectively than individually, is more pronounced in groups of males than in groups of females.[51] Males encourage risky behavior in group situations to enhance their social prestige. As Courtwright puts it, "Men who congregate with men tend to be more sensitive about status and reputation. Even if they are not intoxicated with drink or enraged by insult, they instinctively test one another, probing for signs of weakness. . . . Disreputable, lower-class males . . . exercised much greater influence in bachelor communities like bunkhouses and mining camps. They both

48. Ren Meng, "Confronting Three Populations of 80 Million," *Inside China Mainland*, Vol. 19, No. 1 (January 1997), pp. 78–81.

49. Mazur and Booth, "Testosterone and Dominance," p. 360.

50. See Irving Lester Janis, *Groupthink: Psychological Studies of Policy Decisions and Fiascoes* (Boston: Houghton Mifflin, 1982); Nathan Kogan and Michael Wallach, *Risk Taking: A Study in Cognition and Personality* (New York: Holt, Rinehart, and Winston, 1964); and Norris R. Johnson, Joanne G. Stemler, and Deborah Hunter, "Crowd Behavior as 'Risky Shift': A Laboratory Experiment," *Sociometry*, Vol. 40, No. 2 (June 1977), pp. 183–187.

51. Johnson, Stemler, and Hunter, "Crowd Behavior as 'Risky Shift.'"

tempted and punished, for to fail to emulate their vices was to fail, in their own terms, to be a man."[52]

Thus the behavior of men in groups—particularly young, single, low-status males—will not rise above the behavior of the worst-behaved individual. Collectively, they will take larger risks and be more violent than if they acted alone. Wrangham and Peterson explicate the linkage between risky behavior in male groups and their propensity for violence:

Because of the large potential reproductive rewards at stake for males, sexual selection has apparently favored male temperaments that revel in high-risk/high-gain ventures. At the individual level, this temperamental quality can show relatively trivial effects. Men may sometimes drive their cars faster or gamble more intensely or perhaps play sports more recklessly than women. But the sort of relatively discountable wildness that, for example, hikes automobile insurance rates for adolescent boys and young men also produces a greater willingness to risk their own and others' lives; and that sort of risk attraction becomes very significant once men acquire weapons. And where men combine into groups—gangs or villages or tribes or nations—this driving, adventurous ethic turns quickly aggressive and lethally serious.[53]

In sum, men who congregate with other men tend to be single (which in itself elevates T); they also tend to have higher T levels because of their inclination to compete for status and position within groups. The pronounced risky shift in unmarried male groups is therefore not surprising. If these groups experience the risky shift, the likely result will be a collective effort to capture resources through aggression and violence.

Consequences for High-Sex-Ratio Societies

If these findings hold, what are the likely consequences for societies where, through offspring sex selection in all its forms, the bare-branch population is rapidly and disproportionately rising? What happens when a society consciously selects for bare branches? The result, we argue, will be a significant increase in societal, and possibly intersocietal, violence.[54]

---

52. Courtwright, *Violent Land*, pp. 42–43.

53. Wrangham and Peterson, *Demonic Males*, p. 235.

54. In their study of U.S. locales, Steven F. Messner and Robert J. Sampson found that high sex ratios led to lower levels of family disruption (e.g., divorce and illegitimacy). Lower family disruption levels, in turn, led to lower crime levels. These findings are not applicable to China and India, however, because the authors are making comparisons within a society, not between societies. The movement of women from one locale within the United States to another is not constrained by the presence of international

Crime rates tend to be higher in polygynous societies, and a high sex ratio is the functional equivalent of polygyny.[55] Moreover, the increase in violence will be at both the individual and collective levels. Several researchers, including Mesquida and Wiener, have posited a relationship between young, poor males, unmarriageability, and collective aggression:

Young males participate in collective aggression to acquire the resources needed to attract a mate, and we should expect a great majority of the militants to come from that section of the population with fewest resources. . . . It is likely then that controlling elites astutely underwrite such risky undertakings as territorial expansion or colonization, especially when the alternative is having the aggressive tendencies of the male citizens directed at themselves. . . . Tentatively, we would like to propose that this intergenerational competition for reproductive resources, when exacerbated by the presence of a relatively large number of resourceless young males, might result in the emergence of male collective aggression, which occasionally expresses itself as expansionist warfare.[56]

Boone asserts that in medieval Portugal, for example, the presence of significant numbers of bare branches (whom he refers to as "cadet males") necessitated territorial expansion. He documents the creation of "a highly competitive, volatile situation at the societal level with respect to the problem of excess cadet males. Rulers must choose between dispersing these individuals, for example, in expansionist campaigns, or facing disorder and overthrow on the home front."[57] He further writes, "Territorial expansion does not necessarily arise as an adaptive response on the part of a polity to expand its resource base or to solve productive deficiencies facing the population at large: expansionist warfare often

---

borders. Furthermore, Messner and Sampson examined a society with many types of family disruption, in contrast to other societies where social norms significantly narrow that range. We argue that across societies, including societies with strong norms against family disruption, highly skewed sex ratios will be associated with increasing levels of intrasocietal disruption. This does not contradict Messner and Sampson's findings, but rather suggests that cultural context must be taken into account. See Messner and Sampson, "The Sex Ratio, Family Disruption, and Rates of Violent Crime: The Paradox of Demographic Structure," *Social Forces,* Vol. 69, No. 3 (March 1991), pp. 693–713.

55. See Margaret K. Bacon, Irvin L. Child, and Herbert Barry, "A Cross-Cultural Study of Correlates of Crime," *Journal of Abnormal and Social Psychology,* Vol. 66, No. 4 (1963), pp. 291–300; and Betzig, "Despotism and Differential Reproduction."

56. Mesquida and Wiener, "Human Collective Aggression," pp. 256–260.

57. Boone, "Parental Investment and Elite Family Structure in Preindustrial States," p. 868.

results from attempts by individuals or coalitions to maintain control by directing the competition of their immediate subordinates away from themselves and against neighboring territories. These strategies . . . may be maintained at a considerable resource deficit seen from the point of view of the general population."[58]

Wright is even blunter: "Few things are more anxiety-producing for an elite governing class than gobs of [mateless] and childless men with at least a modicum of political power. . . . Extreme polygyny often goes hand in hand with extreme political hierarchy, and reaches its zenith under the most despotic regimes. . . . Leaving lots of men without wives is not just inegalitarian: it's dangerous. . . . A nation, in which large numbers of low-income men remain mateless is not the kind of country many of us would want to live in."[59] Laura Betzig, in an intriguing empirical study of 186 societies, found the correlation between polygyny and despotism to be statistically significant.[60]

Two observations would seem to flow from the analysis thus far. First, high-sex-ratio societies are governable only by authoritarian regimes capable of suppressing violence at home and exporting it abroad through colonization or war.[61] Second, high-sex-ratio societies that are ethnically heterogeneous are likely to experience civil strife directed against minority ethnic groups, which the government (if it represents the majority ethnic group) may seek to encourage. In our view, the first observation holds for China, and the second, for India.

Consequences for Women

Females in high-sex-ratio societies are likely to experience a variety of negative consequences. First, their already low status in society will probably decline even further. This might seem counterintuitive, as laws of supply and demand would suggest that in high-sex-ratio societies, the

---

58. Boone, "Noble Family Structure and Expansionist Warfare in the Late Middle Ages," p. 81.

59. Wright, *The Moral Animal*, pp. 98–101.

60. Betzig, *Despotism and Differential Reproduction*, p. 94.

61. It is hard to concur with William T. Divale and Marvin Harris that "warfare perpetuate[s] and propagate[s] itself because it [is] an effective method for sustaining the material and ideological restrictions on the rearing of female infants." Nevertheless, we understand how their analysis of 448 populations could result in the conclusion that "we are most likely to find unbalanced sex ratios when warfare is present." See Divale and Harris, "Population, Warfare, and the Male Supremacist Complex," *American Anthropologist*, Vol. 78, No. 3 (September 1976), pp. 531, 528.

relative scarcity of women would increase their value and thus make them more powerful.[62] Yet this has not been the case. When women become scarce, males—particularly powerful men who view females as commodities to be bought and sold—control them even more tightly.[63] Scott South and Katherine Trent describe this dynamic:

It is somewhat paradoxical that the increased "valuation" of women that accompanies high sex ratios severely limits their life options. Our results suggest that an undersupply of women, combined with men's overwhelming structural power, leads to high marriage and fertility rates and low rates of divorce and illegitimacy. But high sex ratios also serve to delimit and constrain the roles women occupy. Hence, where women are in short supply, their levels of literacy and labor-force participation are low, both relative to men in their own society and to women in low-sex-ratio societies. Their suicide rate, relative to men's, is also high. It would appear, then, given the current distribution of structural power, the relative undersupply of females entails few benefits and many costs to women.[64]

Second, when females are already scarce, they are more likely to be kidnapped or sold. In China a chattel market in women and children already exists. According to one source, "From 1991 through 1996, Chinese police freed 88,000 kidnapped women and children and arrested 143,000 police for participating in the slave trade."[65] In 1993 Chinese authorities reported the kidnapping of 15,000 females. Figures from 1997 to 1998 indicate that the police rescued 23,000 women and 4,260 children, in addition to breaking up 8,000 kidnapping gangs.[66] In the late 1990s, the price for an abducted woman was $240 to $480, while a traditional dowry ran upward of $1,200.[67]

---

62. We thus disagree with analyses represented by such works as Marcia Guttentag and Paul L. Secord, *Too Many Women? The Sex Ratio Question* (Beverly Hills, Calif.: Sage, 1983); and Mary Anne Warren, *Gendercide: The Implication of Sex Selection* (Totowa, N.J.: Rowman and Allanheld, 1985).

63. See Scott J. South and Katherine Trent, "Sex Ratios and Women's Roles: A Cross-National Analysis," *American Journal of Sociology*, Vol. 93, No. 5 (March 1988), pp. 1096–1115; and Ashok Mitra, *Implications of the Declining Sex Ratio in India's Population* (Bombay: Allied Publishers, 1979).

64. South and Trent, "Sex Ratios and Women's Roles," p. 1112.

65. Dorinda Elliot, "Trying to Stand on Two Feet," *Newsweek*, June 29, 1998, pp. 48–49.

66. "China Arrests Thousands for Trading Women and Children," Associated Press, June 8, 1999.

67. Li Ji, "Discussions on the Gender Imbalance in China and the Entailed Social Problems," Foreign Affairs College, Beijing, 1999, p. 23.

Chinese authorities suspect that many more women and girls are abducted and sold than is reported. Li Ji explains, "Local policemen complained about the obstacles they faced when trying to save the women: the local people considered women trade reasonable and tried their best to stop them. So the figure of [abducted] women . . . is conservative."[68] Typically, adult women are abducted from the cities and sold in the countryside. Even if an abducted woman somehow manages to escape her prisonlike confinement, her family will probably never accept her back. Anthropologists have noted that in societies where the capture of women is prevalent, a feedback loop can develop such that the desire to capture women promotes offspring sex selection for males likely to engage in this act.[69]

Third, as male members of an older birth cohort search for mates among younger generations of females, the age of female consent tends to drop.[70] A lower age of consent allows for the "transfer" of females to their intendeds before they can become objects of capture by other men. The significantly smaller dowries that the families of these females must pay adds to the temptation to engage in this practice. In the past, it was not uncommon in China and India for brides who had not yet reached menarche to be handed off to their husbands' families. In historical China, even infant girls were sometimes transferred to be raised by the grooms' families and married before menarche.[71] A 1993 survey conducted in Rajasthan, India, revealed that 56 percent of women had married before they were 15. Nineteen percent had married before the age of

---

68. Ibid.

69. This appears to have been the case with the Yanomamo in South America, where a birth ratio of 129:100 was the culmination of tribal bridal-capture practices. See Napoleon A. Chagnon, Mark V. Flinn, and Thomas F. Melancon, "Sex-Ratio Variation among the Yanomamo Indians," in Chagnon and Irons, *Evolutionary Biology and Human Social Behavior*, pp. 290–320.

70. See South and Trent, "Sex Ratios and Women's Roles"; and Courtwright, *Violent Land*. "Youthful brides," notes Courtwright, "were particularly common in regions with very large male surpluses. . . . Marriages of twelve- and thirteen-year old girls were not unheard of in the Chesapeake colonies and were noted during the California Gold Rush. In frontier Michigan the legal age of female consent to sexual intercourse was eleven years." Ibid., p. 137.

71. See James Hayes, "San Po Tsai (Little Daughters-in-Law) and Child Betrothals in the New Territories of Hong Kong from the 1890s to the 1960s," in Maria Jaschok and Suzanne Miers, eds., *Women and Chinese Patriarchy: Submission, Servitude, and Escape* (London: Zed, 1994), pp. 45–76. Another good sourcebook is Arthur P. Wolf and Chieh-shan Huang, *Marriage and Adoption in China, 1845–1945* (Stanford, Calif.: Stanford University Press, 1980).

10.[72] The transfer of infant girls is again becoming prevalent in China. In recent years, China has also witnessed the emergence of a black market in girl babies that serves two types of clients: childless couples who cannot afford a black-market boy baby, and couples who want to ensure that their sons will eventually have wives. Unlike the flow of adult women from cities and towns to the countryside, the flow of girl babies is in the opposite direction.[73]

Fourth, and again counterintuitively, a high sex ratio does not necessarily mean lower population growth. Tighter male control of females in societies where they are already scarce may actually result in more births per woman.[74] This tighter male control also leads to more women than men committing suicide. In low-sex-ratio societies, the opposite is true.[75] Among females, more younger women than older women commit suicide in high-sex-ratio societies. Nearly 56 percent of female suicides worldwide are Chinese women, making this the highest female suicide rate in the world. The overwhelming majority of these women are of childbearing age. In addition, twice as many women as men under the age of 45 commit suicide in China.[76] (For comparison, four times as many men as women take their own lives in the United States). In India, too, the suicide rate for young women is higher than for young men.[77] Observers generally attribute these high suicide rates to the low status of women in patrilocal households, which confers on them both the greatest burdens and the least respect and autonomy.[78]

Fifth, high-sex-ratio societies generally have higher levels of prostitutions. Some evidence also suggests heightened levels of homosexuality

---

72.   John F. Burns, "Though Illegal, Child Marriage Is Popular in Part of India," *New York Times*, May 11, 1998, p. A1.

73.   Damien McElroy, "Chinese Buy Baby Girls on the Black Market," *London Daily Telegraph*, August 1, 1999, http://www.telegraph.co.uk/htmlContent.jhtml?html=%2Farchive%2F1998%2F04%2F02%2Fnlot02.html.

74.   See South and Trent, "Sex Ratios and Women's Roles"; and Mitra, *Implications of the Declining Sex Ratio in India's Population*.

75.   See South and Trent, "Sex Ratios and Women's Roles."

76.   Christopher J.L. Murray and Alan D. Lopez, eds., *The Global Burden of Disease: A Comprehensive Assessment of Mortality and Disability from Diseases, Injuries, and Risk Factors in 1990 and Projected to 2020* (Cambridge, Mass.: Harvard University Press, 1996), p. 448; and Elisabeth Rosenthal, "Women's Suicides Reveal Rural China's Bitter Roots," *New York Times*, January 24, 1999, sec. 1, p. 1.

77.   Murray and Lopez, *The Global Burden of Disease*, p. 444.

78.   See, for example, Ling Li, "China's Suicide Rate," *New York Times*, January 28, 1999, p. A26.

and polyandry.[79] In response, governments have on occasion facilitated the creation of brothels. Officials in nineteenth-century Australia, for example, explicitly recognized the danger of too many men and too few women: "The numerical predominance of males on the first convict ships was from the outset perceived as a social and political problem: those in authority believed that 'without a sufficient proportion of that sex [female] it is well known that it would be impossible to preserve the settlement from gross irregularities and disorders.'[80] Women were needed as an antidote to sexual deviance (read sodomy), rape of 'respectable' (read upper class) women, and rebellion."[81]

Migration of women from other cultures into relatively homogeneous societies, such as China's, may not necessarily alleviate the shortage of marriageable women. Despite numerous reports of the sale of young girls from Burma, North Korea, and Vietnam to buyers from China, it is unclear how many of these girls actually become brides and how many are instead forced into prostitution.[82] In such a cultural context, a "rational

---

79. See Courtwright, *Violent Land;* Wright, *The Moral Animal;* and Nels Anderson, *The Hobo: The Sociology of the Homeless Man* (Chicago: University of Chicago Press, 1961), chap. 10. In chapter 4, we note the widespread practice of female infanticide in Fukien Province in the Yuan, Ming, and Qing dynasties. Thus it is noteworthy that during this period Fukien also appeared to have a more permissive attitude toward homosexuality compared with other parts of China. T'ien Ju-k'ang notes, "Prolonged deprivation of contact with the female sex may also explain the prevalence of homosexuality, called 'sworn brotherhood,' in Fukien. . . . In the criminal codes of the Ch'ing [Qing] Dynasty, the crime of sodomy . . . was punishable by one hundred heavy blows. . . . But in Fukien, the custom of being 'sworn brothers' was still something that could be boasted about in public, rather than being considered shameful." T'ien, *Male Anxiety and Female Chastity: A Comparative Study of Chinese Ethical Values in Ming-Ch'ing Times* (New York: E.J. Brill, 1988), p. 31, n. 54. Concerning prostitution, in the high-sex-ratio society of mid-1800s' Chinatown in San Francisco, the 1850 census shows that of the few Chinese women in the city, 71 percent were prostitutes. See Cheng and Bonacich, *Labor Immigration under Capitalism,* p. 421. In Tibet, high sex ratios traditionally led to polyandry, rather than disenfranchisement of later-born sons: Several brothers would share a wife. See Nancy E. Levine, "Differential Child Care in Three Tibetan Communities: Beyond Son Preference," *Population and Development Review,* Vol. 13, No. 2 (June 1987), pp. 281–304.

80. Martin, *The Founding of Australia,* pp. 22–29.

81. Raelene Frances, "The History of Female Prostitution in Australia," in Roberta Perkins, G. Prestage, R. Sharp, and F. Lovejoy, eds., *Sex Work and Sex Workers in Australia* (Sydney: University of New South Wales, 1994), pp. 27–52 (quotation is from p. 3 of internet version of 18 pages, http://www.hartford-hwp.com/archives/24/230.html); and Martin, *The Founding of Australia.*

82. John Pomfret, "Portrait of a Famine," Washington Post Foreign Service, February 12, 1999.

bachelor" must acquire, by whatever means possible, the resources to win in a hypergynous marriage market.[83]

The Governmental Perspective

Do bare branches pose a threat to the government? If they remain in spree-and-bust mode, the primary victims will be the bare branches themselves. Also, even though bare branches create problems for local law enforcement and perhaps even troubling amounts of collateral damage, during their sprees they also provide a steady source of revenue to their communities. Writing about frontier life in the United States, for example, Courtwright states, "The best that could be done was to fashion a police and court system designed to keep the lid on. Cattle-town justice, to use the term loosely, was aimed at controlling, segregating, and profiting from cowboy vice sprees, not at discouraging them. . . . Open vice was profitable to their towns but attracted criminal elements along with thirsty young cowboys eager to shoot their pistols and blow their wages. The price of separating them from their money was a relatively high level of violence and disorder."[84] In robust economies, governments may simply decide to allow bare branches to burn themselves out, leaving it to the communities to deal with the collateral damage.

What happens, however, if the economy turns sour? What if the bare branches become desperate? Here the potential for a more serious threat arises. Instead of being distracted by vice, the bare branches may turn to appropriation of resources, using force if necessary. As Wilson and Daly note, "Men are not poorer than women, but they help themselves to other peoples' property more often, and they are evidently readier to use violence to do so. The chronic competitive situation among males may ultimately be responsible for a greater felt need for surplus—as opposed to subsistence—resources."[85] The combination of large numbers of bare branches, their outcast subculture, and their lack of stake in the existing social order may predispose them toward organized social banditry.

Below we present several historical cases in which the existence of significant numbers of bare branches acted at the aggravating/amplifying/triggering effect for intrasocietal or intersocietal violence. In these cases, bare branches were part of a larger set of sufficient conditions that

---

83. Mildred Dickemann, "Female Infanticide, Reproductive Strategies, and Social Stratification: A Preliminary Model," in Chagnon and Irons, *Evolutionary Biology and Human Social Behavior*, pp. 321–367.

84. Courtwright, *Violent Land,* pp. 98, 108.

85. Wilson and Daly," Competitiveness, Risk Taking, and Violence," p. 66.

resulted in such violence. To use a metaphor, the mere presence of dry, bare branches cannot cause a fire, but when the sparks begin to fly, those branches can act as kindling, turning sparks into flames.

The Nien Rebellion is an example of how exaggerated offspring sex selection can threaten the stability of entire regions, and even great empires.[86] The rebellion began in 1851 with an organized group of bandits from the poor area of Huai-pei in northeast China whose initial goal was survival. Combined with other factors—including crippling natural disasters, inefficient government, tax increases, and the ambitions of a few charismatic leaders—the activities of the Nien bandits, along with those of the Taiping rebels to the south, eventually led to a massive rebellion against the state.

During the first half of the nineteenth century, counties in the Huai-pei region experienced flood, drought, or locust invasion every three to four years: Crops were destroyed, and many peasants died from starvation. In reaction, the people of Huai-pei turned to female infanticide, believing that boys had value because they could contribute to family income; girls, on the other hand, sapped family resources. Moreover, they could marry only at considerable expense. Nineteenth-century statistics for the Huai-pei region suggest an average of 129 men for every 100 women, an extremely high sex ratio.[87] Because the proportion of women increases over the life cycle, and because men tend to have higher mortality rates, the ratio of males to females in the neonatal years may have been even higher.

As a result, according to David Ownby, "poorer men had to delay their marriages by six years in comparison with richer men, and . . . *twenty-five percent of men were unable to marry at all.*"[88] This accords with estimates of female infanticide in the late imperial period, which are said to have reached levels of 300 per 1,000.[89] James Lee and Wang Feng concur: "Among peasant families in north-eastern China in the century after 1774, between one-fifth and one-quarter of all females were killed as chil-

---

86. This account of the Nien is adapted from the work of Perry, *Rebels and Revolutionaries in North China, 1845–1945*.

87. Ibid., p. 51. For purposes of comparison, the sex ratio in Dodge City, Kansas, in 1880 was "only" 124:100. Courtwright, *Violent Land*, p. 58.

88. Ownby, "Approximations of Chinese Bandits," p. 242 (emphasis in original).

89. Ibid.

dren."[90] Polygamy and concubinage, as practiced by rich men in an estimated 10 percent of Chinese marriages, further contributed to the scarcity of marriageable women.[91] Although the decision by peasant families
to raise sons at the expense of daughters may have seemed a rational
choice at the time, the result was a serious surplus of poor, young adult,
single males. As Daniel Little writes, "Families adopted the practice of female infanticide to increase family income and security, but the long-term
aggregate result was a skewed demography in which there was a large
surplus of young men. These young men became natural recruits for bandit gangs and local militia—thus providing resources for the emergence
of collective strategies of predation and protection."[92] Later dubbed "bare
sticks" or "bare branches," these men would never have their own families: The girls who should have grown up to become their wives and the
mothers of their children had been killed. As one Chinese official, Chen
Shengshao, wrote in 1827, "Since marrying off women is hard, people
raise few women. Since affording to marry is difficult, there are many
bachelors."[93] The high price of marriage would lead many "homeless
bandits" to "kidnap, steal, and feud."[94]

Both Ownby and James Watson have articulated a link in historical
China between violence and permanent, involuntary bachelorhood
caused by high sex ratios. According Ownby, "In the eyes of most Chinese an unmarried man is not truly an adult, not truly a man."[95] Ownby
suggests that a dynamic, which he refers to as "protest masculinity," may
have been at work. According to this view, men who are unable to fulfill
gender expectations are driven toward "hypermasculine displays in order to prove to others, as well as to themselves, that they are indeed 'real

---

90. "6.3 Brides for Seven Brothers," *Economist*, December 19, 1998–January 1, 1999,
p. 57. See also James Z. Lee and Wang Feng, *One Quarter of Humanity: Malthusian Mythology and Chinese Realities, 1700–2000* (Cambridge, Mass.: Harvard University Press,
1999).

91. David Ownby, *Brotherhoods and Secret Societies in Early and Mid-Qing China: The
Formation of a Tradition* (Stanford, Calif.: Stanford University, 1996).

92. Daniel Little, *Understanding Peasant China: Case Studies in the Philosophy of Social
Science* (New Haven, Conn.: Yale University Press, 1989), p. 172.

93. Chen Shengshao, Wensulu 1827, as quoted in David Ownby, "Approximations of
Chinese Bandits: Perverse Rebels, Romantic Heroes, or Frustrated Bachelors?" in Susan Brownell and Jeffrey N. Wasserstrom, eds., *Chinese Femininities/Chinese Masculinities: A Reader* (Berkeley: University of California Press, 2002), p. 241.

94. Chen Shengshao, Wensulu 1827, as quoted in Ownby, "Approximations of Chinese Bandits," p. 245.

95. Ownby, "Approximations of Chinese Bandits," p. 242.

men.'"[96] Watson, who coined the phrase "bachelor subculture" to help explain how antisocial behavior becomes the norm for these men, describes this linkage: "A strategy that [bare branches] sometimes use to enhance their male image is to make a regular practice of challenging the public face of other men. Face is essentially an attribute of married men who have families to protect and obligations to fulfill. Unmarried men have little face to preserve because they do not command much respect in the community. . . . By definition, therefore, bachelors remain perpetual adolescents who cannot play a full role in society. Taking this argument to its logical conclusion an unmarried youth can have no face and is therefore dangerous. . . . These 'bare sticks' had nothing to lose except their reputations for violence."[97]

Ownby notes that the term "bare sticks" or "bare branches" "refers to both violent, petty criminals as well as to bachelors." Quoting a nineteenth-century Western missionary, he writes that for bare sticks, the "sublime ideal" was to make it "a sport and a matter of pride to defy the laws and the magistrates, and commit all kinds of crimes. To give and receive wounds with composure; to kill others with the most perfect coolness; and to have no fear of death for yourself."[98] He also suggests that most bandits in historical China were bare branches. Watson writes that most of the bare branches in his study were semiliterate third, fourth, or fifth sons whose families were too poor to provide them with an inheritance. While still in their teens, many of these noninheriting young men were forced out of their homes by their parents. A number of them would come to live in bachelor houses with other unmarried youths.[99] In their early twenties, many would move into other types of male-only collectives—workers' dormitories, monasteries, religious brotherhoods, or barracks of the local militia—where they would spend much of their leisure time practicing martial arts.

In nineteenth-century Huai-pei, bare branches had two choices: join the military or migrate to the city. Historically, a large portion of China's army had come from this region. On returning home from service, however, many former soldiers could not find work. Meanwhile, bare

---

96. Ibid.

97. James L. Watson, "Self-Defense Corps, Violence, and the Bachelor Subculture in South China: Two Case Studies," *Proceedings of the Second International Conference on Sinology,* Academia Sinica, Taiwan (Republic of China), June 1989, p. 216.

98. Ownby, "Approximations of Chinese Bandits," p. 244.

99. Watson, "Self-Defense Corps, Violence, and the Bachelor Subculture in South China," p. 213.

branches who had moved to the city and were unable to find jobs became beggars, vagrants, or poorly paid day laborers. Some would view banditry as their only means of survival.[100]

Many bare-branch bandits during this period began as salt smugglers. (The government's high tax on salt had made this trade particularly profitable.) Over time, however, local officials came to view such illegal activities with growing alarm. Analyzing the situation, one county magistrate concluded that three categories of men were creating unrest—bare sticks, smugglers, and bandits—and that the overlap between the three groups was considerable.[101] One commentator summed up the attitude of these young men: "They do not fear the imperial laws, nor do they submit to the discipline of their fathers or elder brothers."[102]

The bandits, who initially worked in small, autonomous groups, eventually started to organize. Li notes, "In 1855, most of the 'Nien Zi' [Nien bandits] met at Zhi Heji (a small county in An Hui Province) and united to form a powerful armed force—'Nien Jun.' The goal of the army was to overthrow the Qing Dynasty."[103] Other groups, such as the Taiping rebels, who had a broader political agenda, saw the Nien bandits as potential allies. At its peak, the rebellion included as many as 100,000 bare branches. Active in Anhwei (Anhui), Honan, Hupeh, Kiangsu, and Shantung counties, the Nien's power continued to grow. In 1862 the governor of Anhwei "reported that there were at least two thousand Nien forts in Huai-pei, each with one to three thousand inhabitants. The Nien apparently were in at least nominal control of a population of some two to six million people."[104] In 1868, with the help of foreign arms and the adoption of Western ways of war, the army of the Qing dynasty succeeded in crushing the rebellion.

Robert Kaplan sees parallels between mid-nineteenth-century China and China today. According to Kaplan, "Behind the . . . the steep decline of the Qing Dynasty in the mid-nineteenth century—culminating in armed revolts that killed millions of Chinese—were . . . imbalances be-

---

100. See James Tong, "Rational Outlaws: Rebels and Bandits in the Ming Dynasty, 1368–1644," in Michael Taylor, ed., *Rationality and Revolution* (Cambridge: Cambridge University Press, 1988), pp. 98–128.

101. Perry, *Rebels and Revolutionaries in North China, 1845–1945*, p. 102.

102. Hsiao Kung-ch'uan, *Rural China: Imperial Control in the Nineteenth Century* (Seattle: University of Washington Press, 1967), p. 458.

103. Li, "Discussions on the Gender Imbalance in China and the Entailed Social Problems," p. 11.

104. Perry, *Rebels and Revolutionaries in North China, 1845–1945*, p. 127.

tween soaring populations and precipitous declines in arable land per capita."[105] He notes that, among developing countries in the mid-1990s,
only Egypt and Bangladesh had less arable land per capita than China.
Today China is in the midst of one of its worst droughts in decades, with
the northeast (the ancestral home of the Nien) being the hardest hit. The
parallels to conditions in early nineteenth-century China also extend to
the country's large surplus of young, unattached men: "According to
figures from authoritative departments, China has an indigent population of 80 million, a migrant population of 80 million, and will soon have
80 million single men."[106] Our analysis suggest that the overlap between
these three populations is very significant. China, it seems, is re-creating
the vast army of bare branches that plagued it during the nineteenth
century.

MEDIEVAL PORTUGAL

The case of medieval Portugal, a country that invested heavily in
firstborn sons to maintain familial accumulation of resources over generations, demonstrates the power of bare branches to influence foreign, as
well as domestic, policy.[107] The adult sex ratio in Portugal during this period was approximately 112 males to 100 females; the childhood sex ratio
may have been somewhat higher. Low-status women were much more
likely to marry than low-status men. This confluence of factors bred
extreme political instability, as lower-class bare branches began banding
together in small armies.[108]

Medieval Portugal also had a number of high-status bare branches—
second, third, and higher birth-order sons of nobility who could not
inherit and thus could not marry. According to Boone, "Following ado-

---

105.   Robert D. Kaplan, *The Ends of the Earth: A Journey at the Dawn of the Twenty-first
Century* (New York: Random House, 1996), pp. 299–300.

106.   Ren, "Confronting Three Populations of 80 Million," p. 80.

107.   This case study is adapted from Boone, "Noble Family Structure and Expansionist Warfare in the Late Middle Ages"; and Boone, "Parental Investment and Elite Family Structure in Preindustrial States." In India, primogeniture was more prevalent
among the upper castes. It was not practiced for the most part in China, where
firstborn sons reportedly were more likely to receive land as an inheritance, and younger sons were more likely to receive movable property. In some cases, each son would
receive land, but the firstborn would be given more than his brothers. Of course, the
second factor in the Portuguese case, landed nobility, is no longer a major factor in either India or China.

108.   Boone, "Noble Family Structure and Expansionist Warfare in the Late Middle
Ages," p. 89.

lescence, a period of vagabondage was considered a necessary element in an aristocratic male's development. Vagabondage was not usually solitary, and often bands of 'youths' lived and traveled together: a newly dubbed 'youth' might arm and take with him the sons of his father's vassals who were his own age."[109] One observer offered this account of classic bare-branch behavior in Portugal during this period: "The second and third born sons, and others, who by the custom of the land have little or no portion in the inheritance of their fathers, and who by poverty are often constrained to follow wars that are unjust and tyrannical so as to sustain their estate of noblesse, since they know no other calling but arms; and therein they commit so much ill that it would be frightening to tell of all the pillaging and crimes with which they oppress the poor people."[110]

During periods of political upheaval, bands of bare branches, backed by force of arms, supported challengers to the regime who promised to redistribute the country's wealth. Alternatively, the regime would send bare branches on foreign adventures of conquest and colonization. Boone cites the case of João I, the illegitimate half-brother of the Portuguese monarch, who seized the throne after the latter's death with the help of the cadet sons and their bare-branch bands. When João I discovered that these bands, through piracy and robbery, were beginning to threaten his own rule, he obtained Papal consent to launch the Reconquista—Portugal's military campaign along the North African coast. Boone remarks, "It was above all *the cadets*, who lacked land and other sources of revenue within the country who desired war, which would permit them to accede to a situation of social and material independence."[111] Indeed, Georges Duby notes, "It is obvious that it was the bands of 'youths' excluded by so many social prohibitions from the main body of settled men, fathers of families and heads of houses, with their prolonged spells of turbulent behavior making them an unstable fringe of society, who created and sustained the crusades."[112]

To a certain extent, Portugal's expansionist strategy succeeded. By the mid-sixteenth century, nearly 25 percent of adult noble males had died in war, thereby reducing the overall number of bare branches. Inter-

109. Ibid.

110. Philip de Mezieres, as cited in ibid., p. 86.

111. Boone, "Noble Family Structure and Expansionist Warfare in the Late Middle Ages," p. 94 (emphasis in original).

112. Georges Duby, *The Chivalrous Society*, trans. Cynthia Postan (London: Edward Arnold, 1977), p. 120, as cited in Boone, "Noble Family Structure and Expansionist Warfare in the Late Middle Ages."

estingly, the higher his birth order, the more likely a son would have been killed in a foreign land. Thus in medieval Portugal, the combination of high sex ratios and primogeniture ensured "political instability, warfare, and territorial expansion."[113]

BANDITS AND REBELLION IN OUDH

On discovering the practice of female infanticide in colonial India, British administrators developed a series of policies in an effort to stop it. At the time, British observers noted a link between infanticidal tribes and the level of violence. According to one scholar, "Many of the infanticidal races, particularly in the North-Western Provinces and Oudh, were the most turbulent of people and were in a chronic state of rebellion, their main occupation being to plunder and disturb the peace and security of the country."[114]

The practice of female infanticide in northwest India, home of the Rajputs, appears to have had an effect on the level of violence in the region. William Crooke, a British administrator in nineteenth-century India, wrote of the scarcity of women leading to a rise in the number of *dacoits* (violent bandits): "The lack of brides among Rajputs, in that part of the country where infanticide was most rife, seems also to have been one of the causes which have contributed to that outbreak of violent crime which has been a distinguishing feature of the returns in recent years. Young men, deprived of the chance of enjoying married life, have been forced into connections [i.e., not marriages] with women of the vagrant tribes—Haburas, Beriyas, and the like, who are nothing short of a pest to the country. It is the children of such unions who have been foremost in the outbreak of dacoity in the Central Duab and Rohilkhand."[115]

Other observers of the time found more direct links between female infanticide and violence. For many Rajput clans, the only way to secure wives for their sons was through kidnapping, prompting one observer to note: "The practice of kidnapping of young girls and their sale either for marriage or for prostitution was becoming alarming. The Inspector Gen-

---

113. Boone, "Parental Investment and Elite Family Structure in Preindustrial States," p. 871.

114. Lalita Panigrahi, *British Social Policy and Female Infanticide in India* (New Delhi: Munshiram Manoharlal, 1972), p. 12. The activities of tribes and groups of India's northwest—for example, the martial Sikhs of the Punjab, who were openly called "the daughter-killers"—would make fascinating topic of research, but here we restrict our focus to the geographical area of Oudh.

115. William Crooke, *The North-western Provinces of India: Their History, Ethnology, and Administration* (London: Methuen, 1897), pp. 138–139.

eral of Police of the North-Western Provinces reported in 1870 that 28 young girls had been sold for prostitution and 121 for marriage. He believed that hundreds of cases escaped notice of the police."[116]

As in medieval Portugal, the scarcity of females in parts of India increased competition among males. The higher an Indian family's standing in the community, the more likely it was to commit female infanticide. As a result, firstborn sons from well-off families were much more likely than their younger brothers to find suitable brides. De facto primogeniture among well-to-do families meant that younger sons were sent out to fend for themselves. Many joined the army. In the words of a contemporary, "Our army and other public establishments form a great 'safety valve' for Oude, and save it from a vast deal of fighting for shares in land, and the disorders that always attend it. Younger brothers enlist in our Regiments, or find employment in our civil establishments. . . . From the single district of Byswara, in Oude, sixteen thousand men were, it is said, found to be so serving in our army and other establishments; and from Bunoda, which adjoins it to the east, fifteen thousand."[117] Because the government often could not afford to pay all the soldiers in its bloated armies, it typically gave them license to plunder, a practice that many of these soldiers continued into civilian life.[118]

In other cases, resourceless young adult males formed small armies of bandits to kill their better-off relatives and steal their land. Sons killed fathers, brothers killed brothers, and cousins killed cousins. The more violent one was prepared to be, the more wealth one could amass. The most ruthless bandit chiefs became Oudh's largest landholders, who then extended their reach by seizing lands indiscriminately.

Now the Tallokdars [landholders] keep the country in a perpetual state of disturbance, and render life, property and industry, everywhere insecure. Whenever they quarrel with each other, or with the local authorities of the government, from whatever cause, they take to indiscriminate plunder and murder—over all lands not held by men of the same class—no road, town, village, or hamlet, is secure from their merciless attacks—robbery and murder become their diversion—their sport—and they think no more of taking the lives of men, women, and children, who never offended them, than those of deer or wild hogs. They not only rob and murder but seize, confine, and

---

116. Quoted in Panigrahi, *British Social Policy and Female Infanticide in India*, p. 183.

117. Quoted in P.D. Reeves, ed., *Sleeman in Oudh: An Abridgement of W.H. Sleeman's* A Journey through the Kingdom of Oude in 1849–50 (Cambridge: Cambridge University Press, 1971), pp. 94–95.

118. For numerous cases, see ibid.

torture all whom they seize, and suppose to have money or credit, till they ransom themselves. . . . He first robs the house, and murders all he can of the family of the co-sharer, with whom he has quarreled . . . and then gets together all he can of the loose characters around, employs them in indiscriminate plunder, and subsists them upon the booty.[119]

Bands of bare branches rebelled openly against the government. Their leaders kept garrisons with cannon, prepared to resist even the British army. Inspectors sent to assess the robber barons' lands were frequently murdered and the lands laid waste to avoid their being taxed. The mutinies against the kingdom grew so violent that, following a particularly bloody episode in 1815, the British forcibly annexed Oudh, using martial law to put down the rebellion.[120]

W.H. Sleeman, the primary chronicler of Oudh during the early British colonial period, wondered why the kingdom never sought to unite these robber barons and their bare-branch troops under one banner and send them out to attack neighboring lands—one of the few attractive options for governments facing internal strife. Sleeman concludes that it was only the presence of the British army, hemming in Oudh from all sides, that prevented this from occurring: "The sovereign can never unite them [the robber barons and their armies] under his banners for the purpose of invading and plundering any other country, and thereby securing for himself and them present glory, wealth, and high-sounding titles, and the admiration and applause of future generations. The strong arm of the British Government is interposed between them and all surrounding countries; and there is no safety valve for their unquiet spirits in foreign conquests. . . . They would much rather send out fifty thousand more brave soldiers to fight 'all the nations of the east,' under the banners of the Hon'ble East India Company."[121]

Given this history, it is perhaps not surprising that the one-time province of Oudh—now Uttar Pradesh—still has one of India's highest sex ratios as well as one of its highest crime rates. Nor is it surprising that this area continues to experience significant social unrest.[122]

---

119. W.H. Sleeman, quoted in ibid., pp. 175–176.

120. See ibid.

121. Quoted in ibid., pp. 298–299.

122. After more than twenty years of colonial rule in which female infanticide was vigorously punished, the British reported in 1875 that the juvenile sex ratio in Oudh was 118.6. India's 1991 census shows the overall sex ratio in Uttar Pradesh to be approximately 114.

TURBULENCE IN COLONIAL TAIWAN

Taiwan was a colony of the Qing dynasty from the late 1600s to the late 1800s. During this period, it experienced, on average, a serious revolt every three years. In the eighteenth century, there were nineteen revolts; in the nineteenth century, there were fifty-eight. From 1787 to 1862, revolts averaged one every 1.8 years, falling off in frequency in the late nineteenth century.[123]

Although we do not have official population figures for colonial Taiwan, what we do know suggests an extremely skewed ratio: According to Hsu Wen-hsiung, "The compilers of the *T'ai-wan hsieh-chih* [Taiwan chronicle] in 1720 remarked that it was extremely difficult for Chinese men to marry because women were scarce. That among 257 residents in Ta-p'u (in Chu-lo *hsien*) only one was a woman. Six years later, the governor-general of Fukien and Chiang, Kao Ch'i-cho, reported that new settlers in Feng-shan, Chu-lo, and Changhua were 'all without wives.' A popular saying, 'Having a wife is better than having a god,' aptly expressed the frustration of Chinese men over their bachelorhood. However exaggerated this remark might be, the abnormal sex ratio during the eighteenth century is quite apparent."[124]

A primary aggravating factor in the revolts during this period appears to have been Taiwan's very high sex ratio, which persisted until near the end of the colonial period. From 1684 to 1788, the Qing government sporadically forbade family emigration to Taiwan, favoring instead colonization by males without families.[125] After 1788 the government permitted, but did not encourage, family emigration. The inconsistency in family emigration policy reflected a split in the government. Proponents of single-male emigration argued that it would discourage permanent settlement, which in turn would prevent Taiwan from becoming a rebel base. Supporters of family emigration, on the other hand, asserted that it would have the opposite effect.

Several commentators of the time seemed to agree with family migration advocates that Taiwan's high sex ratio bred the very problems that the Qing had hoped to avoid. Lan Ting-yuan, the high-ranking

---

123. These statistics are from Hsu Wen-hsiung, "Frontier Social Organization and Social Disorder in Ch'ing Taiwan," in Ronald G. Knapp, ed., *China's Island Frontier: Studies in the Historical Geography of Taiwan* (Honolulu: University Press of Hawaii, 1980), pp. 87–106.

124. Hsu, "Frontier Social Organization and Social Disorder in Ch'ing Taiwan," p. 88.

125. See John Robert Shepherd, *Statecraft and Political Economy on the Taiwan Frontier, 1600–1800* (Stanford, Calif.: Stanford University Press, 1993), p. 143.

official who accompanied the imperial forces sent to quash one of the island's many rebellions in 1721, was very outspoken against the Qing's single-male emigration policy. According to John Shepherd,

As examples of the disorder resulting from restrictions on family migration, Lan pointed to the settlements of migrant laborers from the Hakka areas of Kwang-tung. Within these communities, the laborers formed tightly knit gangs that, on the smallest pretext, engaged in murderous brawls. Civil suits abounded, and robbers were so audacious that they even stole branded cattle. The restrictions on bringing wives and families had created a population of rootless vagrants. Lan argued that migrants wishing to farm in Taiwan should be allowed to take families with them and those in Taiwan should be allowed to bring their families over. It was those *without* families who should be barred from crossing, and the vagrants that should be sent back. Once all settlers had families, the sources of rebellion would be eradicated.[126]

The governor-general, Kao Ch'i-cho, was so concerned about Taiwan's highly skewed sex ratio that he wrote a memo to the imperial government asking for a reversal of the family emigration ban. Shepherd writes,

Kao found Taiwanese customs unruly, characterized by excessive drinking and gambling. Whereas immigrants in the old settled areas around Tainan had wives and families, those in the newly opened areas to the north and south had none, and the latter, "whose hearts have nothing to remember with affection," were often involved in disturbances. Living in groups of 20 to 40 men, they spent their leisure and their income on gambling and drinking. When drinking and gambling exhausted their earnings, they turned to robbery. "If each had a wife, inner and outer would be distinguished and there would be no confusion and disorder. If each had to support a wife, drinking and gambling would diminish. If each had to protect a household, robberies would decrease."[127]

The vast majority of the early migrants to Taiwan were young men: "Most were unmarried. Because of Chinese families' strong preference for sons, coupled with female infanticide and daughter neglect, males commonly outnumbered females at marriageable ages throughout late imperial Chinese society. This already unbalanced sex ratio was made worse in Taiwan . . . by government restrictions on family migration, . . . [but these restrictions] merely aggravated and did not single-handedly create this preponderance of males. The many unattached males, with

---

126. Shepherd, *Statecraft and Political Economy on the Taiwan Frontier,* p. 149 (emphasis in original).

127. Ibid.

limited marriage prospects and fond of gambling and brawling, helped destabilize frontier society."[128]

Ownby called these bare branches "entrepreneurs of violence."[129] Chen Shengsao, a chronicler of the time, referred to them as *luohanjiao* (arhat's feet): "*Luohanjiao* is a Taiwanese slang expression for those who have no land or property, no wife or children, who are not officials, farmers, artisans, or merchants, and who do not labor. They gamble, they steal, they feud, and they rise up. So what is a *luohanjiao?* He is single and roams the land, forming bands (*dang*) wherever he goes, never owning both shirt and trousers at one time, remaining barefoot his entire life. In large cities and villages they number no less than several hundred; in small cities and villages they number at least several tens. That is why Taiwan is difficult to govern."[130]

Walter Chen points to the eventual organization of the bare branches as a key to understanding Taiwan's numerous rebellions, most of which were fomented by the Heaven and Earth Society:

The "Heaven and Earth Society" was a civilian organization whose purpose was to overthrow the Manchus and to help other helpless immigrants. The name . . . came from its motto: "Heaven and Earth are our parents, all members are our brothers." To join the club, one had to go through ceremonies of "mixing blood" and "drinking blood," and after exchanging blood cups signifying allegiance, one would be accepted as a member. At that time, since all immigrants were single, by joining the brotherhood one not only participated in anti-Qing activities, but also found relief from loneliness. . . . During the rebellions of Chu Yit-gui and Lon Song-bun, the mobilizing power of the

---

128. Ibid., pp. 311–312.

129. David Ownby, "The Ethnic Feud in Qing Taiwan: What Is This Violence Business, Anyway? An Interpretation of the 1782 Zhang-Quan *Xiedou," Late Imperial China,* Vol. 11, No. 1 (June 1990), pp. 75–98. Ethnic feuds, or *xiedou,* provided opportunities for young men to make money from acts of violence. Indeed, the participants in *xiedou* violence would sometimes hire mercenaries to fight for them. But violence was lucrative in other ways: According to one commentator of the time, "Lineage strongmen delight in *xiedou* activity because it gives them the opportunity to line their pockets. . . . Lineage toughs take delight in *xiedou* activity because it gives them a chance to divide profits among themselves. . . . Pettifoggers delight in *xiedou* because they can make money through their machinations. . . . Evil gentry delight in *xiedou* activity because they can manipulate the situation to their advantage. Yamen underlings delight in *xiedou* activity because it offers them an opportunity to trade on their influence." Quoted in Ownby, *Brotherhoods and Secret Societies in Early and Mid-Qing China,* p. 165.

130. Chen Shengsao, *Wensulu,* Beijing: Shumu wenxian chubanshe, original edition dated 1827, as cited in Ownby, *Brotherhoods and Secret Societies in Early and Mid-Qing China,* p. 20.

Heaven and Earth Society was behind the scenes making it possible to sweep the whole island in a short period of time.[131]

Without the involvement of these bare branches, Taiwan's lawlessness could not have escalated to the point where imperial troops were needed to keep order.[132] When the time came to send troops, the imperial government created new units that would stay in Taiwan to suppress the continuing revolts. According to some historical evidence, the units comprised bare branches from Fukien and Kwantung Provinces. Thus the imperial government was sending bare branches to fight bare branches. Not surpringly, the bare-branch army units engaged in behavior similar to that of the rebels. Troops, for example, were allowed to take part in private business dealings. As a result, corruption, smuggling, and oppression became hallmarks of the Qing official presence on Taiwan. Hsu notes that contemporaries felt that "the Ch'ing government on Taiwan . . . was one of the worst in the empire."[133] Not until 1787, in the midst of one of the worst rebellions, did the Qing realize that the troops deployed to Taiwan were helping to undermine their cause. In response, the government sent a famous general, Fu K'ang-an, and a massive military expedition from the mainland (including crack professional troops) to restore order.

Following the gradual lifting of the ban on family emigration in 1788, Taiwan became a more peaceful place, although families still were not encouraged to emigrate. Susan Naquin and Evelyn Rawski report, however, that sex ratios in Taiwan began to return to normal by the mid-nineteenth century, which coincides with a significant drop-off in the number of island rebellions.[134] In 1874 the Qing appointed Shen Bao-tseng to secure the island. As part of this effort, Shen insisted that the government remove all obstacles to family emigration.

In sum, colonial Taiwan's extremely high sex ratio appears to have been a significant aggravating factor in the outbreak of violence and re-

---

131. Walter Chen, "The Era of the Ch'ing Dynasty," http://www.leksu.com/mainp4e.htm, p. 8.

132. Ownby notes that of those arrested on charges of rebellion in the wake of the Lin uprising of 1787–88, about 60 percent said they were married. These data are unreliable, however. First, a number of those arrested were innocent of any wrongdoing. Second, almost 70 percent of those taken into custody did not indicate or were not asked their marital status. Thus it is difficult to interpret the confession data regarding marital status. See ibid., p. 187.

133. Hsu, "Frontier Social Organization and Social Disorder in Ch'ing Taiwan," p. 94.

134. Susan Naquin and Evelyn S. Rawski, *Chinese Society in the Eighteenth Century* (New Haven, Conn.: Yale University Press, 1987), p. 210.

bellion on the island. Inducting bare branches into the imperial forces sent to suppress these rebellions seems not to have been a wise policy, for these forces exhibited similarly destabilizing behavior.

Other Historical Cases

Several other case studies illuminate the aggravating/amplifying/triggering effects of highly skewed sex ratios on intrasocietal and intersocietal violence. We mention them here only in brief, as their full treatment must await further investigation.

POLYNESIA

According to some historians, Polynesia's skewed sex ratios, coupled with the island's constrained territory, resulted in the sending of second, third, and higher birth-order sons on overseas expeditions. Tribal chiefs believed that if these young men were allowed to stay in Polynesia, they would become a violent and disruptive force. Many never made it to their destinations, however; others simply never returned.[135] As Mildred Dickemann notes of the Tikopia of Polynesia, "The practice of overseas voyaging by males [was] regarded by the Tikopia as tantamount to suicide. . . . Genealogies of chiefly houses prior to 1929 contained 23 males lost at sea out of a total of 69 male deaths. In the period 1929–1952, 30 such voyages occurred, with a loss of 81 and only about 20 survivals. . . . Most of these men were unmarried and under 30 years of age."[136]

EUNUCHS IN CHINA

Eunuchs could be found in both historical India and historical China. Only in China, however, were their numbers significant. By the end of the Ming dynasty, more than 100,000 eunuchs were reportedly in government service.

Eunuchs were considered the perfect employees for emperors with their multiple wives and concubines. Higher birth-order sons were regularly castrated by poor parents in the hopes that one day they might be accepted in the imperial service.[137] Generally, firstborn sons were not castrated, but their higher birth-order siblings could be castrated as young

---

135. James L. Boone, communication with Valerie Hudson, April 11, 1999.

136. Mildred Dickemann, "Demographic Consequences of Infanticide in Man," *Annual Review of Ecology and Systematics,* Vol. 6 (1975), p. 124.

137. See Mary M. Anderson, *Hidden Power: The Palace Eunuchs of Imperial China* (Buffalo, N.Y.: Prometheus, 1990).

as 2 months of age. Given that only about one in ten eunuchs gained a government post, it is not surprising that castration eventually created a class of young men who would ultimately become a problem for the government.[138] One manifestation of this problem was increased banditry. As David Robinson puts it, "Only a small percentage of those castrated actually gained posts in Beijing; a portion of the rest, frustrated, mutilated, and still poor, turned to begging and banditry." He goes on to quote the contemporary commentator Shen Fu: "North of Renjiu, Hejian, there are several dozen eunuchs who hide among the ruins of city walls. Whenever [they] encounter passing carts and horses, the weaker among them mass together to beg for money. The stronger ones take hold of the horses' reins and demand a pay-off. Occasionally, when there are two or three riders traveling unaccompanied in desolate areas, [the eunuchs] pull them down from the saddle."[139]

The cost of retaining the eunuchs on the imperial payroll severely drained government coffers: Each eunuch required about 30 piculs of rice a year (a picul is about 400 pounds). Toward the end of the Ming dynasty, government-employed eunuchs were consuming hundreds of thousands of piculs of rice. How did government officials justify this enormous expense? In part, they did not want to add to the ranks of unemployed eunuchs. As Henry Shih-shan Tsai recounts, "In 1620, some 20,000 [self-castrated men] swarmed into the capital, begging for whatever jobs the government could give them. When their petitions and requests were rejected, the job seekers became angry and turned into a rowdy and militant mob. Supervisors from both the Ministry of Rites and the Ministry of War were undoubtedly alarmed as they began to take measures against any possible uprising."[140]

Eunuchs, however, also contributed to the government's bureaucratic bloat. For example, many important military operations were led by two commanders—one eunuch and one not. Palace guard troops became exclusively eunuch. Some emperors turned the most sensitive intelligence operations over to the eunuchs. Through official corruption and domination of the mining industry and imperial estates, some high-ranking eunuchs also became some of China's richest men. In other cases, their plotting led to palace intrigue and growing turmoil. Indeed, eunuchs carried out several coups d'état in efforts to install more sympathetic emper-

---

138. David M. Robinson, "Notes on Eunuchs in Hebei during the Mid-Ming Period," *Ming Studies*, Vol. 34 (July 1995), pp. 1–16.

139. Ibid., p. 2.

140. Henry Shih-shan Tsai, *The Eunuchs in the Ming Dynasty* (Albany: State University of New York Press, 1996), p. 25.

ors on the throne.[141] In a sense, then, the eunuch system guaranteed that a significant number of bare branches would be brought into government's inner circles. That they did not contribute to the health of that government should not be surprising.

MONKS AND OTHER QUASI-RELIGIOUS BROTHERHOODS IN CHINA

In Chinese history, bare-branch youths could raise their social status by becoming monks. Because monks in historical China were heavily involved in worldly affairs, younger monks often engaged in bare-branch behavior.[142] Martial prowess and the amassing of unearned wealth were not infrequently associated with monasteries and other quasi-religious brotherhoods.

Probably the most famous example is the Shaolin fighting monks, who, having saved the life of emperor Tai Tsung in the Tang era, were given land to build a monastery that eventually housed 2,500 martial monks. The power of monasteries, especially Buddhist monasteries favored by influential eunuchs, grew over the years. In the late 800s, official figures show the existence of more than "a quarter of a million monastics, who controlled some 4,600 monasteries, 40,000 pagodas, and untold thousands of temples, including slaves and attendants, much of the nation's best lands, and much wealth, all existing tax free."[143] By the late 1400s, China had more than 500,000 monks, with one official calculating that the rice needed to feed them all "could easily supply the entire capital population for over one year."[144] According to Robinson, martial monks fought as mercenaries alongside imperial troops in quelling many of China's rebellions during the sixteenth century.[145]

A large number of monks came from provinces where female infanticide was practiced. The natural inference therefore is that they were also bare branches. Referring to Fukien, where female infanticide was rampant during the Yuan, Ming, and Qing dynasties, T'ien Ju-k'ang notes, "One might also be prompted to ask what other social problems could have arisen as a result of a situation such as this. Perhaps this is the key to an explanation of the many peculiar abnormalities of Fukien in compari-

---

141.   For an exposition of the role of eunuchs in palace intrigue, see Anderson, *Hidden Power.*

142.   Indeed certain sects of monks, such as the Taoist monks, did not practice celibacy, though they also did not marry.

143.   Ibid., p. 162.

144.   Ibid., p. 226.

145.   David M. Robinson, "The Management of Violence in the Mid-Ming Capital Region," Colgate University, 1998.

son with other provinces in China. For instance, it was said that nine out of ten wandering monks all over China came from Fukien."[146]

Monastic orders coexisted with more heterodox quasi-religious brotherhoods, many of them secret. The combination of hardship and lack of opportunity led many young men, typically bare branches, to the ranks of these secret brotherhoods in part because conversion to a heterodox sect could supplement a monk's living.[147] Watson speaks of the "bachelor subculture" that spawned such brotherhoods.[148] Fei-ling Davis identifies those likely to have belonged to secret brotherhoods as dispossessed peasants, unemployed artisans, laborers and porters, disbanded soldiers, smugglers, and victims of disasters—who collectively came to be known as the "floating population" (you-min).[149]

The practice of martial arts was sometimes an explicit element of these secret brotherhoods. Boxing exhibitions, for example, were a primary way to seek recruits. Young men who aspired to membership in a brotherhood would begin by becoming pupils of the brotherhood's boxing instructor. The poorer the area, the more likely young male devotees would flock to a secret brotherhood. In the late 1800s, a letter by a former magistrate read, "The road passed through Chiping. The area is bitterly poor, but in hundreds of villages they are studying United-in-Righteousness Boxing."[150] Many of these boxing enthusiasts exhibited characteristic bare-branch behavior: "In this area there are many vagabonds and rowdies (wu-lai gun-tu) who draw their swords and gather crowds. They have established societies of various names: the Obedient Swords (Shun-dao hui), Tiger-tail Whip (Hu-wei bian), the Yi-he Boxers, and the Eight Trigrams sect (Ba-gua jiao). They are overbearing in the villages and oppress the good people. The origin of these disturbances is gambling. They go to fairs and openly set up tents where they take valuables in pawn and gather to gamble."[151]

---

146. T'ien, *Male Anxiety and Female Chastity*, p. 31, n. 54.

147. See Susan Naquin, *Shantung Rebellion: The Wang Lun Uprising of 1774* (New Haven, Conn.: Yale University Press, 1981), p. 48.

148. See Watson, "Self-Defense Corps, Violence, and the Bachelor Subculture in South China"; and Ownby, *Brotherhoods and Secret Societies in Early and Mid-Qing China*, p. 20.

149. Fei-ling Davis, *Primitive Revolutionaries of China: A Study of Secret Societies in the Late Nineteenth Century* (Honolulu: University of Hawaii Press, 1977), p. 90.

150. Cited in Joseph Esherick, *The Origins of the Boxer Uprising* (Berkeley: University of California Press, 1987), p. 223.

151. Ibid., p. 46.

Some members of these secret brotherhoods became bandits and rebels. In 1898 the governor of Shandong reported, "This year the spring rains were late and the grain prices rose. In addition it was a time of troop reduction and consolidation. Dispersed braves and habitual outlaws from elsewhere . . . combined with unemployed vagrants into a mob of several hundreds. . . . Armed with foreign rifles and weapons, they plundered neighboring villages on the pretext of borrowing grain, and extorted horses, weapons, and ammunition."[152] Another contemporary observer noted, "In the provinces of Chihli, Honan, and Shantung, *chiao-fei* [religious bandits] spread their creeds one to another. . . . Once famine occurs they, relying on their numerical strength, plunder collectively in broad daylight, calling their marauding activities 'equalizing the food.'"[153]

Bare branches may have played a role in several major rebellions in China, including the Eight Trigrams Rebellion and the Boxer Rebellion. They also took part in many of the rebel activities of the Black Flag Army. According to Ella Laffey, Liu Yung-fu, the leader of the Black Flag Army, was a bare branch. Liu, she states, "was an impoverished young man without parents, wife, children, or fixed abode. . . . He found odd jobs along the rivers as a boatman or fisherman and in the hills as a fuel-gatherer and charcoal-burner. These latter occupations were known for being riddled with brotherhoods and secret societies. As a vigorous young man without any real roots in the traditional, more stable rural order, he was ideal material for recruitment into the ranks of an illegal group. [When Liu was twenty-one, he], his half-brother, and four fellow villagers simply went in a body from their village to the town of Ch'ien-lung-chou . . . to explore the possibility of joining the rebel army there."[154] There Liu joined the rebels, eventually becoming the Black Tiger General. In his autobiography, Liu's reasons for joining the Black Flag reflect archetypal bare-branch advancement strategy: "It would have been shameful if I did nothing to benefit the people; besides, I could not continue night and day eating thin rice gruel to soothe my hunger."[155]

Some rebel bare branches and their followers enjoyed amazing success. Taizu, the Grand Progenitor of the Ming dynasty, had for most of his

---

152. Quoted in ibid., pp. 176–177.

153. Quoted in Hsiao, *Rural China*, p. 447.

154. Ella S. Laffey, "The Making of a Rebel: Liu Yung-fu and the Formation of the Black Flag Army," in Jean Chesnaux, ed., *Popular Movements and Secret Societies in China, 1840–1950* (Stanford, Calif.: Stanford University Press, 1972), pp. 89–90.

155. Cited in ibid., p. 90.

life been "a vagrant, a beggar, a member of a millenarian sect, and a rebel."[156] In 1629, when the Ming slashed the number of government employees, "Li Zicheng, who eventually emerged as the rebel leader who drove the Ming from Beijing, was among those unemployed workers who threw his lot in with the rebels."[157] In a sense, then, the Ming dynasty was founded by one bare branch and destroyed by another.

Throughout Chinese history, men at the margins of society have been available for work that involves violence. Occasionally they changed the destiny of a nation. According to Gensho Nishimara, most of these men were *wulai*, meaning young male "floaters" who prided themselves on their toughness.[158] Ueda Makato calls the *wulai* urban vagabonds who depended on violence to make a living, often forming "enforcers guilds."[159] During the Ming dynasty, government reports blamed much of the crime in Beijing on the "unregistered ones"—gangs made up of bare sticks whose members were called "fierce tigers."[160] The fate of these criminals was not always bleak. According to Ownby, the Chinese folk saying "If you want to become an official, carry a big stick" refers to the traditional practice of awarding bandits with official posts as a means of co-opting them.[161]

In sum, China's quasi-religious brotherhoods, whether orthodox or heterodox, posed grave security problems for the central government. As one seventeenth-century commentator put it, "Heretical teachings start by inciting, deluding, and gathering people, but end by planning rebellion."[162] Given this history and China's current high sex ratios, Beijing's deep suspicion of movements such as the Falun Gong does not seem especially surprising.

---

156. David M. Robinson, "The Management of Violence in the Mid-Ming Capital Region," Colgate University, 1998, p. 8.

157. David M. Robinson, "Banditry and Rebellion in the Capital Region during the Mid-Ming (1450–1525)," Ph.D. dissertation, Princeton University, 1995, p. 490.

158. Gensho Nishimara, "Ryu roku ryu nana no ran ni tsuite," *Toyoshi kenkyu* [Asian historical research], Vol. 32, No. 4 (1974), pp. 44–86.

159. Ueda Makato, "Minmatsu Shinso: Konan no toshino burai o meguru shakui kankei, dako to kyakufu," *Shigaku zasshi* [Journal of historical studies], Vol. 90, No. 12 (1981), pp. 1619–1653.

160. Robinson, "Banditry and Rebellion in the Capital Region during the Mid-Ming," pp. 126–127.

161. Ownby, "Approximations of Chinese Bandits," p. 240.

162. Quoted in Barend J. ter Harr, *The White Lotus Teachings in Chinese Religious History* (Leiden, Netherlands: E.J. Brill, 1992), p. 237.

Conclusion

At least two broad conclusions can be drawn from the historical cases presented above. First, the strategies that bare branches use to better their lot often have negative repercussions for their societies, contributing significantly to intrasocietal violence and a further decline in the status of women. Second, governments do become aware of the potentially violent dynamics of their high-sex-ratio populations and struggle, at great cost, to implement policies to counteract the resulting destabilization. These strategies may include the recruitment of bare branches into imperial armies, an approach that may lead to greater intersocietal violence in the effort to preserve domestic stability. In the chapters that follow, we examine this conceptual framework from a modern perspective.

Chapter 6

Bare Branches in the Twenty-first Century

Policy Implications

"**A**lready the female shortage is making itself felt. Urmila, a district councillor in the countryside near Rohtak [India], says unmarried young men are turning to crime, and violence against women has increased."[1] So reads a recent analysis in the *Economist*, in one of the first news articles to allude to the linkage between the creation of a large surplus of young males through the manipulation of the natural birth sex ratio and increasing societal instability. Yet this analysis is exceptional: It is virtually impossible to find scholarly or journalistic literature that explicitly recognizes this linkage. No doubt this will change as the baby boom of surplus young males in China, India, and other Asian countries reaches maturity in the early decades of this century. The time is now, however, for security scholars to start asking serious questions about bare branches: What is their role in society? What are the likely domestic, regional, and perhaps even international repercussions if their growth is left unchecked? Although we do not yet have enough information to offer any definitive answers, we can discuss what we do know, confident that others, both in academia and in government, will pick up where we leave off.

In this chapter, we examine what is known about the attributes and behavior of bare branches in contemporary China and India. We address this issue from the perspectives of the Chinese and Indian governments, for whom the question of what to do with their countries' bare branches is becoming increasingly salient. We then discuss several policy interventions, some of which are already being implemented, and consider the advantages and disadvantages of each.

---

1. "Missing Sisters," *Economist*, April 19, 2003, p. 36.

Characteristics and Behavior of Contemporary Bare Branches

Based on the theoretical and historical material presented in chapter 5, the bare-branch populations in present-day China and India should possess many of the same characteristics and behavioral predispositions as their predecessors. They should be from the lowest socioeconomic classes and have less education and fewer skills than other young men. They are likely to be unemployed and disproportionately represented among transient populations. We would expect them to congregate in groups, building distinctive bachelor subcultures. They probably engage in violent criminal behavior—including robbery, rape, and murder—and are at greater risk of joining criminal gangs involved in arms smuggling, extortion, prostitution, and drug trafficking. Finally, they most likely abuse drugs and alcohol, which contributes to their higher rates of violent crime. In sum, we should find that China's and India's bare branches are a volatile, destabilizing force that engenders fear and suspicion.

CHINA'S FLOATING POPULATION

The available evidence suggests that China's bare branches are primarily poor transients who engage disproportionately in crime and substance abuse. They tend to congregate in economically active urban centers, although they can also be found in China's western frontier. In 1997 more than 50 percent of Chinese bare branches were classified as rural residents, even though many had left the countryside in search of work and a better life in China's larger towns and cities.[2] The central government's 1984 decision to relax restrictions against labor migration helped to spur this trend. Until fairly recently, however, rural migrants felt stigmatized, partly for having been denied access to the wide array of social benefits—including unemployment compensation and medical and education benefits—enjoyed by the majority of China's urban residents. In 1998 the Chinese government decided to extend most social benefits to rural migrants living in small and medium-sized cities. Those with stable employment and housing can even register as urban residents. In a related step, the government issued a directive in January 2003 urging the cessation of discrimination against rural migrants in the labor market. As a result, businesses that want to hire migrant workers can do so without first having to obtain approval from municipal administrators.[3]

In the mid-to-late 1980s, unmarried men made up 30 percent of the

---

2. See Ren Meng, "Confronting Three Populations of 80 Million," *Inside China Mainland*, Vol. 19, No. 1 (January 1997), pp. 78–81.

3. Feng Jianhua, "Bright Lights, Big City," *Beijing Review*, April 3, 2003, p. 22.

young adult male population in the following areas of China: greater Beijing, Guandong, Guangxi, Hebei, Henan, Hunan, Shandong, greater Shanghai (including parts of Jiangsu and Anhui), Zhejiang, and farther west in Sichuan.[4] In the early 1990s, these areas, which are also China's most populous, had some of its highest sex ratios at birth.[5] As noted in chapter 4, the proportion of surplus males to all males in China rises the younger the age group. This corresponds to the increase in sex ratios in successive younger-age cohorts. Figures for 1990 (data for 2000 are not yet available in disaggregated form) confirm this finding. For example, about 97 percent of all unmarried persons aged 28–49 in China were found to be male.[6] In the age category 15–34, approximately 13 percent were surplus males; in the 35–55 age group, about 5 percent were surplus males.[7]

The Chinese government does not provide income levels for bare branches. Nevertheless, using other data sources, we have been able to establish a correlation between the education levels of unmarried males in China and income levels. As noted in chapter 5, 1990 data show that approximately 74 percent of all unmarried adult Chinese males failed to graduate from high school.[8] The figures for rural bare branches are even higher: About 97 percent of young males in the countryside never graduated from high school, and about 40 percent were illiterate.[9] Some Chinese scholars link this phenomenon to the practice of hypergyny, as do we. According to Ye Wenzhen and Lin Qingguo, "The existence of lots of unmarried men after marriage age should be attributed to the

4. Population Census Office of the State Council of the People's Republic of China, and the Institute of Geography of the Chinese Academy of Sciences, *Population Atlas of China* (Oxford: Oxford University Press, 1987).

5. See H. Yuan Tien, Zhang Tianlu, Ping Yu, Li Jingneng, and Lian Zhongtang, "China's Demographic Dilemmas," *Population Bulletin,* Vol. 47, No. 1 (June 1992), pp. 1–34; and Terence H. Hull, "Recent Trends in Sex Ratios at Birth in China," *Population and Development Review,* Vol. 16, No. 1 (March 1990), pp. 63–83. As noted in chapter 3, one reason for the higher sex ratios at birth in these metropoles may be easier access to prenatal sex-determination tests.

6. Zhang Ping, "Issues and Characteristics of the Unmarried Population," *Chinese Journal of Population Science,* Vol. 2, No. 1 (1990), p. 87. Zhang's figure of 94 percent is a little low, because he examines only single persons aged 28–49. His figures are also from 1987. Reasonable adjustments to these numbers based on our demographic statistics yield a figure of about 97 percent.

7. U.S. Bureau of the Census International Data Base, "1998: Population by Marital Status, Age, Sex, and Urban/Rural Residence (China)," http://www.census.gov/ipc/www/idbnew.html/.

8. Zhang, "Issues and Characteristics of the Unmarried Population," p. 88.

9. Ibid.

rational 'marrying up' of women at marriage age, and the relatively low social-economic situation of the unmarried men."[10]

Employment data in China are classified, so there is no hard evidence regarding the percentage of underemployed or unemployed males who are bare branches. We can suggest, however, that the figures are significant. Statistics from 2003 indicate record-high levels of unemployment in China's cities and towns, with levels of "idle" (i.e., unemployed) workers in the rural labor force approaching 32 percent.[11] Wang Jian, a research fellow in the State Development and Reform Commission, offered the following assessment: "I estimate China's aggregate unemployment rate to be 12–15 percent if all unemployed people and rural surplus laborers . . . are included. Calculated on the basis of China having 730 million employed people at the end of 2001, its unemployed totals around 100 million."[12]

These high unemployment figures are linked to China's rapid transition to capitalism in the 1990s. Writing in 1994, Linda Wong predicted, "Even within the urban industrial complex, the specter of worsening unemployment is becoming more ominous. Currently, estimates suggest that between 15 and 30 percent of urban employees are really not needed. As state enterprises join the rush to become financially independent and shed excess staff, many urbanites will be forced to join the job chase. This will inflate the ranks of itinerant labourers."[13]

A 1997 study indicated that "as many as 15 million urban workers [were] jobless—equal to 7.5 percent of the urban work force and more than double [the previous] year's level."[14] The same year, Ren Meng wrote that approximately "5% of all urban residents live[d] in a state of relative poverty," and that about 80 million persons nationwide were impoverished.[15] Others suggest that these figures may be too low. Some re-

---

10. Ye Wenzhen and Lin Qingguo, "The Reasons and Countermeasures for Demographic Phenomena in China," *Chinese Demography*, Vol. 4 (1998), as quoted in Ren Feng, "Bare Branches among Rural Migrant Laborers in China: Causes, Social Implications, and Policy Proposals," Foreign Affairs College, Beijing, March 1999, p. 6.

11. Jian Fa, "China Faces an 'Employment War,'" *Beijing Review*, March 20, 2003, p. 26; and Feng Jianhua, "Migrant Workers vs. City Residents," *Beijing Review*, April 3, 2003, p. 21.

12. Wang Jian, "Urbanization: A Long-Term Solution to Unemployment," *Beijing Review*, March 20, 2003, p. 28.

13. Linda Wong, "China's Urban Migrants—The Public Policy Challenge," *Pacific Affairs*, Vol. 67, No. 3 (Autumn 1994), p. 354.

14. "Army of Jobless Threatening China," Associated Press, as published in the *Salt Lake Tribune*, December 26, 1997, p. A6.

15. Ren, "Confronting Three Populations of 80 Million," p. 79.

searchers estimated that in the late 1990s "anywhere from 12 million to more than 22 million urban residents [not poor migrants] out of an urban population of 200 million live[d] in 'absolute poverty,' meaning that they [could not] afford basic food, clothing, or shelter."[16] A 1998 report revealed that in China's northwest "rust belt," the unemployment rate had risen above 20 percent.[17] *Xia gang* workers (i.e., workers laid off from state-owned enterprises) totaled almost 11 million in 1998, and the number continues to rise.[18] Also in 1998, the central government announced that it would lay off approximately 4 million bureaucrats, exacerbating an already bad situation. Meanwhile, the army declared that it would reduce its forces by 500,000 persons; railway officials announced that more than 1 million jobs would be eliminated; and the textile industry released a statement declaring that it would reduce its workforce by about 1.2 million.[19]

China's rural population has fared no better: Statistics from the late 1990s suggest that 150–170 million unemployed workers lived in the countryside.[20] Some studies predicted that the figure would rise to 250 million by the turn of the century, which seems to have been borne out.[21] Vast numbers of rural migrants continue to flood China's cities in search of work: A study in 2000 showed that in one two-week period, 2.4 million unemployed transients, mostly from rural areas, arrived in Guangdong by rail, 1.7 million by road, and more than 100,000 by boat.[22]

---

16. Elisabeth Rosenthal, "Poverty Spreads, and Deepens, in China's Cities," *New York Times,* October 4, 1998, sec. 1, p. 3.

17. Erik Eckholm, "Joblessness: A Perilous Curve on China's Capitalist Road," *New York Times,* January 20, 1998, p. A1.

18. "Chinese Saw Crime Jump 22% in First Nine Months of 1998, Report Says," Reuters, as published in *Deseret News,* February 10–11, 1999, p. A7; and Jian, "China Faces an 'Employment War,'" p. 27.

19. Eckholm, "Joblessness"; Rone Tempest, "China to Close 11 Ministries in Effort to Avoid Fiscal Crisis," *Los Angeles Times,* March 6, 1998, p. 8; and Seth Faison, "China Moving to Untie Its Military-Industrial Knot," *New York Times,* July 28, 1998, p. A1.

20. "Chinese Saw Crime Jump 22% in First Nine Months of 1998"; and Feng, "Migrant Workers vs. City Residents," p. 21.

21. Jeffrey R. Taylor and Judith Banister, "China: The Problem of Employing Surplus Rural Labor," CIR Staff Paper No. 49 (Washington, D.C.: Center for International Research, U.S. Bureau of the Census, July 1989), pp. viii, 75. Although these figures are from 1989, they are largely echoed in more recent studies. See, for example, Li Tan, "Population Flow into Big Cities," *Beijing Review,* July 18–24, 1994, pp. 15–19. See also Li Jingnen, "Challenge to Chinese Population Theory Research on the Eve of the Twenty-first Century," *Chinese Population Science,* n.s., Vol. 4 (1998), p. 10.

22. Wang Rong, "Migrant Labourers to Face Difficulty Finding Work," *China Daily,* February 21, 2000, p. 2.

The largest category of unemployed Chinese consists of young, low-status, unmarried male transients. Many are poor men from the countryside who hope to save enough money to one day return home and marry.[23] One 1993 sample found that 81.8 percent of migrants were male.[24] More recent estimates indicate that 80 percent of this population is under 35 years of age and that 72–75 percent are male.[25] In 2003 the Population Reference Bureau, wrote, "Male migrants make up the largest proportion of the floating population, and are frequently away for 50 weeks a year, living in single-sex dormitory housing."[26] Collectively, these transients are known as China's "floating population" (*liudong renkou*), which is thought to include at least 200 million persons. We estimate that more than half of China's floating population failed to graduate from high school.[27]

The rural-to-urban transition for many Chinese migrants has not been smooth. As Ren Meng reports, "The increase in migrants has placed an added burden on already overloaded city infrastructures. On the out-

---

23. In the words of one migrant worker, "I had planned to get married when I went home this time. But without a real job, that's not very realistic is it?" Interview with Zong Jiaohua, in Elisabeth Rosenthal, "100 Million Restless Chinese Go Far from Home for Jobs," *New York Times,* February 24, 1999, p. A1. Interestingly, one study calculated that these laborers bring home more than 1.6 trillion renminbi (approximately $200 billion), three times the amount of governmental investment in the countryside. Cai Fang, "The Regional Character of Labor Flow in the Transitional Period," *Chinese Population Studies,* n.s. 5 (1998), pp. 18–24.

24. As cited in Ji Dangsheng and Shao Qin, *The Tendency and Management of Chinese Population Movement* (Beijing: Beijing Publishing House, 1996), p. 99.

25. Age data are from "HIV/AIDS—What the Chinese Experts Say," http://www.usembassy-china.org.cn/english/sandt/webaids3.htm. Sex data are from Zhao Yi, *The Population, Resources, Environment, Agriculture, and Continuous Development of 21st-Century China* (Shan Xi: Economic Publishing House, 1997), p. 144; Zhang Xiaohui, Wu Zhigang, and Chen Liangbiao, "Age Difference among the Rural Labor Force in Interregional Migration," *Chinese Journal of Population Science,* Vol. 9, No. 3 (1997), pp. 193–202; and Bruce Gilley, "Irresistible Force," *Far Eastern Economic Review,* April 4, 1996, pp. 18–22. Another revealing statistic is that approximately 82 percent of unmarried men between the ages of 30 and 44 are registered residents of rural areas. Of all unmarried persons between the ages of 30 and 44, more than 94 percent are male. China, State Statistical Bureau, *China Population Statistical Yearbook, 1994* (Beijing: China Statistics Press, 1994), pp. 36–53.

26. Drew Thompson, "HIV/AIDS Epidemic in China Spreads into the General Population," Population Reference Bureau, http://www.prb.org/Template.cfm?Section= PRB&template=/ContentManagement/ContentDisplay.cfm&ContentID=8501.

27. This estimate is based on Gilley's incomplete figures. See Gilley, "Irresistible Force," p. 22.

skirts of major towns, unplanned settlements have sprung up, where not only is public order and safety a problem, but where counterfeit goods and pornography are produced, and where the sex trade is prominent."[28] At one point, more than 2 million migrants were living in or around China's train stations and warehouses.[29]

Over the years, tensions have increased between urban residents and transients. When asked about the effects of the floating population on their daily lives, approximately 78 percent of Shanghaiese responded that the impact has been negative; about 81 percent expressed growing concern over property safety; and nearly 91 percent complained about overcrowding on public transportation systems.[30] To ease such tensions in the past, the government orchestrated periodic drives in which "floaters" would be registered and placed in administration units under the daily supervision of government employees.[31] Since the mid-1990s, the government has again begun to require strict accounting of migrants' whereabouts. Steps include demolishing markets and migrant housing that are unlicensed, as well as requiring the registration of migrants in approved rental housing. As the head of one state public safety bureau remarked, "We realize that the key to establishing a long-term social security is to manage the missions of transient workers in the city in a more effective way."[32]

Despite these attempts at social control, crime rates in China are soaring. Studies by the Chinese Academy of Social Science's Institute of Law suggest that migrants commit more than 50 percent of the country's urban crime: "Many young men, unable to find even $2-a-day jobs in construction or factories, become urban scavengers and predators, stealing everything from manhole covers to wallets."[33] Even though China's

28. Ren, "Confronting Three Populations of 80 Million," p. 79.

29. Ibid., p. 80.

30. Ding Jinhong, "An Analysis in the Extraneous Population Inflow and City Community Integration: Surveys on the Local Shanghaiese's Psychological Acceptance Capacity of Extraneous Population," *Population Survey*, February 1996, p. 48.

31. David M. Robinson, "Banditry and Rebellion in the Capital Region during the Mid-Ming (1450–1525)," Ph.D. dissertation, Princeton University, 1995; see, for example, ibid., p. 16.

32. Quoted in Xiao Wang, "Police Keeping Crime Down," *China Daily*, June 8, 2000, p. 3.

33. Quoted in Michael Dorgan, "Growing Rich-Poor Gap, Economic Growth Spur Crime in China," Knight Ridder, March 27, 2002 (from original report, accessed from Proquest, LexisNexis).

crime data are classified, some statistics still make their way into print. According to one published report, from 2001 to 2002, China experienced an 82 percent rise in crimes involving firearms or bombs and a sixfold increase in organized crime cases.[34] Between 1978 and 1998, the country's crime rate more than tripled.[35]

Both juvenile crime and organized crime are fast becoming significant social threats in China, with organized gangs actively recruiting from the ranks of juveniles—specifically among young bare branches.[36] In a shocking admission, the government announced in 1998 its expansion of the adult penal code to include boys aged 14–18.[37] This year also witnessed the launch of the Strike Hard campaign, which is designed to crack down on urban crime.

The *Beijing Review* reported in 1996 that "outsiders were responsible for 80 percent of criminal offenses in the capital." In addition, 80 percent of individuals arrested in the southern Pearl River delta and other coastal regions came from other provinces."[38] Of the criminal cases and public order disturbances handled by railway authorities in 1994, 82 percent involved migrants. More generally, 69 percent of apprehended criminals were migrants. In 1997, in the Jingdiao area of Shanghai's Pudong region, migrants were responsible for more than 90 percent of all criminal activity, compared with 30 percent in 1990.[39]

Other reports reveal similarly startling statistics. According to Duan Chengrong, "In 1994 . . . the rate of committing crime among the rural migrant laborers was 1.3 percent, which was four times the national average. In Shanghai, Beijing, and other largest cities, . . . rural migrant laborers accounted for more than half of the total criminal cases. Guangzhou even reached 80 percent." Moreover, migrants were "said to be responsible for between one-third to 70 percent of all criminal activities in Chinese cities, with offenses ranging from theft, robbery, prostitution, to drug peddling, extortion, and murder."[40] In Hangzhou, 90 percent of

---

34. Ibid.

35. Feng Shuliang, "Crime and Crime Control in a Changing China," in Liu Jianhong, Zhang Lening, and Steven F. Messner, eds., *Crime and Social Control in a Changing China* (Westport, Conn.: Greenwood, 2001), p. 123.

36. "The Wild East: Guns in China," *Economist,* November 10, 2001, p. 75.

37. Damien McElroy, "China Fears Crime Wave of One-Child Generation," May 7, 1998, http://www.future-china.org/fcn/mainland/et980507.htm.

38. Li, "Population Flow into Big Cities," p. 17.

39. Ren, "Confronting Three Populations of 80 Million," p. 80.

40. Duan Chengrong, "Floating Populations and Their Effects on Rural and Urban Socioeconomic Development," *Population Research,* Vol. 22, No. 4 (1998), pp. 58–63.

criminals in the mid-1990s were migrants.[41] Zhang Haiyang proffered this explanation for the propensity of migrants to commit crime: "Generally speaking, the rural laborers are less educated, are extremely heterogeneous in composition, and lack the sense of law. When their requests cannot be satisfied, they tend to commit crimes."[42] In 1996 two comparative criminologists, Situ Yingyi and Liu Weizheng, offered the following analysis: "Apparently, whereas the regular city residents are responsible for a portion of the crimes, the new migrants constitute a large majority of the problem in the major Chinese cities. Moreover, our study found that many crimes committed by transient people are senseless and ruthless. An argument over a word can lead to a cold-blooded fight; burglars often kill the victims or witnesses on the scene if the offense is observed; highway robbery, rape, and kidnapping usually end with the victims' death; and a complaint about the poor quality of goods sold by transient vendors can cause injury in a severe physical assault."[43] Notable is the authors' mention of characteristics closely associated with bare branches.

Young male transients in China also appear to be disproportionately identified with a variety of other vices. In a 1996 study, for example, "more than 70 percent of the male transient workers surveyed admitted that they often drink and gamble."[44] Also in 1996, more than half of Beijing's known drug abusers reportedly were not city residents.[45] Transients not only abuse drugs in large numbers, but they also disproportionately traffic in them. In Zhenkang County in 1996, for example, thirty-one of the forty-five individuals arrested for selling drugs were migrants.[46] Moreover, the majority of new brothels that sprang up in urban areas in the early 1990s continue to service primarily the unattached migrant communities.[47] As a result, migrants may be disproportionately

---

41. Wong, "China's Urban Migrants," p. 340.

42. Zhang Haiyang, "On Flowing Population in Qiqiha'er: Current Conditions and Management," *Plan Study*, n.s., Vol. 5 (1997), p. 23.

43. Situ Yingyi and Liu Weizheng, "Transient Population, Crime, and Solution: The Chinese Experience," *International Journal of Offender Therapy and Comparative Criminology*, Vol. 40, No. 4 (December 1996), p. 295.

44. Yang Ji, "Transient Workers: A Special Social Group," and "Education Transient Workers," both in *Beijing Review*, June 3–9, 1996, p. 21.

45. Huang Wei, "Continuing War on Drugs," *Beijing Review*, September 2–8, 1996, pp. 17–19.

46. He Jingwu, "War on Drug Trafficking," *Beijing Review*, September 15–21, 1997, pp. 17–19.

47. See, for example, Vincent E. Gil, Marc Wang, Allen F. Anderson, and Guao Mat-

represented among Chinese with HIV/AIDS. In Beijing, of 130 Chinese persons officially reported as HIV-positive in 1997, 75 were migrants.[48] Smuggling, too, especially of firearms, has become big business for bare branches, prompting the minister of public security, Tao Siju, to remark in 1996, "The amount of illegal firearms and ammunition poses a grave threat to law and public safety."[49]

In recent years, China has also experienced an increase in the number of civil demonstrations. According to one report, there were 12,000 labor strikes and other protests in 1996, mostly carried out by migrant workers with grievances over pay.[50] The frequency, size, and intensity of these strikes have only increased. A labor strike in 2003 in Liaoning Province was the largest since the 1949 communist revolution.[51] Further, some of these labor strikes appear to have been coordinated across provincial borders, fueling fears of regional rebellion.

In sum, observers seem intuitively aware of the propensity of China's bare branches for engaging in disruptive behavior. One source refers to them as "a volatile social factor," while another asserts that "the challenge facing Chinese officials—central, provincial and urban alike—is to keep this giant [migrant] work force happy, or at least satisfied with their lot. If they fail, public order will deteriorate as restless migrants tire of being treated as second-class citizens."[52]

BARE BRANCHES AND INDIA'S WILD WEST

The kinds of data on bare-branch characteristics that are available for China are not available for India. Nevertheless we have found a well-researched and repeatedly confirmed link between sex ratios and violent crime at the state level in India. We have also found evidence that surplus

---

thew Lin, "Plum Blossoms and Pheasants: Prostitutes, Prostitution, and Social Control Measures in Contemporary China," *International Journal of Offender Therapy and Comparative Criminology*, Vol. 38, No. 4 (December 1994), pp. 319–337.

48. "AIDS Day, 1997: China Responds to AIDS," http://www.redfish.com/usembassy-china/sandt/aidsdy97.htm.

49. Quoted in "Tougher Actions toward Crime," *Beijing Review*, May 20–26, 1996, p. 6.

50. Ren, "Confronting Three Populations of 80 Million," p. 78.

51. Audra Ang, "Workers in Northeastern China Take to Streets for Back Pay, Better Benefits," Associated Press, March 10, 2003.

52. The first quote is from Li, "Population Flow into Big Cities," p. 17; the second is from Gilley, "Irresistible Force," p. 18. See also Chinese Saw Crime Jump 22% in First Nine Months of 1998.

young men in India are increasingly being recognized as a growing social menace.

India's bare branches reside primarily in the north and northwest states of Assam, Bihar, Punjab, Rajasthan, Uttar Pradesh, Uttaranchal, and West Bengal.[53] Together they make up a region referred to as India's "Wild West." The region is characterized by the same kind of lawlessness that flourished in the nineteenth-century American Wild West, which also had abnormally high sex ratios.[54] India's north and northwest states contain almost half of the country's population. These states also have the highest fertility rates and sex ratios in the country.

Political power in India's Wild West devolves from organized criminal gangs called *goondas*. This is especially true in states such as Bihar and Uttar Pradesh. In fact, the conditions in Uttar Pradesh and Uttaranchal are remarkably similar to those described by the British soldier and colonial administrator W.H. Sleeman in the mid-1800s, when Oudh comprised these two states. Private armies were ubiquitous, with many engaged in long-simmering feuds.

Wide-scale corruption has produced kleptocracies in India's northern region, where gang members are sometimes elected to positions in state government. In 1997 more than 10 percent of Bihar's legislators were well-known criminals. In Uttar Pradesh, 132 of 424 members of the legislature were "suspected criminals."[55] In the state's 1998 general election, a convicted murderer ran for and won a seat in the legislature. Violent crime remains a way of life in these states. Kidnapping, in particular, has become a huge problem. According to one report, "kidnapping is one of the main growth industries. Two people are snatched for ransom every day."[56]

Scholars have made several attempts to quantify the relationship between sex ratios and social disorder in India. Writing in 1999, for example, Amaryta Sen explicated a statistically significant relationship between violent crime rates and sex ratios in Indian states. According to Sen, "Extensive interdistrict contrasts . . . show a strong—and statistically

---

53.   India, *Census of India, 1991, Series-1, Part 2-B(i)*, Vol. 1: *Primary Census Abstract: General Population* (New Delhi: India, 1994).

54.   David T. Courtwright, *Violent Land: Single Men and Social Disorder from the Frontier to the Inner City* (Cambridge, Mass.: Harvard University Press, 1996).

55.   Farzand Ahmed and Subhash Mishra, "Stooping to Conquer," *India Today International*, November 10, 1997, p. 22.

56.   Samar Halarnkar, Sayantan Chakravarty, and Smruti Koppikar, "Fear in the City," *India Today International*, October 6, 1997, p. 14.

very significant—relation between the female-male ratio in the population and the scarcity of violent crimes. Indeed, the inverse connection between murder rates, as an indicator of social instability, and the female-male ratio in the population has been observed by many researchers over the years."[57]

Using 1981 crime statistics, Philip Oldenburg uncovered a striking correlation between sex ratios and murder rates in Indian states generally and in districts of Uttar Pradesh more specifically. (The calculated Pearson's r was -0.72 [sex ratio defined as number of females per 100 males]). Oldenburg's findings prompted him to refer to Indian states with the worst sex ratios as a "Bermuda Triangle for girls."[58] Oldenburg hypothesized that the lawlessness common to these areas has intensified the inhabitants' preference for sons. Greater numbers of sons, he stated, appear necessary "for the exercise of day-to-day power. To be sure, they [are also] needed for the protection of the family."[59] Oldenburg wondered "whether in these areas of violence daughters are seen as an even greater burden than elsewhere because of the greater risk of rape and abduction."[60] On the basis of the theory and historical case studies presented in chapter 5, such speculation seems reasonable. Skewed sex ratios, however, are not merely a consequence of lawlessness; they may also be a contributing factor.

In 2000 Jean Dreze and Reetika Khera replicated Oldenburg's research, correlating murder rates from 1980 to 1982 with the female-to-male sex ratio in 1981, as well as with other variables such as urbanization and poverty and literacy rates. The strongest correlation they found was between murder rates and sex ratios, which were inversely related (when using a female-to-male ratio). As the authors note, "This correlation is very robust: no matter which other variables are included or excluded from the regression, we found that the female-male ratio remained highly significant. . . . Further, the size of the coefficient of the female-male ratio is quite large."[61]

Using India's 1991 census data and 1997 murder rate data, we have attempted to update the analyses of Oldenburg, and Dreze and Khera.

---

57. Amartya Sen, *Development as Freedom* (New York: Alfred A. Knopf, 1999), p. 200.

58. Philip Oldenburg, "Sex Ratio, Son Preference, and Violence in India: A Research Note," *Economic and Political Weekly*, December 5–12, 1992, pp. 2657–2662.

59. Ibid., p. 2659.

60. Ibid., p. 2660.

61. Jean Dreze and Reetika Khera, "Crime, Gender, and Society in India: Insights from Homicide Data," *Population and Development Review*, Vol. 26, No. 2 (June 2000), p. 342.

Although both sets of data are less than ideal, they confirm the authors' findings of a statistically significant relationship between India's overall sex ratios and murder rates (see Table 6.1). The robust and persistent link in the Indian case leads us to the same conclusion as Dreze and Khera: "There is a strong link of some kind between high sex ratios and criminal violence (not just violence against women, but violence in the society as a whole). . . . This issue may be crucial in understanding criminal violence in many societies."[62] Observations on the ground buttress this conclusion. In a visit to the Indian state of Haryana in 2003, journalist Rahul Bedi noted, "With galloping unemployment, shrinking land holdings in a predominantly agricultural state and no family responsibilities, Haryana's vagrant bachelors spend their time playing cards, drinking, harassing local females, and making a thorough nuisance of themselves." One farmer commented simply, "They have become a social menace."[63]

Crimes against women in India, especially those involving kidnapping, trafficking, and rape, are all on the rise. From 1999 to 2000, the incidence of rape rose 6.6 percent.[64] Moreover, while the shortage of brides is becoming acute, girls are being married at younger ages to older men.[65] Potential brides are bought, often from Bangladesh, for 10,000–20,000 rupees.[66] These manifestations of rising social instability will likely increase over the next two decades as India's sex ratios become even more skewed.

Government Options for Dealing With Bare Branches

The Chinese and Indian governments have a variety of options to address the threat that abnormally large surpluses of bare branches may pose to their societies. Some of these options are already being implemented. Others would create such serious legal and moral concerns that they do not warrant more than passing mention. We present them here merely to explain why they would be unsuccessful, even if there were no legal and moral considerations.

---

62. Ibid., p. 347.

63. Rahul Bedi, "Families 'Buying' Girls as Marriage Crisis Deepens," *Irish Times*, March 10, 2003, p. 9.

64. Shefalee Vasudev and Methil Renuka, "Sexual Crimes: Rape!" *India Today*, September 9, 2002, pp. 1, 48.

65. David Gardner, "Where Have All the Girls Gone?" *Financial Times*, February 9, 2003, p. 1.

66. "Missing Sisters," p. 36.

Table 6.1. Indian States, Sex Ratios, 1991, Murder Rates, 1997.

State	Overall Sex Ratio[a]	Murder Rate (per 100,000)[b]
Andhra Pradesh	102.9	3.9
Arunachal Pradesh	116.4	6.3
Assam	108.3	5.7
Bihar	109.8	5.6
Goa	103.4	2.9
Gujarat	107.1	3.0
Haryana	115.6	3.2
Himachal Pradesh	102.5	1.9
Jammu and Kashmir	108.3	8.6
Karnataka	104.2	3.3
Kerala	96.5	1.4
Madhya Pradesh	107.4	4.6
Maharashtra	107.1	3.2
Manipur	104.4	13.0
Meghalaya	104.7	7.0
Mizoram	108.6	3.4
Nagaland	112.9	12.5
Orissa	103.0	2.9
Punjab	113.4	3.3
Rajasthan	109.9	3.1
Sikkim	113.9	2.9
Tamil Nadu	102.7	3.3
Tripura	105.8	6.8
Uttar Pradesh	113.8	4.8
West Bengal	109.1	2.3

[a]Sex ratios were calculated from population totals. See India, Office of the Registrar General, *Census of India, 1991, Series-1, Part 2-B(i)*, Vol. 1: *Primary Census Abstract: General Population* (New Delhi, India, 1994), chap. 3, Table 2.
[b]Figures are from National Crime Records, Bureau of India, http://www.ncrbindia.org.

MORE PROMISING OPTIONS

There are at least six promising policy options available to the Chinese and Indian governments to address problems created by their societies' highly skewed sex ratios, among them: promoting out-migration of males, encouraging in-migration of females, opening up of new frontiers, creating social safety nets, altering society's valuation of females, and establishing different incentive structures.

OUT-MIGRATION OF MALES. Promoting the migration of bare branches to foreign lands as guest workers can benefit both the bare branches and their governments. Bare-branch migrants who find work in other countries frequently send money home to their families, thus contributing indirectly to their states' economies. This was true, for example, of Chinese workers in nineteenth-century California. More recently, migration to the Russian Far East has become increasingly attractive to Chinese immigrants eager to fill positions left empty by Russians seeking their fortunes farther west.[67]

Out-migration has at least two problems, however. First, other countries cannot be expected to absorb significant numbers of bare branches. In addition, many migrants eventually return to their homelands either because they want to marry and start families or because their labor is no longer needed. Chinese farm workers in the Russian Far East, for example, typically return to China after the six-month growing season.[68] Second, migrants may become targets of xenophobic backlashes, especially during periods of economic downturn. Still, a policy of out-migration may be a useful complement to other government initiatives.

IN-MIGRATION OF FEMALES. Another option is to encourage the in-migration of women. Poor women from other countries, in particular, might view migration as an opportunity to marry up. Meanwhile, surplus Chinese and Indian males who marry these women might begin to exhibit less bare-branch behavior. In the case of China, observers wonder whether Taiwan could be a source of marriageable Han women (Han being China's main ethnic group). Taiwan, however, also suffers from abnormally high sex ratios. Even more important, Nicholas Eberstadt calculates that by 2020, "the surplus of [mainland] Chinese males in their 20s will exceed the entire female population of Taiwan."[69]

Meanwhile, given the strong taboos against marrying women of other races (or, in India's case, other castes), many of those who do marry have great difficulty adapting to their new surroundings. Kidnapped and bartered females experience significant challenges in this regard. Indeed, in describing the purchase by Indian men of women from other parts of India or in some cases Bangladesh, a district councillor in northern India stated that despite their status as wives, "many are treated as slaves. Even their children are shunned."[70] Most female migrants, however, are

---

67. Celestine Bohlen, "In Russian East, Chinese Help for Toiling Farmers," *New York Times*, August 1, 1999, sec. 1, p. 3.

68. Ibid.

69. Quoted in "6.3 Brides for Seven Brothers," *Economist*, December 19, 1998, p. 56.

70. "Missing Sisters," p. 36.

bartered as prostitutes. The criminal activity surrounding human trafficking has its own destabilizing effects on society, and in the cases of China and India, it has resulted in the emergence of several new criminal gangs. Unless strictly overseen and controlled by the government, in-migration of females may not help the status and situation of women in the society.

NEW FRONTIERS. In some cases, governments may decide to open up new frontiers for settlement. In China, for example, "'Go West, young Han,' is Beijing's message to the country's educated youth and a focus of the country's current five-year plan."[71] Predictably, however, most of the migrants to heed this call have been uneducated, unskilled bare branches willing to take great risks for an expected large payoff. In the past few years, the government has approved several large infrastructure pro-jects—including a cross-country gas pipeline and the Three Gorges Dam project—that require tens of thousands of Chinese laborers.[72] The leader-ship seems to recognize that such endeavors are not only about econom-ics. According to Chen Dongsheng, a chief engineer with the pipeline project and a member of the Communist Party, "Developing the west is a breakthrough program that concerns overall national security. It has real significance for the economy, politics, society, security, and defense."[73]

Beijing's plan to entice workers to move west faces several chal-lenges, however. First, the national ban on land ownership limits incen-tives to migrate. Second, the western frontier's nearest foreign trading partners are the poor nations of Central Asia. Third, from a historical per-spective, opening new frontiers is successful only when women eventu-ally join the migration. Without women, many men are likely to continue to engage in bare-branch behavior, while others may decide to return home. Moreover, given China's growing shortage of young women, it is extremely unlikely that many would choose to migrate at all. Finally, as the experience of the Nien demonstrates, frontier colonization does not always have its intended effect. As Jack Goldstone observed, "Misery in China's heartland led to massive migration to peripheral areas in the northwest, far west, and south. Such migration, however, did not provide an outlet that relieved social pressure; instead it added another set of ten-sions to China's already difficult situation. For the peripheral areas were

---

71. Craig Smith, "Beijing Tries to Lift Economic Standards in Its West," *New York Times*, November 7, 2000, p. C1.

72. "Western China Pining for Prosperity," Associated Press, as published in *Deseret News*, July 29, 2000, p. D7.

73. Quoted in ibid.

of low fertility and were already settled by various minority religious and ethnic groups. . . . In all these peripheral areas, gentry settlement and control was relatively weak; thus, conflicts quickly produced increased banditry and violence."[74] Similar problems exist in China today.

Another large-scale, government-sponsored infrastructure project in China involves the construction of a vast system of canals, with routes spanning from Tibet to the coast. Completion of the canal system could take up to fifty years and cost more than $100 billion. Such projects, however, may reach a saturation point. Furthermore, in China's case, it is uncertain whether economic conditions will continue to allow the central government to make such capital-intensive investments. Of all the policy options discussed thus far, however, this one appears to have the lowest social costs relative to the potential benefits.

SOCIAL SAFETY NETS. Bare-branch violence thrives on the resentment that income and resource inequality produces in young unattached males. Therefore, shrinking such inequality could reduce intrasocietal violence. Though of great promise, this option is virtually impossible to achieve in a free market economy. Moreover, it would not address one of the major reasons for the volatility of bare branches: the ongoing scarcity of women. Even if incomes were equalized, surplus males would still be unable to find spouses. Thus the inability to marry, to raise families, and to produce heirs cannot be undone by equalizing other resources.

Still, one way that government can reduce inequality—even in capitalist societies—is to establish social safety nets. Beijing's initiatives over the past five years to bolster social insurance programs, for example, are helping to reduce the sense of desperation among those less well off, including the bare branches. In the late 1990s, under Premier Zhu Rongji, the government reviewed the possibility of extending unemployment insurance to migrant and nonmigrant workers alike, as well as providing social security insurance to the elderly.[75] To date, only laid-off urban nonmigrant workers are eligible for unemployment insurance, and the amounts are paltry. Nevertheless, such initiatives could play an important role in managing society's selection for bare branches.

In an even more significant experiment, in the mid-1990s the government in Zhejiang Province began offering old-age pensions to elderly parents in an attempt to offset son preference. According to Xie

---

74. Jack A. Goldstone, *Revolution and Rebellion in the Early Modern World* (Berkeley: University of California Press, 1991), p. 398.

75. Li Chunyi, "'Huji' System, Population Flow, and Instability of Cities," Foreign Affairs College, Beijing, 1999, p. 18.

Zhenming, editor of *China Population Today*, the sex ratio at birth in the province has subsequently normalized.[76] This experiment appears to confirm that social safety nets are an important element in decision-making about offspring sex selection; the manipulation of the former can bring about desired change in the latter.

Scholars in India have also noted the crucial role of old-age insurance in the sex ratio equation. As K. Mahadevan and R. Jayasree have observed, "Since the present children alone form social security for old parents, we need urgent action to introduce other sources of social security."[77] The Indian government, however, has not yet responded to this challenge.

SOCIETY'S VALUATION OF FEMALES. This option has three components: (1) rewarding families that select for daughters, (2) punishing those that select for sons, and (3) raising the overall status of women in society. This option appears to have no disadvantages, although even if all three components were successfully implemented, it would take several decades for the sex ratio of the young adult population to become more balanced. Meanwhile, the government still has to find ways to deal with problems being created by today's high sex ratios.

China and India have taken several steps to improve the valuation of women in their societies. Both, for example, have imposed bans on infanticide and sex-selective abortion (including the use of ultrasound to detect the sex of a fetus). In perhaps a significant move, government officials in Shandong Province announced on January 1, 1999, the banning of prenatal ultrasound scanning. Whether this ban is being enforced, however, is unclear. As noted earlier, ultrasound scanning for the purpose of sex determination is already illegal throughout China.[78] In addition, since 1998 the Chinese government has publicized the punishment of officials who use coercion, such as forced abortion and sterilization, to meet family planning goals. According to the director of international relations for the State Family Planning Committee, Cong Jun, "The committee has issued circulars to branch organizations ordering them to stop forcing women to undergo induced abortions or sterilization."[79] At the

---

76. "6.3 Brides for Seven Brothers," p. 58.

77. K. Mahadevan and R. Jayasree, "Value of Children and Differential Fertility Behavior in Kerala, Andhra Pradesh, and Uttar Pradesh," in Shri Nath Singh, ed., *Population Transition in India* (Delhi: B.R. Publishing Corporation, 1989), p. 131.

78. "China Has 20 Percent Male Surplus," Agence France-Presse, January 7, 1999 (accessed from Proquest, LexisNexis).

79. Quoted in "Coercive Tactics Divulged in China's One-Child Policy," Associated

same time, the government's commitment to enforcing the ban remains uncertain: For instance, in May 1999 a Chinese woman who was nine months pregnant and seeking asylum in Australia was forced return to China to undergo an abortion. The previous year, the Chinese government enacted regulations requiring employers and landlords to report unauthorized births by migrants. Migrant couples found to have violated China's family planning policy would then be "handled" by local governments, implying perhaps compulsory sterilization.[80]

Despite such measures, the sex ratios in both China and India continue to worsen. Tradition can be a stubborn, often inflexible force. In countries with misogynistic cultures, tradition may even trump the law. In an effort to improve the status of daughters in India, for example, the government passed a law in 1956 granting them equal rights of inheritance. The law has been all but ignored.[81]

The continued increase in illegal offspring sex selection in parts of Asia remains troubling. As two observers have noted, "The sudden increases in sex ratios in East Asian societies are impressive—in each country, within a single year the sex ratio has jumped to a high level that has subsequently been sustained. This suggests that people have been anxiously awaiting the availability of sex-control technology . . . and that couples actively use such technology, regardless of fertility level."[82] Re-

---

Press, as published in *Deseret News,* June 14, 1998, p. A17; and Vivien Pik-kwan Chan, "Ban Imposed on Forced Abortions," *South China Morning Post,* October 31, 1998, p. 8.

80. Daniel Kwan, "Tougher Laws for Migrant Birth Control," *South China Morning Post,* September 23, 1998, p. 9.

81. See, for example, Carol Vlassoff, "The Value of Sons in an Indian Village: How Widows See It," *Population Studies,* Vol. 44, No. 1 (March 1990), pp. 5–20.

82. Park Chai Bin and Cho Nam-hoon, "Consequences of Son Preference in a Low-Fertility Society: Imbalance of the Sex Ratio at Birth in Korea," *Population and Development Review,* Vol. 21, No. 1 (March 1995), p. 79. For purposes of comparison, son preference is not as pronounced in other countries, and attitudes toward offspring sex selection are not as positive. In the most recent Shell Poll, 75 percent of Americans surveyed stated that "selecting the sex of a child" was "unethical." Lois M. Collins, "Americans Feel Strongly About What Is Ethical," *Deseret News,* May 8, 1999, p. E1. Another recent U.S. poll found that 41 percent of those surveyed would like to choose the sex of their baby; the birth of a boy was favored by a 2 to 1 margin. "Survey Finds Most Parents Wouldn't Choose Baby's Sex If They Could," Associated Press, March 16, 1999. Therefore, about 25 percent of the total sample displayed a preference for sons. There is some evidence that son preference in the United States was higher in the first half of the twentieth century and was felt most keenly by males, and that son preference was actually slightly lower seventeen years ago than it is today. Lawrence Kilman, "Majority of Americans Wouldn't Choose Baby's Sex If Given a Chance," Associated Press, November 17, 1986. See also Sanford Winston, "Birth Control and Sex

cently, a company in the United States developed a new sperm-sorting technology designed to separate sperm carrying the X chromosome from sperm carrying the Y chromosome.[83] The first overseas office of a company to license this technology is located in Beijing, and though forbidden to sell its services in India, the company is targeting its advertising to Indian-Americans and Indian-Canadians.[84]

These new technologies will increasingly influence parental strategies regarding not only second and higher birth-order children but also firstborns. Judith Banister, a noted expert on Chinese demographics, cautions, "Given that first births are over half of all Chinese births, that's the axe that's waiting to fall." She adds that prenatal sex-selection technologies are already skewing the birth ratios of firstborn children in parts of South Korea.[85] And as William Lavely remarks, "Such practices [in China] . . . not only permit parents to attain transcendent goals [i.e., sons]—they also reduce the birth rate and resistance to administrative controls, and are thus in fundamental harmony with the priorities of local officials in charge of birth planning."[86] In other words, these technologies are used not only because they produce the desired results—sons—but also because the government does not punish parents who abort daughters in the hope of having sons, whereas it does punish those who have more children simply in an effort to have sons.

The Indian government has also intensified its efforts to enforce the country's laws against sex selection. Following international embarrassment over the release of data from the 2001 census on India's child sex ratios, the government decreed that manufacturers of ultrasound equipment can sell the machines only to registered clinics, which must maintain strict records of their use.[87] In addition, the clinics must prominently display signs that read, "This clinic does not perform any sex determination."[88] The government has also established the Cradle Baby Scheme,

Ratio at Birth," *American Journal of Sociology*, Vol. 38, No. 2 (September 1932), pp. 225–231.

83. Gina Kolata, "Researchers Report Success in Method to Pick Baby's Sex," *New York Times*, September 9, 1998, p. A1.

84. Wyndham Murray, communication with Valerie Hudson, October 11, 1998.

85. Quoted in "6.3 Brides for Seven Brothers," p. 57.

86. William Lavely, "Unintended Consequences of China's Birth Planning Policy," University of Washington, July 14, 1997, pp. 18–19.

87. "Doctors Should Abide by Sex Selection Act Norms," *Times of India*, April 29, 2003, p. 1.

88. Gautam N. Allahbadia, "The 50 Million Missing Women," *Journal of Assisted Reproduction and Genetics*, Vol. 19, No. 9 (September 2002), p. 415.

which encourages families to leave their unwanted daughters at state adoption centers.[89] Some Indian localities even require pregnant women to register with area hospitals and attend mandatory gender-equity classes. The purpose is twofold: (1) to counsel these women against killing their female offspring, and (2) to teach them the value of daughters.[90] (Notably, it is almost always the mother or mother-in-law who commits infanticide.)

In recent years, the Chinese government has also begun to address more seriously the issue of the valuation of daughters. To discourage offspring sex selection, family planning clinics in China have begun to post signs that say, for example, "Let Nature Take Its Course."[91] More important perhaps has been the growing number of statements by senior officials criticizing China's high sex ratios. More than a decade ago, Zeng Yi, director of the Demography Institute at Beijing University and a respected voice on Chinese population policies, predicted, "The loss of female births due to illegal prenatal sex determination and sex-selective abortion and female infanticide will affect the true sex ratio at birth and at young ages, creating an unbalanced population sex structure in the future and resulting in potentially serious social problems."[92] But as Martin King Whyte notes, "Chinese analysts seem to worry much more about how these excess males will eventually find brides than they do about the 'missing girls' themselves."[93]

Nevertheless, the Chinese government has launched several initiatives to raise the valuation of daughters, particularly in the eyes of parents. For instance, in an effort to dispel the notion that only sons can provide for their elderly parents, the government has sought to demonstrate that in modern capitalist societies, daughters may actually provide better care than sons. As an example, in 1996 the government erected billboards showing two mothers talking. Dressed in rags and appearing

89. Satinder Bindra, "Grim Motives behind Infant Killings," CNN.com, July 7, 2003, http://www.cnn.com/2003/world/asiapcf/south/07/07/india.infanticide.pt1/index.html.

90. Satinder Bindra, "State Adopts Infants' Cause," CNN.com, July 7, 2003, http://www.cnn.com/2003/world/asiapcf/south/07/07/india.infanticide.pt2/index.html.

91. Celeste McGovern, "Chinese Puzzle: 117 Boys for 100 Girls," *Report*, June 10, 2003, http://report.ca/archive/report/20020610/p56i020610f.html.

92. Quoted in Zeng Yi, Tu Ping, Gu Baochang, Xu Yi, Li Bohua, and Li Yongping, "Causes and Implications of the Recent Increase in the Reported Sex Ratio at Birth in China," *Population and Development Review*, Vol. 19, No. 2 (June 1993), p. 296.

93. Martin King Whyte, "Social Trends and the Human Rights Situation in the PRC," George Washington University, 1998, p. 27.

alone, one of the mothers laments, "I have three sons, but none of them takes care of me." The other, a well-dressed woman whose daughter is rubbing her back, declares proudly, "I have only one daughter, but she surpasses your three sons."[94] Many years ago, Margery Wolf questioned the effectiveness of such campaigns, claiming that "the only women who have succored their aging parents have been in propaganda films or newspaper editorials, or in some other village."[95] More recently, however, some observers suggest that the government's efforts have begun to have an impact: "Already, many urban people say, in a reversal of the old norm, that a daughter is preferable to a son because she is more likely to attend to the parents [in old age]."[96]

Another element in the government's campaign to raise the valuation of women is to dissuade men from practicing polygyny. Cultural practices in India make this all but impossible. In China, however, the government should continue to enforce the ban on polygyny, especially in light of the growing popularity of concubinage. The scarcity of women is one matter, but the hoarding or monopolization of scarce women by wealthy, powerful men makes an already bad situation worse. In the latest revision of China's Marriage Law in 2001, concubinage (like polygyny) remains illegal, and we would urge the government to continue to enforce its prohibition.

The Chinese government has never been shy about using public executions to "educate" the population. In recent years, it has put to death individuals who killed or in some other way contributed to the deaths of girl babies. The execution of a grandmother for killing her granddaughter

---

94. Another interesting point to consider is the demographic structure of China as projected into the future. The only two categories showing marked increases that are expected to continue are (1) bare branches and (2) the older-than-60 population. The World Bank estimates that by 2020, the elderly will account for more than 16 percent of the Chinese population. One cannot help but wonder whether the unprecedented "graying" of this population might cause societies selecting for bare branches to be even more vulnerable to the instability that these young men frequently produce. While the average annual growth rate of the overall population from 1982 to 1995 was about 1.43 percent, the average annual growth rate of the elderly was 3.10 percent. Li Weidong, "To Keep Economic Prosperity under the Double Pressures of Population Aging and Unemployment," *Economics Selection* (1999), pp. 10–11, as cited in Anita Zhong, "China's Aging Population and China's Economy," Foreign Affairs College, Beijing, May 23, 1999, pp. 12–13.

95. Margery Wolf, *Revolution Postponed: Women in Contemporary China* (Stanford, Calif.: Stanford University Press, 1985), p. 271.

96. Erik Eckholm, "Homes for Elderly Replacing Family Care as China Grays," *New York Times,* May 20, 1998, p. A1.

illustrates the government's efforts to curb the practice of infanticide: "A woman who murdered her baby granddaughter because she was angry the child was not a boy has been sentenced to death by a provincial people's court. Lin Xinnu, 63, harbored a traditional preference for male heirs, the *Xinmin Evening News* reported. After Lin's daughter-in-law Kong Yahong gave birth to the girl, the pair continually argued, the paper said. During one fight in March at their home on the outskirts of Nigbo city in Zhejiang Province, Lin snatched the girl from Ms Kong's arms and threw her to the ground, splitting the child's skull. Ningbo Intermediate People's Court gave Lin's daughter a two-year suspended jail term for harboring Lin before her arrest."[97] Those who are found to have profited from the kidnapping and sale of boys to couples who under Chinese law cannot legally try for a second, male child have suffered similar punishment.[98]

Despite such penalties, trafficking in female infants continues in China. In July 2003, twenty-eight girl babies aged 2–5 months were found stuffed two to four together in nylon bags in the back of a long-haul bus. The infants were on their way to be sold as eventual wives for the sons of peasants whose villages had no girls. Shortly after this discovery, President Hu Jintao ordered an investigation.[99]

China's changing cultural values may also play a role in reducing the practice of offspring sex selection. In the television soap opera *Ordinary People*, reportedly watched by more than 11 million Chinese, episodes over the last several years have chronicled the stories of a heartbroken young woman being sold into marriage and of another who decides to keep her baby daughter in defiance of the wishes of her husband and his family. Newspaper columnist Ellen Goodman interviewed Chen Sheng Li of the State Family Planning Commission, which reportedly provided input on the plot lines. She quotes Chen as saying, "Instead of imposing government policies, we are trying to change attitudes."[100]

---

97. "Death for Killing Granddaughter," Associated Press, as published in *South China Morning Post*, July 27, 1998, http://www.scmp.com/news/template/chinaT . . . ina&template=default.htx&maxfieldsize=913.

98. For a discussion of the execution of one of these kidnappers, see "Death for Kidnapper of Twelve Boys," Associated Press, as published in *South China Morning Post*, May 29, 1998, http://www.scmp.com/news/templat . . . ina&template=default. htx&maxfieldsize=898.

99. Elisabeth Rosenthal, "Bias for Boys Leads to Sale of Baby Girls in China," *New York Times*, July 20, 2003, sec. 1, p. 6.

100. Ellen Goodman, "Will China's Values Change? Stay Tuned," *Boston Globe*, November 11, 1999, p. A27.

Providing females with greater educational opportunities—particularly in India where female illiteracy rates are especially high—is another possible approach to raising the status of women. Yet access to better education is not a panacea. The near-universal education of females in China, for example, has failed to slow its spiraling sex ratio. Nor have better educational opportunities coupled with greater affluence had much success. As noted in chapter 3, the sex ratios for educated, affluent Indian families are often worse than those for India's poorest, least educated families. Thus greater educational opportunities and improvements in economic standing must be combined with policies that shift the cost-benefit calculus in favor of daughters. In some parts of southern China, for example, daughters (not sons) have become the key to family prosperity in today's global economy. The strong preference of multinational and joint ventures for employing young women in their manufacturing plants has made many of these women their families' primary wage earners. As awareness of this fact increases, discrimination against female children may wane, though their economic exploitation may be the price.[101]

In addition to these two measures, there are at least other steps that leaders in China and India should be encouraged to take. First, the Chinese government, in particular, should do more to improve the lot of young women who, in desperation, are tempted to kill themselves. Second, every abandoned female infant in China and India should be regarded as a precious national asset and treated as such. Governments in both countries have vested interests in these infants becoming healthy adult women, and both must accept responsibility for their care. To support this effort, they could levy a tax on the birth of every male infant or collect annual taxes from parents of male children. Although this could result in the government raising most of the country's daughters, the potential long-term consequences of unchecked surpluses of young men are far worse. Every female born in China and India today is critically important to the future stability of these countries and the survival of their governments. If parents are unable to recognize this, then it falls to their governments to protect and care for these girls. As the anthropologist Barbara Miller argues, a normal sex ratio is a "public good," and govern-

---

101. Such recognition can become a powerful cultural force. According to a report in the *People's Daily* on April 2, 1983, "Since the initiation of Shao-hsing opera in Chekiang, the characters of which are exclusively made up of females, many baby girls have been saved in Shao-hsing and Hsing-hien. When a baby girl is born, the father often says, 'Don't drown her. Let her grow up to sing in the opera!'" Quoted in T'ien Ju-k'ang, *Male Anxiety and Female Chastity: A Comparative Study of Chinese Ethical Values in Ming-Ch'ing Times* (New York: E.J. Brill, 1988), p. 27, n. 42.

ments that fail to preserve that public good do their societies a tremendous disservice.[102]

DIFFERENT INCENTIVE STRUCTURES. Altering cultural mind-sets about the valuation of females may take more than a century to accomplish. A quicker route may be to change the incentive structures in which parents make life-and-death decisions concerning their children, including decisions involving offspring sex selection.

In October 1997, the director of the Demography Institute, Zeng Yi, said that it would eventually be possible to loosen China's one-child policy. He based this assertion on the successful results of population policy experiments by several local governments. In one experiment in Yicheng County, for example, "Couples which observed the rule of not marrying early and waiting three years to have their first child are permitted to have a second child after age 30 if they wish. The result has been a total fertility rate of 2.35 [only slightly above replacement levels] and a population growth rate considerably less than in neighboring counties and a more normal sex ratio among the children."[103] A year later, Chen Yijun, director of the Institute of Sociology in the ministry of civil affairs, predicted, "The one-child policy is for a certain period of time. . . . I hope it will be changed after five or six years."[104] Other encouraging signs also began to appear in the 1990s. In a small number of counties, municipal governments no longer required that women obtain approval to have their first child. Previously, if a locality or an employer had reached its birth quota, a woman could be denied permission to have even her first child. In other areas, reports have surfaced that couples can have a second child without harassment (but not subsequent children) if they are willing to pay a considerable "family planning fee."[105]

These changes foreshadowed Beijing's decision in 2003 to transform China's population policy. The recently established State Family Planning and Population Commission, successor to the State Family Planning Commission, is to draft China's first-ever five-year (2006–10) population development plan. According to official reports, the decision to adopt a strategic approach to population issues is "the result of looming prob-

102. Barbara D. Miller, "Female-Selective Abortion in Asia: Patterns, Policies, and Debates," *American Anthropologist*, Vol. 103, No. 4 (December 2001), pp. 1083–1095.

103. "PRC Family Planning: The Market Weakens Controls but Encourages Voluntary Limits," http://www.usembassy-china.org.cn/english/sandt/POPMYWB.html.

104. "China One-Child Policy Likely to Be Loosened as Birth Rates Drop," Agence France-Presse, February 11, 1998 (accessed from Proquest, LexisNexis).

105. Quoted in Elisabeth Rosenthal, "For One-Child Policy, China Rethinks Iron Hand," *New York Times*, November 1, 1998, sec. 1, p. 1.

lems aside from birth control issues, such as the immigration of farmers, a rising gender imbalance, the aging population, and increasing unemployment pressures."[106]

The media have portrayed the 2002 and 2003 changes to China's population policy as a loosening of the government's one-child policy. It is not yet clear, however, whether this is an accurate assessment. On the one hand, the September 2002 Law on Population and Family Planning criminalizes the act of having more than the prescribed number of children. In addition, the government has announced its intention to create a nationwide database of all women of child-bearing age, so that it may monitor their reproductive behavior more closely. On the other hand, the law appears to discourage the punishment of couples who have more than one child, requiring instead that they pay a "social compensation fee." In some cases, this fee may amount to several years' income. In addition, there are signs that some exemptions to the one-child rule that until now have been available only in certain localities may become available nationwide. These exemptions would cover couples who remarry as well as couples who wait five years before having a child. More radical approaches are possible, but they could cause greater social unrest than would loosening the one-child policy.[107]

---

106. See "China to Usher in Major Changes in Population Policies," People's Daily Online, August 20, 2003, http://english.peopledaily.com.cn/200308/20/eng 20030820–122707.shtml.

107. An example of a more radical approach would be the reintroduction, perhaps by lottery, of a style of marriage practiced in historical China until the communist period: uxorilocal marriage. *Ciou-zip chua-chut* unions were ones in which the daughter's family "called in" a son-in-law. Sometimes the couple lived with her parents, sometimes with his parents; in both cases, however, the groom assumed support for the bride's parents. In another type of marriage, called *shang-men nu-hsu*, the son-in-law became the legal heir of the bride's parents and assumed their surname. The children born to the couple took the surname of their mother's family, as well. If parents in China—whether of a daughter or a son—all had a 50 percent chance of passing their surname on to their grandchildren, a mighty societal change might be produced. In the current system, a couple with a son has a 100 percent chance of passing their family name on to their grandchildren, whereas the couple with a daughter has a 0 percent chance. If those chances were made equivalent through a mandatory lottery, the status of daughters in society might correspondingly rise. For a discussion of this type of marriage in China's past, see Arthur P. Wolf and Chieh-shan Huang, *Marriage and Adoption in China, 1845–1945* (Stanford, Calif.: Stanford University Press, 1980), chap. 7. Interestingly, China's 1980 Marriage Law states that a woman may become a member of a man's natal family after their marriage is registered, or the man may join the woman's family. Information Office of the State Council, *Protection of Chinese Women's Rights and Interests* (Beijing: New Star, 1993), p. 20. For the resurgence of this type of marriage in present-day Japan, for example, see Howard W. French, "New Pressures Alter Japanese Family's Geometry," *New York Times,* July 27, 2000, p. A1.

In India, because social inequality among castes is a primary factor in offspring sex selection, policies that seek to lessen this social inequality should be pursued. The British had some success in curbing female infanticide in colonial India both by tying resource allocations to locales to their sex ratios and by capping dowry prices. According to this policy, entire locales were punished if colonial administrators discovered that any of their inhabitants had practiced offspring sex selection. The social pressure brought to bear against families contemplating offspring sex selection helped to curb the practice, but only to a point. Meanwhile, restricting dowry prices made it more affordable to have daughters. The policy of encouraging *ekdas*—exchange marriage circles—made dowry caps easier to sustain. Instead of facing bankruptcy, families with marriageable daughters could anticipate only a minor financial setback. It is impossible to know if such policies would be successful in India today, but they may be worth considering—especially in light of a recent report stating that even as brides are becoming scarcer, dowry prices are on the rise. This type of economic irrationality begs government intervention.[108]

LESS PROMISING OPTIONS

There are two additional policy options for dealing with surplus male populations in China and India, but each raises such significant legal and moral concerns that neither is worthy of serious consideration. The first option is official encouragement of certain kinds of vice (e.g., prostitution and drug trafficking) from which the government receives a share of the profits to put toward controlling the bare branches. The encouragement of vice is a double-edged sword, however, and it is unlikely to promote long-term stability or prosperity. In addition, such policies could exacerbate existing problems, including, for instance, Asia's burgeoning AIDS epidemic. In another example, the government of Thailand is having major regrets over its policy of promoting vice, especially prostitution and sex tourism. The resulting societal costs are proving to be immense and potentially devastating. Among its other negative consequences, vice encourages crime and the formation of armed gangs.

The second option is military recruitment, which historically has been a common policy instrument when bare branches became numerous. Military service offers bare branches an opportunity to make a decent living and raise their societal status. But it also gives them valuable training in warfare and arms, skills that under certain circumstances could be turned against the government. Recent government initiatives to downsize the People's Liberation Army and to strip it of its money-

---

108. "Missing Sisters," p. 2.

making industries and smuggling operations thus raise concerns, particularly if they result in the discharge of troops.[109] In his study of the mid-Ming era, Robinson found that many of the foremost bandit and rebel leaders of the period had at one time been in the imperial military. Indeed, some were still in the military when they began to engage in pillage and brigandage. As Robinson puts it, "Managing these men of force was a delicate balance, and the price of failure could be very high. The same factors that made these men attractive to military officers, civil officials, and local gentry were precisely those that made them most dangerous—skill in arms, physical bravery, willingness to use violence, a band of followers, and ties that extended beyond the confines of local society. Allied with proper authorities, these men were a potent addition to the forces of order. If, however, relations between these men and the powers that be broke down, they became a frightening avatar of social chaos."[110]

A page from U.S. history is also relevant here. "The armed forces," according to David Courtwright, "have acted throughout American history as a giant sponge. In times of mobilization and combat they have absorbed the most dangerous elements of society; in times of demobilization and peace they have discharged them and their acquired vices, lethal skills, and war-surplus guns back into society. If, as after World War II, most of the young veterans returned to families or formed new ones, the effects of mass discharge were mitigated. If, however, a sizable number of veterans either did not marry or divorced their spouses, as after the Vietnam War, the negative effects of military service could be of a more serious and long-lasting character."[111] Given China's high sex ratio, the former, more optimistic, scenario seems extremely unlikely. The same is true of India.

In a development that bears continued scrutiny, the Chinese government declared its intention in 1999 to increase the number of troops assigned to the People's Armed Police by fourteen divisions, to about 1 million men. The mission of the People's Armed Police is to maintain internal stability by quelling domestic unrest and rioting spurred by, among other things, high unemployment, corruption, and tax increases. According to John Corbett and Dennis Blasko, "By increasing the size of the People's Armed Police, the leadership in Beijing implicitly acknowl-

---

109. Seth Faison, "China's Chief Tells Army to Give Up Its Commerce," *New York Times,* July 23, 1998, p. A3.

110. David M. Robinson, "The Management of Violence in the Mid-Ming Capital Region," Colgate University, 1998, p. 35.

111. Courtwright, *Violent Land,* p. 46.

edges that internal unrest is a greater threat to the regime's survival and Chinese economic modernization than is foreign invasion."[112]

Many of the new members of the People's Armed Police, however, are what one expert has termed "the dregs" (men from the lowest rungs of society who often have criminal backgrounds).[113] As noted in chapter 5, the use of bare branches by Chinese dynasties to control other bare branches frequently had unintended consequences. Indeed the abuses, corruption, and violence of the "co-opted" bare branches came to rival those of the bare-branch bandits they were supposed to be controlling. Keeping these "troops" close to wealthy urban centers, for example, proved especially unwise.

Some observers might suggest that military recruitment of bare branches could succeed if they were stationed far from cities, perhaps even on foreign assignments. As noted in chapter 5, this strategy proved successful for the Portuguese government in medieval times. A similar strategy could in some cases succeed again. In other cases, however, it could backfire. Wherever a government sends armed forces—whether to troublesome national frontier regions or on foreign adventures—they will likely encounter violent opposition. Sustained conflict can drain a government of resources, legitimacy, and popular support. Indeed it can so weaken a government that it would be vulnerable to collapse from internal or external pressure, or both.

Another variant of this approach might actually be in use in India today. Unlike China's overwhelmingly ethnically homogeneous population, Indian society is a maze of castes, races, and religions. The country's ruling party, the Bharatiya Janata Party (BJP), is unabashedly sectarian and nationalistic. Aiming to move the Hindu nation into the ranks of the world's great powers, the BJP has openly engaged in anti-Muslim rhetoric to gain followers. In response, young Hindu men attracted to this vision of greater India have perpetrated much of the violence directed against Muslims. We wonder if this increasing sectarian violence is related not only to Hindu nationalism but also to the desire of the Indian government to channel the destructive energies of its growing bare-branch population away from itself. If so, it is a dangerous policy that could produce widespread social and economic disruption, thus eroding the minimum stability the government needs to maintain its authority and legitimacy.

---

112. Quoted in Erik Eckholm, "A Secretive Army Grows to Maintain Order in China," *New York Times*, March 28, 1999, sec. 1, p. 6.

113. Ibid.

Conclusion

Many of the policy options discussed above are tools that can help to address societal problems created by highly skewed sex ratios. There is, however, one variable that could drastically alter the security calculi of the governments of China and India, specifically: If either economy falters over an extended period, its bare-branch population could grow increasingly desperate as jobs become even more scarce and their survival more tenuous. The results could include widespread civil strife and direct challenges to the government's legitimacy. For these reasons, China's current high unemployment rate is very troubling, as laid-off urban residents increasingly compete for jobs with migrant workers who continue to flock to the city, and as the country's crime rates continue to rise. Already, a cycle of protests and riots followed by brutal crackdowns has begun.[114] Heavily represented in these protests and riots are the bare branches or, in the words of one observer, China's "army of the discontented."[115]

In this regard, the 2001 accession of China into the World Trade Organization (WTO) carries with it costs as well as benefits. On the one hand, entry into the WTO is likely to contribute to long-term Chinese prosperity. On the other hand, the concessions that the government has had to make as a condition of entry will fall heavily on the country's agricultural and heavy industry sectors, both of which employ large numbers of bare branches. Chi Lo, a senior Asian economist based in Hong Kong, expects urban employment to double as a result of China's WTO membership, and the trend appears to going in that direction.[116] Another suggests, "Millions of farmers . . . would have to leave their homes and find new jobs in urban areas."[117] One unnamed Western economist predicts a "blood bath" for Chinese farmers as a result of China's concessions.[118] Some economists believe that at least 30 million jobs will disappear soon after accession to the WTO is fully implemented by 2005. In the short term, then, the potential for instability may be worse than economists

---

114. Elisabeth Rosenthal, "Factory Closings in China Arouse Workers to Fury," *New York Times*, August 31, 2000, p. A1.

115. See "Army of Jobless Threatening China."

116. Quoted in Paul Eckert, "China's Monumental Leap," Reuters, as published in *Deseret News*, November 21, 1999, p. A1.

117. Ibid.

118. Erik Eckholm, "One Giant Step for Mr. Jiang's China," *New York Times*, November 21, 1999, sec. 4, p. 4.

estimate. Indeed, press reports indicate that a major source of recruits for subversive movements such as the Falun Gong is the ranks of the unemployed.[119]

The nature of the state may also play a role in a society's ability to weather the consequences of high sex ratios in the short run. According to some scholars, the historical record demonstrates that high-sex-ratio societies can be governed only by authoritarian regimes. Under less authoritarian regimes, regionalism, warlordism, and social disorder are likely to result.[120] Although we are not proponents of authoritarianism, we do recognize the logic of this argument.

Finally, in recent years, some Chinese politicians have begun to discuss more publicly the concerns of the bare branches. One candidate in a recent local election even promised, "I will take care of all the bachelors here who do not have the income to find a wife. I will make you rich!"[121] The central government should beware such direct appeals to the bare branches, given their potential to re-create some of the worst violence in China's history.

---

119. Eckert, "China's Monumental Leap."

120. Christian G. Mesquida and Neil I. Wiener, "Human Collective Aggression: A Behavior Ecology Perspective," *Ethology and Sociobiology*, Vol. 17, No. 4 (July 1996), pp. 247–262, are most eloquent in this regard; see also Laura Betzig, "Despotism and Differential Reproduction: A Cross-Cultural Correlation of Conflict Asymmetry, Hierarchy, and Degree of Polygyny," *Ethology and Sociobiology*, Vol. 3, No. 4 (1982), pp. 209–221.

121. Quoted in Thomas L. Friedman, "It Takes a Village," *New York Times*, March 10, 1998, p. A19.

Chapter 7

Conclusion

The Security Calculus of High-Sex-Ratio Societies

What happens to societies that explicitly select for increasing and dispro-portionate numbers of male offspring, or bare branches? This is a ques-tion that China and India, the two most populous nations on earth, will be answering for the world in the twenty-first century.

Offspring sex selection, though initially motivated by the desire to re-strict resource consumption, paradoxically creates increased resource competition. The result, exaggerated gender imbalance and the gender inequality that accompanies it, has the potential to create severe envi-ronmental and human insecurity. The historical cases presented in chap-ter 5 of the Nien and the Reconquista, as well as the turbulence in nineteenth-century Oudh and colonial Taiwan, demonstrate the tremen-dously harmful impact of prevalent offspring sex selection. These exam-ples also suggest possible consequences of the artificially high sex ratios present in contemporary China and India, home to almost 40 percent of the world's population. The evidence suggests that high-sex-ratio socie-ties, especially those with unequal resource distribution and generalized resource scarcity, breed chronic violence and persistent social disorder and corruption. Indeed bare branches in high-sex-ratio societies contrib-ute to this disruption on a larger scale than might be possible in societies with lower sex ratios.

These effects occur as the sex ratio in the 15–34 age category nears 120 males to 100 females. In January 1999, the Chinese Academy of Social Sci-ences in Beijing declared that the birth sex ratio in China had reached 120:100. In addition, the academy calculated that one in six Chinese men was unlikely to find a wife, and that the number of surplus Chinese males had reached 111 million—more than the entire population of

Mexico.[1] Given recent trends, the sex ratio of China's next generation is likely to be even higher. Meanwhile India's sex ratios are forecast to approach 115 over the next several years.

In the historical cases of gender imbalance, the ruling governments eventually became acutely aware of the danger that high sex ratios posed to their societies. Indeed commentators of the time explicitly pointed to high sex ratios to explain both the surge in violence in their countries and governmental efforts to combat it. There is some evidence that the current leadership in Beijing is beginning to understand the potential threat of China's bare branches. In a statement in 1996, a Chinese official captured this growing concern: "By the end of the century, our country could have a great hoodlum army of 70 million single men."[2] In 2002 Ren Yuling, a Communist Party Congress delegate, warned that the skewed gender ratio would "unravel" China's "social fabric."[3] Zheng Zizhen, director of the Sociology and Demography Institute in Guangdong Province, declared in 2003 that "this sustained abnormality in the birth gender rate will have a negative effect on the structure of the Chinese population, society, and morals."[4] Although Indian government officials do not yet appear to have reached similar conclusions regarding their country's highly skewed sex ratios, Indian scholars and journalists have noted the trend with growing alarm. Observers sense that India's abnormal sex ratios may eventually generate negative consequences, but they are uncertain as to what these might be. On the basis of our research, we lay out some of the possibilities.[5]

---

1. "China Has 20 Percent Male Surplus," Agence France-Presse, January 7, 1999.

2. Quoted in "Abortion in Asia," *Wall Street Journal*, September 12, 1996, p. A14.

3. Quoted in "Skewed Gender Ratio Endangers Society, Says Delegate," *South China Morning Post*, March 7, 2002, p. 6.

4. Quoted in "Alarming Gender Imbalance," *China Today*, Vol. 52, No. 1 (January 2003), p. 7.

5. "Doctors Should Abide by Sex Selection Act Norms," *Times of India*, April 29, 2003, http://web.lexis-nexis.com/universe/document?m?cebe7184a90f2eb7390a4f035 fbaddd78. . . . 6/20/2003; Satinder Bindra, "Grim Motives behind Infant Killings," CNN.com, July 7, 2003, http://www.cnn.com/2003/world/asiapcf/south/07/07/ india.infanticide.pt2/index.html; Satinder Bindra, "Indian Women in Short Supply," CNN.com, June 19, 2003, http://edition.cnn.com/2003/WORLD/asiapcf/south/06/ 19/india.women/index.html; Gautam N. Allahbadia, "The 50 Million Missing Women," *Journal of Assisted Reproduction and Genetics*, Vol. 19, No. 9 (September 2002), pp. 410–416; Rahul Bedi, "Families 'Buying Girls as Marriage Crisis Deepens," *Irish Times*, March 10, 2003, p. 10; and Seema Sirohi, "The Vanishing Girls of India," *Christian Science Monitor*, July 30, 2001, p. 9.

Prognostications

By the end of this decade, the politics of handling large numbers of bare branches are likely to play an increasingly significant role in the calculations of the governments of China, India, and Pakistan (another high-sex-ratio society). Leaders in all three countries may soon discover that maintaining control of their high-sex-ratio societies requires strategies different from those crafted for normal-sex-ratio societies. In addition, leaders in other states need to understand the potential threat that vast surpluses of young men pose to these governments and the effect of gender imbalance on decisionmaking. What might seem a sensible course of action to the government of a normal-sex-ratio society might appear wildly inappropriate to the government of a high-sex-ratio society—and vice versa. The potential for overreaction and misunderstanding between these two types of nations is high, particularly in the areas of domestic, regional, and possibly international security.

The findings in this volume make possible two broad predictions regarding likely trends in twenty-first-century China and India, given their large surpluses of young males. First, the prognosis for the development of full democracy in China is poor, and India's ability to maintain its democratic form of government is likely to be challenged. Leaders in Beijing and New Delhi will be hard-pressed to address the potentially grave social instability that their countries' ever-increasing numbers of bare branches may produce in the next few decades. To counter this threat, they may be inclined to move in a more authoritarian direction. In the case of India (and Pakistan), an increase in sectarian and ethnic violence is also likely.

Second, the likelihood of India and Pakistan achieving a permanent settlement of the Kashmir and Jammu conflict is similarly limited in the unstable context produced by skewed sex ratios. The same logic would appear to apply in the case of China and Taiwan. The Chinese government has staked enormous national pride and prestige on its ability to bring about Taiwan's eventual reunification with the mainland. Within twenty years, China may have close to 40 million bare branches to deploy in the event that tensions with Taiwan escalate into a military confrontation. The security logic of high-sex-ratio cultures predisposes nations to see some utility in interstate conflict. In addition to stimulating a steadier allegiance from bare branches, who are especially motivated by issues involving national pride and martial prowess, conflict is often an effective mechanism by which governments can send bare branches away from national population centers, possibly never to return.

Conclusion

The masculinization of Asia's sex ratios is one of the overlooked stories of the century; the scale on which sex ratios in Asian countries are being artificially altered is unprecedented in human history. What are the consequences of this vast demographic shift? Now is the time for serious discussion—within both the subfields of environmental and human security and the field of security studies more generally, as well as within national security policymaking circles—of the potential danger in this huge shift. We have suggested that societies with young adult sex ratios of approximately 120 males to 100 females and above are inherently unstable.

This phenomenon may be only one example of the linkage between the status of women in society and the society's possibilities for democracy and peace. Women's issues, so long ignored in security studies, could well become a central focus of security scholars in the twenty-first century. Francis Fukuyama has wondered whether the democratic peace phenomenon, which holds that democracies are less likely than non-democracies to go to war against each other, is better explained by the status of women in democracies than by the simple existence of democratic institutions.[6] Our analysis takes this question one step further: The very possibility of full and meaningful democracy, of peace within and between nations, may be tied to the status of women in society. Our research has found that high-sex-ratio societies, where women typically have very low status, cannot be expected to emulate normal-sex-ratio societies in terms of either their form of government or of their tendency toward peacefulness. Historically, attempts at such emulation have proved to be short lived. Our research has only begun to explore this important relationship. We hope that other scholars and analysts concerned with national security will continue this effort.[7] Indeed, there may be no more urgent task for security studies, for we believe that the heretofore underexamined relationship between national security and the status and situation of women is critically important, and that it will become a central focus of scholars and policymakers in the twenty-first century.

---

6. Francis Fukuyama, "Women and the Evolution of World Politics," *Foreign Affairs,* Vol. 77, No. 5 (September/October 1998), pp. 24–40.

7. For recent empirical work on the relationship between high-sex-ratio societies and the democratic peace thesis, see M. Steven Fish, "Islam and Authoritarianism," *World Politics,* Vol. 55, No. 1 (October 2002), pp. 4–37; and Rose McDermott and Jonathan A. Cowden, "The Effects of Uncertainty and Sex in a Crisis Simulation Game," *International Interactions,* Vol. 27, No. 4 (October–December 2001), pp. 353–380.

Appendix 1. World Sex Ratios, Ages 0–4, by Country, 2002.

Country	Both Sexes	Males	Females	Sex Ratio
Afghanistan	4,464,862	2,277,923	2,186,939	104.2
Albania	321,236	165,969	155,267	106.9
Algeria	3,495,082	1,779,964	1,715,118	103.8
American Samoa	8,317	4,267	4,050	105.4
Andorra	3,559	1,843	1,716	107.4
Angola	1,816,011	916,638	899,373	101.9
Anguilla	941	476	465	102.4
Antigua and Barbuda	6,595	3,361	3,234	103.9
Argentina	3,360,940	1,720,343	1,640,597	104.9
Armenia	174,467	88,718	85,749	103.5
Aruba	4,590	2,349	2,241	104.8
Australia	1,267,057	649,049	618,008	105.0
Austria	406,756	208,275	198,481	104.9
Azerbaijan	622,050	317,149	304,901	104.0
Bahamas	28,192	14,232	13,960	101.9
Bahrain	64,098	32,392	31,706	102.2
Bangladesh	14,977,628	7,709,590	7,268,038	106.1
Barbados	18,496	9,277	9,219	100.6
Belarus	483,490	247,031	236,459	104.5
Belgium	563,346	288,347	274,999	104.9
Belize	38,942	19,867	19,075	104.2
Benin	1,247,197	629,807	617,390	102.0
Bermuda	3,971	1,921	2,050	93.7
Bhutan	310,848	160,336	150,512	106.5
Bolivia	1,073,012	547,724	525,288	104.3
Bosnia and Herzegovina	248,349	127,798	120,551	106.0
Botswana	213,064	107,536	105,528	101.9
Brazil	15,834,329	8,078,742	7,755,587	104.2
Brunei	35,225	18,005	17,220	104.6
Bulgaria	301,070	154,888	146,182	106.0
Burkina Faso	2,307,727	1,164,695	1,143,032	101.9
Burma	3,938,556	2,013,735	1,924,821	104.6
Burundi	1,093,789	551,908	541,881	101.9
Cambodia	1,869,680	951,474	918,206	103.6
Cameroon	2,528,666	1,277,982	1,250,684	102.2
Canada	1,809,366	926,423	882,943	104.9
Cape Verde	55,038	27,763	27,275	101.8
Cayman Islands	2,559	1,188	1,371	86.7
Central African Republic	56,9392	286,962	282,430	101.6
Chad	176,6396	890,558	875,838	101.7
Chile	1,301,845	666,208	635,637	104.8
China	68,978,374	37,648,694	31,329,680	120.2
Colombia	4,425,244	2,240,012	2,185,232	102.5
Comoros	103,418	51,951	51,467	100.9

Appendix 1. *(continued)*

Country	Both Sexes	Males	Females	Sex Ratio
Congo (Brazzaville)	473,079	238,395	234,684	101.6
Congo (Kinshasa)	10,477,933	5,265,765	5,212,168	101.0
Cook Islands	—	—	—	—
Costa Rica	380,652	194,783	185,869	104.8
Côte d'Ivoire	2,872,903	1,444,049	1,428,854	101.1
Croatia	279,069	143,286	135,783	105.5
Cuba	702,282	360,953	341,329	105.7
Cyprus	50,565	25,841	24,724	104.5
Czech Republic	461,455	237,095	224,360	105.7
Denmark	327,481	168,098	159,383	105.5
Djibouti	79,481	39,938	39,543	101.0
Dominica	6,183	3,140	3,043	103.2
Dominican Republic	1,015,944	518,886	497,058	104.4
Ecuador	1,644,067	836,855	807,212	103.7
Egypt	8,101,775	4,145,316	3,956,459	104.8
El Salvador	853,404	435,968	417,436	104.4
Equatorial Guinea	79,355	39,949	39,406	101.4
Eritrea	790,073	396,735	393,338	100.9
Estonia	60,607	30,975	29,632	104.5
Ethiopia	12,521,590	6,307,061	6,214,529	101.5
Faroe Islands	3,101	1,551	1,550	100.1
Fiji	95,335	48,715	46,620	104.5
Finland	281,470	142,938	138,532	103.2
France	3,637,201	1,866,248	1,770,953	105.4
French Guiana	19,160	9,804	9,356	104.8
French Polynesia	23,276	11,897	11,379	104.6
Gabon	146,933	73,761	73,172	100.8
Gambia	256,298	128,961	127,337	101.3
Gaza Strip	235,037	120,228	114,809	104.7
Georgia	263,270	133,921	129,349	103.5
Germany	3,942,338	2,023,470	1,918,868	105.5
Ghana	2,711,181	1,365,887	1,345,294	101.5
Gibraltar	1,566	803	763	105.2
Greece	517,474	267,282	250,192	106.8
Greenland	4,610	2,337	2,273	102.8
Grenada	10,113	5,066	5,047	100.4
Guadeloupe	36,372	18,595	17,777	104.6
Guam	20,320	10,826	9,494	114.0
Guatemala	2,070,796	1,057,059	1,013,737	104.3
Guernsey	3,241	1,648	1,593	103.5
Guinea	1,256,080	628,272	627,808	100.1
Guinea-Bissau	217,224	108,737	108,487	100.2
Guyana	59,888	30,530	29,358	104.0
Haiti	960,034	487,215	472,819	103.0

Appendix 1. *(continued)*

Country	Both Sexes	Males	Females	Sex Ratio
Honduras	971,746	496,697	475,049	104.6
Hong Kong S.A.R.	410,148	215,493	194,655	110.7
Hungary	472,342	243,983	228,359	106.8
Iceland	20,253	10,507	9,746	107.8
India	157,830,195	81,887,227	75,942,968	107.8
Indonesia	24,225,742	12,336,389	11,889,353	103.8
Iran	5,907,671	3,020,961	2,886,710	104.7
Iraq	3,674,959	1,868,991	1,805,968	103.5
Ireland	277,561	143,012	134,549	106.3
Israel	560,745	286,991	273,754	104.8
Italy	2,630,258	1,355,811	1,274,447	106.4
Jamaica	245,492	125,542	119,950	104.7
Japan	6,232,573	3,195,490	3,037,083	105.2
Jersey	5,223	2,708	2,515	107.7
Jordan	655,251	335,294	319,957	104.8
Kazakhstan	1,310,794	667,987	642,807	103.9
Kenya	4,246,318	2,145,873	2,100,445	102.2
Kiribati	13,844	7,037	6,807	103.4
Kuwait	219,298	111,726	107,572	103.9
Kyrgyzstan	560,233	283,156	277,077	102.2
Laos	926,628	464,736	461,892	100.6
Latvia	91,617	46,827	44,790	104.5
Lebanon	350,120	178,759	171,361	104.3
Lesotho	304,198	153,432	150,766	101.8
Liberia	604,122	305,451	298,671	102.3
Libya	675,580	345,179	330,401	104.5
Liechtenstein	1,926	958	968	99.0
Lithuania	177,335	90,626	86,709	104.5
Luxembourg	28,083	14,482	13,601	106.5
Macau	28,166	14,496	13,670	106.0
The Former Yugoslav Republic of Macedonia	138,927	72,132	66,795	108.0
Madagascar	2,947,528	1,480,354	1,467,174	100.9
Malawi	1,662,744	835,998	826,746	101.1
Malaysia	2,692,306	1,386,589	1,305,717	106.2
Maldives	53,806	27,623	26,183	105.5
Mali	2,170,980	1,094,144	1,076,836	101.6
Malta	24,903	12,995	11,908	109.1
Isle of Man	4,251	2,178	2,073	105.1
Marshall Islands	14,382	7,347	7,035	104.4
Martinique	33,064	16,789	16,275	103.2
Mauritania	514,757	259,441	255,316	101.6
Mauritius	96,611	48,527	48,084	100.9
Mayotte	32,139	16,170	15,969	101.3

Appendix 1. *(continued)*

Country	Both Sexes	Males	Females	Sex Ratio
Mexico	11,321,205	5,778,654	5,542,551	104.3
Micronesia	—	—	—	—
Moldova	275,883	140,640	135,243	104.0
Monaco	1,589	814	775	105.0
Mongolia	264,944	135,314	129,630	104.4
Montenegro	49,217	25,588	23,629	108.3
Montserrat	683	349	334	104.5
Morocco	3,520,206	1,795,105	1,725,101	104.1
Mozambique	2,995,205	1,511,645	1,483,560	101.9
Namibia	278,814	141,154	137,660	102.5
Nauru	1,619	827	792	104.4
Nepal	37,86,819	1,949,068	1,837,751	106.1
Netherlands	966,167	492,940	473,227	104.2
Netherlands Antilles	17,693	9,059	8,634	104.9
New Caledonia	20,854	10,664	10,190	104.7
New Zealand	278,311	142,053	136,258	104.3
Nicaragua	656,650	334,833	321,817	104.0
Niger	2,084,260	1,056,991	1,027,269	102.9
Nigeria	21,843,255	11,026,325	10,816,930	101.9
North Korea	1,929,636	987,060	942,576	104.7
Northern Mariana Islands	6,442	3,305	3,137	105.4
Norway	290,413	149,946	140,467	106.7
Oman	461,717	235,661	226,056	104.2
Pakistan	20,457,124	10,505,142	9,951,982	105.6
Palau	1,818	934	884	105.7
Panama	269,844	137,113	132,731	103.3
Papua New Guinea	744,981	379,378	365,603	103.8
Paraguay	836,968	426,058	410,910	103.7
Peru	3,167,937	1,610,587	1,557,350	103.4
Philippines	10,873,709	5,544,650	5,329,059	104.0
Poland	1,957,618	1,004,985	952,633	105.5
Portugal	571,135	294,648	276,487	106.6
Puerto Rico	299,633	153,756	145,877	105.4
Qatar	62,650	31,946	30,704	104.0
Reunion	78,345	40,101	38,244	104.9
Romania	1,174,228	603,400	570,828	105.7
Russia	6,560,989	3,352,909	3,208,080	104.5
Rwanda	1,079,634	542,377	537,257	101.0
Saint Helena	480	244	236	103.4
Saint Kitts and Nevis	3,633	1,865	1,768	105.5
Saint Lucia	17,031	8,794	8,237	106.8
Saint Pierre and Miquelon	559	285	274	104.0

Appendix 1. *(continued)*

Country	Both Sexes	Males	Females	Sex Ratio
Saint Vincent and the Grenadines	10,378	5,267	5,111	103.1
Samoa	13,690	6,967	6,723	103.6
San Marino	1,577	819	758	108.0
São Tomé and Principe	31,991	16,208	15,783	102.7
Saudi Arabia	3,838,265	1,962,142	1,876,123	104.6
Senegal	1,725,607	871,128	854,479	101.9
Serbia	609,881	316,039	293,842	107.6
Seychelles	7,021	3,545	3,476	102.0
Sierra Leone	994,362	491,669	502,693	97.8
Singapore	261,767	135,687	126,080	107.6
Slovakia	276,164	141,538	134,626	105.1
Slovenia	90,306	46,318	43,988	105.3
Solomon Islands	78,377	39,999	38,378	104.2
Somalia	1,440,107	723,709	716,398	101.0
South Africa	4,324,031	2,179,312	2,144,719	101.6
South Korea	3,553,559	1,869,976	1,683,583	111.1
Spain	1,847,695	953,454	894,241	106.6
Sri Lanka	1,600,128	818,422	781,706	104.7
Sudan	6,132,944	3,136,054	2,996,890	104.6
Suriname	44,006	22,493	21,513	104.6
Swaziland	187,915	94,000	93,915	100.1
Sweden	444,614	228,385	216,229	105.6
Switzerland	381,200	195,571	185,629	105.4
Syria	2,407,770	1,239,392	1,168,378	106.1
Taiwan	1,588,251	827,060	761,191	108.7
Tajikistan	947,633	477,336	470,297	101.5
Tanzania	6,313,344	3,181,977	3,131,367	101.6
Thailand	4,981,367	2,544,117	2,437,250	104.4
Togo	856,149	430,190	425,959	101.0
Tonga	12,781	6,532	6,249	104.5
Trinidad and Tobago	77,206	39,421	37,785	104.3
Tunisia	824,037	426,257	397,780	107.2
Turkey	5,880,127	2,998,161	2,881,966	104.0
Turkmenistan	598,613	307,349	291,264	105.5
Turks and Caicos Islands	2,231	1,137	1,094	103.9
Tuvalu	1,149	586	563	104.1
Uganda	4,897,023	2,462,764	2,434,259	101.2
Ukraine	2,238,896	1,144,825	1,094,071	104.6
United Arab Emirates	209,462	106,949	102,513	104.3
United Kingdom	3,500,740	1,794,466	1,706,274	105.2
United States	18,943,886	9,677,119	9,266,767	104.4
Uruguay	285,083	146,117	138,966	105.1
Uzbekistan	2,971,266	1,515,542	1,455,724	104.1

Appendix 1. *(continued)*

Country	Both Sexes	Males	Females	Sex Ratio
Vanuatu	22,972	11,738	11,234	103.8
Venezuela	2,445,205	1,262,008	1,183,197	106.7
Vietnam	8,203,860	4,248,128	3,955,732	107.4
Virgin Islands	9,647	4,957	4,690	105.7
British Virgin Islands	1,524	773	751	102.9
Wallis and Futuna	—	—	—	—
West Bank	362,127	185,743	176,384	105.3
Western Sahara	—	—	—	—
Yemen	3,441,638	1,753,397	1,688,241	103.9
Zambia	1,751,960	882,335	869,625	101.5
Zimbabwe	1,299,239	656,992	642,247	102.3
World	613,926,156	314,623,942	299,302,214	105.1

SOURCES: U.S. Bureau of the Census, International Data Base; China, Population Census Office under the State Council and National Bureau of Statistics of China, *Zhongguo 2000 nian renkou pucha ziliao* [Tabulation on the 2000 Population Census of the People's Republic of China], (Beijing: Zhongguo tongji chubanshe, 2002), Vol. 1, table 1-17; and India, Office of the Registrar General, *Census of India, 2001* (New Delhi: India, 2002), table 1.
NOTE: Figures for India are for ages 0–6.

Appendix 2. Life Table India, 1980.

	Males				Females		
Age (x to x + n)	1,000 $_nq_x$	$_nd_x$	l_x	Age (x to x + n)	1,000 $_nq_x$	$_nd_x$	l_x
0–1	113.00	11,300	100,000	0–1	115.00	11,500	100,000
1–5	67.83	6,017	88,700	1–5	80.04	7,084	88,500
5–10	16.28	1,346	82,683	5–10	19.57	1,593	81,416
10–15	8.47	689	81,337	10–15	8.27	660	79,823
15–20	10.15	819	80,648	15–20	14.60	1,156	79,163
20–25	11.54	921	79,830	20–25	18.98	1,481	78,007
25–30	11.19	883	78,909	25–30	19.96	1,527	76,527
30–35	16.87	1,316	78,026	30–35	17.70	1,327	74,999
35–40	23.39	1,794	76,709	35–40	22.71	1,673	73,672
40–45	35.46	2,656	74,915	40–45	27.11	1,952	71,999
45–50	47.00	3,396	72,258	45–50	35.99	2,521	70,047
50–55	70.60	4,862	68,862	50–55	50.77	3,428	67,526
55–60	102.29	6,547	64,001	55–60	80.41	5,154	64,097
60–65	161.48	9,278	57,454	60–65	128.02	7,546	58,943
65–70	258.08	12,433	48,176	65–70	187.55	9,640	51,397
70–75	412.47	14,743	35,743	70–75	274.76	11,473	41,758
75–80	659.21	13,844	21,000	75–80	402.53	12,190	30,284
80+	1,000.00	7,157	7,157	80+	1,000.00	18,094	18,094

SOURCE: U.S. Bureau of the Census, International Data Base, 1998, Life Table Values by Sex, http://www.census.gov/ipc/www/idbnew.html/.

Appendix 3. Life Table India, Adjusted, 1990.

	Males				Females		
Age (x to x + n)	1,000 $_nq_x$	$_nd_x$	l_x	Age (x to x + n)	1,000 $_nq_x$	$_nd_x$	l_x
0–1	79.50	7,950	100,000	0–1	80.40	8,040	100,000
1–5	67.83	6,244	92,050	1–5	80.04	7,360	91,960
5–10	16.28	1,397	85,806	5–10	19.57	1,656	84,600
10–15	8.47	715	84,409	10–15	8.27	686	82,944
15–20	10.15	849	83,694	15–20	14.60	1,201	82,258
20–25	11.54	956	82,845	20–25	18.98	1,538	81,057
25–30	11.19	916	81,889	25–30	19.96	1,587	79,519
30–35	16.87	1,366	80,973	30–35	17.70	1,379	77,931
35–40	23.39	1,862	79,607	35–40	22.71	1,738	76,552
40–45	35.46	2,757	77,745	40–45	27.11	2,028	74,813
45–50	47.00	3,524	74,988	45–50	35.99	2,620	72,785
50–55	70.60	5,045	71,463	50–55	50.77	3,562	70,166
55–60	102.29	6,794	66,418	55–60	80.41	5,356	66,603
60–65	161.48	9,628	59,624	60–65	128.02	7,841	61,248
65–70	258.08	12,903	49,996	65–70	187.55	10,016	53,407
70–75	412.47	15,300	37,093	70–75	274.76	11,922	43,390
75–80	659.21	14,366	21,793	75–80	402.53	12,667	31,468
80+	1,000.00	7,427	7,427	80+	1,000.00	18,801	18,801

SOURCE: U.S. Bureau of the Census, International Data Base, 1998, Life Table Values by Sex, http://www.census.gov/ipc/www/idbnew.html/. This table has been adjusted according to 1990 infant mortality rate figures as recorded by the U.S. Bureau of the Census International Data Base.

Appendix 4. Life Table China, 1981.

	Males				Females		
Age (x to x + n)	1,000 $_nq_x$	$_nd_x$	l_x	Age (x to x + n)	1,000 $_nq_x$	$_nd_x$	l_x
0–1	46.33	46,33	100,000	0–1	45.33	45,33	100,000
1–5	17.02	1,623	95,367	1–5	20.62	1,967	95,467
5–10	6.84	640	93,743	5–10	6.15	573	93,498
10–15	4.21	390	93,102	10–15	3.84	357	92,923
15–20	5.69	527	92,710	15–20	5.37	499	92,567
20–25	7.59	698	92,183	20–25	7.86	724	92,069
25–30	7.82	715	91,483	25–30	8.67	791	91,346
30–35	9.39	854	90,768	30–35	9.84	892	90,554
35–40	12.98	1,166	89,916	35–40	12.64	1,132	89,663
40–45	18.69	1,657	88,749	40–45	16.95	1,501	88,530
45–50	28.35	2,468	87,090	45–50	24.48	2,132	87,029
50–55	45.87	3,882	84,621	50–55	38.05	3,231	84,898
55–60	74.24	5,994	80,739	55–60	58.15	4,750	81,668
60–65	123.27	9,213	74,745	60–65	95.91	7,378	76,919
65–70	186.71	12,236	65,531	65–70	146.38	10,180	69,542
70–75	291.87	15,556	53,296	70–75	237.54	14,101	59,362
75–80	411.47	15,529	37,741	75–80	343.90	15,565	45,261
80–85	591.41	13,136	22,211	80–85	524.96	15,589	29,695
85–90	750.32	6,809	9,075	85–90	692.52	9,769	14,107
90+	1,000.00	2,266	2,266	90+	1,000.00	4,338	4,338

SOURCE: U.S. Bureau of the Census, International Data Base, 1998, http://www.census.gov/ipc/www/idbnew.html/.

Appendix 5. Life Table China, Adjusted, 1990.

Age (x to x + n)	Males			Age (x to x + n)	Females		
	1,000 nq_x	nd_x	l_x		1,000 nq_x	nd_x	l_x
0–1	28.20	2,820	100,000	0–1	32.70	3,270	100,000
1–5	9.30	904	97,180	1–5	9.80	948	96,730
5–10	6.84	659	96,276	5–10	6.15	589	95,782
10–15	4.21	403	95,618	10–15	3.84	366	95,193
15–20	5.69	542	95,215	15–20	5.37	509	94,827
20–25	7.59	719	94,673	20–25	7.86	741	94,318
25–30	7.82	735	93,955	25–30	8.67	811	93,577
30–35	9.39	875	93,220	30–35	9.84	913	92,766
35–40	12.98	1,199	92,345	35–40	12.64	1,161	91,853
40–45	18.69	1,704	91,146	40–45	16.95	1,537	90,692
45–50	28.35	2,536	89,443	45–50	24.48	2,183	89,155
50–55	45.87	3,986	86,907	50–55	38.05	3,309	86,972
55–60	74.24	6,156	82,920	55–60	58.15	4,865	83,663
60–65	123.27	9,463	76,764	60–65	95.91	7,557	78,798
65–70	186.71	12,566	67,302	65–70	146.38	10,428	71,240
70–75	291.87	15,976	54,736	70–75	237.54	14,445	60,812
75–80	411.47	15,949	38,760	75–80	343.90	15,946	46,367
80–85	591.41	13,491	22,811	80–85	524.96	15,970	30,421
85–90	750.32	6,993	9,321	85–90	692.52	10,008	14,451
90+	1,000.00	2,327	2,327	90+	1,000.00	4,443	4,443

SOURCES: U.S. Bureau of the Census, International Data Base, 1998, Table 014, http://www.census.gov/ipc/www/idbnew.html/. Life Table Values, by Sex and Urban/Rural Residence. This 1981 table was adjusted for mortality at ages 0–1 and 1–5: Infant mortality rate for 1990 and age 1–5 mortality obtained from Table 1 in Daniel Goodkind, "On Substituting Sex Preference Strategies in East Asia: Does Prenatal Sex Selection Reduce Postnatal Discrimination?" *Population and Development Review*, Vol. 22, No. 1 (March 1996), p. 117.

Appendix 6. Life Table China, Adjusted, 1995.

	Males				Females		
Age (x to x + n)	1,000 nqx	ndx	lx	Age (x to x + n)	1,000 nqx	ndx	lx
0–1	30.45	3,045	100,000	0–1	40.84	4,084	100,000
1–5	9.30	902	96,955	1–5	9.80	940	95,916
5–10	6.84	657	96,053	5–10	6.15	584	94,976
10–15	4.21	402	95,396	10–15	3.84	362	94,392
15–20	5.69	541	94,995	15–20	5.37	505	94,029
20–25	7.59	717	94,454	20–25	7.86	735	93,525
25–30	7.82	733	93,737	25–30	8.67	804	92,789
30–35	9.39	873	93,004	30–35	9.84	905	91,985
35–40	12.98	1,196	92,131	35–40	12.64	1,151	91,080
40–45	18.69	1,700	90,935	40–45	16.95	1,524	89,929
45–50	28.35	2,530	89,235	45–50	24.48	2,164	88,404
50–55	45.87	3,977	86,706	50–55	38.05	3,281	86,240
55–60	74.24	6,142	82,728	55–60	58.15	4,824	82,959
60–65	123.27	9,441	76,587	60–65	95.91	7,494	78,135
65–70	186.71	12,537	67,146	65–70	146.38	10,340	70,641
70–75	291.87	15,939	54,609	70–75	237.54	14,324	60,300
75–80	411.47	15,912	38,670	75–80	343.90	15,811	45,977
80–85	591.41	13,460	22,759	80–85	524.96	15,836	30,165
85–90	750.32	6,977	9,299	85–90	692.52	9,924	14,330
90+	1,000.00	2,322	2,322	90+	1,000.00	4,406	4,406

SOURCES: U.S. Bureau of the Census, International Data Base, 1998, Table 014, http://www.census.gov/ipc/www/idbnew.html/. Life Table Values, by Sex and Urban/Rural Residence. This table was adjusted according to the 1995 reported infant mortality rate, found in China, State Statistical Bureau, *China Statistical Yearbook, 1996* (Beijing: China Statistics Press, 1996), Table 3-9, and mortality rates for ages 1–5 as per China Life Table 1990.

Bibliography

"6.3 Brides for Seven Brothers," *Economist*, December 19, 1998–January 1, 1999, pp. 56–58.

Agnihotri, S.B. "Missing Females: A Disaggregated Analysis," *Economic and Political Weekly*, August 19, 1995, pp. 2074–2084.

"AIDS Day, 1997: China Responds to AIDS," http://www.redfish.com/USEmbassy-China/sandt/aidsdy97.htm.

Aird, John S. *Slaughter of the Innocents: Coercive Birth Control in China*. Washington, D.C.: AEI Press, 1990.

"Alarming Gender Imbalance," *China Today*, Vol. 52, No. 1 (January 2003), p. 7.

Alexander, Richard D., and Donald W. Tinkle, eds. *Natural Selection and Social Behavior: Recent Research and New Theory*. New York: Chiron, 1981.

Allahbadia, Gautam N. "The 50 Million Missing Women," *Journal of Assisted Reproduction and Genetics*, Vol. 19, No. 9 (September 2002), pp. 411–416.

Anderson, Mary M. *Hidden Power: The Palace Eunuchs of Imperial China*. Buffalo, New York: Prometheus, 1990.

Anderson, Nels. *The Hobo: The Sociology of the Homeless Man*. Chicago: University of Chicago Press, 1961.

Aptekar, Herbert. *Anjea: Infanticide, Abortion, and Contraception in Savage Society*. New York: William Godwin, 1931.

Arnold, Fred. "Measuring the Effect of Sex Preference on Fertility: The Case of Korea," *Demography*, Vol. 22, No. 2 (May 1985), pp. 280–288.

Arora, Dolly. "The Victimising Discourse: Sex-Determination Technologies and Policy," *Economic and Political Weekly*, February 17, 1996, pp. 420–424.

Ba, P.V. *Socio-economic Renovation in North Vietnam and Its Effect on Fertility and Development in the Rural Plain*. Hanoi: Institute of Sociology, 1992.

Bacon, Margaret K., Irvin L. Child, and Herbert Barry. "A Cross-Cultural Study of Correlates of Crime," *Journal of Abnormal and Social Psychology*, Vol. 66, No. 4 (November 1963), pp. 291–300.

Bae Wha-oak. "Sex Ratio at Birth in Korea," *Journal of Population, Health, and Social Welfare*, Vol. 11, No. 2 (December 1991), p. 120.

Bahr, Howard M., ed. *Disaffiliated Man: Essays and Bibliography on Skid Row, Vagrancy, and Outsiders*. Toronto: University of Toronto Press, 1970.

Bairagi, Radheshyam, Santosh Chandra Sutradhar, and Nurul Alam. "Levels, Trends, and Determinants of Child Mortality in Matlab, Bangladesh, 1966–1994," *Asia-Pacific Population Journal*, Vol. 14, No. 2 (June 1999), pp. 51–68.

Baker, Hugh D.R. *Chinese Family and Kinship*. London: Macmillan, 1979.

Balakrishnan, Radhika. "The Social Context of Sex Selection and the Politics of Abortion in India," in Gita Sen and Rachel C. Snow, eds., *Power and Decision: The Social Control of Reproduction*, Cambridge, Mass.: Harvard University Press, 1994, pp. 267–286.

Balikci, Asen. "Female Infanticide on the Arctic Coast," *Man: The Journal of the Royal Anthropological Institute*, Vol. 2, No. 4 (December 1967), pp. 615–625.

Balikci, Asen. *The Netslik Eskimo*. New York: Natural History Press, 1970.

Bangladesh. Bureau of Statistics. "1991 Population Census," http://www.bbsgov.org/ana_vol1/Projection.htm.

Bangladesh. Bureau of Statistics. "1999 Demographic Data," http://www.bbsgov.org/data-sheet/DEMO_DATA.htm.

Bangladesh. Bureau of Statistics. "Population Census, 2001: Preliminary Report," http://www.bbsgov.org.

Banister, Judith. *China's Changing Population*. Stanford, Calif.: Stanford University Press, 1987.

Banister, Judith. "Implications and Quality of China's 1990 Census Data," paper presented at the International Seminar on China's 1990 Population Census, Beijing, October 1992.

Banister, Judith. "Son Preference in Asia—Report of a Symposium." U.S. Census Bureau, http://www.census.gov/ipc/www/ebspr96a.html.

Barth, Gunter. *Bitter Strength: A History of the Chinese in the United States, 1850–1870*. Cambridge, Mass.: Harvard University Press, 1964.

Bartlett, Thad Q., Robert W. Sussman, and James M. Cheverud. "Infant Killing in Primates: A Review of Observed Cases with Specific Reference to the Sexual Selection Hypothesis," *American Anthropologist*, Vol. 95, No. 4 (December 1993), pp. 958–990.

Basu, Alaka M. "Is Discrimination in Food Really Necessary for Explaining Sex Differentials in Childhood Mortality?" *Population Studies*, Vol. 43, No. 2 (July 1989), pp. 193–210.

Bayliss-Smith, Tim, and Richard G. Feachem, eds. *Subsistence and Survival: Rural Ecology in the Pacific*. San Francisco, Calif.: Academic Press, 1977.

Beach, Frank Ambrose, ed. *Sex and Behavior*. New York: Wiley and Sons, 1965.

Beck, John B. "On Infanticide and Its Relation to Medical Jurisprudence and Medical Police," in John B. Beck, ed., *Researches in Medicine and Medical Jurisprudence*. New York: E. Bliss, 1835.

Beck, John B., ed. *Researches in Medicine and Medical Jurisprudence*. New York: E. Bliss, 1835.

Becker, Jasper. *Hungry Ghosts: Mao's Secret Famine*. New York: Free Press, 1996.

Benton, D. "Do Animal Studies Tell Us Anything about the Relationships between Testosterone and Human Aggression?" in Graham C.L. Davey, ed., *Animal Models of Human Behavior.* Chichester, U.K.: Wiley, 1983, pp. 281–298.

Berndt, Ronald M., and Catherine H. Berndt. *The World of the First Australians: An Introduction to the Traditional Life of the Australian Aborigines.* London: Angus and Robertson, 1964.

Betzig, Laura. "Despotism and Differential Reproduction: A Cross-Cultural Correlation of Conflict Asymmetry, Hierarchy, and Degree of Polygyny," *Ethology and Sociobiology,* Vol. 3, No. 4 (1982), pp. 209–221.

Betzig, Laura. *Despotism and Differential Reproduction: A Darwinian View of History.* New York: Aldine de Gruyter, 1986.

Bhat, P.N. Mari, Samuel H. Preston, and Tim Dyson. *Vital Rates in India, 1961–1981.* Washington, D.C.: National Academy Press, 1984.

Billington, Ray A. *America's Frontier Culture.* College Station: Texas A&M University Press, 1977.

Birdsell, Joseph B. "On Population Structure in Generalized Hunting and Collecting Populations," *Evolution,* Vol. 12, No. 2 (June 1958), pp. 189–205.

Birdsell, Joseph B. "Some Predictions for the Pleistocene Based in Equilibrium Systems among Recent Hunter-Gatherers," in Richard B. Lee and Irven Devore, eds., *Man the Hunter.* Chicago: Aldine de Gruyter, 1968, pp. 229–240.

Blaikie, Piers, and Harold Brookfield, eds. *Land Degradation and Society.* New York: Methuen, 1987.

Blaikie, Piers, Terry Cannon, Ian Davis, and Ben Wisner. *At Risk: Natural Hazards, Peoples' Vulnerability, and Disasters.* London: Routledge, 1994.

Blok, Josine, and Peter Mason, eds. *Sexual Asymmetry: Studies in Ancient Society.* Amsterdam: J.C. Gieben, 1987.

Blundell, Sue. *Women in Ancient Greece.* London: British Museum Press, 1995.

Boal, Barbara M. *The Konds: Human Sacrifice and Religious Change.* Warminster, U.K.: Aris and Phillips, 1982.

Bohle, Hans-Georg, et al., eds. *Famine and Food Security in Africa and Asia.* Bayreuth, Germany: Bayreuth, 1991.

Bohle, Hans-Georg, Thomas E. Downing, and Michael J. Watts. "Climate Change and Social Vulnerability: Towards a Sociology and Geography of Food Insecurity," *Global Environmental Change,* Vol. 4, No. 1 (March 1994), pp. 37–48.

Boone, James L. "Noble Family Structure and Expansionist Warfare in the Late Middle Ages," in Rada Dyson-Hudson and Michael A. Little, eds., *Rethinking Human Adaptation: Biological and Cultural Models.* Boulder, Colo.: Westview, 1983, pp. 79–96.

Boone, James L. "Parental Investment and Elite Family Structure in Preindustrial States: A Case Study of Late Medieval–Early Modern Portuguese Genealogies," *American Anthropologist,* Vol. 88, No. 4 (December 1986), pp. 859–878.

Booth, Beverley E., Manorama Verma, and Rajbir Singh Beri. "Fetal Sex Determination in Infants in Punjab, India: Correlations and Implications," *British Medical Journal,* November 12, 1994, pp. 1259–1261.

Boserup, Ester. *Economic and Demographic Relationships in Development.* Baltimore, Md.: Johns Hopkins University Press, 1990.

Boserup, Ester. *Population and Technological Change*. Chicago: University of Chicago Press, 1981.

Bossen, Laurel. "Women and Development," in Robert E. Gamer, ed., *Understanding Contemporary China*. Boulder, Colo.: Lynne Rienner, 1999, pp. 293–320.

Boswell, John. *The Kindness of Strangers: The Abandonment of Children in Western Europe from Late Antiquity to the Renaissance*. London: Penguin, 1989.

Bouissou, Marie-France. "Androgens, Aggressive Behaviour, and Social Relationships in Higher Mammals," *Hormone Research*, Vol. 18, Nos. 1–3 (1983), pp. 43–61.

Boulding, Elise. *The Underside of History: A View of Women through Time*. Boulder, Colo.: Westview, 1976.

Bourne, Katherine L., and George M. Walker. "The Differential Effect of Mother's Education on Mortality of Boys and Girls in India," *Population Studies*, Vol. 45, No. 2 (July 1991), pp. 203–219.

Boutwell, Jeffrey, and Thomas F. Homer-Dixon. "Environmental Change, Global Security, and U.S. Policy," in Charles F. Hermann, ed., *American Defense Annual*. New York: Lexington, 1994, pp. 201–224.

Boyatzis, Richard E. "Who Should Drink What, When, and Where If Looking for a Fight," in Edward Gottheil et al., eds., *Alcohol, Drug Abuse, and Aggression*. Springfield: Charles C. Thomas, 1983, pp. 314–329.

Bradford, John M.W., and D. McLean. "Sexual Offenders, Violence, and Testosterone: A Clinical Study," *Canadian Journal of Psychiatry*, Vol. 29, No. 4 (June 1984), pp. 335–343.

Bray, Francesca. *Technology and Gender: Fabrics of Power in Late Imperial China*. Berkeley: University of California Press, 1997.

Breen, David H. *The Canadian Prairie West and the Ranching Frontier: 1874–1924*. Toronto: University of Toronto Press, 1983.

Browne, John Cave. *Indian Infanticide: Its Origins, Progress, and Suppression*. London: W.H. Allen, 1857.

Brownell, Susan, and Jeffrey N. Wasserstrom, eds. *Chinese Femininities/Chinese Masculinities: A Reader*. Berkeley: University of California Press, 2002.

Bruns, Roger. *Knights of the Road: A Hobo History*. New York: Methuen, 1980.

Buikstra, Jane E., and Lyle W. Konigsberg. "Paleodemography: Critiques and Controversies," *American Anthropologist*, Vol. 87, No. 2 (June 1985), pp. 316–333.

Bumiller, Elizabeth. *May You Be the Mother of a Hundred Sons: A Journey among the Women of India*. New York: Fawcett Columbine, 1990.

Burnham, John C. *Bad Habits: Drinking, Smoking, Taking Drugs, Gambling, Sexual Misbehavior, and Swearing in American History*. New York: New York University Press, 1993.

Buss, David. *The Evolution of Desire: Strategies of Human Mating*. New York: Basic Books, 1994.

Cai Fang. "The Regional Character of Labor Flow in the Transitional Period," *Chinese Population Studies*, n.s., Vol. 5 (1998), pp. 18–24.

Cameron, Averil, and Amelie Kuhrt, eds. *Images of Women in Antiquity*. Detroit, Mich.: Wayne State University Press, 1993.

Campbell, Bernard, ed. *Sexual Selection and the Descent of Man*. Chicago: Aldine de Gruyter, 1972.

Campbell, Eugene K. "Sex Preferences for Offspring among Men in the Western Area of Sierra Leone," *Journal of Biosocial Science*, Vol. 23, No. 3 (July 1991), pp. 337–342.

Campbell, Eugene K., and Puni G. Campbell. "Family Size and Sex Preferences and Eventual Fertility in Botswana," *Journal of Biosocial Science*, Vol. 29, No. 2 (April 1997), pp. 191–204.

Cantarella, Eve. *Pandora's Daughters: The Role and Status of Women in Greek and Roman Antiquity*, trans. Maureen B. Fant, with a foreword by Mary R. Lefkowitz. Baltimore, Md.: Johns Hopkins University Press, 1987.

Cao Jinqing, *China along the Yellow River: A Scholar's Observations and Reflections on Rural Society*. Shanghai: Shanghai Wenyi Publishing House, 2000.

Carter, C.O. "Sex Differences in the Distribution of Physical Illness in Children," *Social Science and Medicine*, Vol. 12, No. 3B (1978), pp. 163–166.

Castan, Nicole. "Criminals," in Natalie Zemon Davis and Arlette Farge, eds., *A History of Women in the West*, Vol. 3: *Renaissance and Enlightenment Paradoxes*. Cambridge, Mass.: Belknap, 1993, pp. 474–488.

Catton, William R. *Overshoot*. Chicago: University of Illinois Press, 1980.

Chagnon, Napoleon A. "Is Reproductive Success Equal in Egalitarian Societies?" in Napoleon A. Chagnon and William Irons, eds., *Evolutionary Biology and Human Social Behavior: An Anthropological Perspective*. North Scituate, Mass.: Duxbury, 1979, pp. 374–401.

Chagnon, Napoleon A. *Studying the Yanomamo*. New York: Holt, Rinehart, and Winston, 1974.

Chagnon, Napoleon A. *Yanomamo: The Fierce People*, 2d ed. New York: Holt, Rinehart, and Winston, 1977.

Chagnon, Napoleon A., Mark V. Flinn, and Thomas F. Melancon. "Sex-Ratio Variation among the Yanomamo Indians," in Napoleon A. Chagnon and William Irons, eds., *Evolutionary Biology and Human Social Behavior: An Anthropological Perspective*. North Scituate, Mass.: Duxbury, 1979, pp. 290–320.

Chagnon, Napoleon A., and William Irons, eds. *Evolutionary Biology and Human Social Behavior: An Anthropological Perspective*. North Scituate, Mass.: Duxbury, 1979.

Chambers, Robert. "Vulnerability, Coping, and Policy," *IDS Bulletin*, Vol. 20, No. 2 (April 1989), pp. 1–7.

Chang, Kyung-sup. "Birth and Wealth in Peasant China: Surplus Population, Limited Supplies of Family Labor, and Economic Reform," in Alice Goldstein and Wang Feng, eds., *China: The Many Facets of Demographic Change*. Boulder, Colo.: Westview, 1996, pp. 21–45.

Cheatwood, Derral, and Kathleen J. Block. "Youth and Homicide: An Investigation of the Age Factor in Criminal Homicide," *Justice Quarterly*, Vol. 7, No. 2 (June 1990), pp. 265–292.

Chen, Lincoln C., Emdadul Huq, and Stan D'Souza. "Sex Bias in the Family Allocation of Food and Health-Care in Rural Bangladesh," *Population and Development Review*, Vol. 7, No. 1 (March 1981), pp. 55–70.

Chen, Phillip M. *Law and Justice: The Legal System in China, 2400 B.C. to 1960 A.D.* New York: Dunellen, 1961.

Chen, Robert S., and Robert W. Kates. "Special Issue: Climate Change and World Food Security," *Global Environmental Change*, Vol. 4, No. 1 (March 1994), pp. 1–77.

Chen Shengsao. *Wensulu*. Beijing: Shumu wenxian chubanshe, 1827.

Chen, Walter. "The Era of the Ch'ing Dynasty," http://www.leksu.com/mainp4e.htm.

Cheng, Lucie, and Edna Bonacich, eds. *Labor Immigration under Capitalism: Asian Workers in the United States before World War II*. Berkeley: University of California Press, 1984.

Chesnaux, Jean, ed. *Popular Movements and Secret Societies in China, 1840–1950*. Stanford, Calif.: Stanford University Press, 1972.

China. Population Census Office under the State Council and the Department of Population Statistics of the State Statistical Bureau. *The 1982 Population Census of China (Major Figures)*. Hong Kong: Economic Information Agency, 1982.

China. State Family Planning Commission of China. *China Birth Planning Yearbook*. Beijing, 1996.

China. State Statistical Bureau. *10 Percent Sampling Tabulation on the 1990 Population Census of the People's Republic of China*. Beijing: China Statistics Press, 1991.

China. State Statistical Bureau. *China Population Statistical Yearbook, 1989*. Beijing: China Statistics Press, 1989.

China. State Statistical Bureau. *China Population Statistical Yearbook, 1990*. Beijing: China Statistics Press, 1990.

China. State Statistical Bureau. *China Population Statistical Yearbook, 1991*. Beijing: China Statistics Press, 1991.

China. State Statistical Bureau. *China Population Statistical Yearbook, 1994*. Beijing: China Statistics Press, 1994.

China. State Statistical Bureau. *China Population Statistical Yearbook, 1995*. Beijing: China Statistics Press, 1995.

China. State Statistical Bureau. *China Population Statistical Yearbook, 1996*. Beijing: China Statistics Press, 1996.

China. State Statistical Bureau. *China Population Statistical Yearbook, 1997*. Beijing: China Statistics Press, 1997.

China. State Statistical Bureau. *Major Figures of the 2000 Population Census*. Beijing: China Statistics Press, March 28, 2001.

China Population Information Center. *Analysis on China's National One-per-Thousand Population Fertility Sampling Survey*. Beijing: China Population Information Center, 1984.

"China's One-Child Policy, Two-Child Reality," a U.S. embassy report, Beijing, October 1997, http://www.usembassy-china.org.cn/english/sandt/fert21.htm.

"China's Population and Development in the 21st Century." Information Office of the State Council of the People's Republic of China, December 18, 2000, http://www.china.org.cn/e-white/21st/.

Chiu, Vermier Y. *Marriage Laws and Customs of China*. Hong Kong: Institute of Advanced Chinese Studies and Research, New Asia College, Chinese University of Hong Kong, 1966.

Chivers, David John, and J. Herbert, eds. *Recent Advances in Primatology*, Vol. 1: *Behavior*. London: Academic Press, 1978.

Choe, Minja Kim. "Sex Differentials in Infant and Child Mortality in Korea," *Social Biology*, Vol. 34 (Spring/Summer 1987), pp. 12–25.

Christiansen, Kerrin, and Rainier Knussmann. "Androgen Levels and Components of Aggressive Behavior in Men," *Hormones and Behavior*, Vol. 21, No. 2 (June 1987), pp. 170–180.

Clark, Alice. "Limitations on Female Life Chances in Rural Central Gujarat," in J. Krishnamurty, ed., *Women in Colonial India: Essays on Survival, Work, and the State*. Delhi: Oxford University Press, 1989.

Clark, Gillian. *Women in Late Antiquity: Pagan and Christian Lifestyles*. Oxford: Clarendon, 1994.

Clark, Shelley. "Son Preference and Sex Composition of Children: Evidence from India," *Demography*, Vol. 37, No. 1 (February 2000), pp. 95–108.

Clark, William C., and R.E. Munn, eds. *Sustainable Development of the Biosphere*. New York: Cambridge University Press, 1986.

Clarke, William Carey. "The Structure of Permanence," in Tim Bayliss-Smith and Richard G. Feachem, eds., *Subsistence and Survival: Rural Ecology in the Pacific*. San Francisco, Calif.: Academic Press, 1977, pp. 363–384.

Cleland, John, Jane Verrall, and Martin Vaessen. "Preferences for the Sex of Children and Their Influence on Reproductive Behavior," World Fertility Survey Comparative Studies No. 27. Voorburg, Netherlands: International Statistical Institute, 1983.

Coale, Ansley J. "Excess Female Mortality and the Balance of the Sexes in the Population: An Estimate of the Number of 'Missing Females,'" *Population and Development Review*, Vol. 17, No. 3 (September 1991), pp. 517–523.

Coale, Ansley J. "Excess Ratio of Males to Females by Birth Cohort in the Census of China, 1953 to 1990, and in the Births Reported in the Fertility Surveys, 1982 and 1988," OPR Working Paper No. 93–6. Princeton, N.J.: Office for Population Research, Princeton University, July 1993.

Coale, Ansley J., and Judith Banister. "Five Decades of Missing Females in China," *Demography*, Vol. 31, No. 3 (August 1994), pp. 459–479.

Cohen, Mark Nathan, and Sharon Bennett. "Skeletal Evidence for Sex Roles and Gender Hierarchies in Prehistory," in Barbara D. Miller, ed., *Sex and Gender Hierarchies*. Cambridge: Cambridge University Press, 1993, pp. 273–296.

Cohen, Mark Nathan, Roy S. Malpass, and Harold G. Klein, eds. *Biosocial Mechanisms of Population Regulation*. New Haven, Conn.: Yale University Press, 1980.

Coleman, Emily. "L'infanticide dans le Haut Moyen Age," *Annales: Economies, sociétés, civilisations*, Vol. 29, No. 2 (March–April 1974), pp. 315–335.

Coleman, Emily R. "Medieval Marriage Characteristics: A Neglected Factor in the History of Medieval Serfdom," in Theodore K. Rabb and Robert I. Rotberg, ed., *The Family in History: Interdisciplinary Essays*. New York: Harper and Row, 1971.

Collins, James J. "Alcohol Use and Expressive Interpersonal Violence," in Edward Gottheil et al., eds., *Alcohol, Drug Abuse, and Aggression*. Springfield: Charles C. Thomas, 1983, pp. 5–25.

Conway, G. "The Properties of Agroecosystems," *Agricultural Systems*, Vol. 24, No. 2 (1987), pp. 95–117.

Courtwright, David T. *Dark Paradise: Opiate Addiction in America before 1940*. Cambridge, Mass.: Harvard University Press, 1982.

Courtwright, David T. *Violent Land: Single Men and Social Disorder from the Frontier to the Inner City*. Cambridge, Mass.: Harvard University Press, 1996.

Cowgill, Ursula M., and G.E. Hutchinson. "Sex-Ratio in Childhood and the Depopulation of the Petén, Guatemala," *Human Biology*, Vol. 35, No. 1 (1963), pp. 90–103.

Croll, Elisabeth J. *Changing Identities of Chinese Women: Rhetoric, Experience, and Self-perception in Twentieth-Century China*. London: Zed, 1995.

Croll, Elisabeth J. *Feminism and Socialism in China*. London: Routledge and Kegan Paul, 1978.

Croll, Elisabeth J. "Introduction: Fertility Norms and Family Size in China," in Elisabeth J. Croll, Delia Davin, and Penny Kane, eds., *China's One-Child Family Policy*. New York: St. Martin's, 1985, pp. 1–36.

Croll, Elisabeth J., Delia Davin, and Penny Kane, eds. *China's One-Child Family Policy*. New York: St. Martin's, 1985.

Crook, John H. "Sexual Selection, Dimorphism, and Social Organization in the Primates," in Bernard Campbell, ed., *Sexual Selection and the Descent of Man*. Chicago: Aldine de Gruyter, 1972, pp. 231–281.

Crooke, William. *The North-Western Provinces of India: Their History, Ethnology, and Administration*. London: Methuen, 1897.

Crumley, Carole L., ed. *Historical Ecology: Cultural Knowledge and Changing Landscapes*. Santa Fe: School of American Research Press, 1994.

Dabbs, James M., Jr., and Robin Morris. "Testosterone, Social Class, and Antisocial Behavior in a Sample of 4,462 Men," *Psychological Science*, Vol. 1 (1990), pp. 209–211.

Daly, Martin, and Margo Wilson. *Homicide*. Hawthorne, N.Y.: Aldine de Gruyter, 1988.

Daly, Martin, and Margo Wilson. "Killing the Competition: Female/Female and Male/Male Homicide," *Human Nature*, Vol. 1, No. 1 (1990), pp. 81–107.

Daly, Martin, and Margo Wilson. *Sex, Evolution, and Behavior: Adaptations for Reproduction*. North Scituate, Mass.: Duxbury, 1978.

Dary, David. *Cowboy Culture: A Saga of Five Centuries*. Lawrence: University Press of Kansas, 1989.

Das, Narayan. "Sex Preference and Fertility Behavior: A Study of Recent Indian Data," *Demography*, Vol. 24, No. 4 (November 1987), pp. 517–530.

Das Gupta, Monica. "Selective Discrimination against Female Children in Rural Punjab, India," *Population and Development Review*, Vol. 13, No. 1 (March 1987), pp. 77–101.

Das Gupta, Monica, and P.N. Mari Bhat. "Fertility Decline and Increased Manifestation of Sex Bias in India," *Population Studies*, Vol. 51, No. 3 (November 1997), pp. 307–315.

Das Gupta, Monica, and P.N. Mari Bhat. "Intensified Gender Bias in India: A Consequence of Fertility Decline," Harvard Center for Population and Development Studies Working Paper Series No. 95.03. Cambridge, Mass.: Harvard University, May 1995.

Davey, Graham C.L., ed. *Animal Models of Human Behavior*. Chichester, U.K.: Wiley, 1983.

Davis, Fei-ling. *Primitive Revolutionaries of China: A Study of Secret Societies in the Late Nineteenth Century*. Honolulu: University of Hawaii Press, 1977.

Davis, Natalie Zemon, and Arlette Farge, eds. *A History of Women in the West*, Vol. 3: *Renaissance and Enlightenment Paradoxes*. Cambridge, Mass.: Belknap, 1993.

de Meer, Kees. "Mortality in Children among the Aymara Indians of Southern Peru," *Social Science and Medicine*, Vol. 26, No. 2 (1988), pp. 253–258.

de Sherbinin, Alex. "Human Security and Fertility: The Case of Haiti," paper presented at the annual meeting of the Association of American Geographers, Chicago, Illinois, March 18, 1995.

de Sherbinin, Alex. "World Population Growth and U.S. National Security," *Environmental Change and Security Project Report*, No. 1 (Spring 1995), pp. 24–39.

deMause, Lloyd. "The Evolution of Childhood," in Lloyd deMause, ed., *The History of Childhood*. New York: Psychohistory Press, 1974, pp. 1–73.

deMause, Lloyd, ed. *The History of Childhood*. New York: Psychohistory Press, 1974.

Devasia, Leelamma, and V.V. Devasia, eds. *Girl Child in India*. New Delhi: Ashish Publishing House, 1989.

deVore, Irven. "Male Dominance and Mating Behavior in Baboons," in Frank Ambrose Beach, ed., *Sex and Behavior*. New York: Wiley and Sons, 1965, pp. 266–289.

Dickemann, Mildred. "Concepts and Classification in the Study of Human Infanticide: Sectional Introduction and Some Cautionary Notes," in Glenn Hausfater and Sarah Blaffer Hrdy, eds., *Infanticide: Comparative and Evolutionary Perspectives*. New York: Aldine de Gruyter, 1984, pp. 427–437.

Dickemann, Mildred. "Demographic Consequences of Infanticide in Man," *Annual Review of Ecology and Systematics*, Vol. 6 (1975), pp. 107–137.

Dickemann, Mildred. "The Ecology of Mating Systems in Hypergynous Dowry Societies," *Social Science Information*, Vol. 18, No. 2 (May 1979), pp. 163–195.

Dickemann, Mildred. "Female Infanticide, Reproductive Strategies, and Social Stratification: A Preliminary Model," in Napoleon A. Chagnon and William Irons, eds., *Evolutionary Biology and Human Social Behavior*. North Scituate, Mass.: Duxbury, 1979, pp. 321–367.

Dickemann, Mildred. "Paternal Confidence and Dowry Competition: A Biocultural Analysis of Purdah," in Richard D. Alexander and Donald W. Tinkle, eds., *Natural Selection and Social Behavior: Recent Research and New Theory*. New York: Chiron, 1981, pp. 417–438.

Ding Jinhong. "An Analysis in the Extraneous Population Inflow and City Community Integration: Surveys on the Local Shanghaiese's Psychological Acceptance Capacity of Extraneous Population," *Population Survey*, February 1996.

Divale, William T., and Marvin Harris. "Population, Warfare and the Male Supremacist Complex," *American Anthropologist*, Vol. 78, No. 3 (September 1976), pp. 521–538.

Dixon-Mueller, Ruth. "Abortion Policy and Women's Health in Developing Countries," *International Journal of Health Services*, Vol. 20, No. 2 (1990), pp. 297–314.

Downing, Thomas. "African Household Food Security: What Are the Limits of Available Coping Mechanisms in Response to Climatic and Economic Variations?" in Hans-Georg Bohle et al., eds., *Famine and Food Security in Africa and Asia*. Bayreuth, Germany: Bayreuth, 1991, pp. 36–68.

Downing, Thomas. "Review of Vulnerability in an African Context," paper presented at the First Open Meeting of the Human Dimensions of Global Change Community, Duke University, Durham, North Carolina, June 1–3, 1995.

Dreze, Jean, and Reetika Khera. "Crime, Gender, and Society in India: Insights from Homicide Data," *Population and Development Review*, Vol. 26, No. 2 (June 2000), pp. 335–352.

Duan Chengrong. "Floating Population and Its Effects on Rural and Urban Socioeconomic Development," *Population Research*, Vol. 22, No. 4 (1998), pp. 58–63.

Duby, Georges. *The Chivalrous Society*, trans. Cynthia Postan. London: Edward Arnold, 1977.

Duffield, Mark. "The Political Economy of Internal War: Asset Transfer, Complex Emergencies, and International Aid," in Joanna Macrae and Anthony Zwi, eds., *War and Hunger: Rethinking International Responses to Complex Emergencies*. London: Zed, 1994, pp. 50–69.

Dunlop, Riley E., and William Michelson, eds. *Handbook of Environmental Sociology*. Greenwich, Conn.: Greenwood, 1991.

Durham, William H. "Resource Competition and Human Aggression," *Quarterly Review of Biology*, Vol. 51, No. 3 (September 1976), pp. 385–415.

Dyson, Tim. "On the Demography of the 1991 Census," *Economic and Political Weekly*, December 17, 1994, pp. 3235–3239.

Dyson, Tim, and Mick Moore. "On Kinship Structure, Female Autonomy, and Demographic Behavior in India," *Population and Development Review*, Vol. 9, No. 1 (March 1983), pp. 35–60.

Dyson-Hudson, Rada, and Michael A. Little, eds. *Rethinking Human Adaptation: Biological and Cultural Models*. Boulder, Colo.: Westview, 1983.

Ebrey, Patricia Buckley. *The Cambridge Illustrated History of China*. Cambridge: Cambridge University Press, 1996.

Ebrey, Patricia Buckley. *The Inner Quarters: Marriage and the Lives of Chinese Women in the Sung Period*. Berkeley: University of California Press, 1993.

Eichhorn, Werner. "Some Notes on Population Control during the Sung Dynasty," in *Etudes d'histoire et de littérature chinoises offertes au Professeur Jarolslav Prusek*, Bibliothèque de l'institut des hautes études chinoises, Vol. 24. Paris: Presses Universitaires de France, 1976.

El Badry, M.A. "Higher Female Than Male Mortality in Some Countries of South Asia: A Digest," *Journal of the American Statistical Association,* Vol. 64, No. 328 (December 1969), pp. 1234–1244.

Elliot, Dorinda. "Trying to Stand on Two Feet," *Newsweek,* June 29, 1998, pp. 48–49.

Ellis, William. *Polynesian Researches, during a Residence of Nearly Eight Years in the Society and Sandwich Islands,* Vol. 1. London: Henry G. Bohn, 1859.

Eng, Robert Y. "Fertility and Infanticide," in Thomas C. Smith, Robert Y. Eng, and Robert T. Lundy, eds., *Nakahara: Family Farming and Population in a Japanese Village, 1717–1830.* Stanford, Calif.: Stanford University Press, 1977, pp. 59–85.

Engels, Donald. "The Problem of Female Infanticide in the Greco-Roman World," *Classical Philology,* Vol. 75, No. 2 (April 1980), pp. 112–120.

Ennen, Edith. *The Medieval Woman,* trans. Edmund Jephcott. Oxford: Basil Blackwell, 1989.

Erikson, Kai T. *Everything in Its Path.* New York: Simon and Schuster, 1978.

Esherick, Joseph. *The Origins of the Boxer Uprising.* Berkeley: University of California Press, 1987.

Fantham, Elaine, Helene Peet Foley, Natalie Boymel Kampen, Sarah B. Pomeroy, and H.A. Shapiro. *Women in the Classical World: Image and Text.* New York: Oxford University Press.

Fei Hsiao-tung. *Peasant Life in China: A Field Study of Country Life in the Yangtze Valley.* 1939, reprint. London: Routledge and Kegan Paul, 1962.

Feng Jianhua. "Bright Lights, Big City," *Beijing Review,* April 3, 2003, pp. 22–24.

Feng Jianhua. "Migrant Workers vs. City Residents," *Beijing Review,* April 3, 2003, pp. 21–22.

Feng Shuliang. "Crime and Crime Control in a Changing China," in Liu Jianhong, Zhang Lening, and Steven F. Messner, eds., *Crime and Social Control in a Changing China.* Westport, Conn.: Greenwood, 2001, pp. 123–130.

Fish, M. Steven. "Islam and Authoritarianism," *World Politics,* Vol. 55, No. 1 (October 2002), pp. 4–37.

Ford, Robert E. "The Population-Environment Nexus and Vulnerability Assessment in Africa." Brigham Young University, 1994.

Forum against Sex Discrimination and Sex Pre-Selection. "Using Technology, Choosing Sex: The Campaign against Sex Determination and the Question of Choice," *Development Dialogue* (Uppsala, Sweden), Nos. 1–2 (1992), pp. 91–102.

Foster, Arnold. *Christian Progress in China: Gleanings from the Writings and Speeches of Many Workers.* London: Religious Tract Society, 1889.

Frances, Raelene. "The History of Female Prostitution in Australia," in Roberta Perkins, G. Prestage, R. Sharp, and F. Lovejoy, eds., *Sex Work and Sex Workers in Australia.* Sydney: University of New South Wales, 1994, pp. 27–52.

Frantz, Joe B., and Julian Ernest Choate Jr. *The American Cowboy.* Norman: University of Oklahoma Press, 1960.

Freedman, Ronald, Ming-cheng Chang, and Te-hsiung Sun. "Taiwan's Transition from High Fertility to Below-Replacement Levels," *Studies in Family Planning,* Vol. 25, No. 6 (November–December 1994), pp. 317–331.

Freeman, Milton M.R. "A Social and Ecologic Analysis of Systematic Female Infanticide among the Netsilik Eskimo," *American Anthropologist*, Vol. 73, No. 5 (October 1971), pp. 1011–1018.

Friedman, Richard C., Ralph M. Richart, and Raymond L. Vande Wiele, eds. *Sex Differences in Behavior*. New York: Wiley, 1974.

Fukuyama, Francis. "Women and the Evolution of World Politics," *Foreign Affairs*, Vol. 77, No. 5 (September/October 1998), pp. 24–40.

Furth, Charlotte. *A Flourishing Yin: Gender in China's Medical History, 960–1665*. Berkeley: University of California Press, 1999.

Gamer, Robert E., ed. *Understanding Contemporary China*. Boulder, Colo.: Lynne Rienner, 1999.

George, Sabu, Rajaratnam Abel, and Barbara D. Miller. "Female Infanticide in Rural South India," *Economic and Political Weekly*, May 30, 1992, pp. 1153–1156.

Ghosh, Srikanta. *Indian Women through the Ages*. New Delhi: Ashish Publishing House, 1989.

Giannini, A. James, Robert H. Loiselle, and Brian H. Graham. "Cocaine-Associated Violence and Relationship to Route of Administration," *Journal of Substance Abuse Treatment*, Vol. 10, No. 1 (January–February 1993), pp. 67–69.

Gibbon, Edward. *The Decline and Fall of the Roman Empire*. Chicago: Encyclopædia Britannica, 1990.

Gibbons, Ann. "Anthropologists Probe Genes, Brains at Annual Meeting," *Science*, April 17, 1998, pp. 380–381.

Gil, Vincent E., Marc Wang, Allen F. Anderson, and Guao Matthew Lin. "Plum Blossoms and Pheasants: Prostitutes, Prostitution, and Social Control Measures in Contemporary China," *International Journal of Offender Therapy and Comparative Criminology*, Vol. 38, No. 4 (December 1994), pp. 319–337.

Giladi, Avner. "Some Observations on Infanticide in Medieval Muslim Society," *International Journal of Middle East Studies*, Vol. 22, No. 2 (May 1990), pp. 185–200.

Gilder, George. *Naked Nomads: Unmarried Men in America*. New York: Quadrangle, 1974.

Gilley, Bruce. "Irresistible Force," *Far Eastern Economic Review*, April 4, 1996, pp. 18–22.

Gleick, Peter H. "Water and Conflict: Fresh Water Resources and International Security," *International Security*, Vol. 18, No. 1 (Summer 1993), pp. 79–112.

Goldstein, Alice, and Wang Feng, eds. *China: The Many Facets of Demographic Change*. Boulder, Colo.: Westview, 1996.

Goldstone, Jack A. *Revolution and Rebellion in the Early Modern World*. Berkeley: University of California Press, 1991.

Goodkind, Daniel. "On Substituting Sex Preference Strategies in East Asia: Does Prenatal Sex Selection Reduce Postnatal Discrimination?" *Population and Development Review*, Vol. 22, No. 1 (March 1996), pp. 111–125.

Goodkind, Daniel. "Vietnam's One-or-Two-Child Policy in Action," *Population and Development Review*, Vol. 21, No. 1 (March 1995), pp. 85–111.

Gordon, Manuel J. "The Control of Sex," *Scientific American*, Vol. 199, No. 5 (November 1958), pp. 87–94.

Gorman-Stapleton, Odesa. "Prohibiting Amniocentesis in India: A Solution to the Problem of Female Infanticide or a Problem to the Solution of Prenatal Diagnosis?" *ILSA Journal of International Law*, Vol. 14, No. 23 (1990), pp. 23–43.

Gottheil, Edward, et al., eds. *Alcohol, Drug Abuse, and Aggression.* Springfield: Charles C. Thomas, 1983.

Granzberg, Gary. "Twin Infanticide: A Cross-Cultural Test of a Materialistic Explanation," *Ethos*, Vol. 1, No. 4 (Winter 1973), pp. 405–412.

Greenhalgh, Susan, and Jiali Li. "Engendering Reproductive Practice in Peasant China: The Political Roots of the Rising Sex Ratios at Birth," Population Council Research Division Working Paper, No. 57. New York: Population Council, 1993.

Gregory, Lisa B. "Examining the Economic Component of China's One-Child Family Policy under International Law: Your Money or Your Life," *Journal of Chinese Law*, Vol. 6, No. 1 (Spring 1992), pp. 45–87.

Grosse, Scott. "The Roots of Conflict and State Failure in Rwanda: The Political Exacerbation of Social Cleavages in a Context of Growing Resource Scarcity," University of Michigan, 1994.

Gu Baochang, and Krishna Roy. "Sex Ratio at Birth in China, with Reference to Other Areas in Asia: What We Know," *Asia-Pacific Population Journal*, Vol. 10, No. 3 (September 1995), pp. 17–42.

Gu Baochang, and Xu Yi. "A Comprehensive Discussion of the Birth Gender Ratio in China," *Chinese Journal of Population Science*, Vol. 6, No. 4 (1994), pp. 417–431.

Guisso, Richard W. "Thunder over the Lake: The Five Classics and the Perception of Woman in Early China," in Richard W. Guisso and Stanley Johannesen, eds., *Women in China: Current Directions in Historical Scholarship.* Youngstown, N.Y.: Philo, 1981, pp. 47–61.

Guisso, Richard W., and Stanley Johannesen, eds. *Women in China: Current Directions in Historical Scholarship.* Youngstown, N.Y.: Philo, 1981.

Gunderson, Lance H., C.S. Holling, and Stephen S. Light, eds. *Barriers and Bridges to the Renewal of Ecosystems and Institutions.* New York: Columbia University Press, 1995.

Gurr, Ted Robert. "On the Political Consequences of Scarcity and Economic Decline," *International Studies Quarterly*, Vol. 29, No. 1 (March 1985), pp. 51–75.

Gurr, Ted Robert. "The State Failure Project: Early Warning Research for International Policy Planning," paper prepared for the annual conference of the International Studies Association, Chicago, Illinois, February 21–25, 1995.

Guttentag, Marcia, and Paul F. Secord. *Too Many Women? The Sex Ratio Question.* Beverly Hills, Calif.: Sage, 1983.

Hallissey, Robert C. *The Rajput Rebellion against Aurangzeb: A Study of the Mughal Empire in Seventeenth-Century India.* Columbia: University of Missouri Press, 1977.

Hammel, E.A., Sheila R. Johansson, and Caren A. Ginsberg. "The Value of Children during Industrialization: Sex Ratios in Childhood in Nineteenth-Century America," *Journal of Family History*, Vol. 8, No. 4 (Winter 1983), pp. 346–366.

Han Lei. "Women's Education in China." Foreign Affairs College, Beijing, 1999.

Hank, Karsten, and Hans-Peter Kohler. "Gender Preferences for Children in Europe: Empirical Results from 17 FFS Countries," *Demographic Research,* Vol. 2 (January 2000), http://www.demographic-research.org/Volumes/Vol2/1.

Harris, William V. "The Theoretical Possibility of Extensive Infanticide in the Graeco-Roman World," *Classical Quarterly,* Vol. 32, No. 1 (1982), pp. 114–116.

Hassan, Shaukat. "Environmental Issues and Security in South Asia," Adelphi Papers No. 262. London: Brassey's, Autumn 1991.

Haughton, Dominique, and Jonathan Haughton. "Using a Mixture Model to Detect Son Preference in Vietnam," *Journal of Biosocial Science,* Vol. 28, No. 3 (July 1996), pp. 355–365.

Hausfater, Glenn, and Sarah Blaffer Hrdy, eds. *Infanticide: Comparative and Evolutionary Perspectives.* New York: Aldine de Gruyter, 1984.

Hayase, Yasuko, and Seiko Kawamata. *Population Policy and Vital Statistics in China.* Tokyo: Institute of Developing Economies, 1991.

Hayes, James. "San Po Tsai (Little Daughters-in-Law) and Child Betrothals in the New Territories of Hong Kong from the 1890s to the 1960s," in Maria Jaschok and Suzanne Miers, eds., *Women and Chinese Patriarchy: Submission, Servitude, and Escape.* London: Zed, 1994, pp. 45–76.

Hazarika, S. "Bangladesh and Assam: Land Pressure, Migration, and Ethnic Conflict," Occasional Paper No. 3. Toronto: Project on Environmental Change and Acute Conflict, University of Toronto and the American Academy of Arts and Sciences, March 1993.

He Jingwu. "War on Drug Trafficking," *Beijing Review,* September 15–21, 1997, pp. 17–19.

Hepner, George. "Vulnerability Assessment Using a Geographic Information Systems Approach on the Mexico/U.S. Border," paper presented at the First Open Meeting of the Human Dimensions of Global Change Community, Duke University, Durham, North Carolina, June 1–3, 1995.

Herlihy, David. "Life Expectancies for Women in Medieval Society," in Rosemarie Thee Morewedge, ed., *The Role of Women in the Middle Ages: Papers of the Sixth Annual Conference of the Center for Medieval and Early Renaissance Studies, State University of New York at Binghamton, 6–8 May 1972.* Albany: State University of New York Press, 1975.

Hermann, Charles F., ed. *American Defense Annual.* New York: Lexington, 1994.

Hewitt, Kenneth, ed. *Interpretations of Calamity from the Viewpoint of Human Ecology.* Winchester, Mass.: Allen and Unwin, 1983.

Hirschi, Travis, and Michael Gottfredson. "Age and the Explanation of Crime," *American Journal of Sociology,* Vol. 89, No. 3 (November 1983), pp. 552–584.

"HIV/AIDS—What the Chinese Experts Say," http://www.usembassychina. org.cn/english/sandt/webaids3.htm.

Ho Ping-ti. *Studies on the Population of China, 1368–1953.* Cambridge, Mass.: Harvard University Press, 1959.

Holliday, J.S. *The World Rushed In: The California Gold Rush Experience.* New York: Simon and Schuster, 1981.

Holling, Crawford S. "The Resilience of Terrestrial Ecosystems: Local Surprise and Global Change," in William C. Clark and R.E. Munn, eds., *Sustainable De-*

velopment of the Biosphere. New York: Cambridge University Press, 1986, pp. 292–317.

Hom, Sharon K. "Female Infanticide in China: The Human Rights Specter and Thoughts towards (An)other Vision," *Columbian Human Rights Law Review,* Vol. 23, No. 2 (Summer 1992), pp. 249–314.

Homer-Dixon, Thomas F. "Environmental Scarcities and Violent Conflict: Evidence from Cases," *International Security,* Vol. 19, No. 1 (Summer 1994), pp. 5–40.

Homer-Dixon, Thomas F. *Environmental Scarcity and Global Security.* New York: Foreign Policy Association, 1993.

Homer-Dixon, Thomas F. "Strategies for Studying Causation in Complex Ecological-Political Systems." Toronto: Environment, Population, and Security Project, University of Toronto, June 1995.

Hsiao Kung-ch'uan. *Rural China: Imperial Control in the Nineteenth Century.* Seattle: University of Washington Press, 1967.

Hsu Wen-hsiung. "Frontier Social Organization and Social Disorder in Ch'ing Taiwan," in Ronald G. Knapp, ed., *China's Island Frontier: Studies in the Historical Geography of Taiwan.* Honolulu: University Press of Hawaii, 1980, pp. 87–106.

Huang Wei. "Continuing War on Drugs," *Beijing Review,* September 2–8, 1996, pp. 17–19.

Hull, Terence H. "Recent Trends in Sex Ratios at Birth in China," *Population and Development Review,* Vol. 16, No. 1 (March 1990), pp. 63–83.

Hutchinson, Charles F. "Early Warning and Vulnerability Assessment for Famine Mitigation," Famine Mitigation Strategy Paper. Washington, D.C.: Office of U.S. Foreign Disaster Assistance, 1992.

Hyde, Janet Shibley. "Gender Differences in Aggression," in Janet Shibley Hyde and Marcia C. Linn, eds., *The Psychology of Gender: Advances through Meta-Analysis.* Baltimore, Md.: Johns Hopkins University Press, 1986.

Hyde, Janet Shibley, and Marcia C. Linn, eds. *The Psychology of Gender: Advances through Meta-Analysis.* Baltimore, Md.: Johns Hopkins University Press, 1986.

India. National Crime Records, Bureau of India, 1997.

India. Office of the Registrar General. *Census of India, 1991, Census Data Online,* http://www.censusindia.net/cendat/datatable23.html.

India. Office of the Registrar General. *Census of India, 1991, Series-1: India, Paper 2 of 1992: Final Population Totals: Brief Analysis of Primary Census Abstract.* New Delhi: India, 1992.

India. Office of the Registrar General. *Census of India, 1991, Series-1, Part 2-B(i),* Vol. 1: *Primary Census Abstract: General Population,* New Delhi: India, 1994.

India. Office of the Registrar General. *Census of India, 1991, Series-1: India, Part 4 A-C Series: Socio-Cultural Tables,* Vols. 1 and 2. New Delhi: India, 1998.

India. Office of the Registrar General. *Census of India, 2001, Series 1: India, Paper 1 of 2001: Provisional Population Totals.* New Delhi: India, 2001, http://www.censusindia.net/results.

India. Office of the Registrar General. *Compendium of India's Fertility and Mortality Indicators Based on the SRS.* Delhi: Controller of Publications, 1991.

"Infanticide," in Maria Leach, ed., *Dictionary of Folklore, Mythology, and Legend*, Vol. 1. New York: Funk and Wagnalls, 1949, pp. 522–524.

Ingerson, Alice E. "Tracking and Testing the Nature-Culture Dichotomy," in Carole L. Crumley, ed., *Historical Ecology: Cultural Knowledge and Changing Landscapes*. Santa Fe: School of American Research Press, 1994, pp. 43–66.

Ishii, Ryoichi. *Population Pressure and Economic Life in Japan*. London: P.S. King and Son, 1937.

James, William H. "The Sex Ratio of Oriental Births," *Annals of Human Biology*, Vol. 12, No. 5 (September–October 1985), pp. 485–487.

Janis, Irving Lester. *Groupthink: Psychological Studies of Policy Decisions and Fiascoes*. Boston: Houghton Mifflin, 1982.

Jasanoff, Sheila. *Risk Management and Political Culture*. New York: Russell Sage Foundation, 1986.

Jaschok, Maria, and Suzanne Miers, eds. *Women and Chinese Patriarchy: Submission, Servitude, and Escape*. London: Zed, 1994.

Jeffery, Roger, and Patricia Jeffery. "Female Infanticide and Amniocentesis," *Economic and Political Weekly*, April 16, 1983, pp. 655–656.

Jeffery, Roger, Patricia Jeffery, and Andrew Lyon. "Research Note: Female Infanticide and Amniocentesis," *Social Science and Medicine*, Vol. 19, No. 11 (1984), pp. 1207–1212.

Jhunjhunwala, Bharat. "Sex Ratio Riddles," *Statesman* (India), June 2, 2001, http://web.lexis-nexis.com/universe/docu . . . A1&_md5?f11fe824a367b3b589 54ba7cdd5c72c5.

Ji Dangsheng and Shao Qin. *The Tendency and Management of Chinese Population Movement*. Beijing: Beijing Publishing House, 1996.

Jian Fa. "China Faces an 'Employment War,'" *Beijing Review*, March 20, 2003, pp. 26–27.

Jimmerson, Julie. "Female Infanticide in China: An Examination of Cultural and Legal Norms," *Pacific Basin Law Journal*, Vol. 8, No. 1 (Spring 1990), pp. 47–79.

Johansson, Sten, and Ola Nygren. "The Missing Girls of China: A New Demographic Account," *Population and Development Review*, Vol. 17, No. 1 (March 1991), pp. 35–51.

Johansson, Sten, Zhao Xuan, and Ola Nygren. "On Intriguing Sex Ratios among Live Births in China in the 1980s," *Journal of Official Statistics*, Vol. 7, No. 1 (1991), http://www.jos.nu/Articles/abstract.asp?article=7125.

Johnson, Kay, Huang Banghan, and Wang Liyao. "Infant Abandonment and Adoption in China," *Population and Development Review*, Vol. 24, No. 3 (September 1998), pp. 469–510.

Johnson, Kay Ann. *Women, the Family, and Peasant Revolution in China*. Chicago: University of Chicago Press, 1983.

Johnson, Norris R., James G. Stemler, and Deborah Hunter. "Crowd Behavior as 'Risky Shift': A Laboratory Experiment," *Sociometry*, Vol. 40, No. 2 (June 1977), pp. 183–187.

Johnson, S., and Zhao Xuan. "Live Birth Sex Ratio for China in the 1980s," collected theses of the Beijing International Symposium for China Fertility and Contraception Sample.

Kabir, M., Ruhul Amin, Ashraf Uddin Ahmen, and Jamir Chowdhury. "Factors Affecting Desired Family Size in Bangladesh," *Journal of Biosocial Science*, Vol. 26, No. 3 (July 1994), pp. 369–375.

Kakonen, Jyrki. *Perspectives on Environmental Conflict and International Politics*. New York: Pinter, 1992.

Kanazawa, Satoshi. "Why Productivity Fades with Age: The Crime-Genius Connection," *Journal of Research in Personality*, Vol. 37, No. 4 (August 2003), pp. 257–272.

Kanazawa, Satoshi, and Mary C. Still. "Why Men Commit Crimes (and Why They Desist)," *Sociological Theory*, Vol. 18, No. 3 (November 2000), pp. 434–447.

Kaplan, Robert D. "The Coming Anarchy," *Atlantic Monthly*, Vol. 272, No. 2 (February 1994), pp. 44–81.

Kaplan, Robert D. *The Ends of the Earth: A Journey at the Dawn of the Twenty-first Century*. New York: Random House, 1996.

Karlekar, Malavika. "The Girl Child in India: Does She Have Any Rights?" *Canadian Woman Studies*, Vol. 15, Nos. 2–3 (Spring/Summer 1995), pp. 55–57.

Kates, Robert W. "Drought in the Sahel," *Mazingira*, Vol. 5, No. 2 (1981), pp. 72–83.

Kates, Robert W. "Natural Hazards in Human Ecological Perspective: Hypotheses and Models," *Economic Geography*, Vol. 47, No. 3 (July 1971), pp. 438–451.

Kaur, Manmohan. *Role of Women in the Freedom Movement (1857–1947)*. Delhi: Sterling, 1968.

Kellum, Barbara A. "Infanticide in England in the Later Middle Ages," *History of Childhood Quarterly: The Journal of Psychohistory*, Vol. 1, No. 3 (Winter 1974), pp. 367–388.

Kemper, Theodore D. *Social Structure and Testosterone: Explorations of the Socio-Bio-Social Chain*. New Brunswick, N.J.: Rutgers University Press, 1990.

Kennedy, Robert Emmet. *The Irish: Emigration, Marriage, and Fertility*. Berkeley: University of California Press, 1973.

Kertzer, David. "Gender Ideology and Infant Abandonment in Nineteenth-Century Italy," *Journal of Interdisciplinary Studies*, Vol. 4 (Summer 1991), pp. 1–25.

Khan, M.E., Sandya Barge, and George Philip. "Abortion in India: An Overview," *Social Change*, Vol. 26, Nos. 3–4 (September–December 1996), pp. 208–225.

Kinney, Anne Behnke, ed. *Chinese Views of Childhood*. Honolulu: University of Hawaii Press, 1995.

Kinney, Anne Behnke. "Dyed Silk: Han Notions of the Moral Development of Children," in Anne Behnke Kinney, ed., *Chinese Views of Childhood*. Honolulu: University of Hawaii Press, 1995, pp. 17–56.

Klapisch-Zuber, Christiane, ed. *A History of Women in the West*, Vol. 2: *Silences of the Middle Ages*. Cambridge, Mass.: Belknap, 1992.

Klasen, Stephan. "'Missing Women' Reconsidered," *World Development*, Vol. 22, No. 7 (July 1994), pp. 1061–1071.

Klasen, Stephan, and Claudia Wink. "'Missing Women': Revisiting the Debate," *Feminist Economics*, Vol. 9, Nos. 2–3 (July–November 2003).

Knapp, Ronald G. *China's Island Frontier: Studies in the Historical Geography of Taiwan*. Honolulu: University Press of Hawaii, 1980.

Knight, Olive. *Life and Manners in the Frontier Army.* Norman: University of Oklahoma Press, 1978.

Ko, Dorothy. *Teachers of the Inner Chambers: Women and Culture in Seventeenth-Century China.* Stanford, Calif.: Stanford University Press, 1994.

Kogan, Nathan, and Michael Wallach. *Risk Taking: A Study in Cognition and Personality.* New York: Holt, Rinehart, and Winston, 1964.

Kohl, Marvin, ed. *Infanticide and the Value of Human Life.* New York: Prometheus, 1978.

Krishnaji, N. "Poverty and Sex Ratio: Some Data and Speculations," *Economic and Political Weekly,* June 6, 1987, pp. 892–897.

Krishnamurty, J., ed. *Women in Colonial India: Essays on Survival, Work, and the State.* Delhi: Oxford University Press, 1989.

Krishnan, Vijaya. "Gender of Children and Contraceptive Use," *Journal of Biosocial Science,* Vol. 25, No. 2 (April 1993), pp. 213–221.

Krishnan, Vijaya. "Preferences for Sex of Children: A Multivariate Analysis," *Journal of Biosocial Science,* Vol. 19, No. 3 (July 1987), pp. 367–376.

Kristof, Nicholas D., and Sheryl WuDunn. *China Wakes: The Struggle for the Soul of a Rising Power.* New York: Vintage, 1994.

Krzywicki, Ludwik. *Primitive Society and Its Vital Statistics.* London: Macmillan, 1934.

Kundu, Amitabh, and Mahesk K. Sahu. "Variation in Sex Ratio: Development Implications," *Economic and Political Weekly,* October 12, 1991, pp. 2341–2342.

Kunreuther, Howard C., and Joanne Linnerooth, eds. *Risk Analysis and Decision Processes: The Siting of Liquified Energy Gas Facilities in Four Countries.* Berlin: Springer-Verlag, 1983.

Laffey, Ella S. "The Making of a Rebel: Liu Yung-fu and the Formation of the Black Flag Army," in Jean Chesnaux, ed., *Popular Movements and Secret Societies in China, 1840–1950.* Stanford, Calif.: Stanford University Press, 1972, pp. 85–96.

Lang, Alan R. "Alcohol-Related Violence: Psychological Perspectives," in Susan E. Martin, ed., *Alcohol and Interpersonal Violence: Fostering Multidisciplinary Perspectives,* NIAAA Research Monograph No. 24. Rockville, Md.: National Institutes of Health, 1993, pp. 121–147.

Langer, William L. "Checks on Population Growth, 1750–1850," *Scientific American,* Vol. 226, No. 2 (February 1972), pp. 92–99.

Langer, William L. "Further Notes on the History of Infanticide," *History of Childhood Quarterly: The Journal of Psychohistory,* Vol. 2, No. 1 (Summer 1974), pp. 129–134.

Langer, William L. "Infanticide: A Historical Survey," *History of Childhood Quarterly: The Journal of Psychohistory,* Vol. 1, No. 3 (Winter 1974), pp. 353–365.

Langness, L.L. "Sexual Antagonism in the New Guinea Highlands: A Bena Bena Example," *Oceania,* Vol. 38, No. 3 (March 1967), pp. 161–177.

Lannoy, Richard. *The Speaking Tree: A Study of Indian Culture and Society.* Oxford: Oxford University Press, 1971.

Laub, John H., Daniel S. Nagin, and Robert J. Sampson. "Trajectories of Change in Criminal Offending: Good Marriages and the Desistance Process," *American Sociological Review,* Vol. 63, No. 2 (April 1998), pp. 225–238.

Lavely, William. "Unintended Consequences of China's Birth Planning Policy." University of Washington, July 14, 1997.

Lavely, William, and R. Bin Wong. "Revising the Malthusian Narrative: The Comparative Study of Population Dynamics in Late Imperial China," *Journal of Asian Studies*, Vol. 57, No. 3 (August 1998), pp. 714–748.

Leach, Maria, ed. *Dictionary of Folklore, Mythology, and Legend*, Vol. 1: New York: Funk and Wagnalls, 1949.

Lecky, William Edward Hartpole. *History of European Morals from Augustus to Charlemagne*, Vol. 2. London: Longmans, Greens, 1869.

Lee, Bernice J. "Female Infanticide in China," in Richard W. Guisso and Stanley Johannesen, eds., *Women in China: Current Directions in Historical Scholarship.* Youngstown, N.Y.: Philo, 1981.

Lee, James, Cameron Campbell, and Guofu Tan. "Infanticide and Family Planning in Late Imperial China: The Price and Population History of Rural Liaoning, 1774–1873," in Thomas G. Rawski and Lillian M. Li, eds., *Chinese History in Economic Perspective.* Berkeley: University of California Press, 1992, pp. 145–176.

Lee, James, Wang Feng, and Cameron Campbell. "Infant and Child Mortality among Qing Nobility: Implications for Two Types of Positive Checks," *Population Studies*, Vol. 48, No. 3 (November 1994), pp. 395–411.

Lee, James Z., and Wang Feng. *One Quarter of Humanity: Malthusian Mythology and Chinese Realities, 1700–2000.* Cambridge, Mass.: Harvard University Press, 1999.

Lee, Richard B. "Lactation, Ovulation, Infanticide, and Woman's Work: A Study of Hunter-Gatherer Population Regulation," in Mark Nathan Cohen, Roy S. Malpass, and Harold G. Klein, eds., *Biosocial Mechanisms of Population Regulation.* New Haven, Conn.: Yale University Press, 1980, pp. 321–348.

Lee, Richard B., and Irven deVore, eds. *Man the Hunter.* Chicago: Aldine de Gruyter, 1968.

Lefkowitz, Mary R., and Maureen B. Fant. *Women's Life in Greece and Rome.* Baltimore, Md.: Johns Hopkins University Press, 1992.

Levine, Nancy E. "Differential Child Care in Three Tibetan Communities: Beyond Son Preference," *Population and Development Review*, Vol. 13, No. 2 (June 1987), pp. 281–304.

Levinson, David. "Social Setting, Cultural Factors, and Alcohol-Related Aggression," in Edward Gottheil et al., eds., *Alcohol, Drug Abuse, and Aggression.* Springfield: Charles C. Thomas, 1983, pp. 1–58.

Levy, Mark. "Global Environmental Degradation: National Security and U.S. Foreign Policy," Working Paper No. 9. Cambridge, Mass.: Project on the Changing Security Environment and American National Interests, John M. Olin Institute for Strategic Studies, Harvard University, November 1994.

Li Chunyi. "'Huji' System, Population Flow, and Instability of Cities." Foreign Affairs College, Beijing, May 26, 1999.

Li, Eva B.C. "Modernization: Its Impacts on Families in China," in Phylis Lan Lin, Ko-wang Mei, and Huai-chen Peng, eds., *Marriage and the Family in Chinese Societies: Selected Readings.* Indianapolis: University of Indianapolis Press, 1994, pp. 39–52.

Li Ji. "Discussions on the Gender Imbalance in China and the Entailed Social Problems." Foreign Affairs College, Beijing, 1999.

Li Jieping, and Shao Wei. "Single Children and Their Mothers," in China Population Information Center, *Analysis on China's National One-per-Thousand Population Fertility Sampling Survey.* Beijing: China Population Information Center, 1984, pp. 144–148.

Li Jingnen. "Challenge to Chinese Population Theory Research on the Eve of the Twenty-first Century," *Chinese Population Science,* n.s., Vol. 4 (1998).

Li Li. "Gender Imbalance and Family Planning in China." Foreign Affairs College, Beijing, March 1999.

Li, Lillian M. "Life and Death in a Chinese Famine: Infanticide as a Demographic Consequence of the 1935 Yellow River Flood," *Comparative Studies in Society and History,* Vol. 33, No. 3 (July 1991), pp. 466–510.

Li Tan. "Population Flow into Big Cities," *Beijing Review,* July 18–24, 1994, pp. 15–19.

Li Weidong. "To Keep Economic Prosperity under the Pressures of Population Aging and Unemployment," *Economics Selection* (1999), pp. 10–11.

Li Xiaorong. "License to Coerce: Violence against Women, State Responsibility, and Legal Failures in China's Family-Planning Program," *Yale Journal of Law and Feminism,* Vol. 8, No. 1 (Summer 1996), pp. 145–191.

Lin, Phylis Lan, Ko-wang Mei, and Huai-chen Peng, eds. *Marriage and the Family in Chinese Societies: Selected Readings.* Indianapolis: University of Indianapolis Press, 1994.

Lin Yutang. *My Country and My People.* New York: Reynal and Hitchcock, 1935

Lindert, Peter. *Fertility and Scarcity in America.* Princeton, N.J.: Princeton University Press, 1978.

Lindsay, Jack. *The Ancient World: Manners and Morals.* New York: G.P. Putnam's Sons, 1968.

Little, Daniel. *Understanding Peasant China: Case Studies in the Philosophy of Social Science.* New Haven, Conn.: Yale University Press, 1989.

Liu Hui-chen Wang. *The Traditional Chinese Clan Rules.* Locust Valley, N.Y.: J.J. Augustin, 1959.

Liu Jianhong, Zhang Lening, and Steven F. Messner, eds. *Crime and Social Control in a Changing China.* Westport, Conn.: Greenwood, 2001.

"The Lost Girls," *Economist,* September 18, 1993, pp. 38–41.

Lutz, Elaine. "When the Women Cry, Who Will Listen?" *International Relations Journal* (San Francisco State University), Vol. 14, No. 2 (Spring 1993), pp. 29–32.

Maccoby, Eleanor Emmons, and Carol Nagy Jacklin. *The Psychology of Sex Differences.* Stanford, Calif.: Stanford University Press, 1974.

MacCormack, Carol P. "Health and the Social Power of Women," *Social Science and Medicine,* Vol. 26, No. 7 (1988), pp. 677–683.

Mack, Andrew. "The Security Report Project Background Paper." Human Security Centre, University of British Columbia, Vancouver, Canada, 2003, http://www.humansecuritybulletin.info/archive/en_v1i2.

Macrae, Joanna, and Anthony Zwi, eds. *War and Hunger: Rethinking International Responses to Complex Emergencies*. London: Zed, 1994.

Mahadevan, K., and R. Jayasree. "Value of Children and Differential Fertility Behaviour in Kerala, Andhra Pradesh, and Uttar Pradesh," in Shri Nath Singh, ed., *Population Transition in India*. Delhi: B.R. Publishing, 1989, pp. 123–131.

Makato, Ueda. "Minmatsu Shinso: Konan no toshino burai o meguru shakui kankei, dako to kyakufu," *Shigaka zasshi* [Journal of historical studies], Vol. 90, No. 12 (1981), pp. 1619–1653.

Mandelbaum, David G. "Family, *Jati*, Village," in Milton Singer and Bernard S. Cohn, eds., *Structure and Change in Indian Society*. Chicago: Aldine de Gruyter, 1968.

Martin, Ged, ed. *The Founding of Australia: The Argument About Australia's Origins*. Sydney: Hale and Iremonger, 1978.

Martin, Susan E., ed. *Alcohol and Interpersonal Violence: Fostering Multidisciplinary Perspectives*, NIAAA Research Monograph No. 24. Rockville, Md.: National Institutes of Health, 1993.

Marzuk, P.M., K. Tardiff, D. Smyth, M. Stajic, and A.C. Leon. "Cocaine Use, Risk Taking, and Fatal Russian Roulette," *JAMA*, May 20, 1992, pp. 2635–2637.

Mazur, Allan, and Alan Booth. "Testosterone and Dominance in Men," *Behavioral and Brain Science*, Vol. 21, No. 3 (June 1998), pp. 353–397.

Mazur, Allan, and Joel Michalek. "Marriage, Divorce, and Male Testosterone," *Social Forces*, Vol. 77, No. 1 (September 1998), pp. 315–330.

McCague, James. *Moguls and Iron Men: The Story of the First Transcontinental Railroad*. New York: Harper and Row, 1964.

McDermott, Rose, and J. Cowden. "The Effects of Uncertainty and Sex in a Crisis Simulation Game," *International Interactions*, Vol. 27 (2001), pp. 353–380.

McDonald, Hamish. "Unwelcome Sex," *Far Eastern Economic Review*, December 26, 1991–January 2, 1992, pp. 18–19.

McElroy, Damien. "China Fears Crime Wave of One-Child Generation." May 7, 1998, http://www.future-china.org/fcn/mainland/et980507.htm.

McGovern, Celeste. "Chinese Puzzle: 117 Boys for 100 Girls," *Report*, June 10, 2002, http://report.ca/archive/report/20020610/p56i020610f.html.

McKee, Lauris. "Sex Differentials in Survivorship and the Customary Treatment of Infants and Children," *Medical Anthropology: Cross-Cultural Studies in Health and Illness*, Vol. 8, No. 2 (Spring 1984), pp. 91–108.

McLaren, E.C. *The Story of Our Manchurian Mission*. Edinburgh: Offices of United Presbyterian Church, 1896.

Medhurst, Walter Henry. *The Foreigner in Far Cathay*. London: Edward Stanford, 1872.

Meindl, Richard S., and Katherine F. Russell. "Recent Advances in Method and Theory in Paleodemography," *Annual Review of Anthropology*, Vol. 27 (1998), pp. 375–399.

Melbin, Murray. "Night as Frontier," *American Sociological Review*, Vol. 43, No. 1 (February 1978), pp. 3–22.

Melbin, Murray. *Night as Frontier: Colonizing the World after Dark*. New York: Free Press, 1987.

Menon, Nivedita. "Abortion and the Law: Questions for Feminism," *Canadian Journal of Women and Law*, Vol. 6, No. 1 (1993), pp. 103–118.

Mesquida, Christian G., and Neil I. Wiener. "Human Collective Aggression: A Behavioral Ecology Perspective," *Ethology and Sociobiology*, Vol. 17, No. 4 (July 1996), pp. 247–262.

Messner, Steven F., and Robert J. Sampson. "The Sex Ratio, Family Disruption, and Rates of Violent Crime: The Paradox of Demographic Structure," *Social Forces*, Vol. 69, No. 3 (March 1991), pp. 693–713.

Miczek, Klaus A., Elise M. Weerts, and Joseph F. DeBold. "Alcohol, Aggression, and Violence: Biobehavioral Determinants," in Susan E. Martin, ed., *Alcohol and Interpersonal Violence: Fostering Multidisciplinary Perspectives*, NIAAA Research Monograph No. 24. Rockville, Md.: National Institutes of Health, 1993, pp. 83–119.

Miller, Barbara D. "Daughter Neglect, Women's Work, and Marriage: Pakistan and Bangladesh Compared," *Medical Anthropology: Cross-Cultural Studies in Health and Illness*, Vol. 8, No. 2 (Spring 1984), pp. 109–126.

Miller, Barbara D. *The Endangered Sex: Neglect of Female Children in Rural North India*. Ithaca, N.Y.: Cornell University Press, 1981.

Miller, Barbara D. "Female-Selective Abortion in Asia: Patterns, Policies, and Debates," *American Anthropologist*, Vol. 103, No. 4 (December 2001), pp. 1083–1095.

Miller, Barbara D., ed. *Sex and Gender Hierarchies*. Cambridge: Cambridge University Press, 1993.

Miller, Norman S., Mark S. Gold, and John C. Mahler. "Violent Behaviors Associated with Cocaine Use: Possible Pharmacological Mechanisms," *International Journal of the Addictions*, Vol. 26, No. 10 (1991), pp. 1077–1088.

Mirsky, Jonathan. "Return of the Baby Killers," *New Statesman*, March 21, 1986, p. 19.

"Missing Sisters," *Economist*, April 19, 2003, p. 36

Mitra, Ashok. *Implications of the Declining Sex Ratio in India's Population*. Bombay: Allied Publishers, 1979.

Mohnot, S.M. "Peripheralization of Weaned Male Juveniles in Presbytis entellus," in David John Chivers and J. Herbert, eds., *Recent Advances in Primatology*, Vol. 1: *Behavior*. London: Academic Press, 1978, pp. 87–91.

Monkkonen, Eric H. *Walking to Work: Tramps in America, 1790–1935*. Lincoln: University of Nebraska Press, 1984.

Moore, Trent Wade. "Fertility in China, 1982–1990: Gender Equality as a Complement to Wealth Flows Theory," *Population Research and Policy Review*, Vol. 17, No. 2 (April 1998), pp. 197–222.

Morewedge, Rosemarie Thee, ed. *The Role of Women in the Middle Ages: Papers of the Sixth Annual Conference of the Center for Medieval and Early Renaissance Studies, State University of New York at Binghamton, 6–8 May 1972*. Albany: State University of New York Press, 1975.

Moseley, Kathryn L. "The History of Infanticide in Western Society," *Issues in Law and Medicine*, Vol. 1, No. 5 (March 1986), pp. 345–362.

Moyer, Kenneth E. "Sex Differences in Aggression," in Richard C. Friedman,

Ralph M. Richart, and Raymond L. Vande Wiele, ed., *Sex Differences in Behavior.* New York: Wiley, 1974, pp. 335–372.

Muhuri, Pradip K., and Samuel H. Preston. "Effects of Family Composition on Mortality Differentials by Sex among Children in Matlab, Bangladesh," *Population and Development Review,* Vol. 17, No. 3 (September 1991), pp. 415–434.

Murray, Christopher J.L., and Alan D. Lopez, eds. *The Global Burden of Disease: A Comprehensive Assessment of Mortality and Disability from Diseases, Injuries, and Risk Factors in 1990 and Projected to 2020.* Cambridge, Mass.: Harvard University Press, 1996.

Murray, Christopher J.L., and Alan D. Lopez. *Summary of the Report: The Global Burden of Disease: A Comprehensive Assessment of Mortality and Disability from Diseases, Injuries, and Risk Factors in 1990 and Projected to 2020.* Geneva: World Health Organization, 1996.

Murthi, Mamta, Anne-Catherine Guio, and Jean Dreze. "Mortality, Fertility, and Gender Bias in India: A District-Level Analysis," *Population and Development Review,* Vol. 21, No. 4 (December 1995), pp. 745–782.

Mutharayappa, Rangamuthia, Minja Kim Choe, Fred Arnold, and T.K. Roy. "Son Preference and Its Effect on Fertility in India," National Family Health Survey Subject Reports No. 3 (March 1997).

Muthulakshmi, R. *Female Infanticide: Its Causes and Solutions.* New Delhi: Discovery Publishing House, 1997.

Nan Li, Shripad Tuljapurkar, and Marcus Feldman. "High Sex Ratio at Birth and Its Consequences," *Chinese Journal of Population Science,* Vol. 7, No. 3 (1995), pp. 213–221.

Naquin, Susan. *Shantung Rebellion: The Wang Lun Uprising of 1774.* New Haven, Conn.: Yale University Press, 1981.

Naquin, Susan, and Evelyn S. Rawski. *Chinese Society in the Eighteenth Century.* New Haven, Conn.: Yale University Press, 1987.

Neel, James V., and Napoleon A. Chagnon. "The Demography of Two Tribes of Primitive, Relatively Unacculturated American Indians," *Proceedings of the National Academy of Sciences,* Vol. 59, No. 3 (March 1968), pp. 680–689.

Nelson, Joan M. *Migrants, Urban Poverty, and Instability in Developing Nations,* Occasional Papers in International Affairs No. 22. Cambridge, Mass.: Center for International Affairs, Harvard University, September 1969.

Nichols, R.H., and F.A. Wray. *The History of the Foundling Hospital.* London: Oxford University Press, 1935.

Nigg, Joanne M., and Dennis S. Mileti. "Natural Hazards and Disasters," in Riley E. Dunlop and William Michelson, eds., *Handbook of Environmental Sociology.* Greenwich, Conn.: Greenwood, 1991.

Nishimara, Gensho. "Ryu roku ryu nana no ran ni tsuite," *Toyoshi kenkyu* [Asian historical research], Vol. 32, No. 4 (1974), pp. 44–86.

Nyrop, Richard F., ed. *India: A Country Study, Foreign Area Studies, the American University.* Washington, D.C.: For sale by the Superintendent of Documents, U.S. Government Printing Office, 1985.

Oberai, A.S. *Population Growth, Employment, and Poverty in Third-World Mega-Cities.* New York: St. Martin's, 1993.

O'Donnell, Lynne. "Sex Imbalance Fuels China's Flesh Trade." January 4, 1999, http://www.freerepublic.com/forum/aa36904a553c75.htm.

Oldenburg, Philip. "Sex Ratio, Son Preference, and Violence in India: A Research Note," *Economic and Political Weekly,* December 5, 1992, pp. 2657–2662.

Oldenziel, Ruth. "The Historiography of Infanticide in Antiquity: A Literature Stillborn," in Josine Blok and Peter Mason, eds., *Sexual Asymmetry: Studies in Ancient Society.* Amsterdam: J.C. Gieben, 1987, pp. 87–107.

Olweus, Dan, Ake Mattsson, Daisy Schalling, and Hans Loew. "Circulating Testosterone Levels and Aggression in Adolescent Males: A Causal Analysis," *Psychosomatic Medicine,* Vol. 50, No. 3 (May–June 1988), pp. 261–272.

Ono, Kazuko. *Chinese Women in a Century of Revolution: 1850–1950.* Stanford, Calif.: Stanford University Press, 1989.

Opitz, Claudia. "Life in the Middle Ages," in Christiane Klapisch-Zuber, ed., *A History of Women in the West,* Vol. 2: *Silences of the Middle Ages.* Cambridge, Mass.: Belknap, 1992, pp. 267–317.

Ownby, David. "Approximations of Chinese Bandits: Perverse Rebels, Romantic Heroes, or Frustrated Bachelors?" in Susan Brownell and Jeffrey N. Wasserstrom, eds., *Chinese Femininities/Chinese Masculinities: A Reader.* Berkeley: University of California Press, 2002, pp. 226–253.

Ownby, David. *Brotherhoods and Secret Societies in Early and Mid-Qing China: The Formation of a Tradition.* Stanford, Calif.: Stanford University Press, 1996.

Ownby, David. "The Ethnic Feud in Qing Taiwan: What Is This Violence Business, Anyway? An Interpretation of the 1782 Zhang-Quan Xiedou," *Late Imperial China,* Vol. 11, No. 1 (June 1990), pp. 75–98.

Pakistan. Population Census Organization. "Table-1: Area, Population By Sex, Sex Ratio, Population Density, Urban Proportion, Household Size, and Annual Growth Rate," http://www.statpak.gov.pk/depts/pco/statistics/pop_table1/pop_table1.html.

Pakrasi, Kanti B. *Female Infanticide in India.* Calcutta: Editions India, 1970.

Panigrahi, Lalita. *British Social Policy and Female Infanticide in India.* New Delhi: Munshiram Manoharlal, 1972.

Pantel, Pauline Schmitt, ed. *A History of Women in the West,* Vol. 1: *From Ancient Goddesses to Christian Saints.* Cambridge, Mass.: Belknap, 1992.

Parikh, Manju. "Sex-Selective Abortions in India: Parental Choice or Sexist Discrimination?" *Feminist Issues* (Fall 1990), pp. 19–32.

Park Chai Bin. "Preference for Sons, Family Size, and Sex Ratio: An Empirical Study in Korea," *Demography,* Vol. 20, No. 3 (August 1983), pp. 332–352.

Park Chai Bin, and Cho Nam-hoon. "Consequences of Son Preference in a Low-Fertility Society: Imbalance of the Sex Ratio at Birth in Korea," *Population and Development Review,* Vol. 21, No. 1 (March 1995), pp. 59–84.

Parke, Charles Ross. *Dreams to Dust: A Diary of the California Gold Rush, 1849–1850,* ed. James E. Davis. Lincoln: University of Nebraska Press, 1989.

Parson, Edward A., and William Clark. "Sustainable Development as Social Learning: Theoretical Perspectives and Practical Challenges for the Design of a Research Program," in Lance H. Gunderson, C.S. Holling, and Stephen S. Light, eds., *Barriers and Bridges to the Renewal of Ecosystems and Institutions*. New York: Columbia University Press, 1995, pp. 428–460.

Patel, Vibhuti. "Sex Determination and Sex Preselection Tests in India: Modern Techniques for Femicide," *Bulletin of Concerned Asian Scholars*, Vol. 21, No. 1 (January–March 1989), pp. 2–11.

Pedersen, Frank A. "Secular Trends in Human Sex Ratios: Their Influence on Individual and Family Behavior," *Human Nature*, Vol. 2, No. 3 (1991), pp. 271–291.

Peggs, James. *Cries of Agony: An Historical Account of Suttee, Infanticide, Ghat Murders, and Slavery in India*. Originally published as *India's Cries to British Humanity*, 1830; reprint, Delhi: Discovery Publishing House, 1984.

Perkins, Roberta, G. Prestage, R. Sharp, and F. Lovejoy, eds. *Sex Work and Sex Workers in Australia*. Sydney: University of New South Wales, 1994.

Pernanen, Kai. "Alcohol-Related Violence: Conceptual Models," in Susan E. Martin, ed., *Alcohol and Interpersonal Violence: Fostering Multidisciplinary Perspectives*, NIAAA Research Monograph No. 24. Rockville, Md.: National Institutes of Health, 1993, pp. 37–69.

Perry, Elizabeth. *Rebels and Revolutionaries in North China, 1845–1945*. Stanford, Calif.: Stanford University Press, 1980.

Pomeroy, Sarah B. "Infanticide in Hellenistic Greece," in Averil Cameron and Amelie Kuhrt, eds., *Images of Women in Antiquity*. Detroit, Mich.: Wayne State University Press, 1993, pp. 207–222.

Population Census Office of the State Council of the People's Republic of China, and the Institute of Geography of the Chinese Academy of Sciences. *Population Atlas of China*. Oxford: Oxford University Press, 1987.

Poston, Dudley L., Jr., and David Yaukey, eds. *The Population of Modern China*. New York: Plenum, 1992.

Potter, Sulamith Heins. "Birth Planning in Rural China: A Cultural Account," in Nancy Scheper-Hughes, ed., *Child Survival: Anthropological Perspectives on the Treatment and Maltreatment of Children*. Dordrecht, Netherlands: D. Reidel, 1987.

Power, Eileen. *Medieval Women*, ed. Michael Moissey Postan. Cambridge: Cambridge University Press, 1975.

Prakash, Padma. "Decline in Sex Ratio," *Economic and Political Weekly*, December 19, 1992, p. 2670.

"PRC Family Planning: The Market Weakens Controls but Encourages Voluntary Limits," http://www.usembassy-china.org.cn/english/sandt/POPMYWB.html.

Premi, Mahendra K. "The Missing Girl Child," *Economic and Political Weekly*, May 26, 2001, pp. 1875–1880.

Premi, Mahendra K., and Saraswati Raju. "Born to Die: Female Infanticide in Madhya Pradesh," *Search Bulletin*, Vol. 13, No. 3 (July–September 1998), pp. 94–105.

Preston, Samuel H. *Mortality Patterns in National Populations with Special Reference to Recorded Causes of Death*. New York: Academic Press, 1976.

Prigogine, Ilya, and Isabelle Stengers. *Order Out of Chaos: Man's New Dialogue with Nature*. Boulder, Colo.: Shambala/New Science Library, 1984.

Protection of Chinese Women's Rights and Interests. Beijing: New Star, 1993.

Rabb, Theodore K., and Robert I. Rotberg, eds. *The Family in History: Interdisciplinary Essays*. New York: Harper and Row, 1971.

Rajan, S. Irudaya. "Decline in Sex Ratio: An Alternative Explanation?" *Economic and Political Weekly*, December 21, 1991, pp. 2963–2964.

Rajan, S. Irudaya. "Heading towards a Billion," *Economic and Political Weekly*, December 17, 1994, pp. 3201–3205.

Rajan, S. Irudaya, U.S. Mishra, and K. Navaneetham. "Decline in Sex Ratio: Alternative Explanation Revisited," *Economic and Political Weekly*, November 14, 1992, pp. 2505–2508.

Raju, Saraswati, and Mahendra K. Premi. "Decline in Sex Ratio: An Alternative Explanation Re-examined," *Economic and Political Weekly*, April 25, 1992, pp. 911–912.

Rawski, Thomas G., and Lillian M. Li, eds. *Chinese History in Economic Perspective*. Berkeley: University of California Press, 1992.

Redclift, Michael. *Development and the Environmental Crisis*. New York: Methuen, 1984.

Rees, Sian. *The Floating Brothel: The Extraordinary True Story of an Eighteenth-Century Ship and Its Cargo of Female Convicts*. New York: Theia/Hyperion, 2002.

Reeves, P.D., ed. *Sleeman in Oudh: An Abridgement of W.H. Sleeman's* A Journey through the Kingdom of Oude in 1849–50. Cambridge: Cambridge University Press, 1971.

Ren Feng. "Bare Branches among Rural Migrant Laborers in China: Causes, Social Implications, and Policy Proposal." Foreign Affairs College, Beijing, March 1999.

Ren Meng. "Confronting Three Populations of 80 Million," *Inside China Mainland*, Vol. 19, No. 1 (January 1997), pp. 78–81.

Ren, Xinhua Steve. "Sex Differences in Infant and Child Mortality in Three Provinces in China," *Social Science and Medicine*, Vol. 40, No. 9 (May 1995), pp. 1263–1264.

Renner, Michael. *National Security: The Economic and Environmental Dimensions*, Worldwatch Paper No. 89. Washington, D.C.: Worldwatch Institute, 1989.

Renteln, Alison Dundes. "Sex Selection and Reproductive Freedom," *Women's Studies International Forum*, Vol. 15, No. 3 (May–June 1992), pp. 405–426.

Riches, David. "The Netsilik Eskimo: A Special Case of Selective Female Infanticide," *Ethnology: An International Journal of Cultural and Social Anthropology*, Vol. 13, No. 4 (October 1974), pp. 351–361.

Riddle, John M. *Contraception and Abortion from the Ancient World to the Renaissance*. Cambridge, Mass.: Harvard University Press, 1992.

Risley, Herbert Hope. *The People of India*, ed. William Crooke. Delhi: Oriental Books Reprint Corporation, 1969.

Robinson, David M. "Banditry and Rebellion in the Capital Region during the Mid-Ming (1450–1525)," Ph.D. dissertation. Princeton University, 1995.

Robinson, David M. "The Management of Violence in the Mid-Ming Capital Region," Colgate University, 1998.

Robinson, David M. "Notes on Eunuchs in Hebei during the Mid-Ming Period," *Ming Studies*, Vol. 34 (July 1995), pp. 1–16.

Roizen, Judith. "Issues in the Epidemiology of Alcohol and Violence," in Susan E. Martin, ed., *Alcohol and Interpersonal Violence: Fostering Multidisciplinary Perspectives*, NIAAA Research Monograph No. 24. Rockville, Md.: National Institutes of Health, 1993, p. 3036.

Rooney, James F. "Societal Forces and the Unattached Male," in Howard M. Bahr, ed., *Disaffiliated Man: Essays and Bibliography on Skid Row, Vagrancy, and Outsiders*. Toronto: University of Toronto Press, 1970, pp. 13–38.

Roosevelt, Anna, ed. *Amazonian Indians from Prehistory to the Present: Anthropological Perspectives*. Tucson: University of Arizona Press, 1994.

Root-Bernstein, Robert. "How Scientists Really Think," *Perspectives in Biology and Medicine*, Vol. 32, No. 4 (Summer 1989), pp. 472–490.

Rose, Lionel. *The Massacre of the Innocents: Infanticide in Britain, 1800–1939*. London: Routledge and Kegan Paul, 1986.

Rouselle, Aline. "Body Politics in Ancient Rome," in Pauline Schmitt Pantel, ed., *A History of Women in the West*, Vol. 1: *From Ancient Goddesses to Christian Saints*. Cambridge, Mass.: Belknap, 1992, pp. 296–336.

Rozman, Gilbert. *Population and Marketing Settlements in Ch'ing China*. Cambridge, Mass.: Cambridge University Press, 1982.

Russell, J.K. "Exclusion of Adult Male Coatis from Social Groups: Protection from Predation," *Journal of Mammalogy*, Vol. 62, No. 1 (February 1981), pp. 206–208.

Sachar, R.K., J. Verma, V. Prakash, A. Chopra, R. Adlaka, and R. Sofat. "Sex-Selective Fertility Control—An Outrage," *Journal of Family Welfare*, Vol. 36, No. 2 (June 1991), pp. 30–35.

Sampson, Robert J., and John H. Laub. *Crime in the Making: Pathways and Turning Points through Life*. Cambridge, Mass.: Harvard University Press, 1993.

Sanchez, Roberto. "Vulnerability of Urban Areas in Latin America to Climate Change," paper presented at the First Open Meeting of the Human Dimensions of Global Change Community, Duke University, Durham, North Carolina, June 1–3, 1995.

Sarda, Har Bilas. *History of Ancient Hindu Society: An Attempt to Determine the Position of the Hindu Race in the Scale of Nations*. Delhi: Anmol, 1985.

Scheper-Hughes, Nancy, ed. *Child Survival: Anthropological Perspectives on the Treatment and Maltreatment of Children*. Dordrecht, Netherlands: D. Reidel, 1987.

Schran, Peter. "China's Demographic Evolution 1850–1953 Reconsidered," *China Quarterly*, No. 75 (September 1978), pp. 639–646.

Scrimshaw, Susan. "Infanticide in Human Populations: Societal and Individual Concerns," in Glenn Hausfater and Sarah Blaffer Hrdy, eds., *Infanticide: Comparative and Evolutionary Perspectives*. New York: Aldine de Gruyter, 1984, pp. 439–462.

Sen, Amartya. *Development as Freedom*. New York: Alfred A. Knopf, 1999.

Sen, Amartya. "Missing Women," *British Medical Journal*, March 7, 1992, pp. 587–588.

Sen, Amartya. "More Than 100 Million Women Are Missing," *New York Review of Books*, December 20, 1990, pp. 61–66.

Sen, Amartya. *Poverty and Famines*. Oxford: Clarendon, 1981.

Sen, Gita, and Rachel C. Snow, eds. *Power and Decision: The Social Control of Repro-duction.* Cambridge, Mass.: Harvard University Press, 1994.

Seth, Swapan. "Two-Way Movement of Sex Ratio," *Economic and Political Weekly,* October 5, 1996, pp. 2730–2733.

Seymour, James D., and Richard Anderson. *New Ghosts, Old Ghosts: Prisons and Labor Reform Camps in China.* London: M.E. Sharpe, 1998.

Shah, A.M., B.S. Baviskar, and E.A. Ramaswampy, eds. *Social Structure and Change,* Vol. 2: *Women in Indian Society.* New Delhi: Sage, 1996.

Shahidullah, M. "Breast-Feeding and Child Survival in Matlab, Bangladesh," *Journal of Biosocial Science,* Vol. 26, No. 2 (1994), pp. 143–154.

Shakur, Sanyika. *Monster: The Autobiography of an L.A. Gang Member.* New York: Atlantic Monthly Press, 1993.

Sharma, Brij Narain. *Social Life in Northern India [A.D. 600–1000],* foreword by A.L. Basham. Delhi: Munshiram Manoharlal, 1966.

Shepherd, John Robert. *Statecraft and Political Economy on the Taiwan Frontier, 1600–1800.* Stanford, Calif.: Stanford University Press, 1993.

Shiva, Vandana. *Staying Alive: Women, Ecology, and Development.* London: Zed, 1989.

Simmons, George B., Celeste Smucker, Stan Bernstein, and Eric Jensen. "Post-Neonatal Mortality in Rural North India: Implications of an Economic Model," *Demography,* Vol. 19, No. 3 (August 1982), pp. 371–390.

Singer, Milton, and Bernard S. Cohn, eds. *Structure and Change in Indian Society.* Chicago: Aldine de Gruyter, 1968.

Singh, Shri Nath, ed. *Population Transition in India.* Delhi: B.R. Publishing Corpo-ration, 1989.

Situ, Yingyi, and Liu Weizheng. "Transient Population, Crime, and Solution: The Chinese Experience," *International Journal of Offender Therapy and Comparative Criminology,* Vol. 40, No. 4 (December 1996), pp. 293–299.

Smith, Arthur Henderson. *Village Life in China: A Study in Sociology.* New York: F.H. Revell, 1899.

Smith, Eric Alden, and S. Abigail Smith. "Inuit Sex-Ratio Variation: Population Control, Ethnographic Error, or Parental Manipulation?" *Current Anthropology,* Vol. 35, No. 5 (December 1994), pp. 595–624.

Smith, George. *A Narrative of an Exploratory Visit to Each of the Consular Cities of China and to the Islands of Hong Kong and Chusan on Behalf of the Church Mission-ary Society in the Years 1844, 1845, 1846.* London: Seeley, Burnside, and Seeley, 1847.

Smith, Herbert L. "Nonreporting of Births or Nonreporting of Pregnancies? Some Evidence from Four Rural Counties in North China," *Demography,* Vol. 31, No. 3 (August 1994), pp. 481–486.

Smith, Herbert L., Tu Ping, M. Giovanna Merli, and Mark Hereward. "Implemen-tation of a Demographic and Contraceptive Surveillance System in Four Counties in North China," *Population Research and Policy Review,* Vol. 16, No. 4 (August 1997), pp. 289–314.

Smith, Richard J. *China's Cultural Heritage: The Ch'ing Dynasty, 1644–1912.* Boulder, Colo.: Westview, 1983.

Smith, Thomas C., ed., with Robert Y. Eng and Robert T. Lundy. *Nakahara: Family Farming and Population in a Japanese Village, 1717–1830.* Stanford, Calif.: Stanford University Press, 1977.

Sommerfelt, Elisabeth, and Fred Arnold. "Sex Differentials in the Nutritional Status of Young Children," in United Nations, Population Division of the Department of Social and Economic Affairs, *Too Young to Die: Genes or Gender?* New York: United Nations, 1998, pp. 133–153.

South, Scott J., and Katherine Trent. "Sex Ratios and Women's Roles: A Cross-National Analysis," *American Journal of Sociology,* Vol. 93, No. 5 (March 1988), pp. 1096–1115.

South Korea (Republic of Korea). *2001 Report of the National Statistical Office of South Korea.* Seoul: National Statistical Office, July 2001.

South Korea (Republic of Korea). "Census Population 2000." Seoul: National Statistical Office, 2000, http://www.nso.go.kr.

Srikumar, K.P. "Amniocentesis and the Future of the Girl Child," in Leelamma Devasia and V.V. Devasia, eds., *Girl Child in India.* New Delhi: Ashish Publishing House, 1989, pp. 51–65.

Stacey, Judith. *Patriarchy and Socialist Revolution in China.* Berkeley: University of California Press, 1983.

Stern, Paul, Oran Young, and Daniel Druckman, eds. *Global Environmental Change: Understanding the Human Dimensions.* Washington, D.C.: National Academy Press, 1992.

Suhrke, Astri. "Pressure Points: Environmental Degradation, Migration, and Conflict," Occasional Paper No. 3. Toronto: Project on Environmental Change and Acute Conflict, University of Toronto and the American Academy of Arts and Sciences, March 1993.

Sumner, William Graham. *Folkways.* New York: Dover, 1959.

Svare, Bruce B., ed. *Hormones and Aggressive Behavior.* New York: Plenum, 1983.

Taiwan (Republic of China). *The Republic of China Yearbook—Taiwan, 2002.* Taipei: Ministry of the Interior, 2002, http://www.gio.gov.tw/taiwan-website/5-gp/yearbook/chpt02–1.htm#1.

Tao Chun fung, ed. *General View of the Social Status of Women.* Beijing: Chinese Women's Publishing House, 1991.

Taylor, Jeffrey R., and Judith Banister. "China: The Problem of Employing Surplus Rural Labor," CIR Staff Paper No. 49. Washington, D.C.: Center for International Research, U.S. Bureau of the Census, July 1989.

Taylor, Michael, ed. *Rationality and Revolution.* Cambridge: Cambridge University Press, 1988.

ter Harr, Barend J. *The White Lotus Teachings in Chinese Religious History.* Leiden, Netherlands: E.J. Brill, 1992.

Tern, Warren M. "Health and Demography of Native Amazonians: Historical Perspective and Current Status," in Anna Roosevelt, ed., *Amazonian Indians from Prehistory to the Present: Anthropological Perspectives.* Tucson: University of Arizona Press, 1994, pp. 123–149.

Thomas, Keith. "Fateful Exposure," *Times Literary Supplement,* August 25–31, 1989, pp. 913–914.

Thompson, Drew. "HIV/AIDS Epidemic in China Spreads into the General Population." Population Reference Bureau, http://www.prb.org/Template.cfm?Section=PRB&template=/ContentManagement/ContentDisplay.cfm&ContentID=8501.

Thompson, M. "Postscript: A Cultural Basis for Comparison," in Howard C. Kunreuther and Joanne Linnerooth, eds., *Risk Analysis and Decision Processes: The Siting of Liquified Energy Gas Facilities in Four Countries.* Berlin: Springer-Verlag, 1983, pp. 232–262.

Thornhill, Randy, and Nancy Thornhill. "Human Rape: An Evolutionary Analysis," *Ethology and Sociobiology,* Vol. 4, No. 3 (1983), pp. 137–173.

Tien, H. Yuan. "Abortion in China: Incidence and Implications," in Dudley L. Poston Jr. and David Yaukey, eds., *The Population of Modern China.* New York: Plenum, 1992, pp. 287–310.

Tien, H. Yuan. *China's Strategic Demographic Initiative.* New York: Praeger, 1991.

Tien, H. Yuan. "Provincial Fertility Trends and Patterns," in Elisabeth J. Croll, Delia Davin, and Penny Kane, eds., *China's One-Child Family Policy.* New York: St. Martin's, 1985, pp. 114–134.

Tien, H. Yuan, Zhang Tianlu, Ping Yu, Li Jingneng, and Lian Zhongtang. "China's Demographic Dilemmas," *Population Bulletin,* Vol. 47, No. 1 (June 1992), pp. 1–34.

T'ien Ju-k'ang. *Male Anxiety and Female Chastity: A Comparative Study of Chinese Ethical Values in Ming-Ch'ing Times.* New York: E.J. Brill, 1988.

Tiger, Lionel. *Men in Groups.* London: Marion Boyars, 1984.

Timœus, Ian, Katie Harris, and Francesca Fairbairn. "Can Use of Health Care Explain Sex Differentials in Child Mortality in the Developing World?" in United Nations, Population Division of the Department of Economic and Social Affairs, *Too Young to Die: Genes or Gender?* New York: United Nations, 1998, p. 156.

Tong, James. "Rational Outlaws: Rebels and Bandits in the Ming Dynasty, 1368–1644," in Michael Taylor, ed., *Rationality and Revolution.* Cambridge: Cambridge University Press, 1988, pp. 98–128.

Torry, W. "Anthropological Studies in Hazardous Environments: Past Trends and New Horizons," *Current Anthropology,* Vol. 20 (1979), pp. 517–540.

"Tougher Actions toward Crime," *Beijing Review,* May 20–26, 1996, p. 6.

Trexler, Richard C. "The Foundlings of Florence, 1395–1455," *History of Childhood Quarterly: The Journal of Psychohistory,* Vol. 1, No. 2 (Fall 1973), pp. 259–284.

Trexler, Richard C. "Infanticide in Florence: New Sources and First Results," *History of Childhood Quarterly: The Journal of Psychohistory,* Vol. 1, No. 1 (Summer 1973), pp. 98–116.

Tsai, Henry Shih-shan. *The Eunuchs in the Ming Dynasty.* Albany: State University of New York Press, 1996.

UNICEF (United Nations Children's Fund). *Statistical Review of the Situation of Children in the World.* New York: UNICEF, 1986.

United Nations. *The World's Women, 1995: Trends and Statistics.* New York: United Nations, 1995.

United Nations. *The World's Women, 2000: Trends and Statistics,* http://unstats.un.org/unsd/demographic/ww2000/.

United Nations. Department for Economic and Social Information and Policy Analysis. Population Division. *The Sex and Age Distribution of the World Populations: The 1994 Revision.* New York: United Nations, 1994.

United Nations. Department of International and Economic Social Affairs. *Consequences of Mortality Trends and Differentials.* Population Studies No. 95. New York: United Nations, 1986.

United Nations. Department of International and Economic Social Affairs. *World Population Prospects, 1990.* Population Studies No. 120. New York: United Nations, 1991.

United Nations. Department of Social Affairs. Population Division. *Foetal, Infant, and Early Childhood Mortality,* Vol. 1: *The Statistics.* Populations Studies No. 13. New York: United Nations, 1954.

United Nations. Population Division of the Department of Economic and Social Affairs. "The 1998 Revision of the United Nations Population Projections," *Population and Development Review,* Vol. 24, No. 4 (December 1998), pp. 891–895.

United Nations. Population Division of the Department of Economic and Social Affairs. *Too Young to Die: Genes or Gender?* New York: United Nations, 1998.

United Nations. Population Division of the Department of Economic and Social Affairs. *World Population Prospects: The 2002 Revision* and *World Urbanization Prospects: The 2001 Revision,* http://esa.un.org/unpp.

United Nations Development Programme. *India: The Road to Human Development.* India Development Forum, Paris, June 23–25, 1997, document of the United Nations Development Programme, New Delhi, http://www.undp.org.in/REPORT/IDF97/default.htm.

"Urbanization: A Long-Term Solution to Unemployment," *Beijing Review,* March 20, 2003, pp. 28–29.

U.S. Bureau of the Census. International Data Base, 1998, http://www.census.gov/ipc/www/idbnew.html/.

Vallois, Henri V. "The Social Life of Early Man: The Evidence of Skeletons," in Sherwood L. Washburn, ed., *Social Life of Early Man.* New York: Wenner-Gren Foundation for Anthropological Research, 1961, pp. 214–235.

van Gulik, Robert Hans. *Sexual Life in Ancient China: A Preliminary Survey of Chinese Sex and Society from ca. 1500 B.C. till 1644 A.D.* Leiden, Netherlands: E.J. Brill, 1974.

Vasudev, Shefalee, and Methil Renuka. "Sexual Crimes: Rape!" *India Today,* September 9, 2002, pp. 1, 48.

Visaria, Leela, and Pravin Visaria. "India's Population in Transition, *Population Bulletin,* Vol. 50, No. 3 (October 1995), pp. 2–49.

Visaria, Pravin M. "Indian Population Problem: Emerging Perspective after the 1991 Census, *Demography India,* Vol. 20, No. 2 (July–December 1991), pp. 273–295.

Vishwanath, L.S., "Female Infanticide and the Position of Women in India," in A.M. Shah, B.S. Baviskar, and E.A. Ramaswampy, eds., *Social Structure and Change,* Vol. 2: *Women in Indian Society.* New Delhi: Sage, 1996, pp. 179–205

Vlassoff, Carol. "The Value of Sons in an Indian Village: How Widows See It," *Population Studies,* Vol. 44, No. 1 (March 1990), pp. 5–20.

Wadley, Susan S. "Family Composition Strategies in Rural North India," *Social Science and Medicine,* Vol. 37, No. 11 (December 1993), pp. 1367–1376.

Walker, B.H., and A.R.E. Sinclair. "Problems of Development Aid," *Nature,* February 15, 1990, p. 587.

Walter, Ann. *Getting an Heir: Adoption and the Construction of Kinship in Late Imperial China.* Honolulu: University of Hawaii Press, 1990.

Walter, Ann. "Infanticide and Dowry in Ming and Early Qing China," in Anne Behnke Kinney, ed., *Chinese Views of Childhood.* Honolulu: University of Hawaii Press, 1995.

Walton, John, and David Seddon. *Free Markets and Food Riots: The Politics of Global Adjustment.* Cambridge, Mass.: Blackwell, 1994.

Ware, Helen R. "Differential Mortality Decline and Its Consequences for the Status and Roles of Women," in *Consequences of Mortality Trends and Differentials,* Population Studies No. 95. New York: Department of International Economic and Social Affairs, United Nations, 1986, pp. 113–125.

Warren, Mary Anne. *Gendercide: The Implication of Sex Selection.* Totowa, N.J.: Rowman and Allanheld, 1985.

Washburn, Sherwood L., ed. *Social Life of Early Man.* New York: Wenner-Gren Foundation for Anthropological Research, 1961.

Watson, James L. "Self-Defense Corps, Violence, and the Bachelor Subculture in South China: Two Case Studies." *Proceedings of the Second International Conference on Sinology.* Taiwan (Republic of China): Academia Sinica, June 1989.

Watson, Rubie S. "Afterword: Marriage and Gender Inequality," in Rubie S. Watson and Patricia Buckley Ebrey, eds., *Marriage and Inequality in Chinese Society.* Berkeley: University of California Press, 1991, pp. 347–368.

Watson, Rubie S., and Patricia Buckley Ebrey, eds. *Marriage and Inequality in Chinese Society.* Berkeley: University of California Press, 1991.

Watts, Michael. "Entitlements or Empowerments? Famine and Starvation in Africa," *Review of African Political Economy,* Vol. 19, No. 51 (July 1991), pp. 9–26.

Watts, Michael. *Silent Violence: Food, Famine, and Peasantry in Northern Nigeria.* Berkeley: University of California Press, 1983.

Watts, Michael J., and Hans-Georg Bohle. "The Space of Vulnerability: The Causal Structure of Hunger and Famine," *Progress in Human Geography,* Vol. 17, No. 1 (March 1993), pp. 43–67.

Wen Xingyan. "Effect of Son Preference and Population Policy on Sex Ratios at Birth in Two Provinces of China," *Journal of Biosocial Science,* Vol. 25, No. 4 (October 1993), pp. 509–521.

Westermarck, Edward. *The Origin and Development of the Moral Ideas.* London: Macmillan, 1924.

Westing, Arthur H., ed. *Global Resources and International Conflict: Environmental Factors in Strategic Policy and Action.* Oxford: Oxford University Press, 1986.

"Where Have All the Daughters Gone?" *Sinorama Magazine,* http://www.taiwaninfo.org/info/sinorama/8502/502006e1.html.

White, Gilbert F., ed. *Natural Hazards: Local, National, Global.* New York: Oxford, 1974.

White, Gilbert F., and John Eugene Haas. *Assessment of Research on Natural Hazards.* Cambridge, Mass.: MIT Press, 1975.

Whyte, Martin King. "Social Trends and the Human Rights Situation in the PRC." George Washington University, 1998.

"The Wild East: Guns in China," *Economist,* November 10, 2001, p. 75.

Wildavsky, Aaron B., and Mary Douglas. *Risk and Culture: An Essay on the Selection of Technical and Environmental Dangers.* Berkeley: University of California Press, 1982.

Wiley, Bell I. *The Life of Billy Yank: The Common Soldier of the Union.* Baton Rouge: Louisiana State University Press, 1978.

Williams, Christopher. "Environmental Victims," paper presented at the First Open Meeting of the Human Dimensions of Global Change Community, Duke University, Durham, North Carolina, June 1–3, 1995.

Williamson, Laila. "Infanticide: An Anthropological Analysis," in Marvin Kohl, ed., *Infanticide and the Value of Human Life.* New York: Prometheus, 1978, pp. 61–75.

Williamson, Nancy E. *Sons or Daughters: A Cross-Cultural Survey of Parental Preferences.* London: Sage, 1976.

Wilson, Margo, and Martin Daly. "Competitiveness, Risk Taking, and Violence: The Young Male Syndrome," *Ethology and Sociobiology,* Vol. 6, No. 1 (1985), pp. 59–73.

Winston, Sanford. "Birth Control and Sex Ratio at Birth," *American Journal of Sociology,* Vol. 38, No. 2 (September 1932), pp. 225–231.

Woirol, Gregory R. *In the Floating Army.* Chicago: University of Illinois Press, 1992.

Wolf, Arthur P., and Chieh-shan Huang. *Marriage and Adoption in China, 1845–1945.* Stanford, Calif.: Stanford University Press, 1980.

Wolf, Margery. *Revolution Postponed: Women in Contemporary China.* Stanford, Calif.: Stanford University Press, 1985.

Wolpert, Stanley. *India.* Berkeley: University of California Press, 1991.

Wolpert, Stanley. *A New History of India,* 4th ed. New York: Oxford University Press, 1993.

Wong, Linda. "China's Urban Migrants—The Public Policy Challenge," *Pacific Affairs,* Vol. 67, No. 3 (Autumn 1994), pp. 335–355.

Wooster, Robert. *Soldiers, Sutlers, and Settlers: Garrison Life on the Texas Frontier.* College Station: Texas A&M University Press, 1987.

World Bank. *World Population Projections, 1994–95 Edition: Estimates and Projections with Related Demographic Statistics.* Washington, D.C.: World Bank, 1994.

World Health Organization. *Women's Health in South-East Asia,* http://w3.whosea.org/women/index.htm.

World Vision International. "The Girl Child: Females He Created Them," *World Vision Today* (Spring 1998), p. 2.

Worster, Donald. "The Ecology of Order and Chaos," *Environmental History Review,* Vol. 14, Nos. 1–2 (Spring/Summer 1990), pp. 1–18.

Wrangham, Richard, and Dale Peterson. *Demonic Males: Apes and the Origins of Human Violence.* New York: Houghton Mifflin, 1996.

Wright, David. "Rebellion on the Chinese Frontier: The Lin Shuang-wen Uprising in Taiwan, 1787–1788," *Thetean* (April 1987), pp. 54–84.

Wright, Robert. *The Moral Animal*. New York: Pantheon, 1994.

Xu Song. "A Quest on the Causes of Gender Imbalance in China." Foreign Affairs College, Beijing, May 1999.

Yang Ji. "Transient Workers: A Special Social Group" and "Educating Transient Workers," *Beijing Review*, June 3–9, 1996, pp. 20–21.

Yao, Esther S. Lee. *Chinese Women: Past and Present*. Mesquite, Tex.: Ide House, 1983.

Ye Wenzhen and Lin Qingguo. "The Reasons and Countermeasures for Demographic Phenomena in China," *Chinese Demography*, Vol. 4 (1998).

Yen Chih-t'ui. *Family Instructions for the Yen Clan: Yen-Shih Chia-Hsun*, trans. Teng Ssu-yu. Leiden, Netherlands: E.J. Brill, 1968.

Yu Xie. "Measuring Regional Variation in Sex Preference in China: A Cautionary Note," *Social Science Research*, Vol. 18, No. 3 (September 1989), pp. 291–305.

Yulman, Nur. "On the Purity of Women in the Castes of Ceylon and Malabar," *Journal of the Royal Anthropological Society*, Vol. 93, Pt. 1 (January–June 1963), pp. 42–43.

Yutang, Lin. *My Country and My People*. New York: Reynal and Hitchcock, 1935.

Zeng Yi, Tu Ping, Gu Baochang, Xu Yi, Li Bohua, and Li Yongping. "Causes and Implications of the Recent Increase in the Reported Sex Ratio at Birth in China," *Population and Development Review*, Vol. 19, No. 2 (June 1993), pp. 283–302.

Zerner-Chardavoine, Monique. "Enfants et jeunes au IXe siècle : La démographie du polyptypue de Marseille, 813–814," *Provence historique*, No. 126 (1981), pp. 335–384.

Zhang Haiyang. "On Flowing Population in Qiqiha'er: Current Conditions and Management," *Plan Study*, n.s., Vol. 5 (1997).

Zhang Ping. "Issues and Characteristics of the Unmarried Population," *Chinese Journal of Population Science*, Vol. 2, No. 1 (1990), pp. 87–97.

Zhang Xiaohui, Wu Zhigang, and Chen Liangbiao. "Age Difference among the Rural Labor Force in Interrregional Migration," *Chinese Journal of Population Science*, Vol. 9, No. 3 (1997), pp. 193–202.

Zhao Yi. *The Population, Resources, Environment, Agriculture, and Continuous Development of 21st Century China*. Shan Xi: Economic Publishing House, 1997.

Zhong, Anita. "China's Aging Population and China's Economy." Foreign Affairs College, Beijing, May 23, 1999.

Zillmann, Dolf. *Connections between Sex and Aggression*. Hillsdale, N.J.: Lawrence Erlbaum, 1984.

Zimmerer, Karl S. "Human Geography and the 'New Ecology': The Prospect and Promise of Integration," *Annals of the Association of American Geographers*, Vol. 84, No. 1 (March 1994), pp. 108–125.

Newspaper Bibliography

"Abortion in Asia," *Wall Street Journal*, September 12, 1996, p. A14.

Ahmed, Farzand, and Subhash Mishra. "Stooping to Conquer," *India Today International*, November 10, 1997, pp. 22–24.

Ang, Audra. "Workers in Northeastern China Take to Streets for Back Pay, Better Benefits," Associated Press, March 10, 2003.

"Army of Jobless Threatening China," Associated Press, as published in *Salt Lake Tribune*, December 26, 1997, p. A6.

Bedi, Rahul. "Families 'Buying' Girls as Marriage Crisis Deepens," *Irish Times*, March 10, 2003, p. 9.

Belkin, Lisa. "Getting the Girl," *New York Times Magazine*, July 25, 1999, pp. 6, 26.

Bindra, Satinder. "Grim Motives behind Infant Killings," CNN.com, July 7, 2003, http://www.cnn.com/2003/world/asiapcf/south/07/07/india.infanticide.pt1/index.html.

Bindra, Satinder. "State Adopts Infants' Cause," CNN.com, July 7, 2003, http://www.cnn.com/2003/world/asiapcf/south/07/07/india.infanticide.pt2/index.html.

Bohlen, Celestine. "In Russian East, Chinese Help for Toiling Farmers," *New York Times*, August 1, 1999, sec. 1, p. 3.

Burns, John F. "Though Illegal, Child Marriage Is Popular in Part of India," *New York Times*, May 11, 1998, p. A1.

Chan, Vivien Pik-kwan. "Ban Imposed on Forced Abortions," *South China Morning Post*, October 31, 1998, p. 8.

Chan Yee Hon and Agencies. "Father Killed Girl for Wrong Answer: Fatal Beating Highlights Child Abuse Problems," *South China Morning Post*, July 30, 1998, p. 7.

"China Altering Marriage Law in Bid to Curb Adultery," Reuters, as published in *Deseret News*, October 24, 2000, p. A4.

"China Arrests Thousands for Trading Women and Children," Associated Press, June 8, 1999.

"China Has 20 Percent Male Surplus," Agence France-Presse, January 7, 1999

"China One-Child Policy Likely to Be Loosened as Birth Rates Drop," Agence France-Presse, February 11, 1998.

"China to Usher in Major Changes in Population Policies," People's Daily Online, August 20, 2003, http://english.peopledaily.com.cn/200308/20/eng20030820_122707.shtml.

"Chinese Saw Crime Jump 22% in First Nine Months of 1998, Report Says," Reuters, as published in *Deseret News,* February 10–11, 1999, p. A7.

"Coercive Tactics Divulged in China's One-Child Policy," Associated Press, as published in *Deseret News,* June 14, 1998, p. A17.

Collins, Lois M. "Americans Feel Strongly about What Is Ethical," *Deseret News,* May 8, 1999, p. E1.

"Death for Kidnapper of Twelve Boys," *South China Morning Post,* May 29, 1998, http://www.scmp.com/news/templat . . . ina&template?default.htx&maxfieldsize=898.

"Death for Killing Granddaughter," *South China Morning Post,* July 27, 1998, http://www.scmp.com/news/template/china-T   .   .   . ina&template=default.htx&max fieldsize=913.

"Doctors Should Abide by Sex Selection Act Norms," *Times of India,* April 29, 2003, p. 1.

Dorgan, Michael. "Growing Rich-Poor Gap, Economic Growth Spur Crime in China," Knight Ridder, March 27, 2002.

Dugger, Celia W. "Abortion in India Is Tipping Scales Sharply against Girls," *New York Times,* April 22, 2001, p. A1.

Dugger, Celia W. "Modern Asia's Anomaly: The Girls Who Don't Get Born," *New York Times,* May 6, 2001, sec. 4, p. 4.

Eckert, Paul. "China's Monumental Leap," Reuters, as published in *Deseret News,* November 21, 1999, p. AA1.

Eckholm, Erik. "As Beijing Pretties Up, Migrants Face Expulsion," *New York Times,* April 18, 1999, sec. 1, p. 6.

Eckholm, Erik. "China Plans to Divert Rivers to Thirsty North," *New York Times,* October 17, 2000, p. A19.

Eckholm, Erik. "China's Chief Tells Army to Give Up Its Commerce," *New York Times,* July 23, 1998, p. A3.

Eckholm, Erik. "Homes for Elderly Replacing Family Care as China Grays," *New York Times,* May 20, 1998, p. A1.

Eckholm, Erik. "Joblessness: A Perilous Curve on China's Capitalist Road," *New York Times,* January 20, 1998, p. A1.

Eckholm, Erik. "One Giant Step for Mr. Jiang's China," *New York Times,* November 21, 1999, sec. 4, p. 4.

Eckholm, Erik. "A Secretive Army Grows to Maintain Order in China," *New York Times,* March 28, 1999, sec. 1, p. 6.

Faison, Seth. "China Moving to Untie Its Military-Industrial Knot," *New York Times,* July 28, 1998, p. A1.

France, David. "Testosterone, the Rogue Hormone, Is Getting a Makeover," *New York Times*, February 17, 1999, p. G3.

French, Howard W. "New Pressures Alter Japanese Family's Geometry," *New York Times*, July 27, 2000, p. A1.

Friedman, Thomas L. "It Takes a Village," *New York Times*, March 10, 1998, p. A19.

Gardner, David. "Where Have All the Girls Gone?" *Financial Times*, February 9, 2003, p. 1.

Goodman, Ellen. "Will China's Values Change? Stay Tuned," *Boston Globe*, November 11, 1999, p. A27.

Greenhouse, Steven. "The Greening of U.S. Diplomacy: Focus on Ecology," *New York Times*, October 9, 1995, p. A6.

Halarnkar, Samar, Sayantan Chakravarty, and Smruti Koppikar. "Fear in the City," *India Today International*, October 6, 1997, pp. 12–24.

Herbert, Bob. "China's Missing Girls," *New York Times*, October 30, 1997, p. A31.

Hutchings, Graham. "Female Infanticide 'Will Lead to Army of Bachelors,'" *London Daily Telegraph*, April 11, 1997, http://www.telegraph.co.uk/htmlContent.jhtml?html=/archive/1997/04/11/wchi11.html.

Kilman, Lawrence. "Majority of Americans Wouldn't Choose Baby's Sex If Given a Chance," Associated Press, November 17, 1986.

Kolata, Gina. "Researchers Report Success in Method to Pick Baby's Sex," *New York Times*, September 9, 1998, p. A1.

Kristof, Nicholas D. "Chinese Turn to Ultrasound, Scorning Baby Girls for Boys," *New York Times*, July 21, 1993, p. A1.

Kwan, Daniel. "Tougher Laws for Migrant Birth Control," *South China Morning Post*, September 23, 1998, p. 9.

Li, Ling. "China's Suicide Rate," *New York Times*, January 28, 1999, p. A26.

McElroy, Damien. "Chinese Buy Baby Girls on the Black Market." *London Daily Telegraph*, August 1, 1999, http://www.telegraph.co.uk/htmlContent.jhtml?html=%2Farchive %2F1998%2F04%2F02%2Fnlot02.html.

McElroy, Damien. "Sex Imbalance Fuels China's Kidnap Trade," *London Daily Telegraph*, November 22, 1998, http://www.telegraph.co.uk/htmlContent.jhtml?html=%2Farchive%2F1998% 2F11%2F22%2Fwchin22.html.

Park Chai Bin. "Asia's Female Populations Fall amid Sex-Selection Abortions: Technology Used to Reject Daughters," *Washington Times*, June 30, 1995, p. A19.

Pomfret, John. "Portrait of a Famine," Washington Post Foreign Service, February 12, 1999.

Rosenthal, Elisabeth. "100 Million Restless Chinese Go Far from Home for Jobs," *New York Times*, February 24, 1999, p. A1.

Rosenthal, Elisabeth. "Bias for Boys Leads to Sale of Baby Girls in China," *New York Times*, July 20, 2003, sec. 1, p. 6.

Rosenthal, Elisabeth. "Factory Closings in China Arouse Workers to Fury," *New York Times*, August 31, 2000, p. A1.

Rosenthal, Elisabeth. "For One-Child Policy, China Rethinks Iron Hand," *New York Times*, November 1, 1998, sec. 1, p. 1.

Rosenthal, Elisabeth. "Poverty Spreads, and Deepens, in China's Cities," *New York Times,* October 4, 1998, sec. 1, p. 3.

Rosenthal, Elisabeth. "Women's Suicides Reveal Rural China's Bitter Roots," *New York Times,* January 24, 1999, sec. 1, p. 1.

"Skewed Gender Ratio Endangers Society, Says Delegate," *South China Morning Post,* March 7, 2002, p. 6.

Smith, Craig. "Beijing Tries to Lift Economic Standards in Its West," *New York Times,* November 7, 2000, p. C1.

"Survey Finds Most Parents Wouldn't Choose Baby's Sex If They Could," Associated Press, March 16, 1999.

Tempest, Rone. "China to Close 11 Ministries in Effort to Avoid Fiscal Crisis," *Los Angeles Times,* March 6, 1998, p. 8.

Wang Rong. "Migrant Labourers to Face Difficulty Finding Work," *China Daily,* February 21, 2000, p. 2.

Weiss, Rick. "Anti-Girl Bias Rises in Asia, Studies Show: Abortion Augmenting Infanticide, Neglect," *Washington Post,* May 11, 1996, p. A1.

"Western China Pining for Prosperity," Associated Press, as published in *Deseret News,* July 29, 2000, p. D7.

"World Briefing: China: Drought Hits Millions," *New York Times,* March 31, 1999, p. A6.

Wren, Christopher. "Drugs or Alcohol Linked to 80% of Inmates," *New York Times,* January 9, 1998, p. A14.

Xiao Wang, "Police Keeping Crime Down," *China Daily,* June 8, 2000, p. 3.

About the Authors

Andrea M. den Boer is Lecturer of International Politics in the Department of Politics and International Relations at the University of Kent at Canterbury, where she is the director of the department's postgraduate program in human rights. Her current research is focused on issues relating to gender, human security, and human rights. She received her doctorate from the University of Kent at Canterbury.

Valerie M. Hudson is Professor of Political Science at Brigham Young University. She received her doctoral training at the Ohio State University and previously taught at Northwestern University and Rutgers University. Author, coauthor, or editor of numerous articles, special journal issues, and books, including *Political Psychology and Foreign Policy* and *The Limits of State Autonomy*, her fields of specialization are foreign policy analysis, security studies, and computational modeling. She served eight years as Director of Graduate Studies at the David M. Kennedy Center for International Studies and is the recipient of various awards, including the Karl G. Maeser Award for Excellence in Teaching.

Index

BCSIA Studies in International Security

Published by The MIT Press

Sean M. Lynn-Jones and Steven E. Miller, series editors
Karen Motley, executive editor
Belfer Center for Science and International Affairs (BCSIA)
John F. Kennedy School of Government, Harvard University

Agha, Hussein, Shai Feldman, Ahmad Khalidi, and Zeev Schiff, *Track-II Diplomacy: Lessons from the Middle East* (2003)

Allison, Graham T., Owen R. Coté, Jr., Richard A. Falkenrath, and Steven E. Miller, *Avoiding Nuclear Anarchy: Containing the Threat of Loose Russian Nuclear Weapons and Fissile Material* (1996)

Allison, Graham T., and Kalypso Nicolaïdis, eds., *The Greek Paradox: Promise vs. Performance* (1996)

Arbatov, Alexei, Abram Chayes, Antonia Handler Chayes, and Lara Olson, eds., *Managing Conflict in the Former Soviet Union: Russian and American Perspectives* (1997)

Bennett, Andrew, *Condemned to Repetition? The Rise, Fall, and Reprise of Soviet-Russian Military Interventionism, 1973–1996* (1999)

Blackwill, Robert D., and Michael Stürmer, eds., *Allies Divided: Transatlantic Policies for the Greater Middle East* (1997)

Blackwill, Robert D., and Paul Dibb, eds., *America's Asian Alliances* (2000)

Brom, Shlomo, and Yiftah Shapir, eds., *The Middle East Military Balance, 1999–2000* (1999)

Brom, Shlomo, and Yiftah Shapir, eds., *The Middle East Military Balance, 2001–2002* (2002)

Brown, Michael E., ed., *The International Dimensions of Internal Conflict* (1996)

Brown, Michael E., and Šumit Ganguly, eds., *Government Policies and Ethnic Relations in Asia and the Pacific* (1997)

Brown, Michael E., and Šumit Ganguly, eds., *Fighting Words: Language Policy and Ethnic Relations in Asia* (2003)

Carter, Ashton B., and John P. White, eds., *Keeping the Edge: Managing Defense for the Future* (2001)

de Nevers, Renée, *Comrades No More: The Seeds of Political Change in Eastern Europe* (2003)

Elman, Colin, and Miriam Fendius Elman, eds., *Bridges and Boundaries: Historians, Political Scientists, and the Study of International Relations* (2001)

Elman, Colin, and Miriam Fendius Elman, eds., *Progress in International Relations Theory: Appraising the Field* (2003)

Elman, Miriam Fendius, ed., *Paths to Peace: Is Democracy the Answer?* (1997)

Falkenrath, Richard A., *Shaping Europe's Military Order: The Origins and Consequences of the CFE Treaty* (1994)

Falkenrath, Richard A., Robert D. Newman, and Bradley A. Thayer, *America's Achilles' Heel: Nuclear, Biological, and Chemical Terrorism and Covert Attack* (1998)

Feaver, Peter D., and Richard H. Kohn, eds., *Soldiers and Civilians: The Civil-Military Gap and American National Security* (2001)

Feldman, Shai, *Nuclear Weapons and Arms Control in the Middle East* (1996)

Feldman, Shai, and Yiftah Shapir, eds., *The Middle East Military Balance 2000–2001* (2001)

Forsberg, Randall, ed., *The Arms Production Dilemma: Contraction and Restraint in the World Combat Aircraft Industry* (1994)

George, Alexander L., and Andrew Bennett, *Case Studies and Theory Development in the Social Sciences* (2005)

Hagerty, Devin T., *The Consequences of Nuclear Proliferation: Lessons from South Asia* (1998)

Heymann, Philip B., *Terrorism and America: A Commonsense Strategy for a Democratic Society* (1998)

Heymann, Philip B., *Terrorism, Freedom, and Security: Winning without War* (2003)

Heymann, Philip B., and Juliette N. Kayyem, *Protecting Liberty in an Age of Terror* (2005)

Howitt, Arnold M., and Robyn L. Pangi, eds., *Countering Terrorism: Dimensions of Preparedness* (2003)

Hudson, Valerie M., and Andrea M. den Boer, *Bare Branches: Security Implications of Asia's Surplus Male Population* (2004)

Kayyem, Juliette N., and Robyn L. Pangi, eds., *First to Arrive: State and Local Responses to Terrorism* (2003)

Kokoshin, Andrei A., *Soviet Strategic Thought, 1917–91* (1998)

Lederberg, Joshua, ed., *Biological Weapons: Limiting the Threat* (1999)

Mansfield, Edward D., and Jack Snyder, *Electing to Fight: Why Emerging Democracies Go to War* (2005)

Martin, Lenore G., and Dimitris Keridis, eds., *The Future of Turkish Foreign Policy* (2004)

Shaffer, Brenda, *Borders and Brethren: Iran and the Challenge of Azerbaijani Identity* (2002)

Shields, John M., and William C. Potter, eds., *Dismantling the Cold War: U.S. and NIS Perspectives on the Nunn-Lugar Cooperative Threat Reduction Program* (1997)

Tucker, Jonathan B., ed., *Toxic Terror: Assessing Terrorist Use of Chemical and Biological Weapons* (2000)

Utgoff, Victor A., ed., *The Coming Crisis: Nuclear Proliferation, U.S. Interests, and World Order* (2000)

Williams, Cindy, ed., *Holding the Line: U.S. Defense Alternatives for the Early 21st Century* (2001)

Williams, Cindy, ed., *Filling the Ranks: Transforming the U.S. Military Personnel System* (2004)